"NOT HALF

Having known Harry Bramma since
having worked with him for twelve ye
qualified to sing the praises of this exc
is a masterpiece of Yorkshire understate

Harry's life story is engagingly told
generously sprinkled with amusing an
about his upbringing and offers percept
philosophical matters that have touche

He comes across as a proud Yorksh
of history and a deep social conscienc
perhaps.

Come publication, I'm sure that it v

"Not Half Bad"

A Lifetime of Musical Development and Other Stories

Harry Bramma

AN OXFORDFOLIO PUBLICATION

An Oxfordfolio publication
(www.oxfordfolio.co.uk)

Copyright © Harry Bramma 2025

Harry Bramma has asserted his right to be identified as the author of this Work in accordance with the Copyright, Designs and Patents Act 1988.

Design/typesetting: Nick Allen at Forewords
Project editor: James Harrison
10 9 8 7 6 5 4 3 2 1

A CIP catalogue record for this book is available from the British Library

ISBN 9781068766114

Typeset in 12/16 point Garamond

Printed and bound in India by Imprint Press.

Contents

	Author's Preface	ix
	Introduction	**1**
1	**The Early Years**	**3**
	Origins	3
	Childhood	7
	Adolescence	18
	Holidays	24
	Musical awakening	27
	Widening musical horizons	33
	A lifetime of musical development	38
2	**Oxford**	**43**
	Pembroke College	43
	Arrival at Pembroke	45
	The Music Faculty	48
	Reading Theology	56
3	**Nottinghamshire**	**65**
4	**Worcester**	**73**
	Arrival on College Green, September 1963	73
	The cathedral clergy	76
	The cathedral choir	80
	The cathedral voluntary choir	83
	Three deans	85
	Robert Leslie Pollington Milburn (1957–1968)	86
	Eric Waldram Kemp (1969–1974)	89
	Thomas George Adames Baker (1975–1986)	92

The Three Choirs Festival	95
The cathedral organ	100
The King's School	104
Outstanding pupils	110
Life in Worcestershire	116
Three organists	125
Christopher Robinson (1963–1974)	125
Donald Hunt (1975–1996)	129
Edgar Day (1912–1962)	131
A Worcester postscript	133
5 Southwark	**135**
The challenge – and the way things developed	135
Two Provosts	148
Harold Frankham (1970–1981)	148
David Edwards (1982–1993)	152
The cathedral clergy	154
Canons who were part-time at the cathedral	156
Four assistant organists	158
Garrett O'Brien	158
John Scott (1956–2015)	160
Andrew Lumsden	164
Stephen Layton	166
The Southwark organ and T. C. Lewis	167
Two bishops	173
Mervyn Stockwood (1959–1980)	173
Ronald Bowlby (1981–1991)	180
Southwark diocesan organ adviser	183
The Royal College of Organists	185
Balancing the books	189
A Southwark postscript	191
6 The Royal School of Church Music	**197**
The challenge	197
My predecessor	200
Arrival at Addington	202

CONTENTS

The RSCM staff — 206
The RSCM Council — 207
Three chairmen — 208
    Sir John Margetson — 208
    Roger Butler (Acting Chairman 1994–1996) — 210
    Sir David Harrison (1996–2005) — 212
Work in the United Kingdom — 214
The RSCM worldwide — 217
    Australia and New Zealand — 217
    The United States — 223
    South Africa — 229
    Canada — 237
    Northern Europe and the Channel Islands — 239
The evangelicals — 240
Bringing in the girls — 246
The appeal — 248
The magazine — 254
The move to Cleveland Lodge — 255
An RSCM postscript — 257

7 All Saints, Margaret Street — 261
A long-term connection — 261
How I came to arrive at Margaret Street — 266
Two assistant organists — 268
    Nicholas Luff — 268
    Andrew Arthur — 272
Five organ scholars – a sound investment — 275
Two vicars — 277
    Canon David Hutt — 277
    Prebendary Alan Moses — 279
The choir — 283
The congregation — 285
The restoration of the Harrison organ of 1910 — 290
The William Byrd 450th anniversary (1992) — 294
Final years at Margaret Street — 295

8	**Retirement from full-time work**	**297**
	London life	297
	The Athenaeum	297
	Becoming a composer	298
	The Musicians' Company	300
	The Omphiangelum Society	302
	The Madrigal Society	304
	Salisbury	305
	Teaching at King's College, Cambridge and Christ Church, Oxford	308
	The Diocesan Advisory Committee	308
	A peripatetic organist	310
9	**A spiritual pilgrimage**	**313**
	Faith and doubt 70 years ago; is there a place for God in this?	313
	Memories of social unease	314
	The importance of special friendships	316
10	**Envoi**	**321**
	Upwards and onwards	321

Appendix	325
'Male and female created He them' – In support of Dr Richard Seal and the Girls' Choir at Salisbury Cathedral	325
'Let our merry organ blow' – A detailed examination of the merits of pipe and electronic organs	331
'The labourer is worthy of his hire' – Why church musicians should receive proper financial remuneration	338
'Be still and know that I am God' – The importance of silence in worship	345
Index	

Author's Preface

In writing a memoir which embraces events from over 75 years, it is inevitable the author will have cold feet about what can and cannot be divulged. Sensitivity to the views of very old people or their descendants is crucial. But in not wishing to offend it is important not to be too bland. Much can be implied by humorous comments – and of course what is being written is very much social history with its own remarkable and colourful events. I hope my story will not cause offence; but I hope it will provide vivid information to describe a span of history which deserves to be preserved. My aim is to be of general interest as well as appealing to those with a particular interest in music.

I have been lucky to have been in interesting places at interesting times: at Worcester, where the Cathedral moved from the 18th to the 20th century over but a few years; or at Southwark, where Bishop Mervyn Stockwood's radical agenda had repercussions which are still being felt; or the extraordinary mix of the Shipley Parish Church Choir, which I joined in 1945. Back then, most families didn't own cars, so the children stayed around home. There were not the distractions of today, such as Sunday football. The boys who formed the choir needed to get out of the house – even if this meant singing and dressing up in curious frock-like clothes. There was the added incentive of modest choir pay. Headmasters recommended boys from poor backgrounds with good voices. The more well-to-do boys needed interests to occupy them, even if their parents liked music and saw the value of singing as training for developing the intellect over a wide number of disciplines. I have described this choir community in some detail as it gives a picture of a way of life which is now largely forgotten.

It is a pleasure to speak of distinguished teachers at school and later at university. They were great characters, who should be remembered in all their variety. Throughout my life I have met distinguished and skilful people. It is good to record their work and talents and indeed their idiosyncrasies. These people seen at close quarters come up with a surprising freshness which adds to our knowledge of what they were really like. These accounts are certainly not hagiographical.

I hope this book will be both informative and surprising. Reliving a long life has given me the pleasure of reflection and recall; may it give pleasure to others to discover times long past.

Harry Bramma
2025

Introduction

One sometimes hears upwardly mobile people talk of restructuring themselves as they start out on a professional career. The ambitious novice stockbroker from Cleckheaton loses her broad Yorkshire accent miraculously overnight; the aspiring junior doctor, son of a window cleaner in Bethnal Green, contrives to banish family references from his CV. When I was at Oxford, I found myself tempted to do the same – would that I were the scion of some country house in the rolling acres of Gloucestershire, rather than a lad of relatively humble origins from the West Riding of Yorkshire. Thankfully, when I started to earn my living, such delusions gradually deserted me and throughout my life I have become more and more grateful for my roots. I now realize they were in no way humble.

Reliving my childhood and adolescence in this memoir, I have come to understand what I didn't see at the time: how thoughtful and loving my parents, relations and friends were – and how they took endless trouble to interest me and motivate my personal development. They cared for me and I am now deeply grateful.

I would like to think that recognizing the importance of the early years is a sign of maturity. It is now almost 60 years since I left Yorkshire, but every time I set foot on the platform of Leeds station, I feel I am returning home to the city where at least seven generations of my family lived and worked – mostly as mill engineers. I hope that ultimately the young woman from Cleckheaton and the man from Bethnal Green will revisit their roots, and in so doing grow in self-awareness and to a recognition of what made them what they are – as themselves and none other.

One problem I faced in recounting this memoir is one of chronology. I will therefore complete this Introduction by summarizing the significant events in my life, which I hope will clarify the sequence when thematic digressions intervene.

Born in November 1936, my memories of the early days are hazy. But the earliest is a visit to Blackpool in the summer of 1938. Next, I remember starting school in September 1941 shortly before my father joined the army. He was not demobbed until 1946. During the war years I lived alone with my mother, but with the advantage of my father's parents living in the same road. From then on, things became much clearer. I started at Bradford Grammar School in the Junior School in September 1945 and moved up into the Senior School in 1948, just before it moved from the centre of Bradford to new premises in Frizinghall in January 1949. I left school in 1955 to go to Pembroke College, Oxford where I studied for the Honour School of Music (three years) and then the Honour School of Theology (two years). After a year taking the Oxford Diploma in Education, my first job was in the autumn of 1961 at King Edward VI Grammar School, East Retford, Nottinghamshire. After two years there I moved in September 1963 to take up the post of Assistant Organist at Worcester Cathedral, to which was added the position of Director of Music at the King's School in the autumn of 1965. I stayed at Worcester until May 1976, when I was appointed Organist and Director of Music at Southwark Cathedral, London Bridge. At the beginning of February 1989, I took up the post of Director of the Royal School of Church Music (RSCM) at Addington Palace, Croydon, from which I retired at the end of August 1998. I had already been Organist and Director of Music at All Saints, Margaret Street, London W1 since April 1989. When I retired from the RSCM, I continued at All Saints until 31 January 2004. I moved from Beckenham to Chislehurst in September 2018, and continued to be busy as an organist in the London area and to attend concerts and social events in the capital.

CHAPTER ONE

The Early Years

ORIGINS

It was a matter of great sadness for my father that I did not become an engineer or a scientist. To become a musician was quite out of character for someone born into the Bramma family. This regret was echoed by my father's mother, who one day (when I was already Assistant Organist of Worcester Cathedral) was heard to remark in the local post office to her niece, 'I do wish our Harry would get a proper job!' My father eventually became reconciled to the fact that I was not made in his image – especially after I was awarded an Organ Scholarship at Oxford. For him, that was good enough; thereafter he proudly followed all my professional experiences.

Having become more aware of our family origins in my late sixties, I can now see that my musical vocation was quite at odds with at least 250 years of family history. The Brammas had always been technological, much involved in the machinery used in textile mills. One of my ancestors, Joseph Bramma (1740–1815), was a notable inventor: the originator of the Bramah lock, a highly regarded hydraulic press and the very much improved design of the 18th-century water closet! At his baptism in Silkestone church, South Yorkshire, his name was recorded as Bramma. It was later, when he set up business in London, that he changed it to the more fashionable Bramah!

I had long known something of my distant family history, as I have in my possession the birth certificate of my great-grandfather, Charles Bramma, born in Leeds in 1847. From this I knew that my great-great-grandfather's Christian name was Samuel, and that his wife's maiden name was Hannah Richardson. More importantly, my great-great-grandfather's occupation was recorded as 'millwright' – an old-fashioned term for mill engineer. And that was all I knew – until a very distant forebear from Australia wrote to me to ask if I was related to her. She was an organist too, and thought this might signify a family connection! She had been researching the family tree, and as a result of her work I was able to establish my great-great-great-grandfather as Samuel Bramma, Senior, born in Leeds in 1783; and his father as John Bramma, born in 1758 and baptised at All Hallows church, Kirkburton, three miles south-east of Huddersfield. His father was Jeremy Bramma, who lived at the Green House, Cartworth.

But we discovered much more about these ancestors. They were often referred to in the Leeds Directories of the 1820s, which gave both work and home addresses, and in the 1851 census my great-great-great-grandfather was recorded as living in Lyndon Terrace, Leeds in a large Georgian house with two servants – not of course unusual in those days. We have been able to obtain a picture of this as it was not demolished until 1962 to make way for an extension to Leeds University. We also have a handsome portrait in oils of my great-great-grandfather (born in 1814), which is now in the possession of my cousin Maureen Bramwell. The early Bramma engineering work brought them success and a degree of financial security. How all this went wrong in the 1850s is still a mystery. But it was not uncommon in the 19th century for business successes to be followed by decline for whatever reason.

But there is no question that my grandfather was born into humble circumstances. He refused to speak of his family – he nursed considerable bitterness. I think now that he may have known rather more than he was prepared to disclose. I suspect the demise of the family business may have been caused by drink! But it may alternatively have been a lack of capital to invest in new technology. This was quite a common experience for owners of family businesses in the later 19th century. My grandfather, Ellison Bramma, was born in 1887, and such were the family circumstances that he went to work half-time at the age of 11 in 1898. It seems incredible to us that a child could be released from school, mornings one week, afternoons the next, in order to earn money to augment the meagre family resources. I often thought of my grandfather when I looked at my young choristers at Southwark. I could hardly comprehend how a child was forced to become an adult overnight at a very tender age. But my grandfather was a highly intelligent man who triumphed over his early lack of opportunities. I still have a large exercise book written when he was at night school at the age of 18. The writing, English style and spelling are immaculate. He was clearly intent on self-improvement, eventually becoming manager of the Weaving Department in one of the largest mills in Yorkshire – Salt's of Saltaire. His much improved financial circumstances benefited me directly, as it was he who paid for me to go to Bradford Grammar School.

My father inherited his father's interest in textile design and machinery, and although he started as an apprentice in Salt's Mill, he was appointed in the year of my birth, 1936, as a lecturer at Bradford Technical College, where there was a large textile department. He had worked hard in his spare time for the Diploma of Associate of the Textile Institute, which was a factor in his appointment to the Technical College. He eventually became a lecturer in the College of Technology and then in the University of Bradford (which it subsequently became), where he was awarded the degree of MSc for his research into 'A Study of the influences of materials and mechanisms on cloth geometry – 1972'.

My father, like his father, was a highly intelligent man who achieved a very great deal despite a lack of early opportunities, though my grandparents always said they would have been only too happy to give him a better early education. Apparently he did not want this. My father was true to his roots and was happy in a family which was largely working-class in culture, whilst being financially much better placed. My parents and grandparents were able to buy their own houses, and my grandfather ran a car in the 1930s when motorized transport was still the preserve of the few.

My mother, Christine Wakefield, came from a very different background – still fundamentally working-class, but with a broader view of life and greater cultural sophistication. The Wakefields came from Berkshire. My great-great-grandfather worked at Windsor Castle as a carpenter, and his son, my great-grandfather John Wakefield, born in 1858, was a non-commissioned officer in one of the Guards' Regiments and became a policeman in Paddington in the 1890s. His wife, née Marie Bennett, had been a ladies' maid to a duchess in a very grand house in Suffolk. Tragedy struck the Wakefield family with the death of my great-grandfather, John, in 1904 in the aftermath of the South African war. His widow was forced to move to Yorkshire, where her two sons and one daughter could find work in the mill to support the family. That they moved in several doors away from the Brammas in the village of Saltaire meant that my mother really married the 'boy next door'.

There were tensions between the Brammas and the Wakefields from the start, principally I imagine because my father's family were financially much better off! But the marriage was a good one, and my mother brought to it her own personal gifts. She was sensitive and intelligent and was very musical. She had learned the piano and played with beautiful tone and expression. I remember her when she was quite an old lady, not having played the piano for some years, sitting down at a friend's Bluthner grand piano and playing beautifully. She had a good ear and a highly retentive memory – she found no difficulty in whistling the subject of Bach's great G minor organ fugue, having heard me play it on a number of occasions.

So when people ask me where my music comes from, it must be from my mother's side. She encouraged me – and it is only later in life that I realize how sensible she was and how she had thought out how her son should be introduced to many things, not least music and the Christian faith. My mother had been brought up as an Anglican and was confirmed in her teens, as was her father before her (at St Mary's, Slough). The Brammas were nominally Anglican – and whilst all my family had received some kind of Christian formation in Sunday School, very few of them were churchgoers. I believe my mother wanted it to be different for me – and to that end she persuaded me to join the local church choir at St Paul's, Shipley. She came to support me at Evensong and went with one of our neighbours to the 8 a.m. said Communion at Easter and Whitsuntide – very much the old-fashioned Anglican tradition. Occasionally my Wakefield grandparents would come to Evensong to support – for instance, at the Harvest Festival, after which my grandfather sloped off to The Woodman, an establishment he visited most evenings! It still seems odd that my Bramma grandparents never came to the church to hear me in the choir.

Later, after the early death at the age of 58 of Grandad Wakefield in 1947, my grandmother was confirmed and started to attend church regularly on Sunday mornings. So for much of my time as a chorister, I could look down the church and see grandmother in the morning and mother in the evening. I can't remember my father coming to church in the early days, though later on he attended about once a fortnight (in the mornings), as he said 'to support my mother'. He remained a seeker and considered confirmation, but he remained deeply agnostic as did many of his generation who had served in the war. He made the priceless comment that even if there was nothing in it, it was a very good club!

CHILDHOOD

For my first three years, up to the outbreak of war in 1939, I have very few clear memories. But some stand out. I remember when I was two going to Blackpool with my parents in company with my father's cousin, Lucy, and her husband Alfred Thornton, with their four-year-old daughter Brenda, with whom I have stayed in lifelong contact.

The six of us stayed at a boarding house in a large room, separated by a curtain into two apartments. I have photographs of Brenda with me on the beach – but beyond that I remember very little. I have some memories supported by a photograph of my grandparents taking me out in their car. But I do have clear memories in pre-school days of my Grandma Bramma giving me home instruction. She taught me to enlarge my vocabulary by simply pointing out things in the room or outside and getting me to repeat the name of the object or person after her. She also taught me to tell the time, a simple form of numeracy. For this purpose she used the dining room clock, getting me to count the numbers round the dial, and then eventually to tell the time. I clearly remember her turning the hands on the clock backwards and forwards and saying 'What time is it now, Harry?'

My father's parents lived in the same road as us and played a large part in my upbringing, especially after my father was called up in 1941 to join the army. My grandfather, Ellison Bramma, I much admired. He had style and dressed smartly in homburg hats and smart suits, with stiff white collars and silk pocket handkerchiefs. My grandmother, Sarah, was a powerful character and very much family-orientated. Though they had some long-term friends who were not family, there was no doubt in my grandmother's mind that family came first. She often remarked that 'blood is stronger than water'. Her family, the Jennings, was particularly close-knit. Her father, William Jennings (1850–1923), had been a stone mason, who having saved a thousand sovereigns, a common practice, retired early. He built a row of houses in Alexandra Square, Shipley from which the family continued to receive rents until their demolition in 1962. My grandmother's four brothers held an annual business meeting to administer the property. The sisters were excluded from this, but were expected to provide refreshments, including the occasional glass of whisky!

My grandmother used to visit her elder sister Pat every Friday. Her actual name was Martha Ellen, which my grandmother shortened to 'our-Marth-Ellen' which I thought for a long time was one word. Her eldest brother, Fredrill Croft (his mother had come upon his quaint Christian name in a novel she was reading), was illegitimate, but presumably the child of both my great-grandparents. I could never understand why his surname was Croft, his mother's maiden name, and not Jennings. On a number of occasions I asked my grandmother why this was. The question caused her great embarrassment, and all she would say was 'I can't really explain.' The most colourful of her brothers was Simeon, the youngest. He looked as if he had walked straight out of a Lowry painting. He never changed the style of his dress. Even in the 1960s, he cut a fine figure rolling down the street in his suit, wing collar, bowler hat and shabby raincoat, brandishing an umbrella.

The eldest sister, Pat, lived with her unmarried daughter, Margaret, in the largest of the family houses, which boasted a small kitchen and a front room. On Sunday lunchtimes, they held court in the back living room when family members would call. Both mother and daughter were formidable; one tried hard not to say the wrong thing. Margaret worked as a weaver under my grandfather, and had a reputation for making fine wedding cakes as a sideline. She was very patriotic, a fan of Anthony Eden, and always stood to attention when the national anthem was played on the radio!

I occasionally called in at these Sunday gatherings as my great-aunt's house was on the way home from the parish church where I was a choirboy. As 'our Sarah's grandson', I qualified for attendance! This was around 1945, although in this household it was still very much the Victorian age. The house was lit by gas (as was that of my great-aunt Emily and uncle Joshua). Hot water and heating were provided by the coal-fired kitchen range, though the cooking had progressed to a gas oven in the small kitchen. Most houses like this had a 'set pot', a large copper vat encased in brick with a coal fire underneath. This provided water for washing day, which was otherwise entirely manual, involving a peggy tub, posser, mangle and flat iron heated on the fire. My mother washed like this until 1945, when we purchased a washing machine.

My grandmother's younger sister, Annie Jennings, lived across the square in a smaller house. In some ways this was extremely primitive, but the house itself was not unattractive. In addition to the cellar, there were three decent-sized rooms – a living room which opened onto the street, a first-floor bedroom and an attic. There was no bathroom or kitchen, but a cold water tap above the stone sink at the top of the cellar steps. The coal-fired range was the only source of heating. Cooking was done over the fire and in the fireside oven. The lavatories were at the end of the street. Later she acquired an electric cooker.

My great-aunt had more than a touch of sanctity. She was the one who stayed at home to look after her father when he was widowed at the age of 37. After his death she went out cleaning, and later worked in the canteen at a local ironworks.

I knew her well because she came to my grandmother's for the night every Tuesday. I expect one of the reasons for this was so she could have a bath. As I grew older, she often invited me to tea and to events at the large Methodist chapel nearby at which she was a regular attender. She had a hard life, with very little money; she was also very lame. I know my grandmother helped her financially from time to time. The lesson I learned at an early age was that, like my Aunt Annie, people living in poor circumstances often had high standards in dress, behaviour and morality. I personally realized that nobility of character, happiness and enjoyment of life have little to do with standards of living. She was sustained by a simple Christian faith and the unfailing support of her family.

The Bramma family, as recounted earlier, had gone downhill around 1850. My great-grandfather, William Bramma, had married Mary Ellison, a girl from Cullingworth, at Bradford Parish Church (now Cathedral) on Christmas Eve, 1870. They had eight children, spaced out over twenty years. The oldest was Hannah (known as Pat), who after her marriage moved to Hertfordshire where her husband worked as a painter and decorator. They were the London relatives. One of the daughters was in the theatre, and in general they had rather broken away into a new life. We did see Aunt Pat occasionally on visits to London at her home in Wheathampsted near St Albans, and twice around 1950 she came to Bradford to see her granddaughter perform in the pantomime at the Bradford Alhambra. The thing I remember most about my aunt on these occasions was that she wore gaiters to ward off the cold! My grandfather's other sister Emily lived quite near. Her husband Joshua ran a small firm of joiners and carpenters. We visited quite often and occasionally saw Fred, my grandfather's other brother, who was a male nurse at a lunatic asylum. His wife Annie was a good pianist. On my birthday they used to descend on us with a case full of music, enabling us to have a family sing-song.

The Bramma relation who influenced me most was great-aunt Alice, who had been married briefly before the First World War to my great-uncle Harry Bramma. Like so many others at that time, he died young of pneumonia after only 18 months of marriage. Alice was deeply in love with him and remained so for the rest of her life. When I was born in 1936, she arrived on the doorstep and virtually demanded I should be called after her husband! Having got the family's agreement to this, she opened a bank account in my name into which she paid monthly. When I was 21 I received the accumulated funds. Alice was a stylish person who earned her living as secretary to the owner of Parkinson's Iron Works in Shipley (where my Auntie Annie worked in the canteen). She used to come to lunch with my paternal grandparents on Tuesday once a fortnight, so I saw her frequently. She was musical and had a good soprano voice. I remember her singing the ballad 'There's a long, long road a-winding into the land of my dreams' at my grandparents' Golden Wedding in 1950. She clearly recognized that I had musical ability and set out to encourage me. She gave me a score of Mendelssohn's 'Elijah' and his 'Songs without words'. I also have a copy of Dickens' *Nicholas Nickleby* which I read recently 64 years after she gave it to me in 1948! Sometimes she took me to tea in the restaurant attached to the New Victoria cinema in Bradford. I think the last time I saw her was when she came to Evensong at Bingley Parish Church where

I was organist and choirmaster at the age of 17. Looking back, I am grateful for all the doors that Auntie Alice opened in my favour, although I rather took her for granted at the time.

My mother's side of the family was very different from the Brammas and the Jennings, coming originally from Berkshire and Buckinghamshire. It was an enormous culture shock for my great-grandmother and the children to be uprooted from Slough, where they'd been living. They occupied a small terraced house in Lockwood Street, Saltaire, Sir Titus Salt's famous model village built to house his workers at the gigantic mill nearby. My grandfather had unusually stayed on at school until 16, and was possibly destined for a pathway into professional work. He was confirmed by the Bishop of Oxford at St Mary's, Slough in 1905 and won a prize for religious knowledge. He clearly hated the mill and very soon ran away to sea with another local boy, Alfonso Wall (known as Fonce), who was my godfather's uncle. Eventually his friend's mother 'bought him out' of the navy. My great-grandmother took the view that he had made his own decision and would have to live with it. He stayed in the navy until after the First World War.

My grandfather (known as Don Wakefield) died suddenly whilst walking on Ilkley Moor with a friend in 1947, shortly before my eleventh birthday. He was on his way to The Hermit at Burley Wood Head, to which they repaired quite often on Sundays. In those days before we had a telephone, a neighbour of my grandmother's had to walk the mile and a half to our house to give us the shattering news. I opened the door to him and shall never forget my mother's reaction when he bluntly delivered the message, 'Chrissie, your dad's dead'. He was only 58 and his death was totally unexpected.

Although I was young, I do have clear memories of him. Life was not easy – there was very little money. He worked for the electricity showroom in Shipley and spent his days visiting on foot the homes of those who needed their electric cookers and other appliances repairing. He had known better things in his youth, but he was not bitter. He had a loving wife and liked to look after his garden. He was not very sociable. But it was quite clear he cared very much for me and my mother. His main recreation was his nightly visit to The Woodman, where he met the friend, Fonce Wall, who had run away to sea with him. But he was sufficiently interested to attend Evensong with his wife and daughter to see me singing in the choir at St Paul's Church, Shipley, something my paternal grandparents never did. He hated pretence and was very much on the side of the 'underdog'.

His wife Annie (née Kitchen) was one of a large family and very capable. She also worked during her married life (unusual in those days). She was able to leave my mother with her grandmother who lived with them. Her job was as cook and baker at a pork butcher's shop in Bingley owned by a German, Albert Schick, who had come over before the First World War. There she had to make pork pies, roast meat etc. for sale in the shop. She was obviously talented at her work and was much appreciated by Mr Schick. When his wife died around 1940, she helped him with the house. I remember going there with my parents one Christmas Day. My grandmother was surprised that when her employer died shortly afterwards, he left her the house and its contents. This greatly improved the finances of my grandparents, and indeed I now have much of the fine furniture, including a magnificent grandfather clock which has just chimed as I write.

Looking back, I realize that I was fortunate to have grown up in such a varied family. Some of my relations were relatively prosperous – my godmother, Kathleen Clark, was married to a Bradford wholesale fruit and vegetable merchant. She was in fact a cousin of my maternal grandfather. We visited her home on a regular basis. When I was 12, she gave me as a birthday present F H Crossley's *The English Abbey*, which ignited my already considerable interest in ecclesiastical architecture. I went on to collect many more Batsford books on similar subjects. My other godfather, Jim Wall, was a cousin of my father's. He was the first in our family to go to university, studying English at Leeds, then taught for a time in Derbyshire before going to Hong Kong to work as a Director of Education. Whilst there he was ordained in the Anglican Church, and on his return held various livings in the diocese of Durham. We kept very much in touch, and I was often able to visit him at home in Hartlepool towards the end of his life.

It would be very hard to say precisely where we stood in terms of social status. My father and my paternal grandfather were both very good with machinery and were appointed to jobs of responsibility carrying decent salaries. Though we were financially 'middle class', my family were 'true to their roots' and never sought to move away from their 'working-class' cultural origins. My grandfather was indeed an example of social mobility on a rather extraordinary scale. As his parents were very short of money, he had to leave full-time education aged eleven in 1898. The education authorities still allowed male and female children to go to school on a half-day basis. One week it was the mill in the morning and school in the afternoon, and vice versa the following week. Thus they 'grew up' overnight in what to us seems a brutal system. But Ellison Bramma was of determined personality and clearly intelligent. He became a weaving 'overlooker' – a mechanic in charge of an 'aisle' of 'power' looms. He was soon appointed as an assistant manager and for the last 20 years of his working life was manager of the whole weaving side of Salt's Mill in Saltaire. He had to run two large weaving sheds, organize the workforce, supervise the upkeep of the machinery and advise the directors on new looms. He was also 'quality control', making sure the cloth was woven to a high standard. The responsibilities were considerable and he was paid accordingly. When he retired in 1956, just before his 70th birthday, he was earning £1800 per annum, a decent sum nearly sixty years ago.

My father refused to go into further education, left school at 14 and was apprenticed, like his father, as a weaving overlooker in Salt's Mill. Like his father, he went to night school, taking City and Guilds Examinations, and in 1936 was successful in the examination for the Associateship of the Textile Institute (ATI). Shortly before I was born in 1936, he was appointed to a Lectureship in the Textile Department at Bradford Technical College which in those days attracted students from around the world. They particularly wanted someone capable of overseeing the large number of looms in the Weaving Shed. In this work he prospered and returned to it after the war. When, in 1953, the Technical College was divided off from the new College of Technology which the Government was setting up around the country, he felt his place was to remain in the Technical College. The authorities thought otherwise and my father was promoted to the College of Technology. When this became Bradford University in 1962, my father then became a university lecturer. He still did research and studied, leading to the Fellowship of the Textile Institute (FTI).

In fact after my father came out of the forces in 1946 and right through my adolescence up to the time I left school, we didn't really get on very well. And basically, this was because I was not made in his own image. The Brammas since the middle of the 18th century had had something of a genius with machinery and technological progress. My father would have liked me to become an engineer or a scientist. Instead he got a musician! We just didn't understand one another. However from an early age, I knew I was going to do something different. There was frequent tension right up to the time I was awarded an Organ Scholarship at Pembroke College Oxford. Thereafter our relationship became mutually more respectful. From the time I started working for my living up to my father's death 22 years later, we became great friends and turned to one another for advice. When I asked him whether I should move from my job in Worcester to be Organist of Southwark Cathedral at a third of the salary I had earned as Assistant Organist and Director of Music at the King's School, Worcester, he shrewdly remarked, 'You've got to get your foot in the door!' And he was right. It proved to be a good move for me in 1976.

I have already alluded to my dim memories of before the war. But after 1940, my recollection becomes much clearer. An event that stands out was the 'call-up' of my father in 1941 when I was four and a half years old. His five years away in the army significantly disrupted our family life. My mother and I now lived alone. For the wartime years, we had to become more independent. A factor which eased things was that my father's mother and father, then aged 49 and 51, lived in the same road as us. They were young enough to play a full part in our lives. My grandfather, Ellison Bramma, became a surrogate father to me. I liked him very much. He was quite different from my father, in some ways less fixed in his views. He continued in his responsible job at Salt's Mill and managed to look after his own garden, and two allotments in which he grew vegetables. We were never short of fresh food. He had style, and a more conscious dress sense than my father. I think he also was more sensitive and musical than my father. He had two gramophones – one with an electric turntable – and a venerable acoustic HMV machine in the front room. They also had a good Ritmüller piano bought in 1913, in the hope that my father would learn to play. I have it still and have used it constantly since I was eight years old. My grandfather also liked to listen to music on the radio – particularly *The Messiah* just before Christmas, to which he devoted a whole evening. I admired him very much; he certainly was a good role model in those years. This was a good thing; but it also made difficulties for me and my father when he returned from the war. I continued to relate much more to my grandfather. My grandmother was also an important influence, although she was rather narrow in her views. She had been brought up a Methodist, which in her earlier years was important. But by the time she was approaching marriage, her Methodism had largely died. There was a vague residual faith, but a greater belief in the side issues – the work ethic, puritanism and teetotalism.

About the time my father went to the war, I started school in the autumn of 1940. My parents were keen that I should have a better education than they had received. So instead of going to the local elementary school, I went to a private kindergarten, Parkfield School, Shipley – the type of establishment which took boys from four to eight and girls up to the age of 11. It was really a preparatory school for Bradford Grammar School (boys) and for the Bradford Girls'

Grammar School, and had a good reputation for getting pupils into these schools. I was happy there. We had a good deal of individual tuition and intensive teaching. I remember a formidable teacher called Miss Watmough, who was very disappointed in our ability to spell and read fluently. So we had an intensive extra half-hour reading lesson each day before lunch, when we had to spell out words on the blackboard which she indicated with a large stick. The school itself was housed in a large Victorian house, and I imagine had around sixty pupils. It was just over a mile from our house in the bottom of the valley at Baildon Green. Those now accustomed to the school run should note that I walked to and from school twice a day as I went home for lunch. This meant that from the age of four I was used to walking five miles a day. My mother took me halfway so she could put me across the main road. I then continued alone. This in itself would be considered remarkable today.

As children, we enjoyed remarkable freedom, and were trusted to go out with friends unsupervised. I was lucky in my early years to have a friend in Jim Ogden who lived in Glenaire Drive, very close to us. He was just three months older than me, and as there were no other children in the road of our age, we very much grew up together. Fortunately our interests coincided. He was an intelligent boy, had an ear for music, and was interested in the countryside, buildings and local history. He eventually went to Salt's High School, Saltaire, then to University College, Durham, where he gained a first in English. Subsequently, he taught briefly at Lampeter, and for all the rest of his working life at the University of Aberystwyth. Almost 80 years later, we are still in touch and see one another from time to time. We maintain a regular written correspondence.

When I was eight, I passed the Entrance Examination for Thorneville, the preparatory school for Bradford Grammar School. This too was in a vast Victorian house, but unlike my first school was boys only. It was two-stream in the first two years, to which a third class was added in the third year. Therefore there were seven forms, each with 25–30 boys. So it was quite a sizable school of $c.160$ boys, with some characterful and able teachers. The kingpin of Year 1 was Miss Fisher, a devoted and very good teacher. One of the teachers, a former Anglican priest, was awarded a Doctorate at Durham in my time in English Studies; another, W. Roscoe-Jones, was a commanding presence who later became a non-stipendiary priest in the Church of England. But my favourite teacher was the Headmaster, H. C. Hill, who was a jovial man with a cheery sense of humour. I remember that when he was ill in the Bradford Royal Infirmary my mother took me to see him, though she insisted I went into the ward alone with a handsome potted azalea. I remember how delighted he was. But I now realize that in a practical way my mother was teaching me an important lesson in kindness and compassion.

The school was basically a happy, informal place, where we were well taught and prepared for the Senior School at the age of 11.

ADOLESCENCE

A point which might be of interest was that in my time, Bradford Grammar School did not have a compulsory school uniform. A school blazer was available, and a cap, and some boys did wear both. There was no regulation about the colour of trousers and socks, and very few boys wore a school tie. It was liberal for those days. And indeed in the Senior School, with the influx of many boys on Bradford City or West Riding County Scholarships, school uniform became even rarer. This continued until the appointment of a more public school minded headmaster, the Rev. J. P. Newell from Giggleswick School in January 1954, who gradually made school uniform compulsory, though in my day this did not progress beyond the requirement to wear a school tie.

In other ways, Bradford Grammar School was very old-fashioned. The curriculum was centred round the classics, modern languages, maths and science, with good history and English departments. Discipline was very good and there were very few instances of bad behaviour. Some of the staff had been there since the First World War, including the music master P. P. Dickinson who had been a choral scholar at King's College Cambridge under Dr Mann. There were some colourful characters, including my form master in 1948, R. H. S. Richards, usually known as 'Black Dick' as he always wore a very dark suit and habitually used a monocle. He took infinite pains with the correction of work, writing long comments in perfect copperplate handwriting. He encouraged imaginative literary expression by awarding ticks to colourful phrases. He was very much of a bygone age.

The staff was greatly enriched by a flow of refugees from Nazi Germany and Austria. Hans Krips had been a High Court judge in Vienna before the war, and the Austrian government begged him to go back after the war. Indeed his daughter, Maria (whom I got to know as she was married to a master at the King's School, Worcester), said he could have become the equivalent of Lord Chief Justice of Austria. He was deeply musical, a cousin of Josef Krips the conductor. I got to know him later, through his daughter, in Worcester, where I passed several delightful evenings with him and his family. He was deeply intelligent and sophisticated company.

I have alluded elsewhere to the low-key music department. The art department was much more effective. This was enlivened by Mr Bayer, also from Vienna, who complemented the rather calmer head of department, Reggie Maddocks. David Hockney was a contemporary of mine; I have heard him speak very appreciatively of the help he received from these two teachers. Even to boys of the same age, it was clear to us that in his early teens his talent was outstanding. He was grateful for his education and subsequently has become a considerable benefactor of the school. I had some artistic ability and also received encouragement from these teachers. I wish I had followed through my painting and drawing skills. These took second place to my musical activities; nevertheless, the teaching brought out my appreciation of the visual arts and a love of beauty in architecture and interior design.

I will try not to exaggerate the characteristics of the school. We received a very good grounding – and I met many interesting boys, a few of whom have become lifelong friends. There were talented pupils, many of whom went on to achieve great success. In my final year in Sixth History there were 11 boys, 10 of whom were awarded Open Scholarships at Oxford and Cambridge; the eleventh got a place! This remarkable achievement was only made possible by the school's 'direct-grant' status, which meant that many of the brightest Bradford boys ended up at the grammar school. Today, though the school flourishes, the successes at Oxford and Cambridge are markedly lower than in my day when bright boys from humble homes made it into Oxbridge.

Despite the lack of musical opportunity in the school, some boys went on to become notable in the music profession. One, Malcolm Binns, was a year ahead of me. I remember in 1948, at the Final Assembly in the old school, he played from memory Chopin's Polonaise in A flat. This impressed me greatly, while I was sitting next to the piano. He went on to achieve distinction on the concert platform. The Tunnell brothers were also very successful in the musical world – John as a violinist and leader of the Scottish Chamber Orchestra, and Charles a fine cellist. There were others who played the organ and the piano, but most took lessons outside school. Robert Bell was a fine pianist who went on to study piano at the Guildhall School of Music in London. I have revived my friendship with him recently, as he now lives in retirement at Arnside in the Kent Valley in a large house. He is an old friend of Peter Barker, who is now a neighbour in Kendal. I knew them both at school. Peter I came to know well in my last three years at Bradford Grammar School, when I was in the Sixth Form. In fact we used to meet in the school hall every morning when I was assisting the Director of Music at the organ while Peter was looking after the electrics. He was interested in amateur dramatics and knew about lighting. We shared interests, particularly music. We soon became good friends. I have to say that my musical motivation came from my piano teacher, church music and the wider musical life of Bradford – not from the musical life of the school.

Life as a day boy brought much wider experience and friendship than to those confined within boarding schools. And life was much more *en famille*. This was usually a good thing; even the disagreements and difficulties of family life, though irritating at the time, were real-life experiences which had a profound effect on the development of wisdom, and indeed stoicism, needed for managing personal relationships.

To my parents, family life was important. We sat down to three meals a day together. We usually had something cooked for breakfast. Dinner (lunch), at 1 o'clock, was the major meal of the day. Incredibly my father travelled home by bus for this. It was quite a rush – and my mother had to make sure the meal was on time. I went back to school full of my mother's hearty fare! We had quite a set rotation of menus. Mondays was always cold meat and hot vegetables. For the rest of the week it could be fried fish, broth with dumplings, chops etc. A speciality was fishcakes – two slices of potato filled with fish, covered in batter and deep fried! And there was always a hot pudding – often steamed suet pudding or on some days rice or bread-and-butter pudding. At 5.30 p.m. we had high tea, which might be ham salad or cold tripe with mustard and vinegar, or something cooked – grilled sausages, poached eggs, fried bacon.

We were very well fed. This was essential in a house which was very cold. The only heating was a coal fire in the living room. Upstairs in winter it was freezing cold. As usual in those days, my mother stayed at home to look after the house – a very considerable task before labour-saving machines. I dreaded Mondays, when the weekly wash started at 8 a.m. and continued till the ironing had been completed around 9 p.m. In winter, the clothes had to be dried before a great coal fire in the living room. During the war, I remember listening to Tommy Handley in 'ITMA', which my mother never missed during the ironing. I very much liked the humour, even as a seven-year-old! We bought a washing machine in 1945, which made mother's work easier. Previously she used a peggy tub and an old-fashioned mangle, while the white garments were boiled in an electric boiler. It is hard to believe how few appliances apart from a Hoover we possessed. It was some time before we had a fridge or a telephone; we only acquired a TV in 1955, just before I left school. But we managed, though it made life much slower. If we wanted to communicate with my maternal grandmother, we had to walk the one and a half miles to her house, or send a letter. This was easier when there was a second postal delivery.

I have alluded already to the benefits of a day-school education and the interesting life we led quite independently from school friends. My friend Jim and I went on frequent outings around Bradford. For instance, by the time we were eleven, we had travelled on all the Bradford tram routes, sitting upstairs on the outside balcony. We walked from our homes over the moors, sometimes as far as Ilkley, from where we returned on the bus. We were free to roam widely. The north side of the River Aire where we lived was almost entirely rural – the former estate of Sir Titus Salt. We could cycle for miles up to the gates of his ruined mansion, Milnerfields. A favourite haunt of ours was in the Glen Beck, where we could climb trees and play in the sand by the River Aire. Our outings often involved calling on our aunts and uncles. We were unfailingly made welcome and given refreshments or meals. We went for miles on foot as a matter of course.

A particularly memorable outing Jim and I undertook was to go to stay with his Uncle Clarence and Auntie Lillian who lived in Cheltenham. Every day we went out. This was in 1950 when we were fourteen. We walked from Cheltenham to Tewksbury to see the abbey; to Gloucester where we explored the cathedral; to Worcester by train, then to Malvern on foot, returning to Cheltenham by bus. We also managed to fit in a visit to Hereford, travelling on the line from Gloucester to Hereford, later axed by Dr Beeching. We obviously knew all about the great medieval buildings, probably from the Batsford architectural series which I collected. Of course we investigated Cheltenham thoroughly. One day we were walking in the evening past St Matthew's Church; the building was locked but we could hear the organ pealing out. Rather courageously we knocked on the vestry door, and to our surprise the organist came to the door. I explained that I was very interested in the organ, and to our great delight he took us in and demonstrated the magnificent organ built by the famous 19th-century organ builder, Henry Willis. I still remember its full-throated sound and the blazing quality of the Pedal Ophicleide. It was my first encounter with 'Father' Willis; I have never forgotten it.

In pre-TV days, we had to make our own entertainment in the evenings. Sometimes Jim and I would visit each other's houses to play Monopoly; or we laid out the top of our dining table with farm animals and two villages built of bricks. For this imaginary world we invented names and characters for which we also provided a newspaper with topical local events, concert reviews, an account of the agricultural show etc. These evenings ended with supper – the name of the small meal eaten in Yorkshire before going to bed. Normally it was tea and a slice of parkin – rough gingerbread made with oatmeal, or perhaps a piece of cake or a rock bun. But when we had visitors, the repast was expanded with scones, date and walnut bread and even sandwiches. Occasionally Jim and I went to his grandfather's to play dominoes with him and the man from next door. It was very good for us teenagers to spend an evening with octogenarians. At the close of play, supper would be provided by Jim's Auntie Mary, who would play the piano for us afterwards. It was always Sinding's 'Rustle of Spring', a florid Victorian parlour piece which we all enjoyed!

My organist friends also organized outings, often on Saturdays. These were set up by Frank Greenwood, organist of St Peter's, Shipley, then in his fifties, who for his day job was a wool sorter, a skilled but dirty job. Usually we were driven in an old Ford 8 by another organist, Frank Whitaker, who as a boy had lived next door to my father. He was now a self-employed plumber. Usually there were about five of us – quite a crush in a small car – who normally set out for Evensong at York Minster when Francis Jackson was still the new organist. Afterwards we might have a meal in York before the homeward journey, which always included a visit to a hostelry en route – sometimes at Harewood. This was long before the breathalizer! On special occasions, we would go on to Selby to meet Walter Hartley, the organist of the abbey, who was then getting on a bit. He was a businessman in Leeds; but in order to take choir practice on Fridays and play for the Sunday services, he stayed at the Lanesborough Hotel in the market place. On these Saturdays he took us in to play the fine four-manual Hill organ in the abbey, which had just undergone a major restoration. Then, of course, after this we repaired to his hotel for a restorative.

On one very cold winter Saturday we ventured as far as Beverley, as Greenwood had arranged for us to play the organ in the minster. After this, we went at about 8.30 p.m. to the Beverley Arms Hotel, then a very traditional old coaching inn, where we would have a very traditional dinner – perhaps steak and kidney pudding. I do remember that the head waiter wore tails; I also remember that as we left the hotel, the organ in St Mary's across the road pealed out through the frosty air. I later learned that this was a fine four-manual by T. C. Lewis, and years later I did much to rehabilitate him to his rightful place in the history of English organ building.

I won't say more about the details of my teenage years. But what I have related should give a good idea of how fortunate I was to have a life outside school. Life in those days in the West Riding was still largely unchanged from Victorian times; I also recognize that the way we made our entertainment at home, and how we communicated with our relatives, was not much different from the habits of the characters of a Trollope or George Eliot novel.

HOLIDAYS

Holidays were considered important by my family. In the 1930s, my paternal grandparents owned a car, and before that a motorbike and side-car. They toured extensively, often with my father, covering much of England and Scotland. After the war I went with my parents on some long touring holidays, for which we borrowed my grandparents' car. Memorably we went in 1951 to Devon and Cornwall via Oxford, where I first visited the colleges and was greatly impressed by the magnificence of the architecture. We went as far as Land's End and then came back via Exeter, where I remember seeing masons at work restoring the bomb damage in the south choir aisle of the Cathedral. We followed the south coast as far as Brighton, then headed north to London, where we visited the Festival of Britain site on the South Bank. Returning from London we always called on some of our London relatives, as I have previously mentioned. Actually they lived in Hertfordshire, around St Albans. I remember having tea with my great-aunt Pat. Then on one occasion we visited my father's cousin Edith in Harpenden. She had two sons about my age with whom I got on very well.

Without describing all our travels, I'll note that we did get around; and looking back, I have to acknowledge my parents' tolerance of requests to do a detour to see such and such a parish church or abbey, although they were far less interested in them than I was. One place I remember vividly was Stamford in Lincolnshire. In those days the Great North Road passed right through the narrow streets, passing very close to St Mary's Church. We decided to stop for a tea break, which I used for a quick walkabout. I was particularly impressed by the Corpus Christi Chapel in St Mary's with its beautifully ornamented barrel-vaulted wooden ceiling. It was more than 50 years before I visited Stamford again. I immediately found St Mary's Church to discover whether my memory of this ceiling was correct, and it was. Since then I have often visited Stamford from London and have come to know all the medieval churches. I consider it obligatory to have lunch at the George Hotel, a wonderfully unspoilt institution with excellent English cuisine. Most county towns in the old days had at least one high-class hotel. Sadly many of these old coaching inns have decayed – or in some cases been turned into shopping malls. The

Crown in Broad Street, Worcester or the Spread Eagle in the centre of Epsom spring immediately to mind.

My first visit to London was in 1947, when my parents arranged to stay at a private hotel in Kensington. To an eleven-year-old, the chance to visit St Paul's and Westminster Abbey and all the other sights of London was a great thrill. Here again my parents realized they had on their hands a boy with a precocious interest in buildings, and obviously thought I ought to have a chance to see London. My paternal grandparents also took me away for a few days by car to the West Midlands. We stayed in Hereford at the City Arms Hotel, which is now a bank, and in Tewkesbury and Stratford upon Avon. Little did I realize that less than ten years later, as Assistant Organist of Worcester Cathedral, I would become very familiar with this delightful English region.

In the years after the war, very few people travelled regularly to the Continent. But I did visit Paris on a school trip when I was about 16. We stayed in Versailles and of course visited the palace; then on Sunday morning – I believe it was Easter Day – I was allowed to go alone to the Cathedral in Versailles. I don't remember much of the service except that it was an elaborate affair; but I have a vivid memory of hearing the Cavaillé Coll organ blazing away. I was surprised by the brassy sound of a French organ. Thinking back to this, it is conceivable that the organist I heard was Albert Alain, father of Jehan Alain and Marie-Claire Alain who was organist there. The Bradford Grammar School masters who organized the trip clearly tried to cater for my musical enthusiasms. Unbelievably, they secured me a ticket for the Paris Opera and allowed me to take the train to Paris on my own. My teachers were either extremely trusting of my capacity for self-preservation, or else unbelievably reckless. In the event I survived the adventure without much difficulty!

I did not travel to Europe again until I was 23. I went with an Oxford friend, John Jenkins, for a four-week holiday in South Germany and Austria. But meanwhile I continued to explore places of interest in the UK. Before the Beeching cuts, when many branch lines disappeared, all kinds of delights were possible. A particularly fine journey I did several times was down the Wye Valley from Hereford to Brecon via Hay-on-Wye through Kilvert country. And in 1957 I travelled home from my College Borstal Camp in Wensleydale – catching the train at Hawes and ascending over the Pennines via Garsdale Junction and Ribblehead. Alas, these wonderful branch lines, though not completely defunct, have largely disappeared.

Looking back over my school days up to the point when I went up to Oxford in 1955, I realize how lucky I was in the wealth and breadth of my experience as a day-school boy. I was able to hear a great deal of music, I played the organ and developed my appreciation of organ sound and history. And I knew interesting people of all ages and backgrounds. All this was done from a secure family base. I think I must have been very difficult to manage, since although my parents did have an interest in sight-seeing and in the beauties of the landscape, they did not share my youthful enthusiasm and knowledge of buildings, topography and ecclesiastical architecture. But looking back more than 60 years to our holiday travels, I realize that my parents did try to cater for my wishes and share my passions.

MUSICAL AWAKENING

My parents used to tell me that they realized from an early age I had an ear for music. They noticed I was all attention when I heard music on the radio. But as mentioned earlier, I did not spring from a particularly musical background, though there was latent talent amongst my parents and grandparents. My mother had been taught the piano by a person who was very much on the light music side, so her repertoire was mostly of arrangements of musical comedies and the like. She often played excerpts from 'The Desert Song'! My father was much less musical, but he had had some piano lessons, and could, given sufficient time, fumble his way through a number of hymn tunes – notably 'Deep Harmony' by Handel Parker, very much a West Riding favourite, often played by the Black Dyke Mills Band. My paternal grandfather and maternal grandmother liked music and had done some singing when they were younger.

My first experience of public music making was at the Independent Methodist Chapel at Baildon Green near our home. I was sent there to the Sunday School with my friend Jim Ogden at the age of four. But my mother warned the superintendent that when I was old enough, I would be going to the Church of England Sunday School, a mile away. This I eventually did at about the same time as Jim's parents decided he was old enough to walk up the hill to the Wesleyan Chapel!

It was at the Independent Methodist Sunday School that I first encountered a harmonium – a large Victorian model with much gothic carving and decoration. It was played by Mrs Stead, who brought her large dog. Normally it went to sleep, but when suitably moved, it joined in the singing, much to the amusement of the children. On special occasions, such as the Harvest Festival, Mrs Stead was persuaded, much against her will, to play the pipe organ in the gallery – an attractive-looking instrument with a 'correct' classical case, dating I suspect from the mid 19th century. I was much captivated by its beauty of tone. I now realize that what I was hearing for the first time was an Open Diapason. Thus my lifelong love of organ tone was born!

During the four years Jim and I spent in this church, we acquired a taste for a collection of hymns and made our first acquaintance with Bible stories and the practice of public prayer – particularly the Lord's Prayer, which we knew by heart by the time we were five. They were formative years, particularly in the development of our musical judgement. Jim had a good ear for music, and often when 'playing out' or on a walk we would sing the tunes we had learned in the Chapel – usually to send them up! Even at the tender age of seven or eight, we realized there was something faintly ridiculous in the notion of 'Jesus wants me for a sunbeam', or with the logic of 'Will your anchor hold in the storms of life' where the anchor was strangely 'fastened to the rock which cannot move'. We not only sent up the words; we were well aware how trite some of the musical content was, and we enjoyed caricaturing the sentimentality and banality of the melodies. But we did hear good hymns too. How fortunate we were that our minds were filled with words and melodies at such an early age. It did not matter if some of the material was sub-standard, as we were quite surprisingly, even then, able to differentiate between the good and the bad.

The event which really sparked off my musical pilgrimage was the day I joined the church choir. My mother persuaded me in the summer of 1945, when I was about eight and a half, that it would be a good idea to become a chorister at St Paul's Church, Shipley, a huge early-19th-century building which my mother had attended as a child and young woman – and where many of my ancestors were married and buried. At my first practice I remember quite distinctly the choir was rehearsing S. S. Wesley's anthem 'Blessed be the God and Father'. I was hooked immediately and instantly fell for the beautiful melody of 'Love one another with a pure heart fervently'. It was being sung by a boy with a golden voice – I even remember his name, Jimmy Barber. He was quite a character and a lovable rascal. Nowadays singing is not regarded as 'cool' by many boys. But in our choir at Shipley, that was not a problem. The twenty boys formed a remarkable cross-section of society – the local butcher's son, the boy from the fish and chip shop. Some were a bit more 'up market', but others were distinctly rough, from the slum end of the parish. Sadly it would be difficult to assemble such a group today. But just after the war, before the days of Sunday football or universal car ownership, there was really nothing to do on Sundays. The camaraderie of the church choir – not to mention the choir pay, the annual outing to Blackpool and carol singing at Christmas – provided an opportunity for young boys to get out of the house and experience independent activity. It was worth putting up with acres of Anglican chant, two practices a week and two services on a Sunday.

At first I found exposure to the local youth rather frightening.

Unlike the other boys, I attended a private school and wore a bright red blazer. I was marked out as different. The initiation rights for new boys were horrendous. We were made to lie on our backs on a table tomb by the vestry door and were then tickled by the other boys – the custom was known as 'hen-pecking'. After this ordeal, the new recruit was thrown over the adjacent wall into the lower graveyard – a drop of about six feet. Somehow I survived this barbarity. Indeed the Head Chorister and ringleader – the boy with the golden voice – soon took me under his wing and on one occasion treated me to a visit to the pie and pea shop in Commercial Street, which dealt solely in hot pork pies and mushy peas, ladled from a vast brass cauldron at the end of the counter.

I soon began to enjoy my life as a chorister. We sang a good deal of music in addition to the psalms and hymns. At Matins and Evensong we always sang an anthem. Many of these were Victorian warhorses such as Myles B. Foster's 'O for a closer walk with God' or Varley Roberts' 'Seek ye the Lord'. But our repertoire did include music by S. S. Wesley and Stanford and occasionally larger pieces such as 'How lovely are thy dwellings fair' from the German Requiem by Brahms. As we used the old black *Ancient and Modern*, our hymn repertoire was very 19th century with J. B. Dykes and Barnby much to the fore. Many hymns we sang are now no longer heard – such as Stainer's 'The roseate hues of early dawn' with its dramatic time change in the middle. Nor was our psalm singing any less old-fashioned. We used the *New Cathedral Psalter* with long gathering notes. Sir Sydney Nicholson and his 'speech rhythm' Psalter had not yet arrived in Shipley, though our choir was affiliated to the Royal School of Church Music.

Throughout my time as a chorister – about seven years – I was increasingly attracted to the fine organ which stood high above the choir on the north side. It was a large three-manual instrument by J. J. Binns of Leeds. Built in 1892, it was an outstanding example of his work. The organist rather jealously guarded the console, which was reached by a spiral staircase. But I did manage to get my hands on the keys from time to time, and eventually when I was about 13, I started to play for the monthly Children's Service. Though I did not yet play the pedals, I enjoyed exploring the sounds of the organ and became well acquainted with organ tonal design. It was also invaluable experience in playing chordal harmony, a skill some young pianists find very difficult. I still watch over this instrument and am glad to say it is well maintained and still unaltered after 124 years.

I had started to learn the piano when I was eight, about the time I joined the church choir. My teacher, Mr Downes, came to our house to teach me. He was very conscientious and gave me a grounding in reading music and basic keyboard technique. But the music he gave me to practise was not to my taste. It was rather low-brow. I envied my friend Albert in the choir whose piano teacher gave him music by Bach, Chopin and Heller! The result was that I lost interest, I didn't practise, so my mother decided my lessons were a waste of time and stopped them when I was ten. But I continued to play – largely improvisation for which I had some ability. After a great deal of nagging, I persuaded my parents to send me to Albert's teacher when I was 12. For the next four years, I entered a completely different world. My new teacher, Eric Jackman, was a very good pianist who had been a pupil of Iso Ellinson at the Royal Manchester College of Music. I took much more interest as I was now learning Beethoven sonatas and Bach's Preludes and Fugues. I was not the best pupil – I didn't practise enough – but I learned much about musicianship, playing with fine tone and expression. Often between lessons, Mr Jackman would play one of the great Romantic pieces – sometimes the beginning of Beethoven's Appassionata Sonata or the Liszt Concert Study in D flat. The sound of his fine playing on his Bechstein grand made a profound impression on me and opened my eyes and ears to what music was really about. It may be that much of my keyboard skills were acquired later on the organ, but I owe a great debt to Eric Jackman.

The organist of St Paul's Church, John Mitchell, was not so much of an inspiration. He had a good ear for the sound of the organ, but no technique whatsoever. He was also our choirmaster, and really only taught us the music by rote. Earlier, just after the war, we had a separate choirmaster, Arthur Cordingley, who had a fine tenor voice; but after a short while he went off to join the choir of Exeter Cathedral. He stayed just long enough for me to have a terrific 'run in' with him. He was keen and asked the boys to turn out for a special practice at 9.30 a.m. on Sundays, an hour before the service. This was obviously a good idea – except that he was always late and kept us waiting at the church gates. This was particularly galling as he only lived across the road! One Sunday we found the church open, so we went in and the boys said 'Go on, Harry, you can start the practice!' So I opened the harmonium and start we did. When he arrived, fifteen minutes late, he was incandescent with rage at my audacity. I and the other boys took a very dim view of this very marked lack of generosity of spirit – or indeed of humour.

When I was 12, the organist had a stroke when I was with him after the service in the vestry. I did manage to walk home with him, but it was a shock to have to deal with such a situation. The result of this sad incident had serious musical implications for me. His place was taken temporarily by Robert Andrews, a 17-year-old pupil of the Royal Manchester College of Music, studying with Harold Dawber. He very much encouraged me, and when my voice broke in 1952, I went to be his assistant organist at All Saints Church, Bingley, where he had recently been appointed organist and choirmaster. In return I received free organ lessons and opportunities to play at services from time to time.

At the time of joining the church choir in 1945, I also moved to Bradford Grammar School – firstly to the prep department at Thornville, a large Victorian house with an overgrown garden which was a schoolboys' paradise. I moved up to the big school in 1948, firstly to the very atmospheric old school building in the centre of Bradford, and then in January 1949 to the brand new building in Frizinghall, opened by the Duke of Edinburgh.

My musical education owes very little to Bradford Grammar

School. The music master, Leslie Walsh, was a competent organist and a good musician. But he was progressively ground down by being the only musician on the staff in a school of a thousand boys. He was also of a rather mercenary frame of mind. For any extra help, he had to be paid – and even towards the end of my time at school, when I was able to play for weddings and funerals as his deputy at a church nearby, he made a practice of only giving me half the fee! I took the view that if I was good enough to play, I was good enough to demand full remuneration!

I think the root of the slight frostiness in our relationship stemmed from the fact that I did not go to him for organ lessons. Even when I had won an organ scholarship at Oxford, I was only allowed to practise on the school organ for half an hour once a fortnight before I played for Saturday morning prayers. To do this, I had to collect the key from the Second Master's study. This was quite an ordeal as the Second Master, W. E. Clarkson, was a person noted for his severity. He was extremely formidable. One day when I went to collect the key, he took me quite by surprise. He said that he thought it was ridiculous that I was not allowed to practise on the school organ. As far as he was concerned, I could practise whenever I liked. All I had to do was to get the key from his office – and he rounded off this act of sabotage by saying 'If I'm not in, you know where the key is!'

WIDENING MUSICAL HORIZONS

As a day school pupil, I had a life outside the classroom in my teenage years, which proved invaluable in my musical and social growth. As mentioned earlier, two of my great-aunts were important in bringing the wider world of music to my attention. Alice Bramma was very musical, and when I started to play the organ in churches, she came to hear me. The other great-aunt, Annie Jennings, was a pillar of the local Methodist Chapel. Quite early on she invited me to the annual performance of Handel's *Messiah* there – I was probably only about eight at the time. This became an annual event. Sometimes she invited my friend Jim too, and provided for us a generous tea between the afternoon and evening performances at her home nearby. Even though I was young, the *Messiah* made an immediate impact on me. Perhaps today I might think those performances 'rough and ready'. But the choral singing had fire and commitment and the soloists, well-known local singers, no doubt acquitted themselves well. But whatever the merits of the performance, the inspiration of the music shone through and very soon I came to know Handel's score very well. The accompaniment was played on the organ by Mrs Franks, whose professional name was Madame Ellen Marsden. The organ console, high up behind the pulpit in the traditional chapel style, was mostly hidden by a red velvet curtain. But as Madame Marsden wore a large hat, occasionally she became visible above the curtain at climaxes such as 'Wonderful, Counsellor' in 'For unto us a Son is born'. She clearly had to exert extra pressure on the heavy mechanical action of the instrument and virtually stood on the pedals at moments such as these!

In the days before long-playing records and CDs, I was privileged to hear much standard repertoire for the first time 'live'. I remember quite clearly, aged about eleven, when I was singing in a massed choirs festival at the Eastbrook Hall, Bradford, hearing for the first time Mozart's great Fantasia in F minor (K608). At the end of the service, the elderly Charles Stott of All Saints, Bradford climbed onto the organ bench and proceeded to play this work in a very grand manner, impeccably from memory. He had been a pupil at the Leipzig Conservatoire in the 1880s, and in fact had been examined in his finals by Brahms! He passed out as the top organist of his year and had to play Bach's Toccata and Fugue in F with Brahms sitting in the front row. But for some reason he never left Bradford. His playing on this occasion on the fine Hill organ was electrifying. As we walked out down the side of the organ, we passed the pipes of the pedal Ophicleide just as the stop was drawn – the first time I was ever conscious of the sound of a low pedal reed.

Later in my teens, from 1953 onwards, the Hallé Orchestra under Sir John Barbirolli at St George's Hall, Bradford gave me the opportunity to hear most of the standard orchestral repertoire for the first time in the concert hall. One tends to forget how thrilling and immediate is the impact of works such as Beethoven's 'Emperor' Piano Concerto or Tchaikovsky's Sixth Symphony. At this period, the Hallé Orchestra was on a high, giving memorable performances week by week in provincial cities like Manchester and Bradford. The string tone was outstanding – but so was the overall interpretative conception imparted to the players by Barbirolli, with his fine sense of balance and nuance, together with a clear overview of the architecture of the music. In this respect, his performance of Schubert's great C Major Symphony was outstanding in his judgement of speed, the sense of forward movement and at the same his ability to linger over passing beauties in the score.

Much of the repertoire was built around Mozart and Haydn, Beethoven and Schubert and Brahms and Tchaikovsky. But there was Sibelius too, and a good deal of Elgar at a time when his music was often absent from the concert programme. Barbirolli also championed Mahler when his music was hardly known. I remember hearing the Ninth Symphony sometime in the mid-fifties, then very much a rarity. There were many other opportunities to hear live music, at the Bradford Music Club and in various churches – the *St Matthew Passion* in York Minster and notable visiting organists such as Marcel Dupré, Fernando Germanni and Flor Peeters at Leeds Parish Church.

But in the early 1950s I also began to encounter music through recordings. We could only play 78s at home on our mighty radiogram – and play them I did, buying sets of Mendelssohn's 'Italian' Symphony and the Bach Violin Concerto in E major. But then I discovered that a work colleague of my father's, David Shaw, who lived in the next road, had started to collect long-playing records. I soon became a regular visitor to his house to hear performances of the Vaughan Williams symphonies in the early Boult recordings, Nielsen, Delius and much more. At this distance it is easy to forget our amazement at the hugely improved sound quality, and being able to listen for long stretches without having to turn the disc over. Though I was grateful for this early opportunity to hear much more music, I'm glad I did not possess a gramophone myself until I was 26 years of age. I was still impelled to go out and find new musical experiences in the concert hall and the opera house – and for this I'm grateful. Hearing music live for the first time is still the best way to make the acquaintance of fine music.

I continued my organ lessons with Robert Andrews at Bingley, often playing for services. I also did quite an amount of deputizing at churches in the Bradford area, encountering new organs and new forms of worship in both the Anglican and Free Churches. In 1954, my organ teacher came to the end of his time at the Royal Manchester College of Music, being called up for military service. I then took over the running of the music at All Saints, Bingley – which included training the large choir of boys and adults. As a 17-year-old, I'm not sure how I coped with having 20 boys in the choir twice a week for practices. But somehow I managed and the choir didn't fall apart. It was, of course, an invaluable preparation for my time at university.

At this stage I began to take music lessons from Dr Melville Cook at Leeds Parish Church. I travelled from Shipley every Tuesday afternoon by steam train, alternating harmony and organ lessons. Dr Cook was a fine musician and I learned a good deal from him about how music is put together. My organ playing also progressed; but he was not a good teacher in grading progress step by step. He tended to allow me to choose the pieces I wanted to learn. Sometimes I attended the boys' choir rehearsal at the end of the afternoon, which was conducted on military lines. At the beginning, the boys lined up in formation in the practice room to do vocal exercises. Discipline was awesome; I remember one occasion when Melville asked for the offenders' register and solemnly proceeded to give the culprit a black mark. I'm still not clear what punishment this indicated – whether a fine, or corporal punishment. Sixty years ago, there were still cathedral organists who kept a cane on the piano. Indeed, the practice of giving boys the slipper did not cease at Gloucester Cathedral until the 1980s! The final disappearance of corporal punishment from the educational world has been one of the quieter revolutions of the later 20th century.

The friends I made in the musical world of Bradford proved influential far beyond the confines of music. They taught me to drink beer when inevitably the evening finished in a local hostelry, earning considerable disapproval from my maternal grandmother! The prime mover of these expeditions was a remarkable character, Frank Greenwood (1901–1960). Quite a number of us congregated at his house on Sunday evenings to gossip and play the piano before the obligatory visit to the Branch Hotel at 9.30 p.m. As I imagine I was under-age at the time, I always felt rather self-conscious in the public bar. One Sunday I was horrified to see my grandmother's cousin at the end of the bar – and in fact he offered me a drink! When I pointed out my unease at meeting a relative in such circumstances, Greenwood said, 'Heavens above, don't worry, drinkers don't tell on other drinkers!'

In 1952, when I was about 16, Greenwood organized an expedition to Manchester where he had arranged for us to meet Norman Cocker, Organist of the Cathedral – not long before he died in the following year. We sat in at the boys' practice. I have a clear memory that he had an excellent rapport with the choristers, and the standard of singing was proficient and committed.

He was obviously in 'show-off' mood for, whilst rehearsing the psalms, at the verse 'The Lord looked down from heaven upon the children of men' he stood on his chair and peered down at the boys over his glasses! Cocker was a fine organist – extremely adept in his management of the instrument, and he rarely used thumb or toe pistons (i.e. aids to changing combinations of stops). On one occasion, he got the Assistant Organist to neutralize all the pistons, after which Cocker gave a recital using entirely hand registration! After Evensong (when the Canticles were sung to Stanford in C and the Anthem was 'There shall a star from Jacob come forth' by Mendelssohn) he showed us the new Harrison organ, which at that time was nearing completion. He played us part of his *Tuba Tune*, which I remember was quite stately, unlike the speeded-up performances of the young tearaway organists of today. It was an immense privilege to meet him; he was a great character, but also I deduced a very private man.

A LIFETIME OF MUSICAL DEVELOPMENT

Once I got to Oxford, my lifetime of musical pilgrimage truly got under way… and here I'd briefly like to highlight the many stages of musical discovery I set forth on before delving into them in more detail chapter by chapter.

My interest in early music really took off after my arrival at Pembroke. Though I had known some pre-1750 music as a schoolboy – I collected single copies of anthems and much of this was from the Tudor period – all my new musical tutors were much involved with the early music of Tomkins, Byrd and Palestrina etc. I was able to hear good performances at New College under H. K. Andrews. My centre of interest really changed in my undergraduate years: having been devoted to the Romantic orchestral classics – and of course the organ works of Bach – I chose to take the Renaissance music option in my Schools. I encouraged my parents to buy me a Goble clavichord for my 21st birthday in 1957; and I took out a subscription to the Early English Church Music series when it started in 1957, volumes then being priced at around 3 guineas! Almost 60 years later I still subscribe, and eventually own up to Volume 57. I have now donated these large volumes to my old college. I even taught the Pembroke choir to sing a 14th-century Magnificat by Binchois, which Bernard Rose (my Tutor from 1955 to 1958 at Oxford – see Chapter 2) gave me.

I still have a strong interest in this music; my admiration for the music of William Byrd increases as the years go by. But in 1961, when I became a teacher at Retford Grammar School in Nottinghamshire,

A LIFETIME OF MUSICAL DEVELOPMENT

I needed to widen my interests. In the early 1960s in a boys' school class, singing was not considered unusual. Much of the material I used was traditional. This served to get the 11- and 12-year-olds singing. I was lucky that quite a number of boys sang in church choirs. These formed the backbone of the treble section in the school choir. I found I was able to discover a great deal of singing talent in the classroom; many pupils I persuaded to join the choir. So they might have found themselves initially singing the folk song 'Dashing away with the smoothing iron' and the following week taking part in rehearsals for the Fauré *Requiem*. My singing career took quite a turn when I was persuaded to take the part of Ralph Rackstraw in a performance at the Retford Little Theatre of *The Pirates of Penzance* in 1962!

My move to Worcester in 1963 brought about an enormous widening of my musical experience. Rather alarming was my debut as Assistant Organist. I had to play the loud G minor chord at the climax of the 'Libera me' in Britten's *War Requiem*. Had I been sitting with the choir and orchestra, this might have been easy; but I was sitting 300 feet to the east at the Harrison organ in the choir – full organ prepared. I certainly made a huge amount of noise, and I hope I came in at the right place! The Worcester Festival Choral Society and the Three Choirs Festivals opened my eyes to much new repertoire – all of which I had to play at rehearsals on the piano. This was a demanding task, and sometimes very hard to fit in with a busy work schedule in the school and the cathedral.

There were some amusing moments. Sir Adrian Boult came to conduct with the Festival Choral Society a performance of *The Music Makers* by Elgar. I had done a great deal of practice. Yet he was not easy to follow, as he had an enormous baton wound round with rubber bands which he held in the palm of his hand. At the accelerando before the choral entry 'With wonderful deathless ditties / *We build up the world's great cities*', I obviously didn't do it to his liking. He stopped the practice and shouted 'Oh! you young rascal!' On a subsequent occasion, when I had to play Vaughan Williams' 'Sea' Symphony for him, I practised the piece for a fortnight until I almost knew it by heart. This rehearsal passed without incident; in fact I felt this time he tended to follow me. This was the 1972 Three Choirs performance to commemorate the centenary of Vaughan Williams' birth. At the performance, Sir Adrian brought the brass in at the wrong time; he resolved never again to conduct a choral work in public, though he did go on to do some impressive studio recordings.

In my time at Worcester, I encountered most of the standard choral repertoire and became familiar with the more recent music of Britten and Tippett, and music written specially for the Three Choirs Festival by composers such as Jonathan Harvey, Gordon Crosse and Richard Rodney Bennett. I had to help in the preparation of Dallapiccola's *Canti di Prigionia*, a work which I found very attractive, written in a highly original style but immediately approachable. This led to my discovery of other works by Dallapiccola, including the opera from which the 'Prigionia' were taken.

At the Kings' School, Worcester I put on a wide range of choral works, including Verdi's *Requiem*, various works by Britten including *Saint Nicolas*, the *Cantata Misericordium* and the operetta *The Golden Vanity*. I started a tradition of staging Gilbert and Sullivan operas every two years, starting with *The Pirates of Penzance* in 1977. These involved two girls' schools in Worcester, the Alice Ottley School and the Girls' Grammar School. The combination of the music and the participation of the girls led to the remarkable success of these ventures! The large number of tenors and basses in the King's School choir was directly a result of these G&S performances. Many boys, having discovered a love of singing in operetta, changed their allegiance to Handel, Mozart and Poulenc. I invested much time in the schools' choral singing. Eventually in a senior school of around 600 there were never less than 125 in the choir – around 20% of the school.

Academic teaching of music and Sixth Form General Studies also gave me scope for exploration. I tried to give the talented boys preparing for A levels a wide experience of music, and was occasionally prepared to suspend the A level syllabus to pursue other areas of music. The boys did not realize at the time, but I was sometimes broadening my knowledge as well as theirs! In the General Studies for which a wide range of boys opted to do a musical choice, I studied with them Wagner operas – particularly *The Meistersingers of Nuremburg* and *Siegfried* as well as Britten's *Peter Grimes*. I supplied libretti for all the pupils. After giving an introduction to the music and the text, I then played one side of an LP – about 25 minutes. I was surprised how much the boys took to these works. And I have to confess that preparing for these lessons greatly enhanced my own knowledge, and paved the way for a subsequent exploration of Wagner and other operas.

When I arrived in London in 1976, I was well placed to continue my musical journey. I extended my knowledge of Elgar very greatly. My interest was aroused in my Worcester days. Indeed, my arrival there in the early 1960s coincided with the great Elgar revival. In London I took the opportunity to listen to more Elgar, including a remarkable performance of *The Apostles* around 1980 at the Festival Hall with the Russian conductor Gennady Rozhdestvensky. I also went to chamber music at the Wigmore Hall, often encouraged by my Oxford friend Richard Drakeford, at that time Director of Music at Harrow School; there seemed to be no music in any genre which he did not know.

As choirmaster at Southwark Cathedral and later at All Saints, Margaret Street, I continued to discover new music. Though much of the cathedral repertoire was known to me from Worcester days and before, there were still many new things – especially at Margaret Street where I started to perform a great deal of polyphony, including the earlier English works by Tye, Sheppard and Tallis, as well as the Renaissance polyphony from the Continent which was increasingly heard – works by Lassus and Victoria, but also by previously lesser known composers such as Guerrero or Lobo.

And so the musical pilgrimage continued. When I retired in 2004 from my post at All Saints, Margaret Street, I decided to get to know better all the Bruckner and Mahler symphonies, as well as improving my knowledge of Wagner. I was able to attend the Mahler Centenary

Festival at Leipzig in 2011, when all 10 symphonies were performed over 12 days by the greatest orchestras of Europe. My particularly memorable Wagner experiences in recent years were *The Ring* under Barenboim in Berlin in 2013 and under Ivan Fischer in Budapest in 2014.

Now in retirement, the volume of new works still to be discovered is truly life-enriching. Since I retired from full time work in 1998, I have also been able to devote more time to choral composition. Much of this music was written for my choir at Margaret Street. When I retired from there in 2004, my successor Paul Brough continued to ask me to write music. I was surprised when he asked me for an anthem for the 150th anniversary of the consecration of the church in 2009. This resulted in 'This is the day the lord hath made'. It has subsequently been sung at Trinity College, Cambridge. Another piece I wrote for Margaret Street in 2010 was a setting of the 'Benedicite' which has been performed at Matins at Christ Church, Oxford by Stephen Darlington.

So this final section of Chapter 1 has aimed to chart a summary of my musical encounters through the years: a kind of whistle-stop tour through the many stages of discovery which have enriched and rewarded my years of personal development.

CHAPTER TWO

Oxford

PEMBROKE COLLEGE

My election to the Organ Scholarship at Pembroke was entirely due in the first place to my Form Master at Bradford Grammar, Reginald Petty – Reggie as he was always known. He had an enviable reputation for placing his pupils opportunely for university applications. He took immense trouble to determine which college would offer the best chance for each particular boy. When I was about 16, he came up to me one day and said, 'Bramma, I think the best way for you to get into Oxford or Cambridge will be by way of an Organ Scholarship. I notice in the *Radio Times* that Jesus College, Cambridge is broadcasting Evensong next Tuesday. Listen to it, and tell me whether you think you could cope with that sort of thing.'

As a result of this conversation, I tried unsuccessfully for Clare College, Cambridge in December 1954. It was a depressing episode; I felt underprepared, and it was exceptionally wet. It rained continuously all the time I was in Cambridge. I found Boris Ord (Organist and Director of Music) at King's very unfriendly in the way he conducted the organ trials, and my encounter with John Robinson, Dean of Clare – who later attracted national attention through his defence of *Lady Chatterley's Lover* and his book *Honest to God* – was no less easy. The only thing I remember about the interview, apart from my nervousness, which he did little to relieve, was the question 'Tell me about yourself' – not really an unfair question. But Yorkshire boys were not that used to talking about themselves in those days!

Though I experienced my first serious rejection at Cambridge, the episode left me with unforgettable memories of that city, most notably the interior of King's College Chapel, then entirely lit by candlelight. At night, the fan vaulting was just about visible as if through a haze. I attended Evensong, and was bowled over by the beauty of the singing. My one clear memory is of the anthem, Balfour Gardiner's 'Evening Hymn', then unknown to me. The gradual build-up on the organ and the choral entry was electrifying. I came later to know more of Ord's genius as a choir trainer, but I shall never forget that first live encounter.

The following February, I went to Oxford to try for the Organ Scholarship at Pembroke. My experience at Cambridge proved useful, and Oxford I found altogether friendlier. As it was term-time, the candidates were put up at the extremely old-fashioned and run-down Ross Hotel near Carfax – the sort of place which still had chamber pots in all the bedrooms and Brown Windsor soup on the daily menu. My musical examiner was Dr Thomas Armstrong, Organist of Christ Church, shortly to become the Director of the Royal Academy of Music. I managed the Bach Prelude and Fugue in G quite well on the very rickety Pembroke organ of those days, and I believe I acquitted myself well in transposition, improvisation and score-reading. I have to confess that I knew the sight-reading slightly, a piece (if I remember correctly) by Buxtehude, which I had heard several times on a recording of 18th-century German organs.

My interview with the Chaplain, Colin Morris, later to become Professor of Mediaeval History at Southampton University, was a friendly and stimulating occasion. He had read in the references of my interest in ecclesiastical architecture, so obviously thought he would try me out! He asked the question, 'Did I know the difference between Tierceron and Lierne Vaulting?' I did, and I'm convinced that got me the scholarship. Colin Morris dined out on that story for years. Having secured the Pembroke Organ Scholarship, I returned to my last six months at school, preparing for A level Music and the ARCO (Associate of the Royal College of Organists) Diploma, which I successfully sat in July 1955. The other obstacle to clear was the Oxford Qualifying Examination in Music. In those days, undergraduates had to pass this before embarking on the Honour School of Music. So I went off again to Oxford in the summer. My instructions from Pembroke said that for the examination I had to wear a dark suit, white shirt and white bow tie! This rather alarmed me. I asked my form master whether I had to walk through the streets of Oxford in such attire. His reply was characteristic – 'Oh, don't worry about that; they're used to all kinds of oddities on the streets of Oxford!'

ARRIVAL AT PEMBROKE

October 1955 marked a major turning point in my life. There was quite a crowd of former Bradford Grammar School boys at Bradford Exchange Station in early October 1955, waiting for the 10 a.m. South Yorkshireman for Marylebone on the now defunct Great Central Line. We changed at Banbury to a train for Oxford. I remember the single fare was 28 shillings! I made my way to Pembroke and to my room in the Old Master's House. I discovered that all the first-year scholars were on the same staircase – several to become lifelong friends. Quite astonishingly the person in the next room, John Gray, had been in the same class as me at Bradford Grammar School. Another close neighbour was Don Taylor, who went on to achieve fame as a writer and theatrical producer of stage and screen. I suddenly became 'Mr Bramma'! My fellow scholars thought, when they saw my name on the board at the bottom of the staircase, that I must certainly be from India.

We had the usual introductory talks. The one I remember best was that of the Dean, R. F. V. Heuston, a distinguished Irishman, later to become Regius Professor of Law at Trinity College Dublin. He was rather eccentric of manner, with a plummy voice. The part of his talk which amazed me was the lengths to which he went to explain how we must address various senior members of the college. 'If you write to the Master or the Bursar', he said, 'you must begin 'Dear Master' or 'Dear Bursar'. But if you write to the Dean, you must begin 'Dear Mr Dean'. Such niceties were for a West Riding lad quite a new phenomenon!

In 1955, Pembroke was a small college of 180 undergraduates and 9 Fellows. Its buildings, dating from the 16th to the 20th centuries, were attractive – notably the 17th-century Old Quad, the Chapel of 1732 and the fine neo-Gothic Hall of 1837 modelled on Eltham Palace, south-east London. It was a friendly place with a real sense of its own special identity. The rapport between dons and students was good, strengthened by a fair amount of entertaining and conviviality – though breakfast parties in the Master's Lodgings at 8.30 a.m. could be something of a trial. In those days, most undergraduates took three meals a day in Hall, where the food was generally good and wholesome, and extremely plentiful. Breakfasts were particularly lavish – kippers, bacon and eggs, sausages, herrings – all regularly served in succession, with very decent coffee. At dinner, beer was the common drink, served in the college's large collection of silver tankards, many dating from the 18th century. It is a sad reflection of more recent times that it is deemed expedient not to trust the undergraduates with solid silver tableware these days.

There is no doubt that the undergraduates of the 1950s drank far less than the undergraduates of today. Of course the Rugby Club went to the Jolly Farmers, and there were festive occasions of one sort and another. But most students could not afford to go to the pub every day or drink habitual quantities of wine and spirits, because we lived at a time when overdraft facilities were not available. Students had to balance their books, especially those with restricted financial resources – the majority, I would say, at Pembroke.

As in every Oxford college, there were many luminaries in former generations, including at Pembroke Samuel Johnson, James Smithson, Senator Fulbright and J. R. R. Tolkien to name but a few at random.

In many ways Pembroke was then a conservative institution – largely the legacy of Dr Frederick Homes Dudden, Master from 1918 to 1955 – who had never really moved from the 18th to the 19th century, let alone the 20th. There was one aspect where this really showed. Pembroke was the last but one to abolish compulsory chapel attendance in 1956. I believe Worcester College retained it for a little longer. So my first year coincided with the last year of mandatory attendance at services. Until the death of Homes Dudden, the requirement was three times weekly, which he regarded as extremely progressive! With the election of the Vice-Master, R. B. McCallum, as Master in 1955, changes were quietly implemented. But it was felt that the practice should die gently, so in 1955–56 first-year undergraduates were still required to attend chapel, but only at Sunday Evensong four times a term. The sight of the venerable College Porter, Ponsford, marking the register at the chapel door now seems to us almost unbelievable. Automatic respect for the college authorities was still a characteristic of undergraduate life, so the first-year men, however radical or pagan, deemed it better to turn up rather than risk a fine – or worse, get into the bad books of the governing body.

The chapel services were entirely congregational, led by a small group who turned up half an hour before the service to rehearse the hymns and chants. The organ by Martin of Oxford (1891) was small, and becoming very arthritic, but capable of pleasing sounds. The amateur organ enthusiast, Noel Bonavia Hunt, was a former member of the college, and I suspect he fiddled with the voicing of the instrument. However, the organ was well restored by Harrison and Harrison during my time, in 1957, and the instrument continued to give good service until the new Letourneau instrument arrived in 1995. The case was particularly pleasing. It had been much restored, but did contain some 17th-century carving, having been previously in the Sheldonian Theatre.

The other factor which emphasized the rather old-world atmosphere was that most of the college servants dated from the inter-war years. They still regarded the students as 'young gentlemen'. Ponsford the porter and Duke the high table butler were venerable figures, and the scouts who looked after the college rooms were usually friendly and in some cases great characters. Hector was the scout who cleaned all the shoes. We were well looked after, but had to cope with the Spartan conditions of those days – no central heating, straw mattresses, and long journeys to the loos and washing facilities. In my second year, I had to go down two flights of stairs and across two quadrangles if I required the bathroom in the middle of the night!

THE MUSIC FACULTY

My arrival at Oxford was for me a great liberation. At Pembroke I found freedom to live my life as I wished it in the pleasant and only slightly controlled environment of the college. But it was the stimulation of many new friendships and the experience of really first-class musical tuition that brought about a revolution in my intellectual development.

The most remarkable thing which happened to me – my meeting with Dr Bernard Rose – was really brought about by an historical accident. It had been customary for those reading music at Pembroke to be taught by the music don at Christ Church – the College having no resident musician. But my first Michaelmas term in 1955 coincided with a musical vacancy at Christ Church. Thomas Armstrong had recently left for the Royal Academy of Music, and the new organist, Dr Sydney Watson, was unable to take over until January 1956. This presented the Senior Tutor of Pembroke, Donald McNab, with a problem. He had not foreseen this, and so when I went for my interview with him he had to find a tutor for me. He telephoned Bernard Rose, then Fellow of The Queen's College, and luckily he agreed to take me on. Thus one of the most significant encounters of my life happened almost by accident.

Bernard Rose was 39 when I first met him – but he had the air of someone much younger. He was slightly built, smartly dressed and extremely vivacious in manner – almost theatrical. I had never met anyone like him. He was stylish, something of a wag, and to one used to the accents of the north of England, he had a very 'upmarket' voice. I found him somewhat formidable – he came on rather heavy. But it was not long before we developed a friendly relationship, the ideal climate for learning and teaching. I soon realized that the outward grandeur of personality was very much on the surface. I came to understand that he took a genuine interest in my musical welfare and education. In my first year I shared my harmony and counterpoint lessons with an undergraduate from Lincoln College, but in my second and third years I was taught alone – moving with Bernard from Queen's to Magdalen in 1957 when he took over as Organist and Choirmaster there.

By the standard of today, his teaching methods had no worked-out scheme. It was really a question of turning up with work for him to mark. He expected his pupils to be self-motivated and to a considerable extent to teach themselves. Things are very different now. Having taught harmony to undergraduates at King's College, Cambridge and Christ Church, Oxford in the years 1998–2005, I know how necessary it is to teach them how to do composition exercises, as so few students have received instruction in harmony and counterpoint at school. In the past it was different. Most had been prepared for this kind of work, and in my case I had passed the ARCO before arriving at Oxford.

Sometimes Bernard suggested what I might do for the next tutorial, and made helpful suggestions about how to approach the subject. But he usually left it to the individual to choose what to do; and then he taught subsequently. His corrections were extremely thorough and his comments helpful – often a casual remark for instance about the importance of the second inversion chord in the music of Richard Strauss, or the variety of techniques used in fugal writing. He gave a series of lectures on Fugal Exposition, later made into a small book which was a model – enough detail but not too much. I suppose Bernard's aim was to inspire as much as to instruct. His profound love of music and his ability with notes on paper were truly inspirational. During his first year at Magdalen, he became involved in writing for the chapel choir. I remember his enthusiasm when writing his new Responses for Evensong, and how he played them to me as he wrote them. They are now a cathedral classic and sung worldwide. He was particularly fond of the response which incorporates the chimes of the Magdalen clock. And he would make excellent recommendations – 'Get someone to buy you Haydn's Opus 20 String Quartets for Christmas' or 'Have a look at Hindemith's book on *Traditional Harmony*'. He was full of ideas and keen on music of all eras, whether Tomkins, Handel or Constant Lambert.

As I got to know him, tutorials became more and more a meeting of friends. Of course the instruction came first, but there was a good deal of interesting conversation, often by way of reminiscence. And there was always an element of gossip – he loved that! It was the informal part of tutorials that were often the most informative and inspirational – and indeed convivial. The pupil before lunch almost always was given a glass of sherry, while he had gin and bitter lemon.

One day when we were talking about Stanford's church music, he said, 'Sir Walter Alcock once told me (Bernard had been a chorister under Alcock at Salisbury) that Stanford complained bitterly that choirmasters took his Evening Canticles in C too fast.' They still do, ignoring the metronome mark and turning the Magnificat into a jolly two in the bar, making a mockery of the serious and monumental nature of the piece. I got to the stage where I feared to attend Evensong in a cathedral when Stanford in C was on the list for the day. Such anecdotes were a fascinating and regular feature of my weekly tutorials. The undergraduates who Bernard liked became his friends for life – and many have been grateful for assistance in later years.

He could of course be formidable. God help the people he did not like! The academical clerk in the Magdalen choir who incurred his wrath might be subjected to a torrent of choice army language. It is said he was not above kicking the chorister next to him in the choir stalls, so much so, as legend would have it, that the boy resolved to wear shin pads! I used to find his moods volatile. He could be very direct – like the day he complained I had not shaved before my tutorial. 'I have sent undergraduates back to their colleges for not shaving before now,' he said. He was right, of course. He could however be very magnanimous. At the end of my second year, I had omitted to do any work and turned up with a degree of trepidation saying, 'I have a confession to make.' 'What?' he said. 'You mean to say you haven't done any work? It happens to everyone once in their university career. Come to the buttery and I'll buy you a drink!'

He was unpredictable, and by today's standards politically very incorrect. He chain-smoked through most tutorials, using a cigarette holder which up till then had been something outside my experience. Nor had I seen an ashtray like his: the butt of the cigarette was placed on the top groove, and when a knob at the top was pressed, the fag end disappeared into the cavity below the tray.

Bernard was fun, colourful, occasionally alarming, and very often hugely generous: like the wonderful Sunday lunches at Bampton which he and his wife Molly organized, or his willingness to write music for old pupils. At my request, he wrote a beautiful small Introit, 'Surely Thou hast tasted that the Lord is good', for the choir at Southwark Cathedral; he then made sure he was there at the first performance – though for him this had to be a special performance in the vestry afterwards, as he had missed the beginning of the service because of heavy traffic! He complimented the choir warmly, and was heard to remark that the standard of the choir was 'near miraculous'.

Bernard Rose was unconventional in his approach, which made him truly inspirational. He assumed that an undergraduate would have a natural ability to learn and to enquire. His job was not to spoon-feed, but to enthuse and guide – to light the touch paper. It was a method which worked well for me and many of his pupils, and was in line with what university education is all about.

For my first two years at Oxford, I went alone to Dr Frank Harrison for tutorials in the History of Music. He too was an inspirational figure, but in a very different way. He was not so personally interested in the undergraduates – though he did have a reputation for being rather fond of the women students. What attracted me to him was his pioneering work in the field of English medieval and renaissance music. When I was with him in the mid-fifties (1955–1957) he was in the middle of transcribing *The Eton Choir Book* (published by Musica Britannica) and researching for his own book *Music in Medieval Britain*, which sought to relate the music of the church to its architectural setting. All this interested me very much and I grew to respect him a great deal. My studies were centred round the general history of music, and it became clear that he knew a great deal about all periods.

In my first year, I used to follow David Cawthra, a fine musician from Yorkshire, who ended up teaching at the University of Exeter. He was studying Mozart Piano Concertos for his special subject, and as his tutorial often overran, I listened to the instruction without taking much notice. Harrison was describing the form of some of the movements on the back of a postcard; I remember him getting quite animated about whether a theme which occurred in the orchestral Prelude but not in the exposition proper would reappear in the Recapitulation – or how varied and imaginative were the ways Mozart introduced the piano at the beginning of the Concerto. All this rather went over me until about ten years later I discovered the wonders of Mozart's Piano Concertos for myself. It was only then that I saw the significance of what he had been saying – and the extent of his knowledge. Frank Harrison never became a personal friend; but he remains a considerable figure half a century on, and was a person I still remember with gratitude for opening my eyes to so much of interest across the whole range of music.

In the autumn of 1957 Harrison went on sabbatical, so I was sent for my final year to Dr H. K. Andrews for History and the Special Subject paper. I immediately struck up a rapport with him – rather fortunately, for with Ken Andrews you were either 'in' or 'out'. Those he approved of were treated graciously and occasionally taken for a pint in the King's Arms in Holywell at the end of the tutorial. He was an awe-inspiring figure – physically of great height and lumbersome gait, with a characteristic way of speaking which was slow and something of a drawl. He too was politically incorrect in that he smoked a pipe throughout tutorials, which occasioned the lighting of innumerable matches. Very unusual at that time, he wore plus fours. He certainly was formidable; it was wise to keep on the right side of him. I had first encountered him from a distance as Director of Music at New College, a post he resigned at Easter 1956. During my first two terms I often went to Evensong there, and was much moved by the quality of singing. In fact, it is arguable that King's College, Cambridge was the only other good church choir in Britain at the time. In Oxford, his choir towered over Magdalen and Christ Church, where standards were abysmal. Andrews was a perfectionist and demanded very high standards of tone, intonation and blend. He was satisfied with nothing less than the best, and to achieve this he would often rehearse right up to the time of the service.

His performances were powerful, perhaps by today's standards over-romanticized. But I shall never forget the impact that his readings of Byrd and Palestrina had on me. He could be strangely unauthentic, particularly with regard to organ playing. To hear him playing Purcell's Evening Canticles in G minor was quite incredible. Forte meant the addition of the second Diapason on the Great; fortissimo called for the addition of the Large Diapason and the Open Wood on the Pedal. He was not a good organist – his size 13 shoes must have been something of a hindrance. But as a choirmaster he was pre-eminent at a time when standards were generally low in the English cathedrals.

He had already been out of New College for over a year when I became his pupil. At that time he was preoccupied with his monumental book on Palestrina, which was published in 1958. But like Frank Harrison, he had a great knowledge and love of music over a wide range. He was a particularly appropriate tutor for me as I had opted to do as my Special Subject the music of the Renaissance, including set works by Palestrina. As an undergraduate, I became increasingly interested in Tudor and Elizabethan music, and to this day Byrd is still one of my favourite composers. I learnt a great deal from all my tutors in this area – Bernard Rose was an authority on Tomkins and edited the *Musica Deo Sacra* for the Early English Church Music series.

Andrews, like Rose, was a great raconteur and at the end of tutorials liked to digress. He was full of stories of the mid-20th-century cathedral world, many of which had a rather scornful quality. One such was his description of a visit to Lincoln Cathedral where the choral standards were not good. He had sat in the organ loft for Evensong, during which Dr Gordon Slater, the Cathedral Organist, had gone down to conduct a performance of the difficult anthem 'Laudibus in Sanctis' by Byrd. Slater, who was immensely proud of the fact that Byrd had been a predecessor as organist at Lincoln, said to Andrews on returning to the loft, 'You'll have to go a long way to hear Byrd sung like that', to which Andrews commented to me 'I was forced to agree with him'! Andrews' humour often had that kind of cutting edge – but as long as one was on the right side it was extremely diverting.

There were many interesting musicians in the Music Faculty in my time, including Edmund Rubbra and Dr Egon Wellesz who lectured on Mahler and Bruckner symphonies at a time when these were rarely played in Britain. As a former resident of Vienna, he had known Mahler. Sir Jack Westrup, the Professor, was an outstanding musical all-rounder – an excellent lecturer with a dry sense of humour. But in personal relationships he could be formidable, and I never felt at ease with him. He once said to me with reference to my Yorkshire accent that he liked to hear regional accents around Oxford – a remark that was meant kindly but which I found embarrassing. But like so many university musicians of his generation, he had great versatility. He was the outstanding Director of the University Opera Club, conducting the annual performances. It was he who mounted the first production in Britain of Monteverdi's *Orfeo* and in the 1950s the first performance of Smetana's *The Bartered Bride*. Westrup was a fine musician and a considerable intellectual – the right person to inaugurate the new Honour School of Music after the war. The last time I saw him was in the late 1960s, carrying a very large suitcase down a side street in Worcester. He had come to address the Elgar Society. On that occasion he seemed pleased to see me – but would not hear of me carrying his case! He appeared rather forlorn and unwell, and I believe it was not long after that he died.

The musician in the faculty I knew best after my three tutors was Dr Sydney Watson. As his walking route from Christ Church to the Faculty of Music often coincided with mine from Pembroke, I frequently chatted to him, walking along the street. He had come up to Oxford in the mid-1920s as Organ Scholar of Keble, and after a brief spell as Organist of New College worked in public schools – at Stowe, then at Winchester and Eton. He was a first-class natural musician, a fine pianist and a proficient conductor. I attended his score-reading classes when it was deemed necessary for undergraduates to be able to read from a full orchestral score. His ability in this field was prodigious. He could manage the most complex of scores in the most musical way imaginable. He would play a movement from a Beethoven symphony, for instance, with great panache, making it sound as if it had been conceived for the piano. I also enjoyed his lectures, which displayed a great knowledge of 19th- and 20th-century music. He was not a scholar in the modern sense, but I found the information he was able to impart, in an attractive way, most helpful. Curiously, when speaking in public, he displayed little of the pronounced stammer he experienced when speaking *tête à tête*. He had charm and in some ways his speech difficulties added to this. Stories relating to his stammer abound. A fine example relates to a conversation in the street with an undergraduate who had recently finished his Finals, for which Sydney was one of the examiners. He was alarmed when he was told, 'I am able to tell you, you got a sssssssssssss…first!'

Though Sydney was a fine musician, he made little impact on the choral music at Christ Church. A slight improvement might have been detected when he arrived in 1956, but overall the quality of the singing was at best routine, or at worst downright unacceptable. His work with the Oxford Bach Choir was rather different. I remember some rousing performances, such as Walton's *Belshazzar's Feast* in the Sheldonian Theatre. But I imagine that here he really went for the broad sweep and did not go into too much detail – which might have occasioned H. K. Andrews' remark at the end of the final rehearsal for a concert at which he deputized: 'and when did you say the concert was?!'

Sydney was an imposing presence physically (very tall) and in manner (rather grand). He had clearly revelled in life at Eton and had a distinct preference for good-looking young men from public schools. I felt very much an outsider in this milieu – he was in fact a terrible snob. But later on, when retired from Christ Church, he continued as an examiner for the Associated Board of the Royal Schools of Music. I encountered him when I was training to be an examiner, or later when he moderated me. The children liked his genial and friendly manner – because of which he was able to get away with the most outrageous remarks. To a boy entering the room to take Grade 4 on the guitar, he might say, 'Joseph, you don't mean to tell me you're taking your examination on that dreadful instrument'; or to a girl who had just achieved a distinction in Grade 8 piano, but who was weak in sight-reading, he said, 'Cynthia, you must practise your sight-reading; you must practise it, every day; you must practise it – yes, you must!' I'm sure the poor girl left the room thinking she had failed! He was very against the rules – but he carried it off with aplomb.

READING THEOLOGY

In 1958, Pembroke College elected me for a fourth year as Organ Scholar. This was because I wished to stay for an extra year to study for the Diploma in Theology, as I was at that time considering ordination in the Church of England. In those happy days before student debt, the State Scholarship attached to my Organ Scholarship was extended for an extra year. During this year, I continued to play the organ and direct the choir in the college chapel. By then, I was living in lodgings down the Woodstock Road. Having taken a good second-class degree in Music, I started on the Theology diploma in the Michaelmas Term 1958. I had only been engaged in this for a couple of weeks when I realized that the diploma syllabus formed a very considerable part of that for the Honour School of Theology. I therefore decided to transfer to the degree course. This meant staying two extra years until 1960. Again, the college was able to arrange with the Department of Education for the necessary funding. Launching into the degree course was quite a shock, as in those days it was required to study the Gospels, Acts and the Epistle to the Romans in the original Greek, as well as the Treatise (also in Greek) by Athanasius 'De incarnatione'. To someone who had only studied Latin for O level, this was a considerable challenge – one that I only partially mastered. But the study of the Bible, the Fathers of the early church and Reformation history I found very interesting.

I was particularly fortunate in my tutors. David Jenkins, then Fellow of Queen's, was my Director of Studies. He later became a national figure as Bishop of Durham, and during the miners' strike he became Mrs Thatcher's *bête noire* – or as she famously put it, 'a cuckoo in the land'. I found him friendly and considerably eccentric, as well as alarmingly intelligent. When discussing a point he could become very animated and sometimes descend from his chair onto his knees, then proceed to move round the room kneeling down! I sometimes found him very difficult to understand. But I discovered that if I wrote down his comments, afterwards when I read my notes, I began to see what he was getting at. The fact that he spoke extremely quickly did not help. His mouth could hardly keep up with the speed at which his brain raced ahead! I studied New Testament and Doctrine with him.

Along with this, I found Kenneth Woollcombe's lectures on the

Fathers of the early church a great help – they were both enlightening and amusing. At this time he was Fellow of St John's, later Bishop of Oxford and finally Canon of St Paul's. He had a lightness of touch and clarity of thought which made these early figures come to life. Later on when he was in London, I was able to thank him for what I had gained from his teaching.

For Old Testament studies, I went to Roy Porter at Oriel College. He later became Professor of Theology at Exeter University. He was very different from David Jenkins: polished in manner and very careful about his appearance; he was still young at 35 and probably the best lecturer in the Theology Faculty. He too was alarmingly clever. His lectures on the Book of Judges attracted very large attendances. He was lucid – and for those days radical, in that he related the thinking and customs of the Jews to the cultic history of their Arab neighbours. As a tutor he was stimulating and thorough – but he was often too caustic and intolerant of undergraduates who did not live up to his expectations. I worked hard to satisfy his demands, but I found his scornful comments difficult to handle. He was certainly the most difficult and alarming teacher I have ever experienced in any subject. A Pembroke friend found his tutorials so disturbing that he had to find another tutor! A few months after I graduated, I was on holiday in Germany and attending a concert of Richard Strauss music in the Herkules Saal in Munich. I happened to look round and was amazed to find Roy with a few Oxford undergraduates sitting exactly behind me. On this occasion, he was charming and seemed pleased to see me.

The part of the course I found most congenial was the Reformation History special subject. It fitted well with my interest in Lutheran church music and the late medieval buildings of northern Europe. Here my tutor was Revd T. M. Parker, chaplain and fellow of University College. He was immensely learned. This was summed up charmingly in the Preface to the *Oxford Dictionary of the Christian Church*, on which in the early stages he collaborated with Canon F. L. Cross, the editor, who described him in the splendid Latin phrase

'Cuius eruditionis fontes plurimi gustavimus exhausit nemo' ('Whose erudition, the source of most things we have enjoyed, wearied no one'). He was a kind-hearted man who I took to immediately. He took his priestly vocation very seriously and always wore a black suit and clerical collar; he felt he should always be recognizable as a priest. He used to tell the story of how an Englishman staying in a foreign hotel became seriously ill. He wished to see an English priest, but none could be found. Unknown to the hotel, an Anglican priest was actually in the hotel but was not identified as he did not wear a collar! Parker was short in build and portly and cut quite a figure walking down the High Street in his ten-gallon hat. His facility in Latin was prodigious. He obviously felt this was not unusual, and several times I heard him quote a lengthy passage in Latin in a sermon and then continue, assuming the congregation did not require a translation! He once famously started a sermon by saying 'as most of you will know, in the year 1080 the Pope wrote a letter to the Patriarch of Constantinople…'! It is hard to do justice to his personality in a few words. He had a dry sense of humour and was always low key. He also smoked a pipe, often in tutorials. One felt he had more than a touch of sanctity. He came from Welford-on-Avon, where his family had been butchers for seven generations. When I knew him, he became Master of the Butchers' Company in the City of London. He was very popular with the meat porters in Smithfield Market when he happened to pass that way. They used to greet him in a friendly way and often called out 'Good morning, Father'.

During all this, I continued to live in my Woodstock Road digs and was well looked after by the Miss Lamberds – Nora and Mary. Nora stayed at home and looked after her three undergraduates. This included cooking breakfast, which we had at the civilized time of 8.45; the food was good with excellent coffee. The three of us often got caught up in lengthy conversation, which often caused us to be almost late for our morning appointments. The second Miss Lamberd taught at St Philip and St James C of E Primary School (Phil and Jim) in Leckford Road. She clearly found the work stressful, and didn't take kindly to the three of us. She had a very short fuse; I was frightened of her partly because she disapproved of my friends calling round to see me. Living in someone else's house is never easy; it is easy for tensions to arise.

Reading Theology, I encountered many new friends. One became very close to me: John Jenkins, whom I met at a lecture in January 1959, and we soon became good friends. He had come to do ordination training at Wycliffe Hall theological college, having read Theology at Lampeter. His course also included studying for the Oxford degree. He was rather a fish out of water at a 'low church' theological college, but he was musical and shared many of my interests. We probably spent too much time together for those engaged in a stringent two-year course, and used to go off on expeditions; one such visit was to see the medieval stained glass in Fairford Church on the pre-Beeching branch line via Witney. In the summer of 1960 we went on a four-week holiday to South Germany and Austria, starting with a long railway journey to Ulm from the Hook of Holland. We saw a number of the Baroque abbeys of Bavaria, including Ochsenhausen, Ottobeuren and Weingarten. I shall never forget hearing the exquisite bell-like tone of Weingarten's fine organ, when we were lucky enough to hear someone playing Bach. We went on to Lindau and then sailed to Bregenz on Lake Constance – a very good way of approaching Austria. We then went by train over the Vorarlberg to Innsbruck and onwards by train through the Bavarian Alps to Garmisch and Munich, seeing many sights on the way, including the fairy-tale castle at Neuschwanstein. Then we followed the Romantische Strasse to Rothenburg, and finally turned westwards across Germany to Heidelberg, Metz and Amiens on the way home. It was a wonderful tour. Though we had to be careful with our money, we were able to eat well and stay in good hotels. This was because the exchange rate was extremely favourable to us – something like 10 marks to the pound; so at the Schwarze Adler in Ochenhausen, we were charged 4 marks for the room – at that time about eight shillings and six pence in English money!

The tour was just after we took Theology Schools. John returned to Wycliffe Hall for one year, before being ordained to a curacy at St Paul's, Sketty in the diocese of Swansea and Brecon. We remained in touch till his untimely death at the age of 60 in 1996. This was only occasionally, as he married, had a family and lived a good distance from me. I still see his widow, Jane, from time to time.

For some time whilst reading Theology, I had come to have doubts about the wisdom of ordination for me. I was interviewed by Chesslyn Jones, the brilliant but eccentric Principal of Chichester Theological College, on the day when I had taken the written papers for the FRCO (Fellow of the Royal College of Organists). He kept me up talking till very late, by which time I was exhausted. I had met him before at Pusey House, where he was a librarian. He was a great character and very musical, but I imagine difficult to live with.

I was also interviewed at Wells Theological College by the Principal, Kenneth Haworth (later Dean of Salisbury). I felt more at home here and accepted his offer of a place. I had already been accepted by the church's selection committee (CACTM), which seemed to be a lightweight affair. The Chairman was Archdeacon Sidney Bulley, later Bishop of Carlisle, a very agreeable man. But I did get the impression that in those days if you were a graduate of Oxford or Cambridge, you were unlikely to meet serious obstacles.

However, early in 1960, I was having serious doubts about my vocation. I felt at that stage that I would be unwilling to go to a tough parish, for instance in the industrial North. The allure of cathedrals and church music was too strong. It was because I was unable to accept ordination with no conditions that it seemed wise to withdraw. This meant that I had to decide what I was going to do when I left Oxford. I had applied for music posts in several public schools, and was interviewed at Uppingham unsuccessfully. But I do retain happy memories of a train journey from Rugby Central to Seaton Junction near Uppingham – a line shortly afterwards axed by Dr Beeching.

As a precautionary measure I had applied to the Oxford Department of Education for a place to study for the Diploma in Education. The Principal at the time was highly accommodating. He said that if I failed to get the job at Uppingham, I could do the education year – which in fact was what I did. The experience was useful; it also gave me breathing space to sort myself out. Happily in this final year I had a room in the house of Colin Morris and his family in Pembroke Street. This meant I could share in the life of the college and eat meals in Hall. On a personal level, it was very pleasant as I had become close to the Morris family – and indeed was godfather to Gillian Morris in 1959, a relationship I maintain 50 years later, as Gillian now lives in Wimbledon quite close to me in Beckenham.

I was succeeded as Organ Scholar in 1959 by Lionel Pike, who ran a first-class male voice choir and went on to a long and distinguished career at Royal Holloway College. He had there an excellent mixed voice choir of undergraduates, who sang daily; he was also promoted to a professorship and became well-known as an authority on Peter Phillips.

As I look back almost 60 years, I feel I made the correct decision about ordination. I was in fact too much of a musician to discard lightly the skills natural to me. This feeling has strengthened over the years. Though I am interested in many things, I feel music is the only subject in which I have real expertise in all its aspects: playing and teaching the piano and organ, having a wide knowledge of all music – opera and orchestral music, as well as that for the church. I have an innate harmonic instinct, which enables me to improvise and see how music is constructed. This has enabled me to compose, which has been a key factor in my instrumental teaching and in teaching the techniques of composition, particularly in my Worcester days and later when I taught at King's College, Cambridge and Christ Church, Oxford after I retired from full-time work.

However, I never regret my theological studies. The experience of this very different discipline has been continuously useful to me in relating to clergy and understanding the place of music in the liturgy. It was particularly useful when I became Director of the Royal School of Church Music, when I had to reconcile Christians of many different traditions. I also wrote a regular editorial for *Church Music*

Quarterly in which I tried to look at things across a broad spectrum of belief and practice and sought to remove the not infrequent rancour between the different parties in the church. Thus on leaving Oxford, I reverted to being a musician, a change back to where I began. Throughout my long professional career, I have never regretted this.

CHAPTER THREE

Nottinghamshire

Having decided not to take up my place at Wells Theological College, I then had to sort out where I could start a teaching career. I had been unsuccessful in an application for a junior music position at Uppingham School, so I applied for the post of Director of Music early in 1961 at King Edward VI Grammar School, East Retford. I was so shocked when the Headmaster offered me the job immediately after the interview that I accepted on the spot! I then spent the next six months wondering whether I had made a terrible mistake. Going to the depths of Nottinghamshire was a great risk, as it could mean I was consigned to a lowish level of teaching appointment for the rest of my life. But as often happens, the move turned out to be the best thing I could have done.

Retford was a workaday market town set in quiet but delightful countryside between the Trent Valley to the east and the Dukeries to the west – the grand estates of the Dukes of Newcastle at Clumber and the Dukes of Portland at Welbeck Abbey. But it was also adjacent to the South Yorkshire and Nottinghamshire coalfields. This meant that the boys who came to Retford Grammar School were from extremely diverse social backgrounds. It was a small school of 420 boys, and its catchment area included both Retford and Worksop. So some of the boys came from sleepy rural backgrounds; others from the mining villages round Worksop. All were bright, but those from the mining communities were lively and often something of a handful. There is no one more difficult to teach than the bright naughty pupil. They were always one step ahead.

After Oxford, it was very much a culture shock – and just what I needed to bring me down to earth with a bump. The school at Retford was a pleasant place with a friendly staff, many of whom had been there since before the war. They had had plenty of time to ripen into great characters in many cases. The Headmaster was a Cambridge man – John Gover – very much in the 'low church' evangelical tradition. As with so many evangelicals, he was deeply conservative socially and politically and would very much have preferred Retford to be Repton! He was a hugely magnanimous character – very much larger than life. But looking back, I now see how the aping of public-school tradition in such a school was wrong and did a great deal to create a hostile environment for the boys from working-class homes.

In my first year, I was put in charge of 3B, the most badly behaved form in the school. Some of the boys were quiet country boys, docile and well behaved; but at least half the class came from the mining villages, and they were very difficult. In retrospect I can see they were wonderful characters; but for a novice teacher like myself they were hard to control. As their classroom was the Music Room, I saw a good deal of them. I also taught them Religious Education twice a week – the evangelical Headmaster insisted that all forms had two weekly divinity lessons – something almost unheard of elsewhere.

I battled with them for over a term, and they really had begun to get me down. But then a most remarkable thing happened. On a very wet January day, the boys were in the classroom at lunch time – something which was allowed when the weather was bad. Then one of the boys shouted out, 'Go on, sir, give us a tune.' I duly obliged by playing some popular numbers on the piano – evidently giving pleasure, for after that they never caused me any trouble. Clearly the ringleader, a lovable rogue called Lee, had put out the word that hostilities should cease. So much so that when I arrived to teach them just afterwards, there were two boys waiting inside the double doors of the classroom who duly opened them for me as I arrived. It was all quite extraordinary.

Corporal punishment was still very much part of life at the school. Some of the staff could be physically violent. One, an ex-Indian Army officer, used to knock the boys out of the way with his walking stick as he walked along the corridor. The cane was still much a feature of the Headmaster's study. As it was a state school, beatings had to be witnessed. So as a master in charge of the naughtiest class in the school, I was forever going along to the Headmaster's study. The Head laid into the lads with some force – then shook hands with them. I became convinced that corporal punishment did no good whatsoever. The kind of boys who found themselves on the receiving end became heroes in the eyes of their mates in the classroom. Thankfully, one of the greatest revolutions in schools over the past 50 years has been the gradual, untrumpeted disappearance of the cane.

I was fortunate to inherit a good musical tradition, thanks to my predecessor, Alan Taylor, who had just moved on to be Director of Music at Haberdasher's Askes School in Elstree. There were a good many musical boys, some decent pianists and a number of good brass players who had learned their music in the local Salvation Army Band – a source over generations of fine brass players. The main musical strength of the school was choral singing. There were some very good boy trebles and teenage altos, tenors and basses, and staff also added weight to choral activities. I was helped by the fact that quite a number of boys sang in the excellent all male choir at Worksop Priory or in the choir of St Swithun's, East Retford. But many developed their musical skills at the school. During my time we put on several concerts, including the *Fauré Requiem* and Vaughan Williams' 'Five Mystical Songs'. We also managed a credible performance of Byrd's six-part 'Sing Joyfully' at the Founders' Day Service. Singing was very much evident in the school – and this included regular hymn practices with the whole school.

There was also a strong tradition of boys taking music at O and A levels – again the result of hard work by my predecessor. The orchestral side was not strong. There were peripatetic teachers of instruments, but insufficient full-time staff and instrumentalists to constitute a decent orchestral tradition. Generally the school was very successful academically, with many boys going to university, including quite a number to Oxford and Cambridge.

I made many good friends on the staff, including Ken Birch, the highly successful head of the RE department. The son of a Staffordshire miner, he had been a Methodist minister – but soon forsook this for teaching, at which he was very gifted. He was the mainstay of our regular evening gatherings in various local hostelries – usually organized by the Second Master, Bernard Beasley, with trips to the Angel at Blyth and the Newcastle Arms at Tuxford as well as frequent meetings in the gentlemen's bar at the White Hart in Retford. This last was an incredible survival from an earlier age, where regulars had their own chairs and woe betide anyone who dared to sit in one unbidden. I suppose we drank too much – but there was little else to do in such a very parochial town. There was the Retford Little Theatre, at which I once appeared as Ralph Rackstraw in *The Pirates of Penzance*. There was also the Retford Music Club, organized by Peggy Williamson, a remarkable lady who I came to know well; she seemed to run most things in the town, from her grand Georgian house at Ordsall.

On arrival in Retford, I became Organist and Choirmaster of St Saviour's, Retford, which had quite a decent choir of boys and men. The building was just across the road from my lodgings: a rather austere early-19th-century stock brick Tudor – quite impressive inside, with a good acoustic and the remains of a fine organ by Bevington, regrettably altered by Nelson of Durham. The Vicar, Tom Womack, was an interesting man, then in his 60s. He presided over what was in those days thought of as a 'low church', but he was no Biblical fundamentalist. In fact he was an adherent of the Modern Churchman's Union and very much an admirer of W. R. Matthews, Dean of St Paul's. He was hugely supportive of the choir, and was indeed the chief recruiting officer for boys as he cycled round the parish on his venerable bicycle. The treble section was a hugely varied social mix, with boys from the smart middle-class end of the parish as well as a number of lads from deprived homes in the extremely run-down council estate opposite the church. They were also the best behaved set of boys I have ever encountered. This was because the Vicar was a fierce disciplinarian. When a boy joined the choir, he was interviewed in the clergy vestry and left in no doubt of the standards required of him. I never found out what was said on these occasions – but whatever it was, it certainly worked.

The church was fairly well attended; the Vicar had quite a following for his sermons. There was also good lay support – principally from the church warden Arthur Baker, who in fact was the local baker who ran several shops in the town. He cut an impressive figure as he greeted the congregation. He was very much the local lad made good, a confirmed bachelor who bought his suits in Savile Row and who seemed to spend most of his time in his office behind the bakery, which was dominated by a large photograph of Winston Churchill. I occasionally was asked to visit him there – when at some point he opened a drawer in his desk and produced a bottle of whisky and two glasses. St Saviour's was an interesting church community of a type which has now completely disappeared.

During my time at Retford, I was persuaded to play the fine Father Willis organ for the Parish Mass at the 'Anglo-Catholic' parish in the town – St Michael's, West Retford. The energetic young priest was Frank Pearce, who was doing fine work there, and I enjoyed my weekly exposure to traditional liturgy with incense, even though it made for a very busy Sunday morning: 9.30 at St Michael's, after which I cycled up the hill for Matins at St Saviour's at 11 o'clock.

I made many good friends in north Nottinghamshire – particularly Eileen and David Burnham in Worksop. David was the local probation officer, but also a fine musician who ran an excellent choir of men and boys at Worksop Priory, which he ruled with a rod of iron. He and I hit it off from the beginning, and soon the Burnham houseful became home from home. Their two sons, Patrick and Andrew, were both choristers at Southwell Minster, and both went up to New College, Oxford to read Music. Patrick became Director of Music at Trent College, Long Eaton, whilst his younger brother Andrew was ultimately ordained and eventually became 'flying bishop' of Ebbsfleet (i.e. a bishop opposed to the ordination of women to the priesthood). I occasionally meet him – a very sparky character but very obsessed with his opposition to women priests in the Church of England, a viewpoint I increasingly find incomprehensible. The love affair which some Anglicans have with the Roman Church is hard to understand, considering that church does not accept the validity of Anglican orders. But almost 50 years ago in Retford, these doctrinal skirmishes were very much in the distant future.

Although settled into my work at Retford Grammar School, I was not ignoring my future career. But decisions about this were taken out of my hands by my Oxford tutor, Dr Bernard Rose, who was determined to rescue me from provincial obscurity. Shortly after Christmas 1962, at the beginning of my second term at Retford, I received a letter from him saying that Sir William McKie was looking for a sub assistant at Westminster Abbey following the death of Dr Osborne Peasgood. He asked me whether I thought I would be up to it. Modestly, I said that I thought I was, with the result that I went up to the Abbey for interview and audition. I had little real sense that I would be successful, and quite rightly the far more experienced candidate, Simon Preston of King's College, Cambridge, got the job. But the exercise was hugely helpful subsequently. McKie had obviously taken a liking to me and reported to Bernard Rose that I had given a good account of myself at the organ – when I had improvised and played the Mozart Fantasia in F minor and major.

My visit to Westminster caused some consternation at Retford. The Headmaster was not used to his Director of Music being summoned for interview at places of the prestige of Westminster Abbey. However, I settled back into school work and the social life of Retford. But not for long. A year later I received a telephone call from Christopher Robinson, asking me whether I would be interested in going to Worcester as Assistant Organist. He himself had only been in post about six months as assistant organist to Douglas Guest, having succeeded Edgar Day who had served as assistant at Worcester for 50 years (1912–1962). When Guest was appointed Organist of Westminster Abbey in succession to Sir William McKie, the Chapter at Worcester decided they had the right person to be the new Organist in their midst; they were right. They clearly recognized Christopher Robinson's outstanding gifts, and having sought assurance from Dr Herbert Sumsion of Gloucester that their plans were feasible, Christopher Robinson was appointed.

At the time, it was felt that the new Assistant Organist should be qualified to teach in the King's School, where the Music department was a scandal. It was run by an amiable character, Reggie West, who before the war had been assistant to Sir Percy Hull at Hereford Cathedral and then Organist for a time at Armagh Cathedral. He had clearly showed musical promise when younger, but he had little aptitude for school teaching. The boys ran rings round him. His appearance did not help: long, untidy hair and a bow tie, not unlike a latter-day Franz Liszt. He also had a penchant for best bitter: I doubt whether he drank huge quantities of it, but he drank frequently, and often in the lunch break. Because he often reeked of alcohol, he acquired the nickname of 'Pongo', and his piano was referred to as the 'Pongolium'. The grand piano in College Hall was covered in scratched graffiti applied by the boys during music lessons there; they were not complimentary.

The Headmaster, David Annett, wanted to try to improve the school's music, and it was thought that I might be able to achieve something in this direction as a part-time assistant music teacher. So I was summoned to Worcester, interviewed by the Dean, Robert Milburn, and by the Headmaster, and in due course was offered the job. I learnt subsequently that Bernard Rose had been working behind the scenes on this occasion too!

The appointment to Worcester caused something of a shock at Retford Grammar School – even more so because the Cathedral would not confirm my appointment until I had been interviewed by the whole Chapter, even though I had an offer from the Dean in writing! However, about a month later, I went off to Worcester again to meet the Canons. I arrived late morning to meet three of the Canons sitting with the Dean at a long table in the round Romanesque chapter house. All wore academic dress, and two added gaiters and frockcoat to their black gowns. They were a distinguished group, but very conservative in outlook. The Dean, Robert Milburn, was very much the junior at 55, and had arrived six years earlier from Worcester College, Oxford where he was Chaplain, Fellow and Bursar.

Although I had travelled that morning from Nottinghamshire, the interview was quite perfunctory, though friendly. They were mostly concerned that I should take seriously the Voluntary Choir of men and boys. My meeting with the chapter was quite short, after which I was taken back to the Deanery for a very pleasant lunch. This too was rather old-fashioned – so much so that I remember the menu: braised steak and onions followed by cabinet pudding!

This rather Trollopian beginning led to a happy relationship with all who sat round the table that morning. But for me, for a while, it was a return to Retford to complete my second year at the school and churches there. When the time came for me to leave, I was given a very good send-off. In some ways I was sorry to go. There were excellent pupils in the school, three of whom were just about to start their A Level Music course. And I had made good friendships amongst the staff and in the town. Of course I looked forward to working in a cathedral. But as it turned out, my two years at Retford were the best thing that could have happened to me just then. They quickly erased the 'Brideshead' vestiges from my thinking. I came to realize the true value of people for what they really are, whatever their background. And for this return to reality, I shall be forever grateful.

CHAPTER FOUR

Worcester

ARRIVAL ON COLLEGE GREEN, SEPTEMBER 1963

As I look back, I am aware of moments when circumstances dramatically changed the course of my life. Arrival at Bradford Grammar School and at Oxford brought new opportunities which profoundly affected my subsequent career. My appointment at Worcester was similarly one of these moments.

This was the first time that I had a house of my own. At Retford I had lodged with a pleasant family, but not entirely happily. Now I moved into 9, College Precincts, a large house which today would be considered totally unsuitable for a bachelor by cost-conscious cathedral authorities. It was not in those days considered odd to put a single person into a house with four bedrooms, three reception rooms and two bathrooms! It was like many buildings in the city, originally 16th- or 17th-century timber-framed, to which had been added in the 18th century a brick façade, in this case rather in the Dutch style. There were at least three different types of window and a good deal of old woodwork, including a low-fitted sideboard and panelling from Jacobean times. Though it had been redecorated, it really was in need of total refurbishment. And it was very cold in winter, with no central heating. I relied on coal fires and a stove in the dining room, so that at least one room in the house was always warm.

My initial problem was how to furnish the house, but my family helped me out. A cousin of my father's who ran two newsagent's shops near Bradford had entrée to a wholesale warehouse in Huddersfield, where I was able to buy beds, carpets and many other household items. Then my family decided to thin out their furniture. My maternal grandmother was particularly generous. My piano came from Yorkshire, bought by my father's parents in 1913 – a good, well-made instrument by Ritmuller of Göttingen. It has served me well throughout my career. Other items I found in second-hand shops. The house turned out to be a great resource, as I did a great deal of my teaching there; and I started to entertain. Here I developed my cooking skills, much encouraged by my next-door neighbour, Isabel Braley, a Canon's widow.

In those days the Cathedral was immensely sociable. There were frequent parties and dinners and impromptu meetings for drinks or visits to the Cardinal's Hat, where the organists were almost always included. These days, Cathedral organists often complain that there is insufficient communication between the Chapter and the musicians. But being regularly included in the social round, we in 1960s Worcester had a much better idea of most of what was afoot. In those days, Trollope was very much alive and well, though sometimes one felt that the Cathedral was actually more 18th century. It was significant that the Dean's dog was called Woodforde, after the well-known clerical diarist, Parson Woodforde.

The Canons regarded the Cathedral as very much their private chapel, to which the public were admitted. In fact when I arrived in 1963, the public was largely absent. On weekdays at sung services, however, there were quite a number of regulars; and at weekday Evensong usually more than four or five were present. At weekends, visitors from the countryside and Birmingham swelled the numbers; and in the summer there were many tourists. But on Sundays, the normal attendance was dismal. At Matins in the nave, at best there were 30 to 40 people, swelled by the unwilling addition of boarders from the King's School. They hated the service, which in its traditional formality made no attempt to reach out to them. The Bishop of

Worcester, the impressive Mervyn Charles-Edwards, referred to their presence there as 'the slaughter of the innocents'!

Immediately after Matins at 11.30, the Sung Eucharist took place in the choir. There was no interval between the services. The men and boys processed up into the choir and immediately started the Introit. Choirs had to have strong bladders in those days! The congregation at the Eucharist usually numbered around 75 on a good day. This tended to be a rather 'upmarket' crowd from Worcester and the surrounding county. The liturgy was old-fashioned Tractarian, with the three ministers in copes at the High Altar. It was dignified and had good musical content. The Byrd masses and some Palestrina were sung in English. There was a good deal of the Anglican repertoire by Stanford, Ireland and Wood; frequently the Creed was sung to a choral setting. I suspect the congregation preferred this music. The Archdeacon's wife, Lady Alethea Eliot, was once heard to remark after Palestrina's *Missa Aeterna Christi Munera* – 'It was alright for Palestrina, he didn't have to cook the luncheon!' New music by Walton and Lennox Berkeley was beginning to feature; but the bulk of the repertoire for this Prayer Book Liturgy was deeply conservative.

Evensong was sung twice in the Cathedral on Sundays. The 4 o'clock service was sung by the Cathedral choir, at which there was usually a decent congregation in the choir. A good many came from the parish churches; some sang in the Worcester Festival Choral Society; and others came from as far away as Wolverhampton. At 6.30, the Cathedral Voluntary Choir sang Evensong in the nave in a congregational form. This was a relic of the popular evening services held in many cathedrals before the First World War. At Worcester in 1963, there was still a good following for this service. I suspect that the attendance was often the largest of the day.

When Worcester Cathedral re-opened in 1874 after the major restoration of Sir George Gilbert Scott, there was a surge of considerable new spiritual life. Ninety years later, this tradition had ossified and much about the liturgy was moribund. There were of course notable members of staff, and the musical tradition throughout had remained strong, attracting distinguished organists such as Sir David Willcocks (1950) and Douglas Guest (1957), both formerly at Salisbury Cathedral. But until the late 1960s, the Cathedral remained a deeply conservative place, a remarkable survival.

THE CATHEDRAL CLERGY

In 1963, there were four Crown Canons, appointed by the Prime Minister's patronage secretary. Two were aged 80; the other two were in their early 70s. The Dean at 56 was young! They had one thing in common – they were all Freemasons. This was not unusual then, but would be almost unheard of these days. The Canons were distinguished individuals but were growing old, and only with difficulty could the Dean get them to do anything outside their normal routine. Three of them had academic backgrounds. The most senior in years, Dr Evelyn Braley, had been Principal of Bede College, Durham. Dr Arthur Shepherd had been a much loved parish priest and was an authority on Rudolf Steiner; he was a homely and friendly individual, usually known as 'Uncle Arthur'. Claude Armstrong was Anglo-Irish by origin, a good classical scholar and former Headmaster of St Columba's College, Dublin, a well-known boys' public school. He was formidable, but had a waspish sense of humour. He once remarked that a fellow Canon had strained his back reaching for a prayer book! He had a strong ascetic streak, and into his 90s translated part of a psalm into Greek before breakfast. The fourth Canon was Bishop C. E. Stuart, formerly Bishop of Uganda. He was an endearing character who took his faith very seriously. His reading of lessons was memorably eccentric and delivered in an extremely upper-class voice.

The Canons in post when I arrived gradually retired. They were replaced by an interesting and varied collection. The first to arrive was Coliss Davies, an academic, whose background was Church of Ireland. Like most Irish clergy he was 'low church' – certainly not a rabid evangelical. He moved into the impressive Georgian house by the north porch of the Cathedral – the one that featured on the £20 note next to a portrait of Elgar – a circumstance which much irritated the person who had bought the house from the Cathedral at a time when the Chapter were busy asset-stripping. He felt he should have been consulted. My cherished house in the College Precincts was sold too. But in my time, all the Canons lived in grand houses in the precincts. Canon Davies was well intentioned but not robust in health. Consequently his contribution was low key. But he could flex his muscles, and it was he who opposed the singing of Latin masses and the liturgical changes in the 1960s and 1970s. He did rather give the impression of being 'against' rather than 'for' things.

The second appointment was Peter Eliot, Archdeacon of Worcester, who had previously doubled up as a parish priest at Cropthorne – or Crorpthorne as he pronounced it – a small village near Evesham. He had been a London solicitor who was ordained and became curate at St Martin-in-the-Fields when the incumbent was the Bishop of Worcester, Mervyn Charles-Edwards. Peter Eliot and his wife Lady Alethea, daughter of the Duke of Buxton, really were a breath of fresh air. They were of aristocratic bearing, but nevertheless with a common touch. They became very popular in the Cathedral and city. Both were prepared to exert themselves. Lady Alethea ran the Festival Club at the Worcester Three Choirs, and worked hard to make it a success – sometimes to be seen putting out the dustbins at the end of the day; though she would have been the first to admit she was not particularly musical. Standing on her dignity was not her style. Both she and her husband always joined in – even to the extent of taking part in the play *The happiest days of your life* put on for the boys by the King's School masters. A memorable moment was when Alethea, to great applause, spoke the line 'as far as you can see round her, it all belongs to me'. The Eliots' time at the Cathedral corresponded roughly with mine. They added colour to the community life in the Close, which I much appreciated.

The third Canon to be appointed was William Purcell, who arrived early in my time in 1965 from a post at Coventry Cathedral, which he combined with work for the BBC in the Midlands. A down to earth Yorkshireman, he certainly livened things up. I got to know the family well – his three children were roughly my age. I was a frequent visitor to 10 College Green for the magnificent Sunday lunches put on by his wife Margaret. I also sometimes went out walking with Canon Purcell in Worcestershire, or further afield in the Black Mountains, where on one occasion we got hopelessly lost when conditions changed and we were shrouded in mist. Sometimes we went with the whole family – memorably once to North Yorkshire.

Purcell did much for the Cathedral. He encouraged groups in the city to make use of it; he was also a great supporter of the Cathedral choir. It was he who got in touch with Harry Mudd at Abbey Records to arrange our first recording in 1966. And he was proactive on the pastoral front too. For instance, there was a teenage boy in the Cathedral Voluntary Choir – Michael Latham – who was eager to train as an organ builder with the nearby organ builders, Nicholsons of Malvern. The managing director turned him down because he was a grammar school boy; they thought him unsuitable material for an apprenticeship. This infuriated Canon Purcell, who went across to Malvern and told the managing director he had to take him. And he did!

Purcell was quite a character. His Yorkshire voice was very much in contrast to the velvet tones of the other Canons. His reading of lessons was highly amusing, in that he played fast and loose with the punctuation – for instance replacing commas with full stops in most inappropriate places. When he retired in 1976, his wonderful house overlooking the Severn water meadows with distant views of the Malvern Hills was turned into the Deanery, as the new Dean, a single man, found the Queen Anne house at the other end of the Close too large after the death of his mother and aunt.

The last new clerical arrival in College Green during my time was Eric Turnbull, who replaced the 80-year-old Claude Armstrong. He too had a very pleasing house – largely 18th century but with much older work incorporated into it. It was reputedly the house occupied by Thomas Tomkins in the 17th century, the most illustrious organist of the Cathedral, still very much remembered for his choral and instrumental compositions.

Eric Turnbull came from St Margaret's, Kings Lynn, where he had been Vicar. He was an able man and a fine speaker. He was a Kelham boy – that is he was educated in the monastic community of the Society of the Sacred Mission at Kelham near Newark, which took boys at the age of 14 who were drawn to a vocation in the priesthood. Many boys from humble homes were educated there, and the majority were eventually ordained. The eminent former Bishop of Edinburgh, Richard Holloway, was at Kelham and speaks movingly of the place in his recent autobiography, *Leaving Alexandria*. It may seem strange to us that families were prepared to send their sons to such institutions at a tender age. But it was a way into education for the very many able boys who failed the examination for entry to a grammar school.

Eric Turnbull was a smart and sophisticated man – well read and cultured with a love of music. He was not always appreciated as he should have been by the Cathedral community. It is very sad to say that this was probably because he was gay, though in fairness there was no real hostility to him on this count. When he arrived in 1970, it was not the custom to come out as gay. Indeed, it was only three years after the Labour government repealed the laws against homosexuality between consenting men over the age of 21. But to Turnbull's credit, he did not try to hide his nature, nor did he vaunt it. In those days clerical attitudes were often totally hypocritical and uncaring in such matters – and many others. But he did make an intelligent and cultured contribution to the life of the Cathedral, and became totally accepted as someone who had something to say. I personally found him a bit distant; but I do remember how warmly he congratulated me on my appointment as Organist of Southwark Cathedral. He also recognized the progress of the Diocese of Southwark, which was light years ahead of the diocese of Worcester in its determination to be relevant to life in the later 20th century, under the leadership of Bishop Mervyn Stockwood.

I have tried to do justice to the personalities and abilities of these men, as in their various ways they were people of real qualities. Nowadays it would be harder to find so many distinguished clergy in the chapters of our cathedrals. As the former Bishop of London, Richard Chartres, recently said, there is a shortage of talent at all levels in the Church of England of today.

THE CATHEDRAL CHOIR

Ever since 1950, under Sir David Willcocks and then Douglas Guest, Worcester's choir had maintained a decent standard of performance; but both choirmasters were hampered by the very mixed quality of the lay clerks. Nowadays, many adult singers in cathedral choirs hold university degrees and are thoroughly well qualified as musicians or in other disciplines. But 60 years ago this was not so; some might have been school teachers, but others were quite likely to be shopkeepers or have other forms of poorly paid work in the town. By the time Christopher Robinson took over in September 1963, things had improved slightly. One of the altos, Malcolm Darling, had been a Choral Scholar at Cambridge; the other, Dennis Wickens, a good musician, was Director of Music at the Royal Grammar School. Henry Sandon at this time worked in insurance, but later became curator of the Royal Worcester Museum and as a result became an internationally respected expert on china and porcelain, becoming a much-loved personality on the TV *Antiques Roadshow*. He had been taken on by Willcocks, and when I first knew him was a bass-baritone whose singing had considerable character and professionalism. His performance of the large bass solo in S. S. Wesley's 'The Wilderness', though not perhaps in vocal quality of the very highest calibre, had a dramatic power and understanding I have never heard equalled. Christopher Robinson filled a tenor vacancy by appointing Richard Day Lewis, a fine young singer who later moved to Westminster Abbey. The remaining two lay clerks were both older: Neville Dilkes was an English master at the King's School – a delightful man, but past his best as a singer; and Victor Douse was an Irishman who sang bass. Though he was not really qualified as a lawyer, he doubled up as Chapter Clerk and wore a wig when required to help in the installation of Canons etc. He was an immense character and had a certain panache: he smoked Turkish cigarettes called 'Passing Clouds' in his office, and was known to lock a gin and French in the safe if he saw the Dean approaching his office across College Yard.

Gradually during Christopher Robinson's eleven years in office, other younger singers were appointed to fill vacancies. Graham Hewitt (from Birmingham) and Alan Fairs (a Cambridge man) were basses; three tenors, John Potter, Timothy Hooke and Trevor Owen, were former Oxbridge Choral Scholars; and two new altos were John Southall, who worked for Lloyds Bank, and Barry Still, who had sung at Salisbury Cathedral. Southall had a remarkable high alto voice which caused him to be nicknamed 'Farinelli' by the others; Still taught at the Royal Grammar School and was a published musical editor. His edition of the fine anthem 'Almighty God, the fountain of all wisdom' by Tomkins is in regular use in cathedrals.

So it could be said that the calibre of the lay clerks much improved at this stage. They were all professionals with good sight-reading ability. The vocal standard overall was good, but not outstanding. These men can be heard to good effect in several early recordings made between 1966 and 1969: notably *The Sacred Music of Elgar*, produced by Brian Culverhouse and still available as a CD, which includes Herbert Sumsion's landmark performance of Elgar's Organ Sonata on the old Gloucester organ.

In those days, choirs neither recorded nor toured to the extent that is commonplace today (2016). But in my days at Worcester, we did a visit to Yorkshire in 1970 followed by a memorable tour to France and Germany in 1972, when we sang in Notre Dame, Paris and in the cathedrals at Fulda and Speyer, and at churches in Mainz and Heidelberg. There was also a further tour, in 1975, to the Flanders Festival under the direction of the new organist, Dr Donald Hunt.

Though the overall singing of the choir in this period reached a high standard, it was the quality of the treble line that was outstanding. It is my opinion that there have been no choirs which have exceeded in this respect the Worcester performances of those days. The boys' voices were bright, yet beautiful in tone. They sang with fine expression and total technical accuracy. It is worth noting that there was never a time in the Robinson era when there were no good solo boys. Many of these have been captured on disc, notably the singing of Jonathan Nott and John Davies in Mendelssohn's duet 'I waited for the Lord'. Some of the choristers at this period went on to achieve great success – the conductors Jonathan Nott, Jonathan Darlington and Nicholas Cleobury and cathedral/collegiate organists Stephen Cleobury and Adrian Partington. One, Richard Berkeley-Steele, became well-known as an international operatic tenor. There were very many others too who achieved distinction in various branches of music.

The early 1960s and 1970s were also notable for the changeover to more modern liturgical practice. When I arrived in 1963, the choir still sang on two weekday mornings at 8.30 a.m. – Matins on Thursdays and the Litany plus short anthem on Fridays. I remember how taxing it was to play for Matins on a frosty morning in say February, when the mist rising from the River Severn made it difficult to see across College Green. To perform the Te Deum to Stanford in C or Ireland in F at such an early time was quite a feat of endurance. In the days when the choir regularly conducted themselves, Christopher Robinson and I took it in turns to do the Thursday Matins. On Fridays, the choir did the Litany under their own steam – though often with the organist lurking in the nave to monitor the performance. Both these morning services survived until 1965. At that point the Litany on Fridays was discontinued; Matins moved to Friday and continued to be sung each week until I moved to London in April 1976. It too was discontinued early in Donald Hunt's time. That it survived so long was largely because the six lay clerks liked it. They felt it was continuing a tradition, and some of them were loath to lose this last survival of daily sung morning services, once universal in cathedrals.

Until the departure of Dean Milburn in 1968, all sung services used *The Book of Common Prayer*. The arrival of Eric Kemp as Dean eventually changed all this. Over a period of time he held regular meetings with the Chapter and the organists to discuss liturgical change. Not all the Chapter wanted this. The form of the revised services was thrashed out point by point at these meetings. Somehow during the night, the Dean prepared a memorandum of what had been agreed. This arrived through the letterbox at breakfast time the following morning. Woe betide any of the Chapter who wished to reopen discussion on a particular point. They were told brusquely that if they looked at section 5, number 4, this had already been agreed. And that was that!

All this discussion culminated in the radical events of Advent Sunday 1972, when Matins was abolished, the Eucharist moved from the choir to the nave, and the modern English liturgy was thereafter used at this service. This caused quite a shock! But it did kickstart a whole process of liturgical change. With hindsight the Cathedral has benefited from this. During the time of the next Dean, Tom Baker, things settled down to the kind of liturgical pattern now found in most cathedrals.

THE CATHEDRAL VOLUNTARY CHOIR

Founded in 1874 when the Cathedral reopened after the great restoration, this choir was originally intended to provide musical support for the popular evening service which was inaugurated at this time. At first it was a mixed choir, but before long boys were recruited to provide the treble line. This was very similar to what was happening in other cathedrals. At Worcester, as elsewhere, the service drew huge congregations. But at the time of writing (2016) Worcester is the only cathedral still to have a Voluntary Choir of boys and men, making Worcester unique in having two boys' choirs. When I arrived in 1963, the boys' choir was at a low ebb, really kept going by the indomitable secretary of the choir, Derrick Bollen, who drove round on a Sunday collecting the boys, largely from the large council estate at Warndon. Edgar Day (assistant organist 1912–1962) began to find the boys difficult to handle. What usually happened was that he played the piano and Derek directed the rehearsals.

When Christopher Robinson arrived as assistant in 1962, the standards began to improve. But he only served one year in this post before taking over as Cathedral organist. The Chapter made it clear to me they wanted this improvement to continue! The 6.30 p.m. Evensong on Sundays in the nave still drew a respectable congregation. As in many parish churches, the boys had their own rehearsal on Tuesdays at 6.30 p.m. for an hour, then came again on Fridays with the men at 7.30 p.m.

The standard of the choir began to improve. As a result we attracted good new boys and men for the back row. The original 12 men I inherited included some extremely pleasant characters, quite a number of whom had been boys in the choir. There were also some very inadequate singers, and it was these who resisted change. Quite a number in due course retired or were smoked out. But there was a good spirit amongst the better men, who were pleased to see the choir progressing. The Friday night practice finished with a visit to the White Hart, where probably too much beer was drunk. The men were mostly employed in the city; one was the station master, another was a manager with the Gas Board, and one had been a glove cutter. Throughout my time, I maintained a congregational style service with Anglican chants and hymns. But on most Sundays we sang a substantial anthem. Eventually I was much helped by the good young organists at the King's School, and some former Cathedral choristers who wished to develop their adult voices and gain experience of part singing.

It really was important to have an organist. The organ was situated in the second bay of the choir with the console next to it. In the days before CCTV and sound relay, accompanying nave services was always hazardous. If one played the organ loud enough, then all the singing was obliterated. On Sunday mornings, when the Cathedral choir sang the Te Deum at Matins, they sang from the steps in front of the choir screen so that the organist had a better chance of hearing them. But whenever the organ had several bars rest, it was necessary to come in early in order to synchronize with the choir. Britten in C was particularly difficult to handle. Eventually we got a microphone and loudspeaker on the console. This greatly eased matters. For recordings, such as *The Sacred Music of Elgar*, I wore headphones. This worked very well.

THREE DEANS

It was unusual that my twelve and a half years at Worcester spanned a period when there were three Deans. I arrived halfway through the tenure of R. L. P. Milburn (1957–1968), affectionately known as Bobby; I was there for the whole of Eric Kemp's five years (1969–1974) and had just one year with Tom Baker (1975–1986). They represented distinct but very different types of Anglican clergymen. Milburn seemed old-fashioned – a scholarly and sensitive man who one eventually found was not quite what he seemed on the surface. It was the same with Eric Kemp: it was unwise to rush into facile judgements, as he was something of a dark horse. Tom Baker, a bachelor, was in many ways the most straightforward. I had a friendly relationship with all of them, particularly with Milburn and Baker. I did not always feel quite so sure of my ground with Kemp; he kept his cards close to his chest and could sometimes seem very distant. One was not quite sure of the machinations of his mind – I use the word machinations advisedly. I saw all three regularly as I lived just round the corner. It seems appropriate to try to sketch their characters with a view to illuminating the impact they made on the Cathedral. They were all of great ability with strong but very different views as to how a historic and significant diocesan church should function.

Robert Leslie Pollington Milburn (1957–1968)

Bobby had come to Worcester after a long period at Worcester College, Oxford where he was Fellow, Chaplain and Bursar. A native of East Anglia and graduate of Cambridge, he had passed his whole ministry in the academic world. I suppose he was really a moderate tractarian in doctrinal matters; but it was very difficult to place him in any particular category. He had something of the 18th-century divine about him; he certainly was not very far from the church portrayed by Trollope. He had a mind of great independence and I always thought he had liberal views concerning doctrine and theology. Indeed I felt he was not entirely happy with the idea of a supernatural God, though clearly he was deeply in tune with the wonders of a divinely created world. Even when preaching at Easter, he preferred to quote A. E. Housman rather than St Paul. He actually said, 'if you would prefer it from St Paul…!' I remember him quoting Housman's well-known poem about the cherry tree:

> *Loveliest of trees, the cherry now*
> *Is hung with bloom along the bough,*
> *And stands about the woodland ride*
> *Wearing white for Eastertide.*

To him, the yearly miracle of spring, of death and resurrection, was somehow close to the destiny of human beings. But nature's renewal equated with Christ's resurrection, and the resurrection life shared by believers was never explored. The matter was alluded to as if to encourage individuals to work out their own views on a doctrine which was difficult to explain, let alone to understand. I was never quite sure where he stood. But it was clear he disliked dogma and was suspicious of enthusiasm. But in his life, he was a man of great kindness and sensitivity to others. I suspect he was a follower of Christ the great teacher, but after that was prepared to employ a good number of question marks.

In the business affairs of the Cathedral he really did much of the administration almost single-handed. Yet he never seemed to be busy! He always said he could not get the canons to do anything very much; there was no administrator and the chapter clerk, Victor Douse, was very little help to him. He was a great character. But he had a penchant for the bottle; it was not uncommon to see him getting rid of his 'empties' in a bin attached to a lamp post near his office! The Dean had good secretarial help, but there was no Cathedral office.

Bobby was an experienced man of affairs and was astute in financial matters. Many of his letters were hand-written. But in spite of having little assistance, he left the Cathedral finances in good shape when he moved to be Master of the Temple. Of course his methods only worked in a cathedral where not a great deal happened apart from the usual round of daily services. He could not have coped with the intense activity of today without help. Back then, he actively discouraged too many extra events. He often reminded me of a passage in Trollope's *Last Chronicle of Barset* where Archdeacon Grantley and his son-in-law, Precentor Harding, are discussing whether in their younger days they were rather idle compared with the new generation of younger clergy. Grantley rounded on Harding and said 'he worked hard enough…I believe the work was done a good deal better than it is now…there wasn't so much fuss but there was more reality'. In the days before flipcharts and brainstorming sessions, it was up to individuals to decide what needed immediate attention and what did not. Bobby acted independently in a way which would not be tolerated these days. For instance, in the 1960s there was a great deal of discussion as to whether George Gilbert Scott's screen between the nave and choir should be removed to reveal a through vista from west to east. This had happened at Salisbury and was about to happen at Hereford. Bobby thought this an inappropriate plan – particularly as at Worcester the choir was ten steps above the nave, being built above the early Norman crypt. The eastern arm of the building was a visible but distinct space, as intended by the original builders. There was a stone choir screen, surmounted by a historic organ case until *c.*1870. Scott was reluctant to remove this and the fine 17th-century choir stalls. However, he had to bow to the wishes of Lord Lyttelton who was footing the bill – backed by the Chapter. So he designed a light ironwork screen which only slightly obscured the vista the length of the Cathedral. It was this which many wished to remove. Bobby's answer to this was simple. One day, workmen arrived to erect scaffolding round the screen. Then painters arrived and proceeded to restore and regild it. Thus the argument was settled by a distinctly autocratic act!

Bobby was intensely supportive of the music. He was a help to Christopher Robinson in improving the quality of the singing by facilitating the retirement of some of the older men who were past their sell-by date. He had a particular liking for music from the turn of the century – that meant to him from the 18th to the 19th centuries! He liked Attwood and Crotch, and was particularly fond of the English arrangement of Schubert's 'Where Thou reignest'. He also liked hymns of this period, such as Tate and Brady's metrical psalm 'Through all the changing scenes of life' to the tune Wiltshire by George Smart (1776–1867). Though he might seem an eccentric – his feet not firmly on the ground – this was far from the case. He missed nothing. When I was a new assistant organist he listened through the keyhole of the Chapter House door to me rehearsing the choristers. I know this because he told the Director of Music he liked the way I got on with the practice, briskly without a lot of fuss.

Sometimes what he saw could lead him to unusually frank comment. Shortly before he moved to be Master of the Temple in 1968, I was with him in his study which commanded a long view along the north side of College Green and the entrance to the cloisters. He looked out of the window and saw the four residentiary Canons in eager conversation with Sir John Hewitt, the Prime Minister's Patronage Secretary, who was visiting that day to discuss what kind of person the new Dean should be. He turned to me and said, 'My dear good fellow, what do I see – see how the puppets dance!'

Of course Bobby was old-fashioned, and eccentric. He was just about the last Anglican cleric to wear garters and frock coat – not only on special occasions, but often as daily working clothes. He could be seen cycling down the High Street in this attire with a black Homburg hat worn at a rakish angle; or perhaps on an afternoon walk on the Severn towpath reading a volume of poetry. He was wonderful at the Christmas party held at the Headmaster's house. These became famous for the playing of charades, which for a few years were an established feature of these occasions. The Archdeacon of Worcester and his wife Lady Alethea Eliot loved them and always arrived with a large portmanteau of props. It was all rather Barchester – but it was great fun.

The move of Bobby and Marjorie Milburn from the Deanery did mark the end of an era. But to what extent only became apparent with the appointment of a new Dean, who could not have been more different either in his thinking or in his manner.

Eric Waldram Kemp (1969–1974)

The Canons in conversation with the Patronage Secretary from Downing Street could never have imagined in their wildest dreams the name of the person who was to succeed Bobby Milburn.

I found out who this was to be in an unusual manner. It had been whispered around the close that on a certain day the new Dean was to visit Worcester to have lunch with Vice-Dean Canon Armstrong at 9 College Green, the front door of which could be clearly seen from the Precentor's study. It so happened, not entirely by chance, that the Precentor, Colin Beswick, a minor Canon, myself and the other minor Canon and School Chaplain, Michael Sanderson, were in the Precentor's House at about 2.30 p.m. Sure enough, at 2.40 p.m. the door of Canon Armstrong's House opened and he and the new Dean emerged. Immediately Michael Sanderson exclaimed, 'My God, it's Eric Kemp.' And so it was!

Kemp was only a slightly younger contemporary of Milburn, and like him had been an Oxford don – Chaplain and Fellow of Exeter College (1945–1975). He had previously held a short curacy in Southampton before returning to Oxford in wartime to be a librarian at Pusey House. Unlike Milburn, he was very much part of the Anglo-Catholic scene in Oxford. I first noticed him as President of the Oxford University Church Union, which held a termly Eucharist at the University Church to which I was dragged along by the keen ordinands at Pembroke. His appointment to Worcester Cathedral was something of a shock. I suspect the Bishop of Worcester, Mervyn Charles-Edwards, was operational somewhere behind the scenes. His installation on Ascension Day 1969 was certainly the beginning of five years of radical changes intended to bring the Cathedral kicking and screaming into the 20th century. What he did made him unpopular in many quarters, but later Deans reaped the benefits of his efforts. The dirty work had been done for them. Kemp had a certain legalistic frame of mind and a touch of ruthlessness. It is not surprising that he had been much involved in Canon Law reform instigated by Archbishop Geoffrey Fisher who, as a former headmaster, liked to have things sown up in rules and regulations. Few in the Church of England at the time regarded the project as of any importance whatsoever.

As I have mentioned earlier, Kemp was a deceptive figure. He had a very flat expressionless voice, something I remembered well from my Oxford days. He also looked very much like he did in those days. But he could be charming and was good company, especially after a few drinks, when he poured forth a rich fund of amusing ecclesiastical anecdotes. It was good to have a young family in the Deanery. His wife Pat, daughter of the former Bishop of Oxford, Kenneth Kirk, was a highly intelligent and lovable person. The five children were aged from 4 to 17 years and brought considerable new life to College Green. The family was very generous to me. I spent five happy Christmas Days with them, where there was good food and a good deal of fun. The youngest child, Edward, sang in the Cathedral Voluntary Choir for a few years preparatory to becoming a chorister in the Cathedral choir. I mention all this to underline that there was another side to Eric Kemp, very different from his public persona.

I have already mentioned earlier, the meticulous way he worked towards liturgical change in frequent formal meetings with the Chapter and the organists – it was notable that the congregation was hardly consulted at all. But he did set in motion other changes in the Cathedral generally which brought considerable benefits.

Very soon, he appointed an administrator to manage the business side. This was Colonel Bill Bowen, recently retired from service in the Worcestershire Regiment. He too was a deceptive figure. Externally, he represented something of a caricature of a military figure – he habitually used a monocle with a hint of Colonel Blimp. But in fact he was a highly efficient and likable person who brought a great deal of improvement to how the Cathedral was run. An important project which he masterminded was the installation of central heating. Kemp saw the need, rightly, for this to be a matter of top priority. Previously the building had been heated by coal-fired Gurney stoves, seen in many cathedrals in those days. They were inadequate as regards heating, and also highly labour-intensive in requiring the Works staff to hump coal and clear out ashes. Originally there were five of these stoves in the Cathedral; but Dean Milburn actually got rid of two – those in the north-east transept and in the Dean's Chapel. When people complained, he said that if they felt the cold, they should put on extra clothing. The three stoves which remained, one in the north transept and two at the west end of the nave, were woefully inadequate to warm such a large building in the depths of winter. In fact, on very cold days, the choristers' breath could be seen coming out of their mouths when they sang. The new heating made the Cathedral a much more welcoming place and encouraged many more outside bodies to use it, especially in December when there came to be numerous carol services for local schools, banks and businesses.

There were other projects which made the building more accessible. One of the notable architectural features is the early Norman crypt. Rather remarkably, the only entrance to this was down a narrow and dilapidated staircase in the south transept near the organ. For such a large underground space, it was a health and safety nightmare.

Wulstan's crypt is a remarkably atmospheric place – and not surprising that this Saxon Bishop of Worcester, who was the only bishop to keep his see under William the Conqueror, should produce Norman architecture with such a notable pre-Conquest feel to it. Under Dean Milburn, the crypt had undergone a sympathetic restoration with new lighting which brought out its beauty and numinous quality. Eric Kemp thought it should be used much more, and to this end asked the Cathedral architect to break a new staircase through from the south choir aisle. At first it was something of an eyesore, with rough masonry revealed and very makeshift stairs. This has now been completed with attractive iron railings and a high-quality staircase which blends with Scott's marble pavement in the aisle. Purists might have thought this iconoclastic; but it was a very good idea, well executed, which has made the visiting public aware of beauties which had long been hidden from view. It is also now much used as a devotional space. The extensive forest of pillars and arches cover a very considerable area, accessible as one of the most interesting crypts in any English cathedral.

Many other building projects were undertaken, including cleaning the 19th-century paintings on the choir vaults. It is not possible to mention them all. But what is clear is that under Eric Kemp's brief tenure of five years, much was done to make the Cathedral warmer, more attractive and fit for use at a time when cathedrals were beginning to be much busier – with visitors, worshippers and an amazing variety of musical events causing an enormous growth in the numbers coming through the doors. The liturgical changes which Kemp introduced were highly controversial at first. With the benefit of hindsight, these are now seen to be right and necessary.

Thomas George Adames Baker (1975–1986)
Tom Baker, like Kemp, was also an Oxford graduate. He was academically gifted and took a first-class degree in the Honour School of Theology. I only stayed for his first year, but during that time we became good friends. He had trained for the priesthood at Lincoln

Theological College and was influenced there by Eric Abbott, later Warden of Keble and Dean of Westminster. His connection with the Oxford Theology faculty started early, as the church where he grew up in Southampton had for a curate Christopher Evans, a brilliant scholar and speaker who became Fellow of Corpus Christi College, Oxford and then Professor of Theology at King's College, London. Tom and his friend Dennis Nineham (later Warden of Keble and also Professor of Theology at King's, London) were very much taken under Christopher Evans' wing. I too remember Evans as a fine preacher in my first year at Oxford. How amazing that all these paths should cross! After parochial work in Birmingham, Tom Baker was appointed Principal of Wells Theological College. Eventually with the amalgamation of Wells and the similar college in Salisbury, Tom had to stand down. He was however appointed Archdeacon of Bath and continued to live in the Close at Wells. It was from here that he moved to Worcester in 1975.

He arrived at the Deanery with his elderly mother and an aunt in her seventies. Tom was devoted to his mother, who was quite a character and very lovable. It was sad that both his mother and aunt died during his first year as Dean. The Bakers were a close-knit family and rather unusual. They had a somewhat Bohemian side to them which was delightful; or perhaps I should say they were slightly unconventional, a trait that was very attractive.

Tom arrived in Worcester at the same time as the new organist, Dr Donald Hunt, previously a distinguished organist at Leeds Parish Church. Tom loved music, so it was almost inevitable that the two newcomers should form a friendship that remained central to both during Tom's eleven years as Dean. One could say that these years were a necessary consolidation after five years of upheaval. But to say that would be most unfair to him. He was very much a person in his own right – charming and caring and always friendly. He knew how to relate to others and brought great gifts to his ministry. In my view he was the finest of the three Deans in the pulpit. He always had something to say of interest and said it in a clear and unaffected manner, whatever the occasion.

After a few years in post he was diagnosed with cancer of the throat. This led to much medical treatment. Happily this was entirely successful and he was able to return to work for quite a few more years. He could still speak lucidly, but his voice was much diminished. For someone in a public position this was highly frustrating. It may have been doubts about his physical strength which made him decide to retire slightly early in 1986. This was mainly due to the fact that a major appeal had to be planned to save the central tower. He felt he could not face this. I remember him once telling me that the structural engineers claimed they had until 2000 to do the work on stabilizing the tower – underpinning the foundations and knitting the superstructure together with steel wire; and if they did nothing before 2000, the tower would fall, whatever they did. It was left to the next Dean, Robert Jeffery, a younger man, to mastermind the fundraising and the project through to its conclusion.

The three Deans I have attempted to portray were all significant figures, but each so different. They were all entirely right for their time. Eric Kemp followed a more conservative Dean, who nevertheless in his own way had brought stability and great improvement to the life and fabric of the Cathedral. Kemp's regime was draconian, but radical measures were then required. Under Baker the Cathedral prospered as a result of his wise counsel and his great humanity. He understood people and related to all types with a lack of stuffiness and a warmth of friendship. This does not mean to say he was only a good pastor. He had great presence – and thought deeply about things. His intellectual gifts and clarity of thought were the foundations of his success at a time when the Cathedral needed to settle into the kind of calm and creativity which are the hallmarks of the life of a notable historic church.

THE THREE CHOIRS FESTIVAL

For 300 years, the cathedrals of Hereford, Gloucester and Worcester have hosted the Three Choirs Festival, the oldest music festival in Europe. Originally it was an event organized around the social life of the local gentry – and to some extent it retained vestiges of this tradition up to my arrival in 1963. But it was now a national event and reckoned to be a major arts festival. It was always centred around choral singing, with at first the three cathedral choirs forming the massed choir. But in the middle of the 19th century choral societies were added, presumably to provide forces required for large-scale Romantic works.

In my day, the chorus was the backbone, formed of contingents from the choral societies in the three cathedral cities. The organization of the festival and the training of the choirs fell almost entirely to the organists and their assistants. This added a huge amount of extra work to the normal routine of cathedral services. From Easter through to the festival (now in early August or even earlier, whereas until 60 years ago it was early September) we needed two rehearsals a week, plus several massed practices at the host cathedral. Added to this, at Worcester the Sunday services were sung throughout the summer by the Cathedral Voluntary Choir of men and boys. This entailed maintaining the schedule of two weekday rehearsals. We did not at this stage have visiting choirs at Worcester. Christopher Robinson was of the opinion that it was the Voluntary Choir's right to sing the holiday services. It was not until the arrival of Dr Donald Hunt that visiting choirs became a feature of the Cathedral music programme. Yet we managed. When I had a fortnight's holiday, Christopher Robinson took the Voluntary Choir. The Festival rehearsals were shared between us and were taken from the piano, obviating the need for an accompanist. It was probably too much of a burden. Nowadays, the cathedral organists' load has been much lightened by the appointment of Festival administrators.

From at least the mid-18th century, but more particularly from

1860 onwards, the Festival has gained greatly in prestige from the attendance of well-known composers. Parry, Vaughan Williams and Elgar all attended regularly, as did composers from the continent, Dvorak and Kodaly to name but two. I was present at the Gloucester Festival of 1956, when Vaughan Williams conducted for the last time – it was his 'The Lark Ascending'. There were not so many luminaries around in my time. But Britten visited the Hereford Festival twice. I was there in 1958 when he conducted his *Sinfonia da Requiem*. He wouldn't go to Gloucester and Worcester, but I think Hereford in the hands of Dr Melville Cook was more congenial territory.

From my point of view, as assistant organist, the fact that I had to play accompaniments for a vast variety of choral music was very much a learning curve. When I played for the Worcester Festival Choral Society in term-time at their weekly rehearsals, it was sometimes very difficult finding the time for necessary practice in addition to my normal Cathedral duties, being Director of Music at the King's School and Choirmaster of the Voluntary Choir. To have to turn up to play *Belshazzar's Feast* after a heavy day in school was certainly demanding. But I learned so much from having to do it. I often feel that many young organists lack the feeling for harmony in their accompaniment which comes from the experience of playing from the vocal scores of operas and oratorios, where one gets right inside the composer's mind and technique. But apart from technical matters, the musical benefits of this were huge. We did a good deal of first performances, and much modern music generally. At the three Worcester Festivals in the Robinson era, there were commissions from Jonathan Harvey ('Ludus Amoris'), Gordon Crosse ('Chimes') and Richard Rodney Bennett ('Spells').

I have mentioned that my first experience of the Three Choirs was playing the organ part of Britten's *War Requiem*. This was performed again at the 1965 Gloucester Festival, when I played the chamber organ. But it was not a chamber organ at all but the 4-manual Willis/Harrison instrument on the choir screen! In addition to playing the organ part, I had to direct the choristers. They were crowded around me – about 35 of them – in the organ loft and mostly behind my back. However, we managed to pull it off quite satisfactorily. But this kind of doubling up of roles would, I think, not be expected in these days.

One thing which occurred in my time was applause – also at the 1965 Gloucester Festival. It was the first time since the 18th century that clapping had been heard in the Cathedral. Chapters in the late 19th century were often wary of musical events which they thought had more than a hint of secularism. The proceedings had to be legitimatized by the offering of prayers before the performance – and sometimes at the end. These were dropped in my time, but they continued at Hereford till 1967. There was an attempt to ban applause, but this proved to be quite against public opinion and unworkable.

The outburst of applause after *Belshazzar's Feast* at Gloucester took everyone by surprise. There had been a feeling in the chorus that this difficult work, which never gets any easier, had been starved of rehearsal time. This was strengthened by the fact that Herbert Sumsion, conducting Symonowski's 'Stabat Mater' in the same concert, had considerably overrun his allotted rehearsal time. The chorus was increasingly anxious; quite a number of singers held impromptu rehearsals after lunch on the day of the concert. As it turned out, the performance conducted by Christopher Robinson with the London Symphony Orchestra was an electrifying success. Hardly had the final chord died away before there was a spontaneous outbreak of tumultuous applause. There were some diehards who were appalled. I remember the following year at Worcester a retired public school headmaster storming out during the applause and shouting very audibly 'House of God, my foot – House of Man!' Despite all this, applause had come to stay.

I was fortunate to catch the final four and a half years of Herbert Sumsion at Gloucester. He had been involved in the Three Choirs from 1928 until his retirement at the end of 1967. I believe he had intended to continue for a further six months until the Gloucester Festival in 1968, when he would have completed 40 years. But at the

Hereford Festival of 1967 he decided (he was in his 69th year) to go early. I think he could not face the work involved in another home festival.

Sumsion was a very fine pianist and organist and a very proficient conductor. I remember at the end of the programme of his last festival in 1967 he conducted Kodaly's 'Psalmus Hungaricus'. It was very noticeable that his arrival on the rostrum evoked a considerable increase of interest and alertness from the orchestral players. He was not at his best as a choir trainer. In those days there was little time given to weekly rehearsal with cathedral choirs; perhaps he was a victim of the system. I am reminded of something said by Lady Armstrong, wife of Sir Thomas Armstrong. After they had left Oxford to go to the Royal Academy of Music, she heard that Simon Preston had established a much more extensive schedule of practices, including before services in the Cathedral. She was heard to remark, 'They can't by very good if they have to practise!' I do remember very awkward moments, particularly in a performance of Verdi's 'Te Deum' from the *Four Sacred Pieces*. During the first three pages the unaccompanied 6-part men's voices, mainly in F major, lost so much pitch that when the orchestra joined the full chorus on a fortissimo chord of E flat, the choir came in on a chord of D major, a whole semitone flat. This kind of thing rarely happens these days.

Sumsion was however a remarkable musician and a very interesting person. He was quite radical in his views and extremely anti-clerical. He would not even wear a surplice, but favoured an academic gown instead. His close connection with Elgar was significant. He knew exactly how the composer conducted *Gerontius*, for instance; consequently his own performances had considerable authenticity. He passed this tradition on to his successor John Sanders. In turn this was passed on to Edward Gardner, a former chorister at Gloucester under Sanders. I remember him speaking very affectionately of how John Sanders had advised him when he himself was preparing a performance of *Gerontius*. The instructions were so precise that he was given a list on the back of a postcard of the seven places in the score which had to be rehearsed if all the soloists arrived an hour late for the rehearsal! Sumsion's links with Elgar were further reinforced by his landmark performance of the Organ Sonata in G, written for the Worcester Hill organ in 1897. This is notable for its breadth and lyricism, as well as for its technical mastery. Remarkably it was recorded in one take, and it remains the benchmark performance. A few years ago, I overheard a young organist practising the piece, who had very little idea of the nobility of the music, nor the need for flexible rhythm and Romantic expression; I urged him to listen to Sumsion's performance, which he did, and it transformed his interpretation.

When I arrived in Worcester, it was only 29 years since Elgar's death. Many remembered him well and frequently spoke of him, like Edgar Day (assistant organist 1912–1962), who came out with some splendid anecdotes. He in fact often went to supper on Sundays with Elgar in the closing years of his life at his home, Marl Bank, close to Shrub Hill Station. A story I rather like is of Edgar sitting in the Cathedral listening to a rehearsal of Mendelssohn's *Elijah* with Vaughan Williams and Elgar. When Vaughan Williams remarked that the orchestration was dull and could be much improved, Elgar turned to him and said, 'It could have been orchestrated in no other way'! There was a time when it was fashionable to berate 19th-century orchestration. Schumann suffered in the same way. For years it was considered that his orchestration was incompetent – the doubling of instruments was even regarded as a safety device to make sure leads were covered. Now opinions have changed, and most musicians believe that Schumann produced the sounds on the orchestra he intended.

Another story recalled a rehearsal for *Gerontius* when Edgar was playing the Cathedral organ in the choir. They were rehearsing the remarkable orchestral passage building up to 'Praise to the holiest'. It comes after the tenor soloist sings 'But hark! A grand mysterious harmony: it floods me, like the deep and solemn sound of many waters', a powerful six bars of melodic and harmonic sequence for organ and orchestra leading to a bar marked *molto crescendo*. Edgar built the organ up and made a great deal of noise at this point. After this, the sound of brisk footsteps coming up the organ loft stairs was heard. It was Elgar arriving to say he had never heard the passage more effective – except once before the First World War in Cologne. Most of the time organists miss or ignore the dynamic markings at this point.

I could go on listing my hands-on experience of a great variety of Festival music; and how hard it was having to play for the daily Evensongs at the Festival, and then perhaps in the afternoon to play for example the important organ part in Frank Martin's *Requiem* for a live broadcast. But the Festival was also an enjoyable social occasion. In my time, there was still some feeling of it as a 'county' occasion. Many of the stewards (i.e. those who subscribed to all the concerts) still wore morning dress. Then there were endless parties: lunch at the Deanery and parties at the organists' or Canons' houses; civic lunches at the Guildhall, and sometimes journeys into the county, for instance to an evening reception at the Chairman's House at Birchwood at the end of the Malvern Hills, or Madeira and seedcake at the home of the Bishop at Hartlebury Castle. I doubt whether today there is still this whirl of hospitality. But 60 years ago the old traditions were still very much alive and well. In the 40 years since I left Worcester, it is heart-warming to see how the Festival has continued to develop musically and how new music, always a feature of the Festival, has been very much nurtured and encouraged.

THE CATHEDRAL ORGAN

In the closing years of the 19th century, all three cathedrals had organs by leading builders: Father Willis at Hereford and Gloucester and William Hill at Worcester. The first two had the services of the finest English organist other than W. T. Best of Liverpool: S. S. Wesley was organist of Hereford from 1832 to 1835 and in his closing years at Gloucester from 1865 to 1876. Both Parry and Elgar praised Wesley's improvisations at the Three Choirs Festival. Elgar heard him improvise on the large Hill organ at Worcester, probably in 1874, and later recalled that 'he had built up a wonderful climax of sound before crashing into the subject of the 'Wedge' Fugue by Bach' – an occasion mentioned by J. N. Moore in his *Edward Elgar, a creative life* (Oxford 1987). At this time, the two Hill organs in the Cathedral were new – part of the huge restoration of the building which was completed by 1874. The siting of the organs was a brilliant solution for a very long building. The three-manual instrument had all that was required for accompanying the singers from its position in the second bay on the north side of the choir. The much larger four-manual in the south transept was intended for nave services and the playing of the organ repertoire. Alas, these glory days were of only 23 years' duration: in 1897 the American organ builder, Robert Hope-Jones, a pioneer of electric action and high-pressure voicing, produced what was in effect a new instrument, using some of the Hill material, particularly the longer (and more expensive) pipes.

This is not the place for a detailed technical account of the organ; full information can be found in the National Pipe Organ Register. But something must be said of Hope-Jones. He was inventive, but many of his ideas and inventions were too far outside the European organ tradition and were consequently short–lived. But his employment of electricity for organ actions was ground-breaking and was taken up widely in improved form worldwide, and particularly in the United States. The availability of electricity also made much more powerful organ blowers possible, leading to the development of high-pressure voicing, which again was taken into the mainstream. The tubas and trombas of Harrison and Harrison, and indeed the tonal basis of the theatre organs of Rudolph Wurlitzer, were logical developments. Nor was Hope-Jones a shoddy craftsman. Pipes were well made and the voicing, particularly of string stops and the tibias, showed considerable flair. Having said this, however, the employment of Hope-Jones at Worcester was a disaster and cast a cloud over the organ of the Cathedral for almost 120 years, despite the brilliant salvage work done by Arthur Harrison in the late 1920s.

The truth is that the Dean and Chapter of Worcester were hoodwinked. Whether the musicians were fully aware of the consequences is doubtful. But the crux of the matter was that Hope-Jones said he could unite the two organs and make them playable from a single console by means of electrical transmission. But this turned out to be only a fraction of what actually happened. The organ case in the transept was reduced in size, moved back towards the south wall and housed only the solo organ with the large pedal pipes, including two full-length 32-foot ranks, the Double Open Wood and the Contra Violone from the Hill organ. Meanwhile, a second organ case was placed opposite the existing organ on the south side of the choir in an identical design. The Great, Swell and Choir organs were now housed in the choir behind the singers together with some of the pedal pipes. The sound of the organ was devastating close-up, but was acceptable further down the nave. It was a tonal disaster. It would have been even worse if the proposed Tuba on 50 inches wind pressure had ever been installed above the Dean's stall!

When I arrived in 1963, the organ was very much as revised by Harrison. The instrument had great character, much improved by amongst other things the fine new Mixtures on the Great. But it was hardly possible to use more than a fraction of the organ at choir services. Except very occasionally, the mighty Full Swell in its brick swell box was unusable in accompaniment. The brand new Kenneth Tickell organ of 2008 in the choir solved the problem as far as volume is concerned, but it is my personal view that the complete annihilation of the old organ was unnecessary. I believe other ways could have been found to accommodate the undoubted tonal architecture of the instrument.

As I said, the Harrison organ of 1926 was completely intact when I became assistant organist in 1963. A successful attempt had been made to add upperwork and to develop traditional organ choruses. A great deal of the Hope-Jones pipework remained. Edgar Day said that

Arthur Harrison had worked wonders with this. The quieter stops, for example the chorus of Gambas 16, 8 and 4 feet, the Tibia Clausa 8 foot, the Quintaton 8 foot all on the Swell, were remarkable feats of voicing of great musical and historic value. The Great retained the Diapason Phonon 8 foot; the Choir was a beautiful department, mostly the remains of the Hill instrument. There was a massive Tibia Profunda 16 foot on the Pedal at the back of the south case. The solo organ in the transept had good 16 and 8 foot reeds – the Bombarde and Orchestral Trumpet – and the quite extraordinary double-tongued Tuba which was so loud that it was audible well down the High Street. We occasionally used it in the Nunc Dimittis in A by Stanford. But the tuning of it was such a nightmare for Harry Pearson, Harrison's tuner, that we had it disconnected.

In 1972, when Harrisons did a limited restoration of the organ, quieter stops were added to the Swell, a Diapason from the Nicholson two-stop single-manual organ in the Lady Chapel and a new Mixture and a quieter Principal; the Great lost its Diapason Phonon which was replaced by a Stopped Diapason also from the Lady Chapel organ. This made the organ much more suitable for accompaniment. But with hindsight I regret the removal of the Hope-Jones stops, which were a part of organ history from the time when a group of talented voices such as Thynne, Whiteley and Casson were developing new organ sounds, particularly string stops. Their advances deeply influenced many well-known builders, including Harrison and Harrison, Henry Willis III, and Norman and Beard to name but three.

The Harrison organ did have great character. It can still be heard on recordings, particularly *The Sacred Music of Elgar* (EMI 1969), produced by Brian Culverhouse, and the fine disc by Christopher Robinson in the Great Cathedral Organ series. Heard live in the nave, it was impressive. I remember once entering the building by the North Door: Stephen Cleobury, then at the King's School, was playing Messiaen's 'Dieu parmi nous' and making a great deal of noise. At one point he added the Swell reeds and opened the box; I shall never forget the magnificence of that moment. As is often the case when the tonal architecture of an organ is tampered with, things gradually get worse and the integrity of the instrument is compromised. At Worcester, the minor changes were well-meaning and the organ made fit for use. But one cannot avoid the view that every time changes were made, the instrument was diminished.

I have tried to keep this brief account of a general nature, not too technical. But it is important that there should be some observation about the organ which plays such a part in the life of the Cathedral. The very fine case by George Gilbert Scott, which still remains in situ in the south transept, is a sad reminder of past glories. It is to be hoped that one day it will again have a new life of its own and once again house distinguished pipework, including the Hill and Harrison ranks still sitting in the transept case.

THE KING'S SCHOOL

When I was appointed to the Cathedral in 1963, the Headmaster of the King's School hoped that as a part-time teacher on a two-thirds timetable I would be able to make a contribution to enliven the music department. One cannot avoid saying that things were at a very low ebb. Reggie West, the first Director of Music there, single-handed tried to keep things going, but his personality was not suited to a major reformation of the department. He was affable and had had cathedral experience at Hereford and Armagh. But he didn't have the required talents to be a schoolmaster. In fairness to him he worked in appalling conditions. There was no Music School. Instrumental teaching and practice took place in his large house in College Yard. Class teaching was held in College Hall, the old refectory of the Cathedral priory. It seated 600 people and was totally unsuitable as a classroom. Music was very much the poor relation. Early in my time, however, the school acquired a row of three small cottages in Severn Street, which were converted in a makeshift manner into a small Music School. Upstairs there were seven practice rooms and a music store; downstairs a classroom and an office/teaching room for the Director of Music. It was all done on the cheap and there was no sound insulation; but it was better than nothing. I usually did my teaching at home in the study at my large house in College Precincts. For the first time, boys were able to take O Level Music, which I taught twice a week after school. Later this developed into a full academic programme, including A Level and scholarship work. My main occupation initially was individual teaching – mostly piano, but two of the choristers, Nicholas Cleobury and Roger Parkes, I taught on the Cathedral organ. The fact that I had a relatively light schedule in my first two years meant that I had time to get acclimatized to work in the Cathedral and to my duties as pianist and Assistant Conductor of the Worcester Festival Choral Society. I was even able to get out in the afternoon sometimes, walking over the Malvern Hills.

But all this changed in 1965. Near the beginning of the summer term, I was summoned to the Headmaster's study and asked whether I would be prepared to take over as Director of Music. This was unexpected; and it put me in the unenviable position of having to change places with Reggie. He accepted this stoically, since he had no choice. But he did say he would do anything I asked him to do. So we continued for the next four years until he retired in 1969. It was not easy. He continued to do the bulk of the class teaching and also taught the piano.

So my workload increased greatly from 1965. My salary went up, but I was still only employed on a part-time basis. This was problematic to say the least. How can a Director of Music in a school of 700 boys be part-time? I immediately took over the choral work. I also did a small amount of class teaching in the Lower School, which I found useful for discovering good potential singers. Improving the orchestral side had to wait until the appointment of a new Assistant Director of Music. It was totally impossible for me to run the orchestra, as I had to do the major part of the academic work. This soon became a major factor, as a good number of boys from now on opted to take O and A Level Music. But also the number of pupils gaining organ and choral scholarships at Oxford and Cambridge, together with those applying for musical conservatoires, made a lot of extra work. There were also a number of boys taking the examinations of the Royal College of Organists. I really was very busy; but I was young enough to have the necessary energy.

So I had to prioritize. Top of the list came the school choir. I developed a weekly schedule of three practices for altos, trebles and tenors and basses. Nearer the concerts, we put all the voices together in College Hall. And the Headmaster, David Annett, was willing occasionally for boys to miss lessons for combined choral practices. It was hard work having to do the sectional practices in the lunchtimes, but this was the only time I could get the boys. The sports department (cricket, rugby and rowing particularly) maintained an iron grip on free time in the afternoon after classes. This was a constant source of friction, and led to some sharp exchanges at staff meetings. I shall never forget one occasion when the Head of History, Alex Natan, a refugee from Nazi Germany, came down heavily on my side. He said, 'Headmaster, it is not as if I am against sport; I myself ran for Germany in the Olympic Games of 1936.' And so he did. There was no answer to this! I think some of the boys thought some of the sporting staff a bit dim. I remember one of the brighter Cathedral choristers saying to the Head of PE, 'Sir, who wrote Bach's Air on a G string?' He said he didn't know! I discovered that the best way to vanquish the organizers of sport was to get many boys from the First Fifteen, the rowing eights and the cricket elevens into the school choir. This also sent out a message that singing was not unmanly! Eventually there were a great many tenors and basses. And as time went on, many of the trebles moved down to the lower parts.

In the year before I arrived, Christopher Robinson had organized a very successful choral and orchestral concert on a summer Sunday evening. The chorus and orchestra practised in the afternoon. Many of the players were local professional players or from further afield, augmented eventually by some of the better boys. I thought this a very good idea. The Summer Concert became a regular feature throughout my time. After a year spent getting the school singing going, we put on the first concert on a Sunday in June 1966. The choral work was Mozart's *Coronation Mass*, preceded by a performance of his charming Piano Concerto No.17 with Stephen Cleobury as soloist, just before he took up the Organ Studentship at St John's College, Cambridge in the Michaelmas term of that year. In the following two years we again had a Mozart Piano Concerto: in 1967 No. 23 in A major played by Roger Parkes, a former Cathedral chorister who went on to be Organ Scholar of Corpus Christi College, Cambridge; and in 1968 No. 24 in C minor played by Christopher Tolley, who then went to be Organ Scholar at New College, Oxford. He read English and continued to do research for a doctorate on 'The Clapham Sect'. He taught for nearly 40 years at Winchester College, involved with the Chapel Music and the English department. He always appeared rather shy and diffident in manner, but underneath there was a real touch of brilliance. I soon realized this when I read his essays as a sixth former. They taught me a good deal!

The Summer Sunday Concert continued as a feature throughout my Worcester years. We attempted some challenging repertoire: for example the Verdi *Requiem*, Britten's *Cantata Misericordium* and Poulenc's *Gloria*. The orchestra was formed of mainly professional musicians, with on several occasions Christopher Robinson playing double bass. I also introduced an Autumn Concert, usually with organ. On one occasion I conducted Britten's charming operetta for boys, *The Golden Vanity*, a challenging piece. I was lucky to have a first-rate boy in the lead role, Geoffrey Stout, who negotiated the complexities with ease. I last saw him in Durham where I believe he was reading Music.

In order to attract as much choral talent as possible, I started a tradition of performing Gilbert and Sullivan operas every two years. The first was *The Pirates of Penzance* in 1967, with Nicholas Cleobury taking the role of the Pirate King. We had an enormous cast with 30 policemen and 30 pirates. The confrontation between these two groups was so realistic that it was rumoured an ambulance had to be called at one performance! For the younger boys, there was a staged performance of *Captain Noah and his Floating Zoo* by Joseph Horowitz. There were also a number of away events, the most memorable of which was the trebles providing the boys' choir in Britten's *Spring Symphony* at Birmingham Town Hall. All this indicates the rise of singing as a serious factor at the King's School.

I found the organization of all this became a major part of my work. One had to have the apostolic touch – spotting and netting talent. There also had to be sprats to catch mackerel; for instance, introducing boys to singing by joining with girls from two local schools; or taking part in *The Mikado*; then progressing to singing in Verdi's *Requiem* the following term. I found the personal appeal essential in recruitment. Directors of Music who think that putting up notices is the right approach inevitably fail. Long gone are the days when, for instance in 1949, the Dean and Chapter of York put up a printed notice around the city saying that there would be auditions for probationers in the Minster Choir on a certain day; it merely said that boys should turn up at the Song School at a specified time! Or in 1918, when Sir Sydney Nicholson was in his first year as organist at Westminster Abbey, he received a thousand applications for chorister places, of which he auditioned 350! Those were the days. Now we have to work much harder to compete for the commitment of children.

In 1969, we managed to install a good small pipe organ in the gallery of College Hall. By now there were so many organ pupils that this was an essential requirement. It could not have been achieved without the generous assistance of Stanley Lambert, Managing Director of the long-established Worcestershire organ building firm of Nicholson's. It was based on good 19th-century pipework from the redundant organ at Holy Trinity, Shrub Hill, which was given to us by the Diocese of Worcester. Some new pipework for the higher registers was added to make an extremely attractive *multum in parvo* instrument. Quite a number of years after I had left Worcester, I was visiting when I heard to my dismay a boy practising on a large flashy electronic organ. On enquiring, the boy told me they no longer used the pipe organ. I'm afraid I went into meltdown! But I have been relieved to hear that a new Director of Music has caused the pipe organ to get spring-cleaned and it is now fully operational again.

An interesting consequence of the new organ was when Edward Heath came to see it during the 1969 Worcester Festival, prior to his Prime Minister days. The MP for Worcester, Peter Walker, asked if he could bring him as he was staying with him for the Three Choirs. Unlike my later meetings with him, when I found him entirely devoid of small talk, on this occasion he was relaxed and charming. He improvised on the organ in a rather rudimentary manner, but seemed pleased enough. Then Peter Walker looked at his watch and said they must be off as they were due at an engineering works. In fact I was surprised when he said, 'Ted, we must go. Do you want to see some machine tools?'! Later on, when I had a flat in Salisbury, I lived very near to Heath and saw him from time to time. But my longest exposure to him was at a Royal College of Organists dinner, which he had arranged in the House of Commons dining room. As Honorary Treasurer I sat on his left, but I found it virtually impossible to get him to communicate. I did however discover that if I said 'Thatcher', he would fulminate for 20 minutes about 'that woman'. He was equally loquacious in his response to the mention of Europe, and talked volubly and interestingly about the European Community. This was of course after he had ceased to be Prime Minister.

As far as the King's School was concerned, I much enjoyed being able to score a few points against the sports department by managing to get music firmly on the school agenda. My regret is that orchestral playing never really took off. The Assistant Director of Music, Alan Young, appointed in 1969, made some progress in this area; but he was possibly hampered by the fact he was not the Director of Music.

OUTSTANDING PUPILS

I have described the great developments at the school in the field of choral singing, for which I think I am remembered; also for the expansion of the academic side of the music department. This was driven by the fact that there came to be many highly talented boys in the school who were hungry for instruction. Apart from those who were generally interested and who took O Level Music and perhaps A Level, there were many who wanted to prepare for life as a professional musician. In the ten years from 1966 up to my move to Southwark in 1976, twelve boys gained Oxbridge organ scholarships – at Cambridge at St John's, King's, Downing, Corpus Christi and Christ's; and at Oxford, Christ Church, New College (three times), Worcester (twice) and Pembroke. Four boys were elected to choral scholarships at St John's College, Cambridge. Others went on from the universities of Durham and London (Goldsmiths' College) to distinguished careers. Four former Worcester boys are now well-known international conductors: Jonathan Nott, Jonathan Darlington, Nicholas Cleobury and Nicholas Kok. Then there are the Oxbridge dons and cathedral organists: Stephen Darlington, organist at St Albans then Student (Fellow) and organist of Christ Church, Oxford; Andrew Millington, organist at Guildford and Exeter; Adrian Partington, organist at Gloucester and conductor of the BBC National Chorus of Wales; and Geoffrey Webber, Precentor and Fellow of Gonville and Caius College, Cambridge. Also there were singers: Richard Berkeley-Steele, a well-known international operatic tenor, and many others who, like Thomas Hunt, sing in cathedrals and churches in various parts of the UK.

In the field of education, many Worcester boys have been evident. Two have given a lifetime of service to the same school: Christopher Tolley, English teacher and Director of Chapel Music at Winchester College; and John Penny, Director of Music at Woodbridge School, Suffolk. Adrian Leang taught at Marlborough and Sutton Valence and now in Berlin; Peter Hewitt was Director of the Junior Royal College of Music; Jonathan Shardlow has run for many years the wind section of the North Yorkshire Music Centre; and Stephen Dagg became Director of the London Schools' Symphony Orchestra and Centre for Young Musicians. There is no knowing where former Worcester pupils will turn up! Martin Holmes took charge of the music collection at the Bodleian Library, and Richard King became commissioning editor of Faber Music. Paul Hughes decided he wanted to specialize in music late in his school career: he did a crash A Level course with me and went on to be General Manager of the BBC Symphony Orchestra. And then Peter Irving became organist of Solihull School. Of course many old pupils opted to work in non-musical jobs: Roger Parkes, a former Cambridge Organ Scholar, taught for a time at Shrewsbury School, then moved into IT. Robin Jéquier went into the Army and did very well. And of course inevitably there are many I have lost touch with.

Why so many musical boys from the King's School becoming professional musicians – at least 25 in a short period? Well, one answer must be that the Cathedral choir was a good breeding ground for musical talent. Many were not in the choir, though were influenced by the prevailing ethos of the place. Talented boys were 'discovered' in the school. But even this is an inadequate explanation. I have a feeling that the Severn Valley is a part of England which has always breathed music. Elgar thought so. He said in conversation with R. J. Buckley in 1896: 'My idea is that there is music in the air all around us, the world is full of music [here he raised his hands and made a rapid gesture of capture] and you simply take as much as you require.' He also said in a letter to Sir Sydney Colvin in 1921, 'I am still at heart the dreamy child who used to be found in the reeds by Severnside with a sheet of paper trying to fix the sounds and longing for something very great.'

It does seem remarkable that the region has been associated with so many outstanding composers: Parry, Vaughan Williams, Howells, Gurney, Ivor Novello, Holst, Tomkins and not least the greatest of them all, Elgar. The cathedrals of Worcester, Gloucester and

Hereford and the Three Choirs Festival have been for 300 years places where music is performed and composers given a platform. In the Middle Ages, the Severn Valley was very much Benedictine territory. The Worcester Cathedral Priory was a noted centre for musical performance and composition. The latest volume of *Early English Church Music* which I have on my desk – Volume 57, *English Thirteenth-Century Polyphony* – has page upon page of facsimiles of music which originated in Worcester at this time. The other great Benedictine houses were nearby: Malvern Priory, and the Abbeys of Evesham, Pershore, Tewkesbury; and greatest of all, the Abbey Church of St Peter at Gloucester, though not a cathedral until 1541. Apart from Evesham, where only the magnificent bell tower survives, all these monastic churches are still extant. All except Gloucester are now parish churches. That the townsfolk of Tewkesbury bought the Abbey for their parish church was quite remarkable – and there it still is, a building of European significance. But I wax too lyrical. The point is that monastic communities in the later Middle Ages were considerable educational establishments. In all of them, music was central. Boys and young men were taught to sing plainsong and polyphony. Some of these would go on to be organists, composers and choir trainers. Is it too fanciful to think that the music of the Severn Valley is a legacy of the Benedictines? I think not, especially when one considers that the great flowering of music in Tudor England after the Reformation was entirely built on the tradition of music which flourished in the greater English churches of the late Middle Ages and saw the foundation of Henry VI's colleges at Eton and King's College, Cambridge. The *Eton Choirbook* is remarkable evidence of creative activity; and of course the musical tradition at King's has never looked back. All this is speculation; but the evidence is such as to make it highly probable that this expertise has, to quote John Major, cascaded down the generations and that we today only exist as musical practitioners because of our remarkable British ancestors.

I am reminded of a quotation by Erasmus when he complained of the dominance of music in the later medieval English church. In

1516 in a sour comment on 1 Corinthians xiv.19, he said 'they have so much of it (choral music) that the monks attend to nothing else. A set of creatures who ought to be lamenting their sins fancy they can please God by gurgling in their throats. Boys are kept in the English Benedictine monasteries simply to sing hymns to the Virgin. If they want music, let them sing psalms like rational beings, and not too many of them.'

Returning from this historical diversion to the King's School, Worcester, I will speak of a few distinguished alumni for another reason which will become clear. Stephen Cleobury, the current Director of Music at King's, originated in Worcester. He was the first pupil in my time to gain an organ scholarship – at St John's College, Cambridge. His career took him by an interesting and surprising route – St Matthew's, Northampton, Westminster Abbey (Sub-Organist), Westminster Cathedral and finally King's. St Matthew's, Northampton has been a famous place of music-making – and as a footnote to musical history, I would mention that I was on the shortlist for the job when Cleobury was appointed. They quite rightly appointed someone with the energy and musical commitment of a young man. But I remember with a wry feeling that when I went into the interview room, George Guest – the musical adviser for the appointment – asked me whether I had come to be an additional consultant! As so often happens – but regrettably not always – the bumpy ride most people have in the pursuit of jobs turns out with the blessed assurance of hindsight to have been for the best. I was lucky to have an interesting and varied musical pathway which was entirely suitable for me.

I am tempted to digress again! I recently re-visited St Matthew's, Northampton – this time to hear and play the restored Walker organ of 1895. The former vicar, Walter Hussey (later Dean of Chichester), had put the church on the map by commissioning music and works of art – for example Britten's 'Rejoice in the Lamb' in 1943; but most remarkably, Graham Sutherland's painting of 'The Crucifixion', and a 'Madonna and Child' sculpted by Henry Moore out of a two-and-a-half-ton block of Hornton stone. Having unlocked the church and walked down the nave as far as the transepts, I looked to the right and saw the Sutherland, and to the left the Moore. I felt a distinct frisson and was glad I did not have the responsibility of locking the church after choir practices – a similar feeling I had when let into King's College Chapel to practise on the organ some years ago by the Organ Scholar Tom Winpenny (whose Yorkshire grandfather I know well from my childhood). He was the first person to address me as Mr Bramma when I was playing for a hymn practice he was taking at St Paul's Church, Shipley. This shocked me greatly as I was barely 13 years of age at the time! I was greatly alarmed when his grandson told me he could not return to lock King's Chapel. So he had to explain the locking-up procedure and how to set the alarm. I was mightily relieved when listening to the 8 o'clock news next morning to find Rubens' 'Adoration of the Magi' had not been stolen, nor had the chapel burnt down in the night!

I can't resist another anecdote. I am reminded of an episode in 1982 to do with job-seeking. This was when Stephen Cleobury moved from Westminster Cathedral. My assistant at Southwark, John Scott, had applied for this and been shortlisted. The week of his interview I went to York Minster to be interviewed with three others for the organist's job, vacant when Dr Francis Jackson retired. It suddenly occurred to me that if we were both appointed, Southwark Cathedral would lose both its musicians. Fortunately, neither of us was appointed!

I have been speaking of King's School pupils who became professional musicians. But before this chapter ends, it is important to speak of all the boys who were involved in music at the school but who did not seek a career in music. There were a great many who became excellent pianists and instrumentalists, some of whom I taught. I normally taught organ pupils, but also had a good number of piano pupils. And I always tried to have at least one beginner. It is a privilege to see a young child learn to read and make music and to connect with a universe of sound and feeling. Of course, it is tempting for teachers to view their efforts as rewarding to themselves.

It is very easy to write off or become exasperated with those who don't find that learning to play comes naturally to them. I shall always remember a housemaster taking me aside in the common room one day and saying (I hasten to add very civilly) he'd noticed that I didn't think his son David, who I taught, was very good. He went on to say that his son enjoyed his lessons and got a lot out of them – how to read notation, to realize that keyboard skills needed hard work, and to develop an enhanced appreciation of music which comes from hands-on experience. I felt humbled – and resolved to think differently about instrumental teaching in future.

Of course in all teaching, motivation is the key factor. I have found in recent years that pupils tend to be spoon-fed too much, rather than learning how to discover and learn for themselves. I remember with pleasure how after a course of lessons on Wagner's *Ring* one of the boys was so fired up that he went out and bought tickets for the *Ring* cycle at the English National Opera – almost certainly I think conducted by Reginald Goodall. Then there was another pupil who was learning Bach's 5th Trio Sonata on the organ and was doing extremely well, but he never played it without a couple of slight slips. I decided this was one of those occasions when I had to insist on a perfectly accurate performance. The following week he arrived without the music. I commented, 'Aren't you going to play Bach's 5th Trio Sonata then?' At this, he sat down and played the work note perfect from memory. Instances such as these make everything worthwhile. Motivation is a key factor in teaching anybody anything.

As I draw this section to a close, I think of more and more pupils I ought to name; but this is virtually impossible to achieve. Any I have failed to include will I hope be tolerant of my omission. And one further point: some brilliant executants are very unwilling to teach. As far as I am concerned, handing on the tradition and the expertise is an obligation. Bach thought so; and Beethoven begged Haydn to give him lessons. And at less exalted levels throughout the ages, the relationship between teacher and pupil has been an essential factor in the continuation and enrichment of the European tradition we are privileged to inherit. My years at Worcester gave me the opportunity to inhabit a rich field of musical talent which had to be nurtured and grown – and for that I am grateful.

LIFE IN WORCESTERSHIRE

I look back with great pleasure on my days living in the West Midlands, which I find a very special part of England. I had been there several times before. Whilst I was still at school, my Bramma grandparents took me for a short holiday by car when we stayed in Tewkesbury, Hereford and Stratford-upon-Avon. This was pre-motorways when travelling on the uncrowded country roads was a real pleasure. I am reminded of a passage in Dom David Knowles' very readable *Religious Orders in England* Part 3 where he describes the last days of the monasteries in Tudor England. It is where he is writing about Prior More of Worcester, when he suddenly goes off at a tangent and waxes lyrical about the local countryside. He says, 'Worcestershire is to this day a county of moated farms and manors, where the shallow pools, overhung by branches of pear and cherry, are stirred only by the moorhen or the birds of the farmyard.' This is as I remember it – peaceful and well-wooded pastoral landscape. During my twelve years living here, I got to know this countryside very well. I missed it very much when I moved to live in central London next to the Thames.

The two hills of the Severn Valley, the Malverns and Bredon, were frequent haunts. In 1963 it was possible to start walks from village railway stations, places long ago axed by Dr Beeching. A favourite outing was to catch the train from Worcester to Eckington to climb Bredon Hill, ascending past Woolass Hall, then over the top and down into the picturesque village of Elmley Castle with its attractive pub, the Queen Elizabeth, where a lunchtime stop for beer and sandwiches was imperative. The only drawback to this outing was the long trudge on the main road to Evesham, where we caught a train back to Worcester. A visit to the two interesting medieval churches, St Laurence and All Saints, standing almost side by side and very close to the remaining part of Evesham Abbey, the fine 15th-century bell tower, amply compensated for the slog along a busy road. The Malverns were more easily accessed by public transport. A bus from Worcester to Malvern Wells enabled a walk up to British Camp, stopping on the way to visit Elgar's grave at St Wulstan's RC church. It was a delightful walk along the ridge and down into the deer park at Eastnor, then going by way of the castle – an amazing 19th-century confection in the Norman style. The woods and meadows above this led to Ledbury, where the excellent beef sandwiches in the Talbot were very welcome. It was then on to the main street, past the delightful black and white cottages in Church Row, leading to the spire of the impressive church. It was possible to catch a train at Ledbury station back to Worcester. I often did this walk with the Precentor of Worcester, Colin Beswick, who was a fount of knowledge on the area and the buildings there. He was subsequently Canon and Precentor of Norwich Cathedral. He was a good amateur musician and an authority on Victorian church history. He was also an amusing conversationalist with a rather interesting turn of phrase and an unusual vocabulary, much of which I think were invented. He had a fund of anecdotes, not all of which could be told in any drawing room!

Over fifty years ago, the Worcestershire countryside, villages and pubs were largely unspoilt. The drinking of beer could be varied in those days, when there were still many small breweries producing excellent beer – Kelseys, Mitchells and Butlers and Ansells to name but three. Round the cathedral in Worcester, there were many pleasant inns, quite a number of which have now closed, including the Crown in Broad Street which claimed to have a chair in the gentlemen's bar used by Elgar. The landlords were great characters. Wally at the Cardinal's Hat in Friar Street was not always entirely sober. On leaving one night, I said tongue in cheek that it was time I was going home to my 'virtuous' couch; for a long time afterwards he asked me if it was time I was going to my 'verminous' couch!

Another landlord at the Farriers Arms was a great fan of the music of Delius. On one occasion I went home with a heap of excellent LPs of Sir Thomas Beecham conducting Delius which he had lent me. These records made about 60 years ago were superlative. That Delius himself said he would never find a better advocate for his music than Beecham is worth noting.

Sometimes our rural escapades had a rather different flavour. I remember one evening when a few of us were driven by a young lay clerk at Worcester, Tony de Rivas, in his Peugeot to the Malverns. We were at the Wyche cutting when someone remarked, 'Doesn't that track lead to the top of the Worcester Beacon?' Tony said 'Let's find out' and we set off in his car – and in fact we did get to the top. One wonders how hazardous this was! However, we got up and down in one piece. Sometimes we had rather grand picnics on the Malverns. I remember one near Castlemorton Common with my friends John and Edith Bleney. We packed a splendid hamper of food and chilled bottles of white wine wrapped in copies of *The Guardian*. I believe I also took a thermos flask of gin and French – a popular drink in the Close at Worcester. At times we really did quaff quite a lot. We were very young! In later life I have gradually became more abstemious – enjoying a drink occasionally, but also spending long periods on the wagon.

One of the most remarkable hostelries we frequented was the Mug House, three miles to the north of the cathedral in the churchyard at Claines. It was a small 14th-century building, presided over by a real old-timer of a landlord, Wally Trow. He kept excellent Banks's Bitter – indeed he considered he ran an ale house. It was possible to get gin and tonic, but no ice and lemon were available. Wally considered that sort of thing rather cissy! He ran an orderly house, so much so that the local police constabulary HQ nearby turned a blind eye to his rather flexible closing times. In one of the small stone-flagged rooms was a piano, and sometimes we managed to persuade one of the regulars, Harry Jones, to give us a tune. He was a good pianist in the lighter style – and in fact he earned his living playing for the patients in Powick Mental Hospital, a large Victorian building on the outskirts of Worcester. Today he would be called a music therapist. We used to pull his leg and say he was Elgar's successor – for it was at this institution that Elgar in his young and impecunious days conducted an orchestra for the enjoyment of the patients. I don't suppose they called it music therapy in those days.

Over many centuries, the local pub has been central to the life of singers and players – and bell ringers. Singing is a tiring and thirsty activity, as is playing the trombone or the bass tuba. And the concentration and physical effort required in ringing a quarter peal of Steadman Triples calls for a visit to the local. On this subject, it is appropriate to sidetrack to London – to the Wheatsheaf in Borough Market. This was still in 1976 an old-fashioned place patronized by people from all walks of life: the Southwark choir, the bell ringers, the clergy certainly; but also the market porters and those who worked in the City having a few drinks on their way to London Bridge station. That this very assorted social mix worked was largely because of the landlord, Sid Leader, very much a South Londoner from the Old Kent Road who was one of nature's gentlemen. He knew all his customers and took an interest in what they did. The pub was eventually taken over by Gary, Sid's son. And when Sid died a few years later, almost the first thing he did was to inform the organist of St Paul's Cathedral, John Scott. John had been an habitué of the Wheatsheaf when assistant organist at Southwark Cathedral. The funeral in the Cathedral was a great occasion. I played the organ and David Hutt, later a Canon of Westminster Abbey, was asked by the family to speak. At the end of the service, the congregation poured down Cathedral Street behind the hearse. When this turned right, bound for the crematorium, the congregation kept on straight ahead into the Wheatsheaf, where continuous free beer and jellied eels were available. This occasion, founded on the camaraderie of people from across the social spectrum, would be harder to find these days; it spoke of the local community. But choirs still generally have their local pub. Friendship is an important part of choral singing, and choristers who know and like one another sing well. As Sir Adrian Boult once remarked, music making is 70% personal relationships.

This may sound as if singers are a drunken lot, but this is generally far from the case. The need to relax and relate amongst those of shared interests is a natural habit. I think also that the church and pub as important meeting places for the community risk being diminished nowadays. But it is heartening to know that choirs still drink and maintain community life.

The social factor in our lives was certainly considerable! I began to entertain in my own house, picking up cooking tips around the Close when I ate out. My next-door neighbour, Isabel Braley, actually gave me lessons and made meringues for when the Bishop was coming for dinner. In those days there were many very good hotels in country towns – for instance the Swan at Upton-on-Severn, or the Hop Pole at Bromyard – where a good meal for two with a bottle of wine cost around £5. It was also a time when many rural pubs were beginning to rediscover their catering role. So there were many visits to village inns in the county – places with such delightful names as Upton Snodsbury, Broughton Hackett or Wyre Piddle. My friend Laura Perrée, who had come to work in Worcester, was my companion on many of these convivial evenings. She had recently left the University of Montpellier, and being musical entered into the life of the Worcester Festival Choral Society and the cathedral. She eventually married a Pembroke friend of mine to whom I introduced her. This was my only ever successful occasion of matchmaking!

I had plenty of musical work outside my obligations in Worcester – the most important being with the Kidderminster Choral Society, to which I was appointed in 1972 as Chorusmaster and Conductor. It was an organization which still had a Victorian feel about it. The three principal officers were 'carpet kings' who owned carpet factories for which Kidderminster was famous. The oldest, Cyril Johnson, was the President. He had been organist of the Baxter church for fifty years. He and his father, who was the first organist, had held the post for a total of 100 years. The church housed a very fine Walker organ of the late 19th century. Very shortly after I arrived, I had to congratulate the old man who marked the register at the door on his 90th birthday. He had actually sung at the first concert of the Society in 1899! Things changed slowly in Kidderminster. When I took over, the choir numbered about 80 with good soprano and alto sections. The men were rather a mixed bag; but overall the choir was of a decent standard, with great potential.

Over my seven years as conductor, we attracted singers to the maximum of 120, the number of singers who could get onto the stage of the Town Hall. This was a fine Victorian building which accommodated an audience of 500, together with the choir and orchestra. The building was magnified by the outstanding Hill organ of 1854, largely in its original condition. There was a real community feel to the concerts, with the Mayor in his chain of office seated in the gallery, and everyone adjourning to the pub across the road in the interval!

During my time we performed much of the traditional repertoire, including Verdi's *Requiem* and Bach's *St John Passion*. But additionally we did challenging music like Vaughan Williams' 'Dona nobis pacem' and several works by Britten, Honegger and Tippett. The society had a good reputation locally; my predecessor as conductor, Merlin Channon, did the Bach *B minor Mass* just before I arrived. But the person who led the society with great success over many years was Frank Edwards, whose repertoire was always interesting.

It came as no surprise that the Kidderminster Society was very sociable. One of the sopranos I came to know well: Peg Jordan, widow of a local doctor, who dispensed ample hospitality at her comfortable Georgian house on the outskirts of town. After the rehearsal, where we went by car each Thursday with a King's School boy as accompanist, we were sometimes invited back to Mrs Jordan's for refreshments, which included lethal scotches. We then had to motor back to Worcester. It was, I remember, still the early days of the breathalyser, when its potency and terror did not yet strike so deep. Though the Kidderminster responsibilities added considerably to my workload, I was grateful for the opportunity to develop my conducting skills, and for the weekly journey 16 miles north. It made a change.

I occasionally acted as guest conductor to the Malvern Operatic Society, which was run by a formidable Italian lady, Maria Lloyd-Foulkes. She was dynamic and successful but occasionally alarming, when on occasion she would flare up in rehearsals and engage in a fit of Italian tantrums. She was a powerful operatic soprano who could ride over the top of a performance and almost take over the direction from the choir stalls. My first event was to conduct excerpts from *Aida* at the Winter Gardens in Malvern. My next assignment was quite different, a performance of Menotti's charming operetta *Amahl and the Night Visitors* at Holy Trinity Church, Malvern Link. This I enjoyed greatly. It was also an occasion when I was given good advice by the principal flautist, a Yorkshireman who was not given to circumlocution. I had experienced some difficulty in getting the orchestra to move forward in the March, where there is a considerable *accelerando*. Tactfully, the flautist came up to me at a break in the rehearsal and said 'Ee, Harry lad, if tha wants us to go faster, beat smaller!' He was right. I have never forgotten this advice.

In addition to conducting, as Assistant Organist of the Cathedral I was asked to play for concerts and recitals – for instance at Halesowen Parish Church for Bach's *Christmas Oratorio*, accompanied solo on the organ – a feat not to be undertaken lightly, particularly the rushing hemi-demi-semiquavers in the chorus 'Christians be joyful' at the beginning of Part 1.

In those Worcester years we certainly worked hard and played hard. My musical commitments involved most weekday evenings, and at weekends I spent a lot of time in the Cathedral, starting with 8.30 till 10.00 a.m. on Saturday mornings for the full practice of the Cathedral choir – the only one in the week except for half an hour at 8.30 a.m. on Tuesdays. Choirs did not rehearse much then – apart of course from the boys. All this activity did sometimes take its toll, and occasionally I went down with flu and had to be visited by the school doctor, Dr Duncan. He was very old school, and once remarked to the Precentor when he was letting him into my house, 'There's not much wrong with him. All he needs is an electric blanket or a wife!' On one occasion he advised how to cut down on drinking at parties: 'Take a bottle of Lucozade, which everyone will think is whisky and soda!' Strangely, on moving to London I never again experienced these bouts of flu! Perhaps it was the sea air blowing up the Thames outside my front door which kept me healthy.

During my Worcester years, my parents were still living in Guiseley, so every now and again I would visit them, particularly in the holidays. Though I had frequent run-ins with my father in school and Oxford days, as mentioned before, once I started working, everything changed. My parents became a great support. I had always got on well with my mother – I lived alone with her during the five years of the war. She was rather north country and undemonstrative towards me on the surface; but when she met other mothers, she gave an altogether different account of me. In the 15 years of her widowhood, when she lived alone in quite a large house, though I lived 200 miles away, she came to rely on me a good deal. She also used to visit me at Southwark and Addington with her cousin Doris Beanlands, whose funeral I played for in 2013.

Once my mother said something I found devastatingly moving. This was a year or two before she died. Quite out of the blue she said that when she knew she was having me, people at work said they could tell her what to do to terminate the pregnancy – a kind of home-made abortion. She took no notice, she said, 'because she wanted me!' She was of in fact referring to conceiving out of wedlock, just before she married my father. This happened a good deal in those days, and my parents had actually been going out together for some years – as he was the boy next door!

My mother had a genius for friendship and was often called upon by the neighbours. There was a sad incident at the house opposite one day when a woman put her head in the gas oven. The first thing her son did was to send for my mother. In her last months, she was visited in her nursing home by my friend Nicholas Frayling while I was working abroad. She remarked that she found it hard to pray there, but she added, 'I'm not worried. I've put a lot of prayers into the bank over the years and now I'm living on the interest!' She had a dry sense of humour and was good at cutting things down to size.

My father also had quite a sharp wit, as well as a Yorkshire directness. But much of it was 'huff and puff'. Underneath he was very sensitive. Maybe as a former rugby player and a motorbike eventer, he tried to cultivate something of a macho image. But it was only skin deep. I experienced much closeness with him in later years, particularly when I was able to talk to him about his illness. I remember some lifelong friends telling me how good and patient he was with their Downs syndrome daughter whenever they visited my parents, and how he sat down with her showing her how to draw and colour – something the little girl always remembered. When I was younger, he didn't really understand this unusual creature he had for a son; I also lacked commonsense in my teenage years. But later this became past history and we became very close. Both my mother and father were fortunate in that they both had extremely peaceful ends to their lives. I'm glad I was able to be present at both.

I have possibly given the impression that Worcester life was arduous. Well, not entirely. There were pleasant visits to the continent, usually with young masters from the King's School – to Italy, the Netherlands, Germany and Austria. Surprisingly not often to France, but I have made up for that deficiency in later life, and still manage to get there several times a year.

I was lucky to have such a stimulating and interesting job in my Worcester days. Friendships made there have continued for over 50 years. It was noticeable at my 80th birthday lunch at the Athenaeum that more than a third of the 36 guests were friends made in those years who have remained in touch and enriched my life with their friendship.

THREE ORGANISTS

Christopher Robinson (1963–1974)

Christopher has already figured a good deal in the account of my time at Worcester. But I would like to add some personal reminiscences over a longer period. He was a year ahead of me at Oxford, taking his Schools in the summer of 1957. It was about this time we first met. I remember visiting with him the fine Father Willis organ in Oxford Town Hall, even today a well-kept secret. From then on we met occasionally before he went off to Birmingham University to take the Diploma of Education course, which he passed with distinction. Afterwards he was on the music staff of Oundle School for several years. He followed Edgar Day in 1962 as Assistant at Worcester to Douglas Guest, only months before the latter was appointed Organist of Westminster Abbey. This led to Christopher being appointed Organist of Worcester Cathedral little more than a term after he had moved from Oundle. Again a new Assistant had to be found – and that is how I fit into the picture. I went to Worcester with some ability on the organ and as a choir trainer. I was also an experienced teacher. But there were areas where I had to make a rapid ascent up a steep learning curve.

Unlike me, Christopher had long experience of cathedral music. He was a chorister at St Michael's College, Tenbury – he was actually interviewed by Sir Sydney Nicholson, Director of the RSCM, who was running Tenbury during the war. A music scholarship at Rugby School was followed by the Organ Scholarship at Christ Church, Oxford. He knew so much about the Anglican choral repertoire and how pieces should go. Having to play S. S. Wesley's anthem 'The Wilderness' and other classics under his direction at Worcester gave me an instinctive feel for the style of this music – something I carried through to my subsequent appointments at Southwark, the RSCM and All Saints, Margaret Street.

I found Christopher easy to work with when it came to dealing with choristers. They worked well for me because he instilled in them the idea that they were young professionals performing for the good of the choir and the Cathedral and not for the choirmaster's personal satisfaction. Hero worship was not on the agenda. But respect there certainly was. He expected much from the boys and he worked them hard, something they very much liked. They felt their job was important. All this was achieved without tantrums. Christopher had a consistent manner and only very rarely raised his voice – again something much appreciated by the boys. He got them to sing with a beauty of tone which was bright and natural. To this was added unanimity and flexibility of rhythm, perfect intonation and a great sensitivity in phrasing and expression. Recently I was listening to a recording of Schubert's four-part setting of 'The Lord is my Shepherd' for upper voices, made in 1966, where all these qualities were demonstrated to perfection. It was only three years after Christopher's arrival and already the style of singing was recognizable as very much the 'Worcester' sound. And it was no flash in the pan. The standard was constantly maintained.

Amongst the boys there were always a few who had outstanding solo voices: for instance, Jonathan Nott and John Davies singing Mendelssohn's duet 'I waited for the Lord' from the oratorio *St Paul* in 1974. I doubt whether better solo singing has existed anywhere. It was certainly in the tradition of the Temple Church under Sir George Thalben-Ball, particularly the virtuoso performance of Mendelssohn's 'Hear my prayer' by Ernest Lough.

The singing of the Worcester boys at this time was probably the finest to be heard in cathedrals in the 1960s and 1970s. It was special, and its reputation travelled far. I can say this with real authority, as I was part of this tradition. But I did not instigate or create it; that was the work of Christopher Robinson. It was a good period. And whether it was a quiet Evensong on a very cold winter day or a great occasion, the aim was to maintain a consistent standard. This was not easy when it came to singing Matins at 8.30 a.m. on Thursday mornings when the mist from the Severn hung low over College Green.

I remember one week when I was on duty, we had just finished the Te Deum in C by Stanford, rather a marathon for that time of day. At the end of this, before the Second Lesson, there was considerable altercation in the choir stalls. One of the bass lay clerks was not at his best at this time of day, and on this occasion the boys on his side had been turning round and staring at him. This brought forth a great rebuke from the man concerned, who was obviously extremely rattled. When I arrived to take the boys' practice after the service, I asked them what on earth was going on. The leading boy immediately said they had tried so hard to do their very best but this man just did not care. I felt I had to take issue with their behaviour which, whatever their feelings, was not acceptable during a service. Whereupon the boy in question explained indignantly, 'Oh but sir, he's awful, sir!' I felt we had to move on and just told them to put out the copies of 'Lord for thy tender mercies' sake!'

Christopher was a great support to me in the school. When there was a concert, he taught the boys the music and they then joined their friends in the school choir for the final rehearsals and performance. He even did this when the work in question was the Verdi *Requiem*. Previously the boys had not been allowed to sing in school concerts. Christopher also gave piano lessons – and in their final year, organ lessons to the most talented boys. He was a fine pianist and teacher of the piano. He usually took one of the boys to act as accompanist when he rehearsed the City of Birmingham choir on Tuesday evenings.

In around 1970, when Andrew Millington and Stephen Darlington were exact contemporaries at the school, he could not decide who he should take. So he gave them both a copy of *Belshazzar's Feast* by Walton to learn during the summer holidays so that he could decide when they returned for the autumn term who was better at it. In the event he couldn't decide who the winner was, so he chose both of them, taking them to Birmingham alternate weeks.

One rarely managed to get Christopher to play the piano. But there was one hilarious occasion when we had unusually gone together to the Mug House at Claines, just to the north of Worcester. He was prevailed upon by one of the regulars to do a turn on the pub piano. He sat down and gave an immaculate performance of Scott Joplin's 'Maple Leaf Rag' from memory. This was hugely well received; but one habitué rather blotted his copy book by asking him whether he could play it in three flats!

Christopher and his wife Shirley (who I had also met at Oxford when she was reading Music at St Anne's) were very hospitable to me, including inviting me in my early days to Sunday lunch. We occasionally went off to have dinner in a country hotel – a great favourite was The Elms at Abberley where there was exceptional cooking and great log fires in winter. There were just two menus available – at 27 shillings and 32 shillings and sixpence. On Christmas Day after Evensong we drove over to Bredenbury near Bromyard where Christopher's father, Prebendary John Robinson, was the incumbent. Even in the late 1960s, large country vicarages were still common – now mostly sold off as part of a policy of asset-stripping. Christopher's mother Hilda was a wonderful cook, producing superb Christmas dinners very much in the manner of Mrs Beaton. After staying the night, we were sent off next morning after a large cooked breakfast. For us, it was back to work as the choir stayed on for the three Holy Days after Christmas to sing Evensongs, a custom abolished fairly early on in our time. Parents understandably were not happy that the boys could not go home until 28 December.

It was at Bredenbury that I came to know Christopher's sister, Catharine, rather better. I was delighted to conduct the choir in the Cathedral at her wedding to Adrian Edwards in the autumn of 1974, just before Christopher and Shirley and their two children moved to Windsor.

The 11 1/2 years I worked with Christopher were highly formative for me. I learned so much. When I was appointed, some doubted the wisdom of having an organist and his assistant of roughly the same age. I would like to think we proved them wrong. Through all the succeeding years we have kept in touch, and it is a pleasure to see Nicholas my godson from time to time; he was baptised by his grandfather in Worcester Cathedral in the summer of 1970 and is now Director of Music at St Peter's, St Albans, and teaches at Wycombe Abbey School. It all seems so long ago. Worcester, like most cathedrals, has changed out of all recognition. But to me those days 50 years ago are still vivid in my memory – and for that I am grateful. My Worcester years were the making of me as a musician.

Donald Hunt (1975–1996)
Christopher Robinson moved from Worcester to be Organist of St George's Chapel, Windsor Castle, just after Christmas 1974. There was an interregnum of five weeks before the arrival of Dr Donald Hunt in early February 1976. I ran the choir and all the daily services during this interval. In many ways, it was a difficult period for me. I had worked with another boss for eleven and a half years. It was no secret that many in Worcester, including the Bishop, thought I should have been the successor. Eric Kemp, the Dean, thought differently; he was anxious to avoid a tenure of 40 years. He was probably right in this. But his unwillingness to discuss the matter was a serious omission on his part. Looking back, I think his decision was right, but for other reasons. I am now glad I was not appointed. With the Worcester Three Choirs on the horizon in six months' time, my lack of sufficient experience in orchestral conducting would have caused me much anxiety and stress. Had I had three years to prepare, things might have been different.

Donald Hunt had the necessary experience in this field. As a distinguished organist of Leeds Parish Church for 18 years, where he followed my teacher Dr Melville Cook on his appointment to Hereford Cathedral, he was widely experienced as a conductor at the Leeds Triennial Festival, at the Halifax Choral Society and elsewhere. I made up my mind to support Donald fully and to help him get used to the local Worcester customs, which I hoped might help him to settle in. I was determined to be a good assistant. In fact this was only for just over a year before I moved to Southwark in April 1976.

I found Donald very friendly, and he and his wife Jo were hospitable in welcoming me to their home. He was a support to me in the school, and actually sang tenor in the Mozart *Requiem* at my summer concert. We were soon in the midst of the Three Choirs Festival, for which I had much to do – including playing the important organ parts in Mendelssohn's *Lobgesang* and in the unfamiliar and challenging *Requiem* of Frank Martin. This was quite stressful as it was an afternoon live broadcast conducted by John Sanders of Gloucester. At the end of the Festival's final concert, Donald called me onto the stage to take a bow – a gesture which I much appreciated for all I had done to prepare for the week's music. He was very supportive of the Voluntary Choir, and involved them more in the Cathedral's music. He did in fact lighten their load in the holidays by encouraging visiting choirs to sing at weekends, something which had never happened before. In some ways it was a good idea, but it did not meet with approval in all quarters. During 1976 the Cathedral choir sang several concerts at the Flanders Festival. Meanwhile a good deal of new music was introduced to the repertoire, which kept us all on our toes.

At Leeds, Donald kept the choral tradition of the Parish Church in good shape – a tradition which started with the opening of the new church in 1841, when the Vicar, Walter Hook, persuaded one of the foremost organists of the day, S. S. Wesley, to move from Exeter Cathedral to inaugurate the new musical arrangements. These continued to be directed by men of real ability, principal amongst them Sir Edward Bairstow, who moved to York Minster in 1913. It was a great tradition, but one which became more difficult to maintain in the later part of the 20th century. There was no choir school; boys had to be recruited and enthused. There was also little money, and the lower parts were mainly sung by able volunteers.

Donald had been a chorister at Gloucester Cathedral and a pupil of Herbert Sumsion – as had his predecessor, Melville Cook. Between them for over 40 years they ably maintained the musical tradition of the church. It was natural that Donald should return to the West Midlands to preside over the music of Worcester Cathedral for 21 years. I think his greatest achievement was with the Three Choirs

Festival. He was a good organizer and entrepreneur, bringing a good deal of useful change to the programming and the organization.

My abiding memory of Donald was that he loved music and music-making. He had a remarkable knowledge of all kinds of music. When he retired from the Cathedral, he continued as Principal of the Elgar Music School located in the Countess of Huntingdon's Chapel in Deansway. And into his eighties he continued to conduct the Great Witley Operatic Society. He was very much a person who thought things could be done. During the year I spent with him, we formed a good working relationship. I look back with pleasure on my last months as Assistant Organist of Worcester Cathedral as his colleague.

Edgar Day (1912–1962)

This is a kind of postscript to what I have written about Christopher Robinson and Donald Hunt, for I feel that Edgar Day's long years as Assistant Organist (1912–1962) should be mentioned. I have already spoken of him in connection with Elgar. He did however inspire a great deal of affection as a teacher and friend, and should have a place in any musical account of Worcester. I got to know him well in retirement, as he lived round the corner from me in (appropriately) Edgar Street. When I first met him he was very active, going for long country walks. He didn't come in the Cathedral much, but sometimes when we performed his music, he could be seen lurking behind a distant pillar in the nave. He was essentially a very shy man. I think his terrible experiences as a soldier in the First World War had a lot to do with his nervousness. He was wounded and spent considerable time in a military hospital in Sevenoaks.

He was born on a farm in the Cotswolds near Northleach. He obviously showed musical talent as a young man and came to Worcester at the age of 21 as Assistant to Sir Ivor Atkins, Organist of the Cathedral 1897–1950. It is true to say that he was dominated by Atkins, who treated him like a batman. This cannot have done much for his self-confidence. He was expected to pour the tea at Lady Atkins' Sunday afternoon tea parties! I think Edgar respected

Atkins, but he had a much more equal and friendly relationship with his successors, Sir David Willcocks (1950–1957) and Douglas Guest (1957–1963). Willcocks was particularly kind to him, played golf with him, and when he was ill went round to the house to look after him, and on occasions to shave him.

Edgar was a likable man and very well informed about music. Many thought he had a touch of sanctity and that his kindly nature prevented him from speaking ill of anyone. This was in fact not quite true. When one got to know him well, it became clear that he was a man of deep feelings. He could be outspoken and sometimes angry when speaking to a considerate friend. I was able to get to know him through regular visits after he ceased going out. But he did sometimes come to me on Saturdays for lunch, when I always made cauliflower cheese, his favourite dish. He had been a lifelong vegetarian and often spoke of the butcher as 'a naughty man'. He gradually became more infirm and was visited regularly by my two successors as Assistant Organist, Paul Trepte and Adrian Partington. At Christmas they took some of the Voluntary Choir to sing in his house.

Though he did not write much, his music is well crafted and imaginative. Two of his pieces published by the Oxford University Press are still sung in cathedrals and college chapels – the charming setting of 'Round me falls the night' and an impressive setting of the Magnificat and Nunc Dimittis in B flat, originally written for a Worcester Three Choirs Festival. Several of his Anglican chants are very well known and appear in most collections. I remember his friendship with affection.

When he died, he left me £100 – the only time anyone other than family has bequeathed me anything. Using some of this, I bought Gerald Northrop Moore's monumental book on Elgar, which I thought a fitting memento of one who had known the composer so well during the last 20 years of his life.

A WORCESTER POSTSCRIPT

I was 26 when I went to Worcester and 39 when I left. I was full of youthful energy and able to cope with a very full programme of work. And that was just as well as employers expected good measure in those days.

My grandfather, even in his late 60s, had a huge job at Salt's Mill, Saltaire, where he was in charge of the weaving department. He ran two large weaving sheds with the help of an under-manager. He had to make sure the cloth was of a high quality, supervise a large workforce and when it came to buying new looms he had to advise the directors. Nowadays there would have been quite a team to do all this work, but he coped. He arrived at 7.30 a.m., with the workforce and left with them at 5.15 p.m., after only three-quarters of an hour for lunch.

We likewise had to put in many hours at Worcester. I usually had only two free evenings in the week – that is if I was lucky. But the memory of those days is of hard work mixed with leisure and the making of long-term friendships. Some of the men of the Voluntary Choir, many of whom had started as boys, were very sociable – usually in the White Hart, where a good deal of arm lifting was customary after the Friday evening practice. George Bourne was stationmaster at Shrub Hill station, and Den Morris worked for the Gas Board.

The venerable Alderman Walter Amphlett had been a glove cutter and sometime Mayor of Worcester. He didn't join us in the pub! Like many old-fashioned choirmen, he sang with considerable attack. When the conductor lifted his arm, he was in slightly ahead of the beat. David Willcocks when organist at Worcester played a practical joke on him. He crept up behind him in the choir stalls during the opening responses. Just as Walter was about to get in first, he grabbed his arm and shouted 'Stop'!

John Bleney I invited to join the choir in 1964, and I recently went to a lunch in his honour given by the Chapter to celebrate his 50 years in the choir. When he joined, he was an organ builder working for Nicholson's, where he had served his time. When he married Edith White in 1968, he moved to more lucrative work at a large mail order company. I played for the wedding and soon Edith too became a great friend. She was a country girl from near Malvern, who had much *savoir faire* and instinctive understanding of human nature. She was a good cook and wonderful host. She welcomed many of the musical boys from the King's School to meals and was a good friend to many. Sadly she died before her time at the age of 50. I played for the funeral in the Cathedral, and it was moving to see how many former King's School musicians came to honour her friendship.

John has remained a close friend and now lives with his second wife Marion in an idyllic location at Grafton Flyford, with views across the Vale of Evesham to Bredon Hill in the distance. As I grow older I realize that despite the importance of honing our skills and talents, the only thing that really matters in the end is friendship and a respect for and enjoyment of the variety of people one encounters at every turn.

Worcester gave me the opportunities to improve my skills as a musician. But this was in a context where I mixed with a great variety of people from right across the social spectrum. This was an education which left me wiser and more sensitive to others. People were generous to me and I would like to think that I learned there to treat others in a similar manner.

CHAPTER FIVE

Southwark

THE CHALLENGE – AND THE WAY THINGS DEVELOPED

During the later part of my time at Worcester, I had tried to move position on several occasions and had been shortlisted for organists' appointments at Llandaff, Hereford and Birmingham without success. I was nearing the age of forty; I felt it essential to move on. Eventually in January 1976, aged 39, I was appointed as Organist and Director of Music at Southwark Cathedral. And as can happen after disappointments, this seemed to be the right job for me. It fitted very closely with my previous experience at Worcester and elsewhere.

I had only been in Southwark Cathedral once before: in October 1974 when I played the organ and the Worcester choir sang for the consecration of Dr Eric Kemp, Dean of Worcester, as Bishop of Chichester by Archbishop Michael Ramsey – in fact his last consecration before retirement. I had travelled up the day before to familiarize myself with the organ and the liturgical arrangements. This turned out to be providential as the choir was held up by points' failure at Didcot. In fact they only got to the cathedral minutes before the service began and performed without practice in the building. Fortunately the mass was unaccompanied: the Mass in five parts by Lennox Berkeley.

I was much taken by the beauty and atmosphere of Southwark

Cathedral and was enraptured by the Lewis organ, even in its damaged state. Henry Willis iii did revoicing in 1953, and as he often did with his grandfather's instruments, altered the essential tonal architecture. Fortunately these amendments were done on the cheap, and it was found in 1990 when Harrisons restored the instrument that these were entirely reversible! I little thought on that October day in 1974 that 18 months later I would actually be Organist of the Cathedral!

I suppose I had an advantage over the other shortlisted candidates, as the Chapter had already heard what I could do on a great occasion. The actual interviews were on 14 January 1976 at the Provost's Lodgings on Bankside on a gloriously sunny day. As was usually the case in those days, there were no auditions with the choir and at the organ – just a one-hour interview with the Provost, Harold Frankham, and two of the Canons, Peter Penwarden and Peter Delaney. On leaving, the Provost pointed to the small house next door and said it would be a very desirable residence for a single man! Within three months I was moving in. I finished at Worcester on Low Sunday, which that year was the last in April; and started at Southwark the following Sunday, 2 May. There were no gap periods or sabbaticals in those days!

The house, 52 Bankside, was one of three 18th-century houses which had survived the industrialization of the south bank in the 19th century. The middle house was occupied by the Provost; and at the far end, a remarkable character, Guy Muenthe, lived in what used to be known as Christopher Wren's house. It was in fact a pub – The Cardinal's Cap. A fascinating account of this house and the whole row can be found in the recent book by Gillian Tindall, *A House by the Thames*. Muenthe was very much a playboy with a wide circle of friends ranging from Rudolph Nureyev to Princess Margaret. I once arrived home to find the street full of photographers waiting outside, hoping for a shot of Princess Margaret who was thought to be visiting!

Southwark was a place of great opportunity – but also of massive challenges. The first was financial. The Cathedral had been through a very difficult time in the late 1960s, and by 1970 it was bankrupt.

THE CHALLENGE – AND THE WAY THINGS DEVELOPED

My annual stipend on arrival was £1,500 per annum, one third of what I got at Worcester from the Cathedral and the King's School. I did – as at Worcester – get my living costs at the house free of charge. This just about made things possible. I was worried about the great drop in salary and remember discussing this with my very Yorkshire father. He said, 'Well, you've got to get your foot in the door!' He was right. The risk was worth it and soon all kinds of opportunities started to open up. I had some family backing as my father gradually handed over to me the proceeds of my grandfather's estate. I was also helped by the foresight and sagacity of Frank Richardson, the Comptroller of the Cathedral. A former hop merchant, aged about 80 at the time, he was very canny. For instance for the purposes of my pension, he added to my salary all the other factors – what I would have to pay in rent and the value of other benefits. He also said he was going to put me in SERPS (State earnings related pension scheme). It was only many years later when I started to draw the state pension that I realized the wisdom of this move.

The second risk was musical. Though Southwark had once had a good musical reputation, particularly in the days of Dr E. T. Cook (1909–1953), on my arrival standards were low. I followed three organists – Dr Sydney Campbell, Harold Dexter and E. H. Warrell, none of whom had ultimately been successful. Campbell was extremely difficult and volatile. Stories of his exploits are still told – as when, disgusted by the singing of the choir in an unaccompanied anthem, he tore up the copy, threw it over the choir and walked out during the performance. Harold Dexter was a distinguished man, a Professor at the Guildhall School of Music. He had a very quick temper and didn't always have sufficient tact in what was a volatile situation. He had a good deal of time for the embattled Provost, Ernest Southcott, who had to cope with a Chapter of prima donnas appointed by Bishop Mervyn Stockwood to modernize the cathedral. This resulted in 'South Bank Religion' and 'Sunday Nights at Southwark', spectaculars with celebrities from a wide spectrum of opinion. There was little room for the choral tradition of the Cathedral, though it has to be said, from a glance at the music lists from the 1960s the repertoire was deadly dull.

The Canons were a strange collection: Sydney Evans was a communist and John Pearce-Higgins a believer in ghosts. The man who stood out was Eric James. He had been an organ pupil of E. T. Cook, a cultured and intelligent man who later became a distinguished writer and broadcaster. He probably found it difficult to go against the flow, but I believe later much regretted what had happened in those heady days in the 1960s. When Harold Dexter resigned after a furious row with Eric James in a local pub, the Chapter turned to a former Assistant Organist and articled pupil to E. T. Cook: E. H. Warrell, who at that time was Organist of St John the Divine, Kennington. They thought, I believe, that they were downgrading the post (they were mistaken in my view), and that to have a good parish organist would make life much easier. In this they could not have been more wrong. Warrell (1915–2010) had a deep love of the Cathedral and worked very hard during his six years (1969–1975) to keep a vestige of the Cathedral's musical tradition alive – against insuperable odds.

The problem was that the Cathedral was virtually bankrupt, so money was in short supply. His salary was a mere £750 per annum, meaning he had to supplement his income from elsewhere. In 1970 Stockwood ordered the Chapter to sack the six professional lay clerks – mainly because of the profligate spending on 'South Bank Religion'. To crown it all, St Olave's School, which had provided boys for the choir on scholarships since the late 19th century, had moved from Tower Bridge to new premises in Orpington in 1968. Thus Warrell had to set about recruiting boys and amateur men for the lower parts. That anything survived was nothing short of a miracle. He once told me that though he realized musical standards were not good enough, he had at least been able to keep something going. That was true – and indeed it made my job of rebuilding the choir a good deal easier.

There was still a very considerable challenge. But there were other problems of a political nature. Warrell had a stormy relationship with the new Provost, Harold Frankham, who was highly musical, having played the organ in his younger days. He was dissatisfied with the standard of music and in the end, in autumn 1975, he decided to ask Warrell to resign: to deliver his keys and go immediately. This not surprisingly caused a furore amongst Warrell's supporters. I had to live with the fall-out from this for some time after my arrival. This was not made easier by the Assistant Organist, Garrett O'Brien, having to step into the breach and run the music for seven months during the interregnum. In fairness to him, he managed to stabilize the situation; indeed, things began to improve. It was not surprising, therefore, that O'Brien resented my arrival. He felt, as the rescuer, that he should have been appointed.

When I took over in May 1976, there were fourteen boys in the choir. Half of these were musical; the others had little ability and were very difficult. The two best boys were aged 14, but with completely unbroken voices. One, Ian Coleman, had a golden voice. He and the other boy, Andrew Hagyard, supported me up to the hilt. They showed considerable maturity. Fortunately both survived until they were 15. A few of the better younger boys lasted longer. The weaker boys gradually left. Recruitment of new boys was an immediate priority. I was much helped in this by the Succentor, David Hutt, a former soldier with the Greenjackets who organized the campaign on military lines.

But my first new chorister, Benjamin Tingle, arrived by a most extraordinary route. About three weeks into my new post, a former Worcester pupil, Nicholas Woods, studying at the Royal Academy of Music, invited me out for a drink at a pub near his student hostel in Camberwell. I expressed my anxiety about chorister recruitment, which prompted him to say that the following morning he was going to give a piano lesson to a boy who lived nearby. This was because he was going out with the family's Danish au pair, and the boy's mother had asked her to enquire if her boyfriend could give him piano lessons! At this, I said you must ask whether he can sing. It turned out the boy had had a traumatic experience at the Temple Church at an audition with Sir George Thalben-Ball, when he was obviously totally unprepared. So his mother brought him to see me. He didn't know much about music but he had a pleasant voice. So I took him on. I then discovered that he went to a progressive state primary school, Prior Weston in the Barbican, where the well-known Headmaster Henry Pluckrose turned out to be his godfather – and more incredibly a former Head Chorister of Southwark Cathedral. Within a week, I had six new boys from the school.

Over the next 12 years, many very able boys of character came from this source. The music mistress, Margot Fagin, a remarkable person, became a great supporter. She would sometimes phone to say there were some boys I ought to see. Over the course of my first year, we formed relationships with a good number of other schools, particularly Archbishop Tenison's Grammar School at the Oval, where the distinguished music master, Alan Gibbs, kept me supplied with boys right up to the end of my time at Southwark. When news got around, parents eventually started to approach us. Keeping the choir stalls full became less of a problem. At Southwark, with rehearsal time limited, it was essential to look for intelligent boys with good voices in order to make rapid progress. When auditioning for the choir, I found that asking candidates to read a suitable column from a newspaper was a good way of assessing intelligence and reading ability. If a boy could not read English reasonably fluently at the age of eight, he would flounder when he came to learn how to read music.

Attempting to integrate many new probationer-choristers with the boys already there was a tricky exercise. I decided to have a reception class for the new boys once a week for an hour after school. This was relaxed and fun and gave me a chance to gain their confidence, then to give vocal training and sight-reading exercises and teach some choral music. A piece I found useful for inducting them to two-part singing was the melodious piece by Marcello, 'Give ear unto me'. I also taught the Latin words of the Mass from some of the easier Viennese masses. A particular favourite was the opening of the 'Missa sancti Nicolai' of Haydn. When the recognizable red copies were produced, there was always an outburst of enthusiasm and pleasure.

The boys learned to love the music I gave them. That they liked it was the main thing; it was of little importance to them whether it was by Haydn or Mozart!

After a period in the reception class, I gradually fed them into the choir. By this time, most of them were eager to be promoted. It was during one of these Wednesday afternoon sessions that a remarkable thing happened. The boys from Prior Weston School were used to addressing their teachers by their Christian names. So looking back on it, I should not have been surprised when one day a small boy arriving for practice said 'Hello, Harry'. I realized he was not taking the mickey, so I said nothing. Within a fortnight, all the boys started to call me 'Harry'. I rather liked it and eventually became irritated when they addressed me as 'Sir'. I remember on one occasion barking at a boy 'For God's sake, don't call me Sir!' 'All right, Harry,' he replied. From then on I was always 'Harry'. I think it emphasized the generally friendly and happy atmosphere that prevailed, and certainly was not the cause of discipline problems. Quite the reverse. That did not mean that sometimes I could not be angered. The boys talked for years about the time I threw a tin of biscuits across the practice room!

The social background of these boys was very varied. Some came from disadvantaged backgrounds, but most were from good homes which were often affluent. Some were the children of professional parents – teachers, doctors, architects, barristers. Occasionally the social mix caused tensions, but not often. Virtually all the younger boys attended state primary schools, so were used to social variety. It is interesting that when they moved to secondary schools, the transition was usually seamless. Thus after the age of eleven, it was quite usual for the boys to have to travel long distances to the Cathedral – from St Paul's School at Hammersmith, Westminster and Alleyns or Dulwich College. Quite a number of boys attended comprehensive schools, including Haverstock School in Hampstead and a variety of schools in South London. I thought it was important that the Cathedral should have boys from the Elephant and Castle as well as boys from the suburbs.

It must be remembered that all the choristers were volunteers. They were bound together by a love of singing and by the camaraderie which goes with it. This was one very great advantage of a non-choir school system. The boys did not have to come. They decided themselves to do so; it was this that was the foundation of their loyalty. People often asked how we managed to run a voluntary choir in central London. One rather opinionated headmaster in South London who helped on RSCM residential courses said 'it was impossible'. We showed him otherwise. There were of course some financial benefits – travel costs and choir pay at the end of each term, but this was quite modest.

In the early years we attracted some excellent boys who began to develop very rapidly. With the men, finding good volunteers was less easy. But when I arrived, there was a nucleus of good tenors and basses – medical students from the local hospitals, for instance, or men who sang in London choral societies. There were gaps, particularly in the alto section. Gradually, as news got round the diocese that developments were afoot at Southwark, quite a number of good new volunteer men appeared on the horizon. The Cathedral was also able to fund two choral scholarships for students at the Royal College of Music.

Though the choir's composition was all the time improving, I feared that when the experienced nucleus had to leave in a short while, things could become very shaky. So I took the bold and, I believe, in the circumstances the right decision to appoint a young professional soprano to give support to the treble line. She was someone I had known well in Worcester days – Harriet Leigh-Spencer, who had sung in my productions at the King's School. Her voice, though capable of power, blended ideally with the sound of the boys. And just as importantly, she had the right temperament to exist in an all-male environment. She was very popular with the boys and the men, and gave us wonderful support for four years till 1980, when she left to have her first child. By this time the boys had become capable of holding the top line with confidence.

The choir gradually improved and in 1978 received a considerable boost when we were asked to broadcast Choral Evensong on BBC Radio 3. This arose out of the appointment of John Scott as the new Assistant Organist at Southwark. When he came down from Cambridge in the summer of that year, he became assistant at Southwark and second assistant at St Paul's. In order to finalize the arrangements for this dual post, Barry Rose, then Choirmaster at St Paul's, had come to see me at my house on Bankside. On leaving, he paused on the doorstep and said, 'I have a vacancy for choral evensong in six weeks' time. Do you think the Southwark choir could do this?' I said I thought we could. That we did it successfully with John Scott at the organ raised the morale of the choir enormously and was the beginning of annual broadcasts. Had Barry Rose mentioned the reason for this unexpected vacancy, my background from the West Riding of Yorkshire might have caused difficulty. The broadcast was intended to be from Bradford Cathedral, where the Director of Music, Keith Rhodes, had done remarkable work. It is no secret that his relations with the Provost of Bradford, Brandon Jackson, had reached a low ebb. The Provost thought that the choir could only think of the Cathedral in musical terms and had got their priorities out of balance. This led him to cancel the broadcast. It was a sad episode – but like all such cases, there was probably something to be said on both sides.

At Southwark, in addition to regular services, the choir sang at a great variety of events. There were the regular consecrations of bishops by the Archbishop of Canterbury, a TV broadcast in honour of Arthur Askey, and the first choir tour to Yorkshire, when we sang in York Minster, Bradford Cathedral, St Wilfred's Harrogate and St Martin's Scarborough. But the most remarkable special event was the 75th anniversary of the diocese of Southwark in 1980, when Bishop Mervyn Stockwood celebrated the Eucharist on the centre court at Wimbledon in the week after the lawn tennis championships! It had first been thought that the largest auditorium in the diocese was the Royal Festival Hall, until someone pointed out that the centre court at Wimbledon seated 12,000. So it was decided to go there – a risky business considering the unpredictable weather in July. In fact that year the championship had overrun because of heavy rain. Fortunately, by Sunday 13 July they had finished and all went well in glorious sunshine. But after lunch, it clouded over and there was torrential rain!

The Bishop and his suffragans officiated at an altar in the middle of the court. Numerous concelebrating priests enabled the sacrament to be administered to the capacity congregation with flawless efficiency. The hymns were accompanied by the military band of Tiffin's School, Kingston conducted by David Nield, who together with a choir of 500 drawn from 25 churches in the diocese occupied the Royal Box! John Scott accompanied some parts of Schubert's Mass in G on an electronic organ, and a memorable performance of Byrd's 'Ave verum corpus' was given during the communion. It was a truly great occasion, made the more so as it came near the end of Stockwood's 21 years as Bishop. At the end of the service, he did a lap of honour in the manner of John McEnroe.

The choir was further stabilized in 1979 when the Cathedral decided we should have three professional men. We were able to recruit some excellent singers. We started with Philip Lawson, who eventually joined the King's Singers; Wilfred Swansborough, who would move to St Paul's; and Julian Andrews, who after three years joined the RAF and ultimately became Administrator at Hereford Cathedral. We expected these men to move on. One, Michael Lees, went to Westminster Abbey; and another, Alex Donaldson, became Headmaster of the York Minster Choir School. Then in 1988 the Cathedral was able to fund six professional lay clerks, to which were added six good amateur men who were given expenses. The support for all this came from the Precentor, Canon Gerald Parrott, who rightly thought that the choir should have a sure foundation based on financial remuneration. It is worth noting that the composition of the choir now reverted to what it was up to 1970, when six paid men were supplemented by good amateurs.

In the administration of the choir, the Organist was assisted by the minor canon (the Succentor). We were fortunate in my time in having five excellent Succentors. My first, David Hutt (1973–77), later became Vicar of All Saints, Margaret Street and the Sub Dean of Westminster Abbey. He had done a great deal to hold the boys together during the interregnum. On my arrival, he threw himself into the campaign for new choristers, producing recruitment leaflets and giving general support for me as we forged links with South London schools. Before ordination he had been a professional soldier; he was used to administration and was often seen around carrying a clipboard. He was very much identified by his range of Homburg hats in the streets of Southwark. The boys used to call him 'Hutt the hat'! He was eventually succeeded by Neil Heavisides (1978–81), who came to us from a curacy at St Peter's, Stockton-on-Tees. He and I got on well; he was musical and perceptive. He was extremely good with the boys who had just left the choir, who felt at ease in his company. He was humorous but informal, and perhaps a little chaotic in manner. This put the teenage boys at their ease. Many years later, some of them still kept in touch with him. He ended up as Precentor and Residentiary Canon of Gloucester Cathedral.

The next Succentor was quite different, but brought very special gifts. He was Roly Bain (1981–1984), an old boy of St Paul's School, and just before Southwark, curate of St George's, Perry Hill, where he had had a great deal of trouble with a lady in the parish who stalked him. Roly was very much a one-off, who pursued a vocation to be a Christian clown in the belief that the clown's attitudes and thinking were very close to the Christian gospel. He gave much to Southwark and was a great help to me in organizing the annual choirboys' camp. After leaving us and after a brief incumbency at Furzedown, he went freelance as a clown. He and his wife moved to Bristol, and frequently his antics were in the newspapers. It was a precarious existence, but he was in great demand. He was very proud of the number of bishops he had custard-pied! Sadly he died recently (in 2016) at the early age of 62. His obituaries were prominent in all the newspapers, including a particularly fine one in *The Spectator*.

My fourth Succentor was David Adlington, who was also distinguished in the job. He was quite a contrast to Roly. He had been an incumbent in the East End. With us he was invaluable in his support of my work, especially in extra-curricular activities and the choir camps. He too progressed to a distinguished career: as Director of Education for the Diocese of Llandaff; then Team Rector of Folkestone; after which he moved to three country parishes in Kent, where he was very happy. But this was not for long: his personal gifts were so considerable that he was persuaded to move back to Folkestone as Team Rector, where he had to be in charge of a group of parishes of different traditions. Towards the end of 2018 he died suddenly and unexpectedly; obviously a great sadness for his wife Kim, who he had met when she was a member of the congregation of St John's, Walworth.

My fifth Succentor, who was in post for my last year, was Nigel Worn. We definitely hit it off together, and he soon became a great support and friend – a friendship which has continued to the present day. He was until retirement Vicar of St Anne's, Kew, an immensely thriving south-west London church with very good music.

I really valued the support of these five men, my colleagues during my twelve and a half years at Southwark. They were a remarkable group with many personal gifts, who all progressed to important jobs in the church; we remain in close touch.

I mentioned one task which fell to the Succentor: the organization of the annual summer choristers' camp. This was a long-standing tradition dating back to before the war, when all the boys from the parish organizations joined in this venture. By the time I arrived, Provost Frankham had gradually wound down these parish activities. The Mothers' Union and the Boy Scouts had recently folded; so the camp became choir only. Attendance was not compulsory, but during my time most of the choristers came several times. It was good for a non-residential choir to spend more time together. We had some excellent camps in Suffolk and Devon, and quite a number at Melbury Abbas near Shaftsbury in Dorset. I made it my job to do the catering. I was glad not to have to go out on expeditions, and enjoyed the daily routine of cooked breakfast, packed lunch and a substantial evening meal. The boys were amused to see their choirmaster slaving away at the cooker – and of course they could be pressed into service as kitchen assistants.

Two other aspects of the job deserve a mention. Looking for talented children always had to be on the agenda. We continued to develop links with South London schools. The headmaster of Macauley School, Clapham said he had two boys who were interested: one had a mother who was an actor, and the other sang in the chorus at Covent Garden. Thus Joe West (son of Prunella Scales and Timothy West) and Edward Bright (son of Joan Bright, a former member of the Covent Garden Chorus) came into the choir. But increasingly as the choir became better known, parents started to approach us. They wanted their sons to be exposed to good singing and musical training, but did not want their boys to be locked into a 'choir school' situation. I received many enquiries. One of the most interesting was from the wife of a United Reformed Church minister at East Dulwich: she recommended two boys who came from a home where there had been family difficulties, and she wanted to do something for them. One was too old, but the other I took. Subsequently she brought him every Wednesday to the probationers' practice. She was not young. When one day I remarked it was good of her to bring him then wait in the Cathedral, she said, 'Don't worry about that – he's worth it.' With that kind of support, it seemed hardly possible to fail!

The other aspect I would like to mention is the special occasions we were increasingly asked to fulfil. One was a concert with Sir Philip Ledger at the Royal Festival Hall, when the boys sang the treble parts in Honneger's *Cantate de Noël*. They sang well on the night. I was relieved at this, as the previous day Ledger had come to Southwark to rehearse them, which I found rather a disturbing occasion. He made no friendly remarks to the boys, and throughout played the piano *fortissimo*. He almost crashed it through the floor. It seemed to be an object lesson in how not to treat children you were meeting for the first time. But we survived.

Two other occasions were entirely different. The first was the part the boys played in the Festival of Remembrance in November 1984 at the Royal Albert Hall. They were asked to start the evening by singing Vaughan Williams' song 'Linden Lea', for which I made a special arrangement with John Scott playing the organ. It was quite a nerve-racking occasion and the only time I got the boys to learn the notes by heart. They in fact rose to the occasion and acquitted themselves with great honour.

The second memorable occasion was when they sang the *ripieno* part in Bach's *St Matthew Passion*, conducted by Jeffrey Tate at the Barbican. Before the main rehearsal we were taken to a side room so he could hear them sing. We started off on the opening chorus, which the boys delivered with great confidence. After several pages, Tate stopped and said, 'Boys, your German is excellent; who taught you to do it so well?' After that the boys redoubled their efforts. This occasion was an object lesson in the art of human relationships. Quite a few years later, I encountered Tate at All Saints, Margaret Street. I asked him whether he remembered the occasion. He said he did and again remarked 'Their German was good. We ought to know, as we speak it all the time at home.'

TWO PROVOSTS

Harold Frankham (1970–1981)

The head of the Cathedral in my day was called the Provost. Later the terminology was standardized, but originally the so-called 'parish church' cathedrals were run by Provosts, not Deans.

There had been distinguished predecessors to Frankham. Cuthbert Bardsley became Bishop of Croydon and then of Coventry – he officiated at the consecration of Basil Spence's new cathedral in 1962; Hugh Ashdown went to Newcastle as Bishop, and George Reindorp to the see of Guildford, then to Salisbury. They were a distinguished trio. On the resignation of Reindorp, a totally different person was appointed – Ernest Southcott, the parish priest at Halton, a parish formed almost entirely of a large council estate on the eastern outskirts of Leeds. Mervyn Stockwood felt that he was a more appropriate figure for a South Bank London Cathedral, which in the late 1950s was still an area of considerable deprivation. Mervyn's intention was to make the cathedral parish more relevant. But alas, it was not quite so simple. Southcott, a dedicated priest, had had a remarkable ministry in Leeds. The Parish of Halton was a model of the 'parish and people' movement. He was on a mission to help the disadvantaged, and was for a time a Labour member of Leeds City Council.

But in Southwark, Southcott had a hard time. He had to cope with a set of Canons who were all prima donnas, their main interest being 'Sunday Nights at Southwark', spectaculars with star-studded casts aimed at pulling in the crowds. It was the Provost who had to maintain the daily Cathedral services. In the end it all got too much for him and things were brought to a head by the virtual bankruptcy of the Cathedral. He became ill and resigned. He did, however, go on for some years to a parish in Lancashire, where he was again able to exercise his talents in the parochial ministry.

This was the background situation which Harold Frankham inherited when he arrived after a distinguished term as Vicar of St Mary's, Luton. A firm hand and business ability were called for. I believe it was Cuthbert Bardsley (formerly Provost of Southwark) who put the idea into Stockwood's mind that Frankham might be the man. This turned out to be the case. When he arrived he had moved far from his evangelical roots at the London College of Divinity. He was now 'middle of the road', but with 'low church' leanings. And he did understand cathedrals, and particularly two of the factors crucial to them – the building and the music. At Luton, he had employed George Pace of York, a distinctive though not universally admired modern architect. He also rebuilt the organ. He was in fact very musical and had played the organ himself in his younger days. He had a good ear. I remember him telling me one day that the 2-foot stop on the choir organ was very out of tune and that I should get it attended to. He was right. He was also keen to improve the standard of the choir. At my interview, he told me that he didn't mind whether it was girls or boys on the top line, or an adult mixed choir, as long as it was good. I have already described how I decided to keep and improve the boys' choir. There had been a long tradition of boy trebles singing in the Cathedral, and I felt this should be honoured.

I got on well with Frankham. I was next-door neighbour to him and his wife Margaret. They were generous in their hospitality and they became good friends. But neither of them was always easy to deal with: they were strong characters, and like many evangelicals, socially deeply conservative.

I have never worked anywhere under such an autocratic figure as Frankham. He in effect ran the Cathedral single-handed, relying on assistance from the Vice Provost, Peter Penwarden, and the Precentor, Canon Gerald Parrott. But he rarely relied on them for their opinions! I remember at his funeral at Salisbury Cathedral, the former Archbishop of Canterbury, Donald Coggan, who had known him at the London College of Divinity, said 'Harold didn't like committees. His idea of the ideal committee was one of two members when the other person was away with flu.' His tendency not to consult was legendary. On several occasions he made musical decisions without consulting me – for example, the restringing of the Cathedral grand piano or commissioning a case to house the small Willis organ in the nave. I only knew of this when the case arrived. In this instance, my advice would have been helpful. The instrument was very poor and the architect had no idea what an organ case should look like. It was a complete waste of money. But I got so much support from the Provost in most matters that I decided this was one of those occasions when I should grit my teeth.

His wife Margaret could also occasionally interfere, in the manner of Mrs Proudie. She got an idea into her head once that the kind of robes choristers wore were out of date and were in any case not very manly. She thought we should try for something completely different. I was totally opposed to this. If choirboys were going to wear any kind of robes, they should wear what they had been wearing since the Middle Ages – cassocks and surplices. Quite out of the blue at this stage, a woman in the congregation offered to buy two completely new sets of choristers' surplices! So the battle was narrowed down to what the boys wore round their necks! The Provost's wife thought that Tudor ruffs were not the thing for boys. I think she thought they were 'cissy'. She found it was possible to buy the neck pieces only of polo-necked sweaters. These were of heavy wool, and in her view would be much more the thing, despite the fact they would be unbearably hot in the summer. In the end she decided to ask the boys what they thought. She waltzed into the vestry and showed them her proposed neckware. They all spontaneously said they preferred things as they were. And that was that!

That Harold and Margaret were strong characters was greatly to the good of the Cathedral. She gave much time to the organization of the cathedral bookshop, and he in many ways revolutionized the whole place. It became financially more secure and began to look cared for. A great deal of work was done to improve the appearance of the Cathedral interior, which involved gilding some statues on the reredos and the restoration of the many fine monuments. Again this was not to everyone's liking. One of the choirmen, the Clarenceux King of Arms, complained that the heraldic colours applied to the coats of arms were not authentic. This was an example of the Provost's vigorous approach, which brought great benefits but which sometimes caused him to take shortcuts.

His outstanding work was the development of the Cathedral to the north, with the addition of new buildings designed by Ronald Sims, George Pace's successor. This involved massive fundraising and lengthy negotiations to reclaim the land which had previously been occupied by the monastic buildings of the medieval Augustinian Priory of St Mary Overie. Subsequently this had been filled with large warehouses, the largest of which came up to within feet of the northern boundary of the Cathedral. This was still standing when I arrived. That there is now a pleasant open space leading to the riverbank was largely a result of the Provost's vision – helped by a mighty fire which providentially destroyed a very large warehouse next to the river! It is hard to imagine nowadays how derelict and neglected this whole area leading into Clink Street was around 1980. It had hardly changed since Dickens' day – except it was silent. The docks had closed, the buildings were empty and hustle and bustle were now absent.

There is no doubt that Provost Frankham restored the Cathedral's dignity. He believed in it. As a result of his work, this incomparable place of worship regained its place as a spiritual and cultural centre in South London. It is now a vibrant and busy place, largely as a result of Frankham's vision and his determined hard work to achieve it.

David Edwards (1982–1993)

The new Provost who succeeded Frankham was a distinguished cleric of a completely different personality. Just as it could have been said of Frankham that he was the right person at the right time, this could be said too of David Edwards. His predecessor was a businessman and very much an entrepreneur. Edwards was scholarly, rather shy and somewhat eccentric in a delightful way. A graduate of Oxford, he was at first a Fellow of All Souls. Subsequently he was Dean of King's College Cambridge, Canon of Westminster and Vicar of St Margaret's church. He was then until 1982 Dean of Norwich. It was unusual for a Dean of an ancient cathedral to become a Provost. But as he said in his installation address, he had been told that 'Deans had more dignity, but Provosts had more power'. A scholar and a good preacher, he brought a new dimension to the Cathedral. The administrative matters were now largely overseen by the Vice-Provost, Peter Penwarden, an able man who was now liberated from playing second fiddle to the Provost. The combination of Edwards and Penwarden worked well. This is not to say that the Provost abdicated from all management decisions. He made two simple decisions that helped me early on: he insisted that the choir should have half-term breaks; and he fixed Evensong earlier, at 3 p.m. on Sundays, which meant that the choristers were free to go home at 4 o'clock, having been at the Cathedral since 9.30 a.m. This, and some free time at half-term, took the pressure off the boys and their parents. The Canons were not pleased with 3 o'clock Evensong. They complained in true Trollopian fashion that it did not give them enough time for their lunch!

Edwards was a prolific author and reader, and never happier than in his study. Yet in the public life of the Cathedral, he brought an insistence on the importance of the daily services which he attended with regularity. The 'Opus Dei' was important to him. This resulted in the Cathedral clergy becoming a much more bonded group, centring on regular attendance at Cathedral services throughout the week.

Early in his time at Southwark, the Provost married Sybyl Falcon, whom he had known at Norwich. She had worked for many years in South Africa, based at the church in Kimberley. She was now able to give sympathetic support to her husband, as a real anchor. I got to know both David and Sybyl well. They were hospitable neighbours, and I have fond memories of Christmas dinners in the Provost's lodgings and of getting to know David's children.

David was a considerable character. He was in his element reading and writing. He was not quite so much so in practical matters. When a new Bishop of Southwark – Roy Williamson – was appointed, it was agreed that the Chapter should have him with other guests to dinner. The Provost said he would take care of the arrangements. A day before the dinner, it was found that he had done nothing about getting a caterer! A lady who worked at the Cathedral and did very good home catering was persuaded to take it on. When it came to the time for the dinner, no guests appeared. A taxi was sent round to the Provost's lodgings, where all the guests were waiting on the pavement outside the front door wondering what had happened. Well, the wrong venue had been put on the invitation!

David Edwards' eleven years as Provost were very successful. Practical affairs might not have been his forte, but intellectually he brought lustre to the Cathedral. His sermons were worth listening to, and he was also charming and well disposed, which did much to foster the right kind of atmosphere. That he had his eccentric foibles rather added to his success rather than detracted from it.

THE CATHEDRAL CLERGY

I have already spoken above of the five Succentors with whom I worked closely. Technically they were minor Canons and not on the Chapter – though at Southwark the distinction between the Canons and the minor Canons was not so hard-edged as in many of the older cathedrals.

There were additionally two residentiary Canons who worked with the Provost – the Vice-Provost and the Precentor. I will speak of them now.

Peter Penwarden, the Vice-Provost, has already been mentioned. He increasingly filled an important role as an administrator, at which he was very able. When I arrived in 1976 he was 55 and had been in post for around five years. He had spent the whole of his ministry in the diocese of Southwark as incumbent successively of three Anglo-Catholic parishes. He was an Oxford graduate of some note. He had a fastidiousness of character which verged on the pedantic. He dressed smartly and everything he did was in good taste. He could sometimes be prickly and difficult to live with; but at heart he was a likable person who was very committed to all he did in the Cathedral. He certainly could be a bit 'old maidish', a trait which occasioned the nickname 'Petronella' amongst the choirmen. Like many celibate clergy of his generation, I think he was deeply lonely, though he lived with his very pleasant sister, and still with his widowed mother when I first arrived in Southwark. He had independence of spirit and often used to explore alone on his summer holidays the length and breadth of the United States, travelling by Greyhound bus. He was a compassionate priest, and in cases of real need he would drop everything to sort out whatever the problem was. Peter really came into his own during David Edwards' time as Provost, when he found he was suddenly needed to keep the Cathedral running efficiently.

Gerald Parrott arrived as Precentor quite early in my time, and left just before I did when he became Vicar of Wimbledon. He had come to us from St John's, Catford, a parish in the diocese of Southwark. He and his wife Angela, a nurse, were a breath of fresh air; with their attractive children, they brought a touch of normality to the place. Gerry (as he was known) was quite a character. He had read English at St Catharine's College, Cambridge, and always joked that he only got in because he was a good oarsman. There was probably some truth in this. I doubt whether I would have got into Oxford if I had had to gain normal A Level results. When Oxbridge colleges did a good deal of the selection themselves, they often spotted potential or special gifts which would enrich the college. They had an eye for the talented late developers. At the examination for the Pembroke organ scholarship, my Latin translation paper was greatly inferior to that of most of the other candidates. My musical abilities were sufficient to render that of lesser importance.

Gerry Parrott as a colleague became very important to me. Precentors are expected to make a major musical contribution, which Gerry did with great success. He had a love of music and a good singing voice. He coped very well with the responses at Evensong. Rather like BBC announcers of 50 years ago, his singing and spoken voice had a rather 'upmarket' quality, but that did not affect the effectiveness of his contribution, which was always marked by perfect intonation. Gerry was also great fun. He and I always sang a duet at the choristers' Shrove Tuesday pancake party – quite often 'The Gendarmes Duet' by Offenbach; or Gilbert and Sullivan's 'The Policeman's Song' from *The Pirates of Penzance*, or 'What a tale of cock and bull' from *The Yeomen of the Guard*, in which Gerry always made the most of the possibility for *double entendre*. The boys themselves performed turns at the pancake party, as did the parents. One of them, Sandy Borthwick, sometimes gave us a bagpipe solo, which in the confined space of

St Saviour's Primary School was deafeningly loud and reminded me of Dr Johnson's observation that the best place to hear the bagpipes was 'on the highroad to England'! Gerry knew all the choristers by name and where they lived – and also those who could be difficult to handle. That he knew them so well was a very useful sounding board for me when I needed to deal with a chorister who was being a bit difficult; his response was always caring and human.

Precentors are usually expected to plan and arrange the liturgy – very important at great occasions, which were frequent at Southwark. The Vice-Provost had fulfilled this role when there had been a Precentor who was not much interested in the niceties of liturgy. Indeed he considered he was something of an authority. That he was unwilling to let go of these matters when Gerry arrived caused a great deal of frustration for the new Precentor, who quite simply found an important part of his job taken away. Gradually things improved between the Vice-Provost and the Precentor – but there was always an element of tension. Clergy one imagines should be above empire building and petty wrangling; but my long experience of clergy has made me realize that they often have all the foibles and weaknesses common to the human race. Having said this, by the standards of many cathedrals, Southwark was a 'happy ship' where people related well and everyone tried to do what was right for the life of the institution.

CANONS WHO WERE PART-TIME AT THE CATHEDRAL

There were quite a number of clergy who worked principally for the diocese, for instance the Director of Ordinands. We most frequently saw them when they were 'in residence'. This meant they had a month in the year when they had the right to preach at the main Sunday morning service themselves, or invite others to do so. In fact some of the best preaching at Southwark was by the diocesan Canons. Sitting near the pulpit, I came to look forward to what some of them had to say. In my view, the finest orator was the Canon Missioner Ivor Smith-Cameron. He was a remarkably fluent speaker and had much of interest to say. As someone who has endured many sermons in my life from the confines of the organ loft, if I remember what was said – perhaps only something of what was said – it is an indication that the sermon was worth listening to.

Ivor was radical, and did not endear himself greatly to the powers that be. He was Anglo-Indian, brought up in Madras. Before coming to Southwark as Diocesan Missioner, he had a distinguished time as a chaplain at London University. He was a great supporter of the Cathedral choir and felt it was the only activity which was attractive to young people. This view did not go down well when publicly expressed! He and I got on; I have a very nice ikon he gave me at my farewell service, the only time he had been known to attend Sunday Evensong. He only came on four or five Sundays in the year when in residence, when he preached each week at the morning Eucharist. I got a great deal from him.

One month he did a course of addresses on the relationship between Christianity and the other major world religions. For instance, he compared Christian and Buddhist monasticism, the relationship between Eastern mysticism and Christian mysticism, and the common roots of Islam, Judaism and Christianity. It was ahead of its time, before inter-faith movements developed to the extent seen widely in the great cities of the United Kingdom today. The one actual phrase I remember from these addresses was that the ecumenism of the future would be between the great religions, rather than between the various branches of Christianity. Many years later, when Christians still squabble endlessly about points of doctrine, as they have for 2,000 years, such a statement seems to belong to a far distant future. But I believe it is an ideal towards which all people of faith should continually strive – and Ivor 40 years ago was right to say so.

Other occasional preachers who remain in the memory were the two Dereks. Derek Tasker was diocesan Director of Ordinands when I arrived. He was a much loved character who spoke with the common touch. Many of his sermons were in the form of parables – colourful and amusing stories with a pertinent message – such as the one in which the landlord of the Dog and Gun, who never set foot in the church, turned out to be more Christian in his lifestyle than many of the regulars at Sunday worship. They reminded me very much of the delightful passages in William Law's 'Call to a holy and devout life', where 18th-century grandees thought they could buy divine favour by their largesse, such as the landowner who provided his parish church with a fine new ring of bells; just as in the 19th century the building of churches by brewers was often referred to as 'fire insurance'.

The other Derek was Derek Watson, whom I came to know well. He had been Chaplain to Mervyn Stockwood and took over from Derek Tasker as Director of Ordinands. He too was a thoughtful and interesting preacher with a fine feeling for words. He eventually became Dean of Salisbury (where I saw him occasionally when I had a home in the Close there), and as a retirement job Preacher to Lincoln's Inn. His sermons were beautifully crafted, relevant and always accessible.

I give these examples of the quality of thought we were routinely exposed to at Southwark. There were many others who would merit a place in this list. But the point which needs making was that Southwark was a place where it was possible to meet with lively thinking aimed at tackling the difficult questions and trying to make the faith relevant to a rapidly changing modern world. I felt that the church in Southwark had an unusually strong sense of purpose which I found personally helpful and which I had failed to find elsewhere. It had a spring in its step.

FOUR ASSISTANT ORGANISTS

Garrett O'Brien

When I arrived at Southwark at the end of April 1976, Garrett had been running the music for nine months during the interregnum.

He had done this well and given new heart to the choir after the sad event of E. H. Warrell's sudden departure. He had a gift for choral training and ran a good adult mixed choir, the Exultate Singers, which rehearsed in the Cathedral vestry on Monday evenings. At services, he quite often directed the choir whilst Warrell played the organ. This was logical as Garrett was not a highly proficient organist. It was difficult for him when I arrived – he was a few years older than me – and particularly as the rebuilding of the choir demanded that I should rehearse and conduct the choir. I felt he had to become the accompanist. I could see he didn't like this as it did not play to his strengths.

However, we worked together for two years and generally the relationship was reasonably cordial. But I never really got close to him; I felt he wanted to support me, but remain at a distance. He was an interesting character and rather charmingly flamboyant in his manner. He wore informal clothes – sometimes a poncho – and routinely took snuff. He had been a mature student at the Royal School of Church Music in the College of St Nicolas at Addington Palace, where he had taken on board many good ideas about how choirs should be run. I think he thought things had rather 'gone to the dogs' after my arrival. That was because I had to recruit new boys to prevent the treble line folding – and the large influx of new potential choristers was in fact quite difficult to handle in the early stages. This required a degree of experiment and informality. It did come right, but I felt Garrett thought I should have taken a tougher line.

I realized I needed to have an assistant who was a good organist, but I let the matter rest for a couple of years. In the end, the matter was taken out of my hands. The Provost from time to time remarked that it was time I had my own assistant. But I was totally taken by surprise when, one day, he called me in and said that he had seen Garrett that afternoon and had arranged for him to leave. I never knew how these negotiations were conducted; but I imagine the Provost had organized a golden goodbye!

John Scott (1956–2015)

I first met John at the Three Choirs Festival at Hereford in 1976. We had a good deal in common as émigrés from the West Riding of Yorkshire. He had been a chorister at Wakefield Cathedral and eventually became Organ Scholar at St John's College, Cambridge in 1974. I met him again soon after when I gave an organ recital at St John's in 1977; I spent a good deal of time with him and David Hill during the weekend I stayed in the college. He was a prodigious organist who obviously had a great future. In 1978 he was coming to the end of his time at Cambridge and would need a suitable move. It occurred to me that an organist of his ability might want to come to London. So I got on the train to Cambridge and went to ask him whether he might consider Southwark. The Cathedral had a spacious flat available, which I thought might have some attraction as a London base. During our very friendly talk, he said that Barry Rose had just asked him whether he might go to St Paul's, where they needed a third organist. To put it briefly, Barry Rose and I cobbled together a deal in which St Paul's provided a stipend and Southwark provided accommodation. This specified that John should play at Southwark on Sundays and on Tuesdays and Fridays at Evensong. This worked well for seven and a half years, and John became a first-rate support and a very good friend. It was something of a culture shock for him coming to Southwark – but not that much as the cathedral at Wakefield where he had sung as a boy and learned to play the organ was a parish church cathedral, but a fine building with a good tradition of music and liturgy. I suppose the West Riding lads were not that different from those from South London.

His playing soon came to be much admired, especially at the Sunday morning Eucharist. He took great trouble to prepare suitable voluntaries – and indeed all aspects of the service. It was the custom to have a short improvisation after the reading of the gospel. In order to strike the right mood, John habitually read the passage of scripture appointed and prepared ideas which would illuminate the meaning of the text. He was so good at this that Canon Ivor Smith-Cameron once remarked in his sermon how effectively John conveyed the spirit of the words: 'more so than many sermons'. In whatever John did, he was a perfectionist and drove himself very hard.

He entered into the social life of the choir and was good with the boy choristers, if at times rather fierce. One boy complained to his father, who came into the vestry after the service in his boiler suit (he was a dustbin man) to remonstrate. I feared that this could turn into more than a strongly worded complaint. John probably thought that I let the boys off too lightly when they did not give of their best. Years later, in an article he wrote on my retirement from the RSCM, he confessed that he had come to realize that in a situation where we were attempting to re-establish a tradition, it was important to take the long view. I thought in terms of years, he in days!

We became very good friends and remained so during his time as organist of St Paul's and St Thomas's, Fifth Avenue, New York. He was very supportive and at times when I was wavering unduly about something he would say, 'Come on, Harry, get a grip!' He and his wife Jane drove me to Heathrow when I made my maiden flight at the age of 45. I was going to the US to run a choral course. I was so terrified by the whole idea that they said they only got me inside the airport with difficulty. Subsequently I had to fly quite often when I was at the RSCM, but I have never liked travel by air. Not long before John's untimely death in 2015, he and another good friend, Ben Hutto in Washington, tried hard to get me to visit the States by sea on the QM2. I was seriously considering this, but it was not to be. Both of these friends sadly died within six weeks of one another in the summer of 2015.

There were many occasions when John's fine playing came to the fore: the annual broadcast of choral Evensong from Southwark, TV appearances, or on the choir tours in 1980 and 1981 to Yorkshire and East Anglia, and particularly so during our tour to America in 1984. We little thought when we gave a concert in New York at St Thomas's that he would be moving there 20 years later as Organist and Director of Music.

This concert was memorable for me in a special way: we met Dorothy Hammerstein, widow of Oscar, who with her husband had been a great supporter of Southwark Cathedral. They loved the Shakespeare connection and often visited when in London. Indeed, in 1962, she endowed the head choristerships in memory of her husband, to be known as the Hammerstein Chanters. She made two impressive silver badges for them, and I'm glad that on this trip to New York I took the medals. I was able to introduce the two Hammerstein Chanters, Jeremy Bowyer and Marc Milmo, in their full regalia! Dorothy was quite overcome. At this concert, Jeremy had just given a magnificent performance of the taxing treble solo in S. S. Wesley's anthem 'The Wilderness', which greatly added to this encounter.

John and I covered the services well. Occasionally one or the other of us had to be away. So I was able to appoint a Deputy Organist, Nicholas Luff, who could come in when we needed a spare pair of hands. In 1989 he became my assistant at All Saints, Margaret Street. He had an important role at Southwark, and never more so than on New Year's Day 1985, when the Croydon Archdeaconry, which had always been part of the Diocese of Canterbury because of the Archbishops' historic links with the town, was transferred to the Diocese of Southwark. This was a sensible move, though there were people who thought the transfer to Southwark rather *infra dig*. Archbishop Robert Runcie decided that there should be a grand service in Southwark Cathedral on the day the transfer took place, 1 January. Unfortunately the organists were not consulted, and neither of us was available. I was to be in South Africa conducting the annual RSCM Summer School in Grahamstown, and John in Jerusalem playing the organ for the Bach Choir! It was at this stage that Nicholas Luff came magnificently to the rescue. There were times when I had to be away examining, giving recitals etc. when I could rest assured that John and Nick would hold the fort. They were both popular with the choirmen and the boys.

It was during this time I had to have a prolonged absence around my father's death on 8 May 1983. Prompted by John, the choir sent a veritable florist's shop to our home in Guiseley. My father had been ill with leukaemia for two years, and sadly went into Bradford Royal Infirmary for the last time on my mother's 70th birthday, 22 April. He had been wonderfully looked after by the infirmary for two years, when he was able to live an almost normal life. But this time it was not possible to fight infection. He caught pneumonia and died a fortnight later.

Fortunately I was at home when he was admitted to hospital, as I had travelled north for my mother's birthday. I had to go back to work at Southwark, but within a week my mother telephoned to say my father was dying. I had to go immediately. I found him conscious and peaceful, not saying much, but not looking desperately ill. He sat up in bed, smoothing and folding the sheets, which prompted my mother to recall my Grandma Bramma's view that when this happened it would not be long: a curious old wives' tale. And indeed he gradually became unconscious and died three days later. We spent much of the time with him. On the last day we were at the hospital all afternoon. My mother thought we should go home briefly for tea, as a neighbour was driving us back to the hospital. When we returned, the sister was waiting for us and told us he had just passed away. We went in and found him lying peacefully. He had obviously just faded away. He still had a wonderful head of white wavy hair and a good complexion. We were very annoyed that we had gone home. However we stayed in the room for some time, then went home to prepare for the funeral at St Paul's Church, Shipley.

On the day of the funeral, my mother insisted the undertakers should bring Dad home. His coffin stayed in the dining room for a few hours. Then the relatives arrived and were put in the sitting room. Before we set off for the church, everyone gathered in the dining room; my father's cousin, Jim Wall, said a few prayers. Leaving from home was very much a tradition in the old days, one my mother thought was important. She was of such a practical turn of mind that she arranged for us to see the solicitor the day after the funeral, before I went back to London, so we could sort out the business affairs. I had a wonderful caring welcome from John Scott and the choir on my return to Southwark.

John eventually left Southwark in 1985. That was when Barry Rose moved from St Paul's and Christopher Dearnley, the organist there, needed a full-time assistant, largely to run the choir. This was a good move for John, from which he was promoted five years later to the top post after Christopher Dearnley retired in 1990. Perhaps John was the only cathedral musician to progress from third to second organist and then to the top job. This was well deserved: he was obviously cut out to be Organist of St Paul's Cathedral.

Looking back, I realize how fortunate Southwark was to have the services of John for over seven years. He contributed enormously to the quality of the music and to the life of the Cathedral. He was a highly intelligent man who was very 'aware'. He came to understand me as a person and became a good friend. We might have had some moments of tension – but very few. During our time together the standard of music improved very considerably, and he played no small part in this transformation.

Andrew Lumsden
Andrew, like John Scott, came to us straight from St John's College, Cambridge. He soon fitted in at Southwark and quickly got to know the boys and the men of the choir. He had progressed through a traditional route as chorister at New College, Oxford and Music Scholar at Winchester College – where incidentally he was taught by my old Worcester pupil, Christopher Tolley. The cathedral music world in those days was close-knit and it was inevitable that there should be many cross-relationships. Over the past 25 years with the welcome growth of girls' choirs in the cathedrals, the number of children singing there has doubled – a very good thing. As a result the number of organists and choirmasters has also increased considerably to cope with the expanding activity in cathedral music departments. As a result, appointments have been made from a much larger pool of applicants. Again this is all to the good.

In terms of personality, Andrew was very different from his predecessor. He had a friendly approach, which suited the ambience of Southwark. He was a formidable organist, and seemed to have little difficulty in reading and assimilating new music very quickly. He was a first-rate accompanist and soloist. Not having to juggle the requirements of Southwark and St Paul's, he had more time to devote to his duties with us. He coped very well with a sabbatical I had in the summer of 1986. In the following year, when we were planning a choir tour to Canada and America, he of his own accord took a great deal of the burden of administration off my shoulders – producing an attractive illustrated programme and organizing various duties to be shared out among the lay clerks, down to who should be responsible for the two laundry baskets of music and robes which had to be got on and off the aircraft. On our previous tour of America in 1984 I had done virtually everything myself. This time, thanks to Andrew, I was able to concentrate on the music.

We went to America initially at the request of Harvard University to sing at the final service of their 350th anniversary celebrations. John Harvard, son of a Southwark butcher, had sailed out with the Pilgrim Fathers in 1620. The university which bears his name was remarkably founded just seven years later. The visit to Harvard was an outstanding occasion. At the service we sang the Te Deum in C by Benjamin Britten, and Andrew managed to tame the savage Fisk organ which was an extreme example of neo-classical post-war organ building. It was so caustic in tone that professor Peter Gomes, the Chaplain of the Memorial Church, described it as having fangs! I gather it has now been replaced. But whatever instruments we encountered, Andrew coped without flapping and made nasty or difficult organs sound more pleasant than one might have felt possible.

Andrew stayed with us for three years before moving in September 1988 to be Sub-Organist at Westminster Abbey. It was right for him to move to a position of greater responsibility – which in turn led to his appointment as Organist of Lichfield Cathedral in 1992 and then to Winchester in 2002.

Stephen Layton

Stephen came to Southwark in September 1988 on leaving King's College, Cambridge, where he was Organ Scholar. He had evidently had a gilded educational pathway, after being a chorister at Winchester Cathedral and Music Scholar at Eton. But this was not the whole story. He came from Derby, where his father was organist of a Pentecostal church. He had something of the North country about him, which was an asset when dealing with Southwark where the choristers were volunteers, very unlike boys in choir school situations. In many ways it was easier to run a choir like Southwark, where the boys had themselves made the decision to join. I have experienced difficult situations where pushy parents had locked their son into a choir school system they did not like. Such instances are rare, but when they occur, things can become very difficult. Early on at the King's School, Worcester, I came to accept that a boy with a golden voice does not always wish to sing in a choir – or even much care for music.

Stephen and I only worked together for five months before I left to be Director of the RSCM. They were, however, significant months. Indeed, Stephen's first service was the dedication of the new Cathedral buildings, which were later that autumn visited by the Queen and the Duke of Edinburgh to attend a short service. They actually sat in the same chairs used by Edward VII and Queen Alexandra when they attended the service of inauguration for the new diocese of Southwark in 1905. Alas, soon after, they were stolen and have not been seen since.

Having made a decision in 1987 when I was appointed to the RSCM that I would keep up the pressure at Southwark, I decided to round off my time there with a choir visit to Worcester at the beginning of January 1989. This was arranged by the Worcester Cathedral Voluntary Choir. And as it happened, the weather was perfect – mild with continuous sunshine which enabled us to climb the Worcester Beacon at Malvern. We sang the Sunday services in Worcester Cathedral and Evensong in Tewkesbury Abbey the day before; their Vicar's son, Benjamin Moxon, had been a chorister at Southwark when they lived in London.

Although my time with Stephen was short, we laid the foundations of enduring friendship. Southwark gave him time to develop the professional group of singers, Polyphony, which he had formed whilst still at Cambridge, and to conduct the Holst Singers. He stayed for nine years at Southwark before moving to the Temple Church. He then became Director of Music at Trinity College, Cambridge in 2006, succeeding Richard Marlow, a former chorister of Southwark Cathedral.

The three assistants I appointed at Southwark were musicians of very considerable calibre. They all of them contributed greatly to the Cathedral music; and all of them, though very different in personality, identified with the Cathedral. For all of them it was a considerable learning curve to come to the Cathedral of the South Bank from the Elysian fields of Cambridge. It gave them a sense of reality, which all of them readily acknowledged.

THE SOUTHWARK ORGAN AND T. C. LEWIS

Planning the restoration of the organ by T. C. Lewis (1897) was a source of great satisfaction to me. This instrument is now widely regarded by many as the finest organ in a major London church. It is a thoroughbred. Others, like St Paul's Cathedral's, are mongrels, having suffered so many subsequent changes that the intentions of the original builder have been almost completely lost and consequently the sound much diminished. At Southwark the specification of the organ is unaltered and all the pipework is by Lewis. True, in 1953 Henry Willis III tinkered with the sound; but the physical changes made to the pipework were slight and found to be reversible.

When I arrived, Thomas Christopher Lewis had been dead for 61 years. He was very much a 19th-century person (1833–1915), who initially trained as an architect. He came to organ building in the

1860s. Like many, he had been inspired by the remarkable instrument by Schulze from Paulinzelle in Saxony which was exhibited at the 1851 Exhibition in the Crystal Palace. It was much admired, but particularly by two people: E. J. Hopkins of the Temple Church and Jeremiah Rogers, organist of Doncaster parish church. It was the latter who, after the church at Doncaster was rebuilt by Sir George Gilbert Scott because of a disastrous fire, recommended Schulze as the builder of the new organ. It was a large instrument, suitable for the magnificent church. It was soon recognized as a masterpiece. In fact the tonal quality of the instrument became a significant influence in the UK. Foremost amongst the admirers was T. C. Lewis, who visited Edmund Schulze on several occasions at Doncaster, where the organ was completed in 1862. He wrote that on occasions he conversed with him for a whole day and sometimes well into the evening. Lewis admired the fullness of tone achieved on low wind pressures and set out to work along Schulzean principles, copying his pipe scales and his tonal ideals – very much Romantic organ voicing in the classical tradition. I have always felt that Schulze coming from Saxony, where the organ builder Gottfried Silbermann flourished several generations earlier, is not without significance. Silbermann was admired by Bach, and to this day many instruments by him survive in the Freiburg area as he left them. I feel that Schulze inherited something of this tradition. Lewis also was considerably influenced by the French organ builder, Aristide Cavaillé-Coll, especially in his reed stops and harmonic flutes.

I became acquainted with the organs of T. C. Lewis at about the age of 15, when I played his fine instrument in Ilkley parish church. Though it was a moderate sized 3 manual, I remember being very impressed by its forthright tonal qualities. I was aware of Lewis's reputation, but at this time he was very much under a cloud – considered old-fashioned by the more recent organ builders and organists. This was still the case to some extent when I arrived at Southwark. Aware of the greatness of Lewis organs, I was determined to set matters right. The initial impetus for this came from an unexpected source. When the Father Willis organ in St George's Hall, Windsor Castle needed restoration, Christopher Robinson invited Ralph Downes (designer of the Royal Festival Hall organ) to give advice. During the course of conversation, Christopher mentioned that I had moved to Southwark and was keen on Lewis. On hearing this, Downes rang me up immediately and said he was going to offer his services gratis to help draw up plans for the Cathedral organ – something he had never done before. I was unaware that Downes was almost fanatical in his admiration of Lewis and had incorporated many Lewis features into the Festival Hall organ. He had been Assistant Organist at Southwark to Dr E. T. Cook for two years (1923–1925) when the organ was only 26 years old. He confided in me that he had been much helped financially as an impecunious student by one of the Canons, so would like to give something back.

This was the unexpected beginning of a rather tempestuous relationship over a period of ten years, when we worked together to plan the restoration. Ralph was intellectually rigorous and saw things in black and white; compromise was anathema to him. There was one occasion when I said to him that despite the tonal alterations made by Willis, the sound of the organ was still impressive. To him this was unacceptable. The Lewis voicing had been seriously mutilated and as far as he was concerned, that was that! Our relationship was much chilled by this rather off-the-cuff sentiment I had made casually to him, which he took as deadly serious. In time there was a thaw. When he actually heard the restored organ in 1991, he was thrilled by it. He wrote to tell me that Harrisons, the organ builders, had done a fine job and 'short of getting back T. C. Lewis himself, it could not have been done better'.

In the 1980s the cathedral recognized that work needed to be done, as the action of the organ was failing. In 1983, it was necessary to re-leather the actions of the pedal reeds as many notes were off. Willis had used synthetic rubberized leather called 'Tosh', rather aptly named. By this time it was shot through with holes, causing notes to become silent. This was a necessary running repair. Major work was done to the actions in 1986, as the first stage of the eventual restoration. The console was restored and the transmission – that is the connection between the keys and the soundboards – was renewed. This kept the organ going until a full restoration took place in 1990–1991 by Harrison and Harrison. The mechanisms were renewed and all the pipework set back on its original speech. This was a marathon task. The wind pressures had been raised by Willis as part of what he thought of as necessary modernization. As a result, the whole organ had to be revoiced. Fortunately, Willis had raised the pressures by a simple method – knocking up the feet so that the pipe could still speak on the higher weight of wind. The organ builder, John Budgeon, confirmed to me that this had happened as he had heard the 'knocking up' going on when he made a visit to the Cathedral in 1953. When the holes of the feet of the pipes were opened up, it was remarkable how the pipes with some relief came back onto speech at the original pressure.

The rebirth of the organ was more than we could have hoped for. The responsibility rests with Peter Hopps, the Head Voicer of Harrison and Harrison, assisted by Mark Venning, managing director, who together revived the characteristic Lewis sound. Ralph Downes had written two reports and visited several Lewis organs. I went with him to St John's, Upper Norwood; he even went to look at the instrument in St Marie's Cathedral, Sheffield, which he found had suffered serious alterations. I went with Peter and Mark to see the Schulze organ at Doncaster from which Lewis derived so much inspiration. We also went to Lancashire to see the large Lewis at the Albion Chapel, Ashton-under-Lyne, and in the same town the remarkable survival at Christ Church, a fine small 3-manual, entirely unaltered. This gave us very good ideas. One of the things Downes suggested was that the pipework should be lengthened. Like so many organs of the late 19th century, they spoke about a quarter of a tone sharp (A=), making it difficult to use them with orchestras at the now standardized lower pitch (A=440). A decision in 1953 was made to lower the pitch, but it was achieved by shortcut measures – by altering the tuning slides and by putting shades on the tops of the longer pedal pipes. This method seriously affected the tone quality. For instance on the Pedal Bombarde, the tuning slides were so far up the reeds that they were only speaking on about a third of their full length. Thus it was decided to lengthen most of the pipes (about 4,000 of them) by a fraction of an inch to a foot by soldering extensions on to the pipes using metal of the alloy used by Lewis (spotted metal) of 55 parts tin to 50 parts lead. This was a time-consuming and tedious operation, but it turned out to be well worth it. The pipes, both reeds and flues, had much more freedom of speech and the column of air inside the pipes and resonators vibrated at the required length compatible with the pitch of the note being sounded.

It will be apparent, even to those unacquainted with the details of organ building, that it is only possible to achieve the original sound by getting the design, the scaling, the wind pressure and the material right. It was a question of reversing the ideas behind the alterations made by Willis III in 1953. He probably thought he was doing the modern and correct thing. But he seemed unable to refrain from imposing his ideas on notable work of the past, and in fact he was responsible for altering much of the work of his visionary grandfather, Father Henry Willis, in the first half of the 20th century – even at St Paul's Cathedral. Since the work done at Southwark in 1990–1991, the critics have been unusually unanimous in praise of what has been achieved. The organ is now much visited and sought after for recitals, and the Royal College of Organists holds its presentation recitals at Southwark. Wider recognition has evoked admiration from foreign organists and builders, and the organ builder Ralph Richards of the American firm of Richards, Fowkes & Co. admitted to me recently, when I heard his new organ at St George's, Hanover Square, London, that Lewis was a great influence on his thinking. Lewis was esteemed in his life-time. But it is heartening to think that his reputation has now been firmly re-established internationally as an innovative organ builder of genius.

I feel I ought to try to explain what it is that makes a Lewis organ so special in its tonal character. It is of course difficult to write about organ sound. But a good starting point would be Lewis's pamphlet published in 1897, 'A protest against the modern development of unmusical tone'. Here he emphasizes the need for fine materials and the necessity of having 50% tin in the alloy of metal pipes. He also stresses the need for unlimited time for the construction of an organ, reminding me of William Morris's dictum that craftsmen can't hurry. To Lewis, the diapason tone must be voiced on low pressure in order to achieve the maximum harmonic development of the sound; and the pipes must be designed with modest scaling to get the best result. Lewis remarked, 'the pipe being voiced to sound its note firmly, yet leaving it securely within that verge beyond which it might fly off to sound its octave'.

I was reminded forcibly of this when I recently played the restored Lewis organ in the village church at Titchmarsh in the wilds of Northamptonshire. The pipework quite buzzed with harmonic overtones, which made me remark to Andrew Scott, Head Voicer of Harrison and Harrison, that the sound was very near the edge, to which he replied 'it certainly was'. Playing it, one felt one was living dangerously! But the way in which sound waves from the pipes reacted with one another, throwing down resultant tones and a halo of overtones, made it possible for a small number of stops to create a brilliance of sound which was both exciting yet very beautiful – very much the hallmark of Lewis organs, where peals of golden tone carry far in the building without a punishing degree of volume and abrasiveness, which as one organ builder remarked are liable 'to take the enamel off one's teeth'!

As with all Victorian builders, those who came later and thought they knew better often seriously compromised the intentions of the original makers. Sufficient Lewis organs survive, large and small, to testify to the genius of their creator. Sometimes it is the smaller organs, languishing uncared for in village churches, which reveal the greatest secrets of the voicer's art. That Southwark's organ has been reclaimed is a matter of great satisfaction to me. It has merited universal praise, sometimes from unexpected quarters. It stands as a living monument to T. C. Lewis's genius, who was very much a man on a mission.

TWO BISHOPS

Mervyn Stockwood (1959–1980)

It is widely held that Stockwood's appointment to the see of Southwark in 1959 was influenced by Harold Macmillan in the days when Prime Ministers were still able to wield considerable power in the appointment of bishops. It is to be doubted whether he would have made it onto the Bench of Bishops in present-day circumstances. He would have been regarded as unsafe and far too left-wing, with a flamboyance of character and, even worse, a strong and volatile personality. At the present time, when the officials behind the scenes at Lambeth Palace prefer to appoint managers rather than pastors, his outlook would have been bleak. Mervyn was a pastor par excellence and most particularly to his clergy. He left management to others. That he should have been appointed by a Conservative Prime Minister speaks volumes about Macmillan, who clearly realized that a man of vision was required – someone who would take radical steps to revitalize the church in South London, always the poor relation of the City and London north of the Thames. But in fact, this was not entirely true as there was much prosperity in the affluent suburbs of south-west London and in what Mervyn described as 'the soft underbelly of the diocese'. There were many delightful country parishes in the beautiful Surrey countryside stretching as far as Gatwick airport; in fact the diocese covered approximately two-thirds of the county of Surrey, to the east.

Mervyn was brought up in Bristol, where he was influenced by the fine music and worship at All Saint's, Clifton, a well-known Anglo-Catholic parish. He also occasionally went with his mother to the Unitarian church to hear the preaching of Dr Beckham, who attracted large congregations of up to a thousand people. From school days at Kelly College, Tavistock he went up to Christ's College, Cambridge in 1932, and then for his theological training to Westcott House. Very early in his ministry, he was appointed curate, then Vicar, of St Matthew's, Moorfields in Bristol, a large working-class parish where he stayed for 18 years, developing a remarkable ministry in an extremely deprived part of east Bristol. In his autobiography, *Chanctonbury Ring*, Mervyn says 'it is difficult to describe the squalor, misery and hopelessness to a generation that is largely ignorant of real want. Housing and overcrowding were deplorable. Within a few yards of the mission building was a family of nineteen and another of sixteen. They slept six in a bed, three at the top and three at the bottom.' These social conditions made an indelible mark on his consciousness and shaped his attitudes throughout his ministry as priest and bishop.

His success in Bristol led to his appointment as Vicar of Great St Mary's, the University church in Cambridge (1955–1959), a post he initially wanted to turn down. Here his approach was legendary.
On arrival, he found the church terribly run down. He first of all repaired the windows, cleaned the church and then set to work on repairing the congregation. He invited distinguished outside speakers both to liturgical services and to special courses of lectures. The politicians came, including Nye Bevan. As Mervyn remarked, 'the top brass came, because no political party in Cambridge would provide an audience, let alone an uncommitted audience of a thousand'. It was estimated that at some times in the year between two and three thousand undergraduates passed through the doors of Great St Mary's. To achieve all this, Stockwood worked with great commitment and imagination. It was a remarkable story.

When the letter came from the Prime Minister inviting him to Southwark in 1959, he was inclined not to accept. Even after an interview with Archbishop Fisher, he still dithered. But eventually, persuaded by friends, he did accept. He was consecrated in Southwark Cathedral on 1 May 1959, the date chosen by the Archbishop, though he had forgotten it was Labour Day!

I have outlined his background up to this point as it makes clear what it was that shaped him – indeed changed him from a member of the University Conservative Association and Tory representative at Christ's College into a convinced socialist. In later years at Southwark he was sometimes called a 'pink socialist' or by others a 'champagne socialist', to which he quipped 'it depends on the vintage'! He was a complex character: he liked mixing with the good and the great, including royalty who were sometimes to be found at his dinner table, and he was certainly something of a *bon viveur*. All this masked a deeply serious side and considerable asceticism. He was strictly disciplined about saying the daily offices and celebrating the Eucharist. Even if he had been out late at a function the night before, he would still meet his Chaplain in the house chapel at 7.30 a.m. for Matins and the daily Eucharist.

He took his responsibility for the welfare of his clergy very seriously, whatever the shade of churchmanship. I remember an evangelical priest from Kennington telling me how, after a breakdown, Mervyn sent him and his wife to the Mediterranean to recuperate for three weeks. He seemed to have considerable slush funds available for such purposes. And when a young priest got himself into difficulties and needed to see the Bishop urgently, even if he had been out on engagements all day, he would see the man at midnight and talk to him for three hours, probably over several glasses of whisky. Even so, Mervyn would be at Matins at 7.30 next morning. He must have had a remarkable physique and an amazing tolerance of alcohol.

Stories of Mervyn abound. In fact many of his former clergy now in their seventies and eighties love swapping Mervyn stories to this day. But though Mervyn was a colourful and sometimes outrageous character, his total dedication to his work, regardless of the toll it took on him, was remarkable. He had his finger right on the pulse of the diocese and was always there when needed. This showed in his attention to detail. When St Mark's, Wimbledon was destroyed one night by fire, the congregation attended the United Reformed Church instead as an alternative home; when they arrived there the following

Sunday, they were greeted in the vestibule by a large display of flowers bearing the message 'With love from your Bishop Mervyn'.

In order to achieve his objectives, he needed to build a new team of bishops, archdeacons and clergy. This he did with considerable flair, sometimes taking risks which usually paid off. He appointed Hugh Montefiore as Bishop of Kingston, who had succeeded him at Great St Mary's and later became a distinguished Bishop of Birmingham. Then he appointed David Sheppard, formally England cricket captain, to be Bishop of Woolwich, who later became Bishop of Liverpool. Another appointment as Bishop of Woolwich was Michael Marshall, Vicar of All Saints, Margaret Street at the age of 39. But his best-known appointment to Woolwich was that of John Robinson, Dean of Clare College, Cambridge, whose book *Honest to God* sent shock waves through the church establishment in daring to question central Christian doctrines. It was widely read and sold a million copies. This brought him notoriety, but was nothing compared with the outcry which followed his support as a witness for the defence for the publication by Penguin Books of *Lady Chatterley's Lover* at the trial at the Old Bailey brought by the Crown in 1960. Eric James, former Canon of Southwark and well-known writer and broadcaster, used to tell the story of the visit of the Bishop to St George's, Camberwell where he was vicar, for a confirmation shortly after the trial. A local character in the congregation caused a stir when she said audibly as the Bishop processed down the aisle, 'Cor – if it ain't Lady Chatterley's Lover himself!' Eventually John Robinson returned to Cambridge academic life, to which he was probably more suited.

These four bishops were all of outstanding ability and great communicators. Mervyn should be given credit for drawing from such widely different backgrounds for his senior appointments. He liked the stimulus of having independent-minded people around him. Though he was himself a liberal Anglo-Catholic, he got on well with evangelical churchmen and appointed many to senior positions in the diocese. I think one of the reasons the 'low church' clergy liked him was because of his amazingly comprehensive knowledge of scripture.

If he was visited by one of them, he would unzip his Authorized Version of the Bible and suggest they start their meeting by sharing some verses from the prophet Habakkuk! Yet old rogue that he was, if a young mincing high church curate arrived, he would reach for his Rosary and suggest they should start by saying the Rosary together. Joking apart, he was extremely fair in the way he treated evangelical clergy, and I think that even today the comparative absence of party politics in Southwark is a result of Mervyn's ability to get on with the evangelicals.

Many of the archdeacons he appointed were from this wing of the church. They fitted in and made a significant contribution – individuals like Michael Whinney, Archdeacon of Southwark, a direct descendant of Charles Dickens; and Peter Coombs, Archdeacon of Wandsworth. They were low church clergy of a type not seen much these days. Thoroughly Anglican, they were light years away from the 'happy clappies' both in liturgical practice and doctrine. They were caring, intelligent people with none of the arrogance or judgementalism to be found in some evangelical churches today.

Mervyn was indeed larger than life. Having been used to the gentler kind of bishops in the Diocese of Worcester, I found when I arrived at Southwark that his presence in the Cathedral was almost terrifying. His personality seemed to fill the place. There was no doubt who was the boss and the centre of attraction. In the sermon at his final service, he actually said that he was the last of the 'prince bishops' – and added tongue in cheek 'you had better take a good look, you will never see another'! He reminded me of a formidable Cardinal Archbishop of Palermo, of whom it was said that the sound of his limousine passing into the courtyard of his residence caused a frisson to run through all the corridors and rooms of the palace.

Mervyn was certainly powerful in church. There was one Sunday afternoon when he was commissioning a new stewardship adviser – a person responsible for teaching the parishes how to organize committed giving. His address started predictably; but suddenly the mood changed and he became violently angry. He said that the rich churches in the south of the diocese should be ashamed of giving less than the poorer parishes in the north. He went on to say that unless things improved, he would suspend licences and amalgamate parishes. He became extremely heated, in a tirade that went on for all of ten minutes. The choirboys talked about it for years after, always enjoying Mervyn's antics. I remember the head chorister turning to me in the choir stalls and saying 'He's a character, isn't he?'

I had dealings with him about the choice of music. In fact every Lent, the Vice-Provost and I were summoned to the *palais* (as it was known) to discuss the music for the Easter services. Mervyn considered himself to be in charge of the Cathedral services, whereas at most cathedrals the Dean and Chapter thought they were. On one occasion, we were discussing the Easter Sunday morning service – at which he did the Easter ceremonies at 11 a.m., lighting the new fire in broad daylight – when we suggested that an essential part of these rites was the Proclamation of the Easter Gloria. We proposed that the choir should sing it to a setting by Mozart. But it was clear that this idea found no favour. We argued with Mervyn a little. Eventually he became exasperated and banged his fist down on his desk and said, 'I will not have the Gloria. I am the Ordinary, and I repeat I will NOT have the Gloria.' That was the end of the discussion. Mervyn hated long services. He once famously said, 'I am neither 'high' nor 'low' church – I'm 'short' church!'

He had some very strange musical tastes. On great occasions he liked to sing the hymn 'At the name of Jesus' to the tune of 'Land of Hope and Glory'. I told him I thought this unwise, as Elgar's tune was all right if sung twice; but to sing it seven times was more than flesh and blood could endure – it was exhausting. He obviously remembered this, for when at his farewell service John Scott accidentally played the Vaughan Williams tune, all hell was let loose. The Bishop's Chaplain came up to me in the first verse and said, 'This is not the tune his Lordship intended.' I stood my ground, for I thought to change the tune in mid-stream would make matters worse, but I apologized to the Bishop after the service. I was so upset that I actually went, unbidden, to see the Bishop at 9 a.m. the next morning at his house in Streatham to apologize again. He greeted me graciously, but could not talk long as he was about to go off to a meeting with the Prince of Wales. I thought that was that: I had gone out of my way to say I was sorry, but I was wrong. The whole affair rumbled on for three months. The palace courtiers tuned the Bishop up, saying 'But of course, Bishop, it was a snub.' In the end the Provost and I went to see the Bishop to discuss the whole matter again. We sat round his desk, each with a large glass – rather a vase – of dry sherry, usual practice at that hour of the day. In the end Mervyn drew matters to a close by saying 'Shall we have a few words of prayer' and then gave us his blessing. The whole saga was totally ridiculous and it did not show Mervyn in a good light. But I genuinely believe that if he had not been 'tuned up', he would have let the matter drop.

As will be clear from this account, life with Mervyn was not easy. But I am impelled to say that, despite my personal difficulties and his flamboyant and despotic behaviour, I believe that he was a very great Bishop of Southwark. Like many outstanding men he was flawed. But unlike most bishops, he had the courage to speak out on major public matters and achieved a national hearing. He was a faithful pastor to his clergy and people. And he was way ahead of the times. He died shortly before the first women were ordained in the Church of England, a development he had championed for many years. He was also a groundbreaker when it came to the compassionate recognition of homosexuality as an undeniable fact of life. Many of his best parish priests were gay; he urged them to use discretion – but he understood and supported them. Mervyn himself, despite his hectic social life, was, I believe a lonely man. He was deeply hurt when six weeks before he died, he was 'outed' by Peter Tatchell. This was unjust for two reasons. Mervyn was a celibate who exercised iron discipline. But he was also a person who did a great deal to promote a better understanding of gay relationships.

I feel that what I have said about Stockwood is maybe rather shallow. I was only around for his last four and a half years. It may be that his glory days were much earlier. It is possible that he became latterly something of a caricature of himself. But he remained a fine speaker, full of wit and humour – though his wit had a tendency to be at other people's expense. And at the end of the day, the affection he inspired was testimony to the regard in which he was held. Yes, he could be impossible; but one felt it was worth putting up with his lapses as the broad sweep of his ministry was marked by kindness and friendship, along with a powerful commitment to social justice. That he was popular with the great and famous was to me a plus. The well-known wanted to enjoy his company.

His friendships were sometimes rather surprising. I remember him leaving a service early from a clergy conference I attended at Butlins in Minehead, Somerset, to fly to London so that he could be in time to speak at Barbara Cartland's 80th birthday lunch. This would have caused outrage in other dioceses, but in Southwark it was accepted almost as normal behaviour – just as it was accepted that the Bishop did not take his meals with the clergy on these occasions, but usually got his chaplain to drive him to restaurants in the surrounding countryside!

Mervyn was certainly out of the ordinary. He was also someone one could not ignore. He thought big and achieved much. He was a tireless worker and knew the parishes and the clergy with an intimacy which I doubt has ever been equalled. Life was never dull; there was always much to amuse. This I believe, along with the long days he worked, was the foundation of his great success as Bishop of Southwark.

Ronald Bowlby (1981–1991)
To have to follow Mervyn Stockwood was no easy matter. But the appointment of Ronnie Bowlby, then Bishop of Newcastle, turned out to be an inspired choice. He was a rather unlikely Old Etonian – a fact which at one time he removed from his biography in *Who's Who*, but later reinstated, in my view rightly. He was a friendly and

thoughtful man; and the fact that his character was the exact opposite of Mervyn's was very much a bonus. Of course there were those around who said it was now all rather dull. But after the virtuoso antics of Stockwood, a touch of dullness was no bad thing. Indeed Ronnie was very much his own man: a diligent and faithful priest who soon earned considerable respect. He was enthroned in the Cathedral at Candlemas on 2 February 1981. The following year Candlemas fell on a Sunday, and we had a special service to mark his first year. This was a musically significant occasion for me, as it marked my debut as a serious composer. I had always written occasional music (*Gebrauchsmusik* as the Germans call it). But when I was asked to write an anthem to cover the lighting of the candles at the beginning of the service, I took the task very seriously. For the anthem 'God is Light' I assembled, after the manner of S. S. Wesley, a series of Biblical texts about light. Eventually this was published in America by the Roger Dean Publishing Company. This was because Sir David Willcocks had been asked to assemble a group of pieces by English Cathedral organists. It is now sung widely and every February at Southwark Cathedral and All Saints, Margaret Street. I became more motivated as a composer, and after my retirement from the RSCM in 1998 I started to produce a steady stream of choral pieces for the choir of All Saints, Margaret Street where I was fortunate in being able to try out my music. I was also increasingly asked to write music for other churches.

Ronnie Bowlby was a rather private man – not for him the wide canvas on which Stockwood operated. But his quietness of manner was deceptive. He had inner strength and considerable perception. In church his manner was devotional and he always had things to say in the pulpit which were worth listening to, expressed in a well modulated voice and not without a touch of quiet humour. It soon became obvious why he was the right man for the job. For some years there had been talk of transferring the parishes of the Croydon Archdeaconry from Canterbury to the diocese of Southwark. Archbishop Runcie was keen on the idea; Bowlby as a former Vicar of Croydon had the knowledge and experience to accomplish this important change, which came into force on 1 January 1985.

Croydon's historic links with Canterbury went back to the Middle Ages. The Archbishop had a palace there. In 1807, with proceeds from the sale of this residence, Addington Manor was bought as the country residence of the Archbishop during the episcopate of Charles Manners-Sutton. This became known as Addington Palace and was home successively to six archbishops. Then the advent of the railways and easier travel I imagine removed the need for a staging post for coach travel from Lambeth to Canterbury. So in 1897 it was sold to a South African diamond merchant, Frederick English. His grandson became Master of St Catharine's College, Cambridge and once visited me when I was Director of the RSCM.

As always with any ecclesiastical change, the transfer of Croydon parishes to Southwark provoked controversy. Some were opposed to breaking historical links; but I suspect the opposition was mainly for the snobbish reason that a new South London diocese was a considerable come-down. But 32 years later, people have got used to the idea. It was rather ridiculous to have an outpost of another diocese completely cut off from the mother see, as it always had been by the substantial ancient diocese of Rochester.

It is inevitable that a record of Bowlby's time at Southwark is much shorter than that of his long-serving predecessor who courted publicity and for whom the oxygen of public life was an essential part of his personality. In no way should brevity be seen as a mark of insignificance. Bowlby was a very good Bishop of Southwark and entirely right as successor to Stockwood. Being quiet, devout and intelligent felt a welcome change from the 'larger than life' qualities of Mervyn, which in any case would be impossible to replicate. But the shadow of his predecessor continued to fall for some time across the landscape. Gradually things settled down and Bowlby should be honoured as an able and kindly man who managed very well what was never going to be an easy transition.

A portrait of my great-great-grandfather,
Samuel Bramma, senior, born in Leeds in 1783.
[chapter 1]

Aged one in 1937.
[chapter 1]

Aged eight in 1944.
[chapter 1]

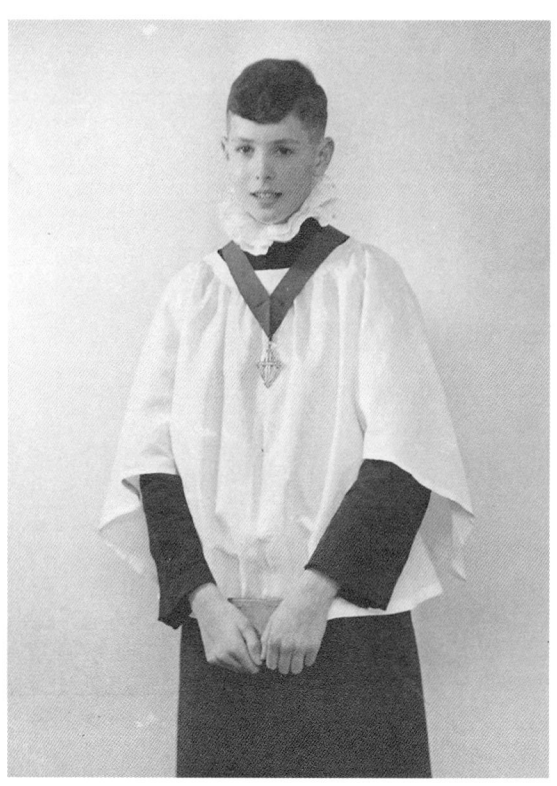

As a choirboy in the choir of St Paul's church, Shipley.
[chapter 1]

My father, Fred Bramma, in the Royal Armoured Corp (Tank Regiment), c.1945.
[chapter 1]

With my paternal grandparents, Ellison and Sarah Bramma.
[chapter 1]

Salt's Mill, Bradford – my grandfather, Ellison Bramma was manager of the weaving department.
[chapter 1]

My organ teacher, Dr Melville Cook seated at the organ of Metropolitan United Church, Toronto where he was organist and choirmaster, 1967–1986.
[chapter 1]

The choir of St Paul's, Shipley, 1945
(I am in the front row, second from right).
[chapter 1]

The organ of St Paul's Shipley, built by
Leeds organbuilder J J Binns (1892).
[chapter 1]

Me (right) with John Jenkins
outside King's College,
Cambridge, May 1961.
[chapter 2]

John Jenkins at Trinity Hall,
Cambridge, May 1961.
[chapter 2]

Me (front row, centre) with Class 3B (1961–62).
Peter Lea is on the back row (third from left).
[chapter 3]

HMS Pinafore production, c. 1962. Left: Me as Ralph Rackstraw.
Below: I am in the front row, second from left.
[chapter 3]

Rehearsing Retford Grammar School choir for Fauré's *Requiem*.
[chapter 3]

The Choir of St Saviour's, Retford. I am in the back row, centre right.
[chapter 3]

Outside the front door of my house in the College Precincts, Worcester c.1974.
[chapter 4]

Me with the Worcester Cathedral Voluntary Choir, Donald Hunt and cathedral clergy c.1975.
[chapter 4]

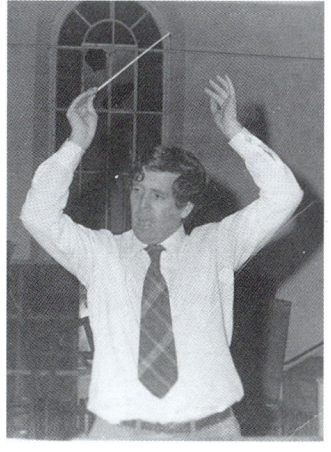

Conducting a rehearsal of the Kidderminster Choral Society. c. 1975.
[chapter 4]

Gloucester Three Choirs 1965. Left to right: Assistant Organist Roger Fisher (Hereford), me (Worcester), and Richard Latham (Gloucester).
[chapter 4]

A 'thank you' from the Kidderminster Choral Society for all the performances I conducted with them, 1972–1979.
[chapter 4]

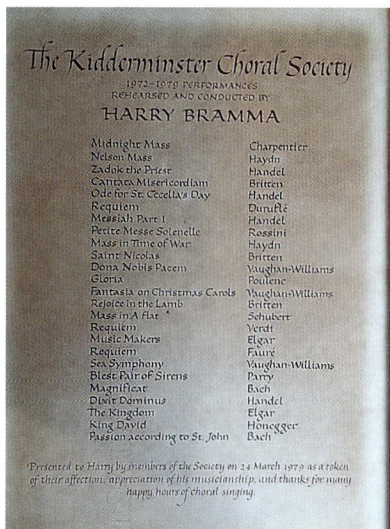

With my mother in the back yard of the College Precincts, Worcester, c. 1964.
[chapter 4]

A portrait photograph taken for the Three Choirs Festival brochure 1966.
[chapter 4]

Me (centre) on an outing with the Purcell family; Canon William Purcell is second on the left.
[chapter 4]

Rehearsing a chamber music ensemble at King's School, Worcester, c.1967. Andrew Millington is seated at the piano.
[chapter 4]

My leaving gift from the Worcester Cathedral Voluntary Choir, with (left to right) Derrick Bollen, Dean Tom Baker, Donald Hunt and Michael Smith, 1976.
[chapter 4]

Mr Edward Heath playing the new organ in College Hall as I and Basil Edmunds (Chairman of the Three Choirs Festival) look on, 1966.
[chapter 4]

Conducting the choristers of Worcester Cathedral Voluntary Choir in its centenary year, 1974.
[chapter 4]

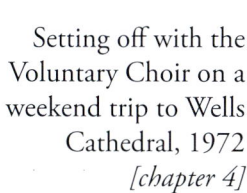

Setting off with the Voluntary Choir on a weekend trip to Wells Cathedral, 1972
[chapter 4]

The College Precincts, Worcester, where I lived whilst Assistant Organist.
[chapter 4]

A Southwark organists' dinner at The Cheshire Cheese, Fleet Street. Left to right: me, Peter Wright, and John Warrell.
[chapter 5]

Portrait photograph taken in front of the organ case at Southwark Cathedral.
[chapter 5]

In conversation with Ralph Downes at a Royal College of Organists Diploma Awards Ceremony.
[chapter 5]

Meeting HM Queen Elizabeth II during her visit for the opening of the new buildings at Southwark Cathedral, 1988.
[chapter 5]

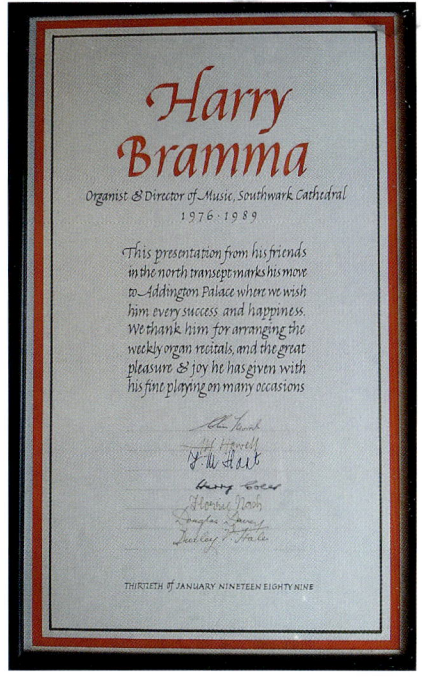

Framed presentation from my 'friends in the north transept' in recognition of my services as Organist and Director of Music 1976–89.
[chapter 5]

The Southwark boys singing at the Festival of Remembrance at the Royal Albert Hall, November 1984
[chapter 5]

With the Southwark boys on a choir outing to Margate.
[chapter 5]

The Southwark Choir singing carols at the Savoy Hotel.
[chapter 5]

Officers of The Royal College of Organists at their Summit, c.1982. Left to right: David Lumsden (former President), Martin Neary (President), me (Treasurer), Stephen Cleobury (Secretary) and Barry Lyndon (Clerk).
[chapter 5]

Bishop Mervyn Stockwood in his study; '… certainly the most colourful and controversial diocesan bishop of his generation' (*The Independent*).
[chapter 5]

At the Wurlitzer organ, formerly of the Trocadero, Elephant and Castle and subsequently rehoused in the University of the South Bank.
Left to right: Nigel Ogden, me, Simon Gledhill, and Phil Kelsall.
[chapter 5]

As Director of the RSCM sitting at the piano in the Great Hall at Addington Palace.
[chapter 6]

At the launch of the RSCM Appeal in The Guildhall, with the Duchess of Kent and Sir John Margetson (centre), 1992.
[chapter 6]

One of several overseas visits as Director of the RSCM. This was my first trip to New Zealand in 1991, here at the Maori Girls' College, Hukarere with the Reverend Brororii Turei, Chaplain.
[chapter 6]

In Canada, with Geoffrey Steele at the Steinmeyer organ in the Cathedral of Christ the King, Hamilton, Ontario, 16th November 1991.
[chapter 6]

Photograph taken during an event at the Athenaeum Club, c. 1989. Left to right: Denzil Freeth (Churchwarden), Nigel Worn (a former Succentor at Southwark Cathedral), and Prebendary Alan Moses (Vicar of All Saints, Margaret Street).
[chapter 7]

Conducting the choir of All Saints, Margaret Street,
c. 1992.
[chapter 7]

With my mother at her home in Guiseley.
[chapter 8]

At my flat in The Close at Salisbury.
[chapter 8]

SOUTHWARK DIOCESAN ORGAN ADVISER

Arriving in 1976, I immediately became a member of the Diocesan Advisory Committee (DAC) for the care of churches. This was an important role, as the Church of England is exempt from planning regulations because it has its own legal system. The DAC has to advise the Chancellor of the Diocese in all cases where changes are being made in parish churches, from comparatively minor matters such as the renewal of a boiler or the colour of new carpeting to large-scale projects like plans for a new organ or the complete reordering of a historic listed building.

I became suddenly aware of this legal system in the summer of 1976, when the church of St Mary's, Balham had gone ahead with ambitious plans to enlarge and alter the existing organ without getting a faculty. This became a *cause célèbre*. The plans did not really add up either artistically or financially. The decent 19th-century 2-manual organ by Hill had been broken up; the intention was to use only the pipework, together with that of a redundant Nicholson organ from Holy Trinity, Malvern Link. A small builder from Wiltshire had undertaken to do this work, which included a new console to operate a sizable 3-manual organ for the sum of £9,000. It was clear that this scheme, which included new pipework, could not be achieved for this sum, even forty years ago. It was a tricky situation, as work was already in progress. As there was no permission for this work, the diocese decided it must reluctantly hold a consistory court, at which the Chancellor came down heavily on the parish. The vicar was accused of not giving sufficient leadership. In fact he was likened to the Duke of Plaza Toro in Gilbert and Sullivan's *The Gondoliers*, who led his troops from behind! It was however all too late: the damage had been done. An order was made appointing a professional adviser, Herbert Norman, to supervise the work. But this too was difficult to effect. The parish still suffers from the lack of a pipe organ, as the new organ failed many years ago. It has now, as a dangerous structure, had to be removed. For me, involvement in this case was certainly a baptism of fire. Fortunately it was a rare instance, the like of which did not recur.

I enjoyed getting to know the fine organs of the diocese, some from the late 18th century and many from the 19th. Fine new churches by Scott, Bodley, Pearson and Temple Moore, to name but a few, often housed very fine instruments by leading builders such as Harrison and Harrison, Father Willis, T. C. Lewis, Hunter, Walker and Norman and Beard. There are many early organs of very considerable scale and magnificence, for instance the Byfield at St Mary's, Rotherhithe (1763) and two notable Bishop instruments at St James', Bermondsey (1829) and St Giles, Camberwell (1844), both large organs remaining basically unaltered since they were put into these new churches. In my time, there has been the usual round of restorations and an impressive list of new organs installed in the past 40 years, about 20 in number. There are British organs by Mander, Collins, Lammermuir, Drake and Tickell, as well as many by builders from the Continent, including two by the Danish firm Frobenius at All Saints, Kingston and St John's, Shirley, a Marcussen at St Mary's, Putney and a Swiss instrument by St Martin at St Peter's, Petersham. This indicates that the pipe organ is still very much appreciated in the Diocese of Southwark. As I have been an organ adviser for 41 years, and my colleague Dr William McVicker for 24, it has been possible for us to build up a good working relationship with the parishes. I have found it rare for a parish with a fine instrument, whatever the level of churchmanship, not to value their musical heritage. In Southwark, it is certainly a myth that evangelical churches fail to value their organs; several such churches have recently carried out extensive renovations to their instruments. The Southwark DAC is known to have a pastoral heart – not ruled exclusively by matters of conservation and authenticity. Sometimes the committee has to take a firm line. One evangelical church with a fine Hill organ which had received lottery money for its restoration had to be told they could not remove the instrument to make space for a children's playroom! In recent years it has become easier for churches to face the high cost of organ restoration because of generous grants from the Heritage Lottery Fund.

Generally speaking, the parish formulates their plans and the diocese comments. It is usually helpful for the DAC to be involved at an early stage. I have often had friendly discussions about proposed schemes, and occasionally some of my suggestions have been adopted – for instance for 16-foot tone on the Great organ, or for an extra stop here and there. I am rather proud of my influence at St John's, Upper Norwood where the outstanding Lewis organ was restored 20 years ago. The Pedal Trombone rank was not by Lewis; it had been added later by Willis, and to my ears made completely the wrong sound. The parish accepted my view and replaced the Trombone with a brand new stop in the style of Lewis. They were able to fund this by selling part of a graveyard at Elmer's End.

From what I have written, I think I have demonstrated the range of work undertaken by the organ advisers. At the age of 80 I have become an emeritus member of the committee. I am able to keep in touch, and occasionally attend meetings. I am grateful for this as the DAC has been an important part of my life since I came to live in South London. It is good to be consulted – and sometimes to provide useful information.

THE ROYAL COLLEGE OF ORGANISTS

During my time at Southwark, I became actively associated with the Royal College of Organists. It was a considerable surprise to receive a letter from Sir John Dykes Bower in the autumn of 1979 to say that the Council had co-opted me to fill the place vacated by George Guest on his becoming President. It had never crossed my mind that this might happen. I began to attend meetings of the Council, an august gathering of many of the leading church musicians in the country – most of the well-known names were there. Soon I was asked to examine for the written papers of the Associate examination – something

I did for many years. I was impressed by the method which had evolved over time for achieving a fair result, principally by rotating the questions so that each candidate was marked by all the examiners. It was quite fun. Sitting down one side of a table, the three examiners were able to ask for advice in difficult borderline cases. But it was hard work. Marking the papers of 50 candidates took a whole day. It was a good way of getting to know the fellow Council members. A very experienced examiner, Dr William Cole, I found was most helpful to a novice examiner. He was charmingly old-fashioned – the only person who ever introduced me to his wife by saying 'May I introduce you to Mrs Cole'. It was all rather Jane Austen! He had earlier been Secretary of the Associated Board; he was also an expert on stained glass. I met him in Southwark in his role as a liveryman of the Glaziers' Company, whose Hall was next to the Cathedral.

In those days the College inhabited Dickensian premises in Kensington Gore. There were Turkish carpets, long-case clocks and solid Victorian furniture. It was leased from the Trustees of the 1851 Exhibition in 1903 for 100 years at a peppercorn rent of £1 per annum. I had never really understood the prevalence of peppercorn rents in the past. The rent of course was a way of safeguarding ownership – and it was useful to the Trustees to find a body who could use and maintain it. But I don't think it was as simple as that. I believe peppercorn rents denoted a public-spirited intention to assist worthwhile institutions to function. At the present time (2025) when the making of money seems to be top of the agenda, the idea of a peppercorn rent seems hardly credible. But they still just existed in 1953.

When the RSCM lost its base in the Close at Canterbury – the Dean and Chapter wanted to use the building – Archbishop Fisher had some influence in persuading Croydon Town Council to lease Addington Palace (the former country seat of the Archbishops of Canterbury) to the RSCM at a rent of £1,000 per annum for 50 years. This was equivalent to the rent the RSCM received per annum from letting the Lodge Cottage at the entrance to the estate! It was an extremely favourable lease. The RSCM had to maintain the interior, while the Council took responsibility for the external fabric, which in my time turned out to be quite a heavy responsibility. It was all very old-fashioned. The RSCM took over a palatial Georgian mansion wonderfully transformed inside by the well-known architect Norman Shaw. This kind of thing just would not happen today.

The Royal College of Organists were fortunate to have a headquarters in central London, where there could be musical events, examinations and members could visit the library. It was all presided over by the Clerk, Barry Lyndon, a remarkable man who was totally dedicated to the College. He had been recruited in the 1960s by Sir William McKie, who had known him years before when Barry was one of his choristers at Magdalen College, Oxford. He had great charm and personal characteristics which are rather hard to describe; he was a real one-off. He worked very hard, assisted by his wife Hessie. He was Spartan in his habits, and very much a traditionalist. He didn't like change over much, which affected all manner of things. For instance the College owned its own china, made specially in Stoke on Trent, which was used for social occasions such as after the Diploma award ceremonies. Lyndon went to endless trouble to find a firm who could supply slab cake, richly fruited, which had always been served on these occasions since the time of Sir John Stainer.

He was insistent that the Council members should process in the right order into the Organ Hall on great occasions. I could never understand why I had to walk second in the procession, after the President and before the Secretary. He claimed I was the most senior person after the President. Yes, a great deal of trouble was taken to maintain tradition. But the College was a friendly place, and many members look back with real affection on their meetings and their friendship with Barry Lyndon. He had a charming sense of humour and was in his element and very relaxed at the staff Christmas lunch held in the Council Chamber, at which he produced varieties of wine, port and liqueurs.

Those who visited him and his wife at their home in Welwyn

Garden City found the same charming hospitality. I visited there once after he had retired from the College, when he was Clerk of the Ouseley Trust. He was arranging a visit of the Chairman, Harry Pitt, to my house at Addington where I was to give him lunch with a view to getting financial help for the RSCM. One of the main reasons for my visit to the Lyndons' home was to discuss the menu for this lunch! Barry insisted that soup must be served – the chairman always had soup. We went through all the details of the visit. Looking back, this all seems rather amusing; but it was a good example of Barry's attention to detail.

Another such example was when he and I practised giving the ARCO Ear Tests on the piano at the College. I had to get the volume and speed right – and I must make sure that all four playings of the test should be exactly the same. There was a story that on one occasion a candidate put up his hand and said 'Which of the two versions are we to write down?'

Barry was an amazing man who commanded great affection through his lack of pretence, his humour, his quirkiness and his thoroughness. When the College moved in 1990, after surrendering the lease, he retired slightly before the actual move took place as he felt he could not face it. On no account should he be taken as a comic character. He had amusing traits, but he was rock solid, the most conscientious and thorough servant of the College it is possible to imagine. Perhaps he was sad at the idea of leaving Kensington Gore and was glad to go.

Barry was succeeded in 1990 by Vincent Waterhouse, a colleague of mine at the RSCM, and it was he who was responsible for the physical move to new premises at St Andrew's, Holborn Viaduct. As Honorary Treasurer, I had been much involved with the Archdeacon of London, George Cassidy, in finding a new HQ. Virtually all prospective venues, principally city churches, were out of the question because of the expense involved. Finally we found suitable accommodation at St Andrew's. We had two fair-sized rooms at gallery level on either side of the tower for the Clerk and the administrative staff, and the use of a large basement across the yard which, though very cramped, housed the library. And of course we were able to use the church and its very good Mander organ for events and the practical exams of the ARCO. It was a distinguished well-lit space, one of Wren's finer churches. We stayed there for most of the 1990s before the planned but ill-fated move to an old railway building in Birmingham. This scheme eventually collapsed for financial reasons after a great deal of work had been done, including plans for a new Swiss organ by Kuhn. I suspect the College lost quite a lot of money in the process. As someone who negotiated the surrender value of the lease at Kensington for a sum of £600,000 which had subsequently grown to a million pounds, I felt unhappy about the whole venture. But all this happened after my time at the College. I resigned as Treasurer in 1996 as my work at the RSCM meant too many demands on my time.

Since then I have not had any official connection with the College. In the computer age, much of the administrative work is done online. The official address of the College is now a front room somewhere in South London. I can see why this makes some sense, but the lack of a place where members can visit is a distinct loss. However, Southwark Cathedral has become the venue for the Diploma presentations and organ recitals. This works well. And it is most encouraging to see how the outreach work, particularly amongst young organists, has developed amazingly. The College is far more active in musical education and in promoting and encouraging people to take the organ seriously, which is all to the good.

In my nostalgia for past days, I think much of the College's character and personal touch have disappeared. But it is good to see it flourishing under its new dispensation. And as someone deeply involved in its past, I am grateful.

BALANCING THE BOOKS

As my remuneration at Southwark was not enough to live on, I had to find ways of increasing my income. My appointment as an examiner for the Associated Board of the Royal Schools of Music in 1979 was a great help in augmenting my finances. I made it clear that overseas work was out of the question; but I did do three weeks in the year (Monday to Saturday) and quite a number of extra days usually in the London area. Philip Cranmer, a former chorister of Margaret Street, was the Secretary. It was by today's standards a cottage industry, but it was a friendly and genteel environment that I found agreeable.

The examining was taxing at first – having to make important decisions quickly about candidates and always with an eye on the clock. Gradually I got used to it and came to enjoy my periods away, often in new places. Cities like Leicester and Glasgow I found fascinating, with superb architecture and open spaces. Sometimes I was able to meet old friends or perhaps visit a notable organ I had always wanted to hear. I continued this work throughout my time at Southwark, but a year after moving to the RSCM in the summer of 1990, I decided I had to resign.

My predecessor, Lionel Dakers, continued as an examiner throughout his RSCM career, sometimes doing overseas tours which he hooked on to visits to the RSCM branches abroad. I was in a different position as I had become Organist and Director of Music at All Saints, Margaret Street, which principally involved Sunday work. It was important to me that I should have my own choir and organ. So I felt that I had to free up time to do this. It turned out to be the right decision. In fact, many of the RSCM members valued the fact that I was a hands-on Director, though it meant that I often worked a seven-day week. Had I been married with a family, it would have been impossible.

My other main outside work was giving organ recitals. I did in fact receive a considerable number of invitations, including a return visit to Worcester and playing at King's and St John's Cambridge, York Minster, and on the great Harrison organ at Durham Cathedral. I enjoyed all this. But I never set out to specialize as a solo organist. I realized that I had a feel for the instrument and a decent technical standard, but I knew I didn't have the top-class ability necessary for a solo career. Rather than looking back with regret at my level of musical skills, I think I have a fairly good idea of where I stood: whereas I was not top of the league in some areas, I certainly was in others. Delusions of grandeur can be common amongst musicians, but I think I avoided these. Only a few have the ability to make a career as an outstanding soloist. That may be a good thing, as Dame Gillian Weir, pre-eminent as she was, once remarked that the career of solo organist does not exist!

Throughout my Southwark days there were enjoyable interludes: like taking the boys to sing at a Livery Company Service, or being asked to contribute to the opening recital on the Wurlitzer from the Trocadero, Elephant and Castle, with Phil Kelsall from Blackpool's Tower Ballroom, Nigel Ogden of *The Organist Entertains* and the well-known theatre organist, Simon Gledhill. When the instrument was moved to the University of the South Bank, I was expected to show that it could play 'straight' music; but to be honest, I was quite out of my depth on that occasion. By contrast, we took the choristers to Margate fun fair for the day on the train with the obligatory fish and chip tea. Although my main work at Southwark was in the Cathedral, I was grateful for the many interesting diversions the job afforded – and for the additional income which many of these activities generated.

A SOUTHWARK POSTSCRIPT

The changes in my life and attitudes occasioned by my move from Worcester to Southwark were monumental. People thought that I was so rooted in provincial life that I would not survive the transfer to London. In this they were entirely wrong. I found the transition enormously liberating. Life at Southwark Cathedral had a touch of reality.

This was particularly so in the matter of human sexuality. Worcester in 1976 was closeted and hypocritical; Southwark had moved on. The congregation at the Cathedral was very well balanced: married people with families, ethnic diversity, a wide age range and many single young to middle-aged people, many of whom turned out to be gay. The Cathedral, always in the catholic tradition of the Church of England, had moved on to be welcoming, inclusive and non-judgmental. This agenda has gradually developed in most of the parishes of the diocese, where the majority of churches are catholic in tradition. The Oxford Movement had an enormous influence as South London developed outwards along the routes of the railways. The majority of churches are welcoming and inclusive; and many of the evangelical parishes have a gentler, more nuanced approach to theology. Indeed, there are a few churches of this tradition with gay parish priests.

At the same time as the church was becoming a place of healthy change in the life of South London, the area south of the Thames was still old-fashioned and Dickensian. The built environment around the Cathedral had hardly changed at all since the mid 19th century, and many characters around looked as if they had stepped right out of the pages of a Dickens novel. The locations too – for instance the Marshalsea Prison (*Little Dorrit*), London Bridge (*Oliver Twist*) and the Thames itself (in the dramatic opening chapters of *Our Mutual Friend*) were as in the novels. Dickens himself used to enjoy attending bell ringing practice at the Cathedral – then known as St Saviour's Church. The Southwark tower has an honoured place in the history of change ringing and houses the oldest ring of 12 bells in England (1735). Sometimes on Tuesdays, the Ancient Society of College Youths practised. This was a nuisance, as I held a choir rehearsal at the same time. When I complained to the Captain of the Tower, suggesting they might change their evening, he replied that this was impossible as they had been practising at Southwark on Tuesdays since the 17th century!

The Head Verger when I arrived was Philip Chancellor, an impressive figure with a well-cut beard. He was of somewhat ample proportions, had a great wit and an uninhibited style of conversation with those who became his friends. He was very musical, going to lots of concerts, and very well read. He had not had the easiest of starts in life, but his native intelligence made up for his lack of early education. He was in fact a highly cultured and sophisticated man – but also someone who had not a trace of pretence. He had great perception, which went with a wicked sense of humour. In private he could certainly cut people down to size. His impressive appearance meant that he was much in demand as a mace bearer at livery dinners in the City, particularly at the Musicians Company where he acted as Beadle. Later he moved to a succession of verging jobs, ending up working for the Duchy of Lancaster as Verger at the Savoy Chapel. I have kept in touch with him over the years, and from time to time we meet for a pint at the White Hart in Whitechapel Road before going round the corner for a curry in Brick Lane. I look forward to an evening in his company – there is never a shortage of humour and much gossip.

The congregation at Southwark certainly attracted characters – Georgina lived somewhere down in Bermondsey; we never knew her surname. She came to Mass at the cathedral every day, and wherever she went she brought a shopping bag on wheels which she parked at the end of the pew. She didn't fraternize much with the congregation, but she and her bag where very much part of the scene – so much so that one of the Canons, Peter Delaney, once referred to her as 'Our Lady of the Bag'. The name stuck, and for ever after that was how she was known.

Another regular who came to the Cathedral every day was Jim Webb. He was slightly physically handicapped, and when working at Remploy he came after finishing work. No one knew exactly how he arrived or had any idea of his provenance; but not long after I arrived, he retired and came every day in the morning and stayed for the rest of the day. He sat for hours on the stone bench along the north aisle of the nave; he came to all choral services, where he joined in in a high falsetto voice. He rather fancied himself as a counter-tenor! He helped with simple tasks – folding service sheets for instance and repairing dozens of dilapidated choir anthems and services. I used to buy him large rolls of sellotape. He then went off to his Peabody flat in Marshalsea Road with anthems to be repaired. The Cathedral was a real lifeline. He came to the choir lunch every Sunday, where he fitted in with the boys and men. He was quiet of manner and did not socialize much. Shortly after I left in 1989, he fell ill and died. The Cathedral paid for a dignified funeral, which was attended by a good-sized congregation, as was only right.

Then there was the North Transept Brigade. At the Monday lunchtime organ recital about a dozen men and one woman came and sat at the front of the north transept. They said the organ sounded best there, and they were probably right. They rather remarkably started grouping themselves as an informal club soon after I became organist in 1976. They were quite elderly even then, and had a very old-fashioned air. They were presided over by Dudley Hale from Goodmayes in Essex, who was rather grand in manner and held court in an authoritative style. The oldest was Leslie Pattison from Catford, who each week arrived with a carpet bag of old organ recital programmes dating back as far as the Karg-Elert Organ Festival at St Edwards, Lombard Street, where this famous German organist gave a series of recitals in 1930. I was once asked to lunch by Leslie and his sister at their house in Sangley Road, Catford, where I was given the best ham sandwiches I ever tasted – excellent white bread, liberally buttered and filled with delicious home-baked ham.

To mention all the members of the North Transept Brigade would take too long, but I must mention three others. The one lady in the group was Flo Nash, who also came on Sundays. She used sometimes to bring me bags of fruit and vegetables she had bought in Lewisham Market. She was quite formidable – she did not mince her words. Harry Coles was a former chorister and had the dubious distinction of singing treble in the 1937 Coronation at the age of eighteen. Dr E. T. Cook, the much-revered organist (1909–1953), used to keep boys until well after their voices broke by getting them to sing falsetto. One boy went up to Dr Cook to tell him he would not be at the practice on Saturday morning as he was getting married! And finally I must mention Alf Howell, who had been happily married to an Austrian lady. When I knew him he lived alone, a widower, in a house at Colliers Wood, opposite Christ Church where he was the organist. I visited him there once for a very nice lunch. He had been a professional draughtsman and artist and did wonderful calligraphy. When I left the Cathedral, he produced an illuminated address which all signed and was touchingly inscribed 'from his friends in the North Transept'.

There were so many more wonderful characters. One was Syd Edginton, a retired docker from Bermondsey, who attended the Cathedral till he was 90. He too helped in moving chairs and other tasks. He had a dry sense of humour. He was smart and articulate and always good to spend time with. Then I must mention the two women who cleaned the cathedral. They lived somewhere near the Elephant and Castle, and were a wonderful cockney duo. The leader was Kate who had a strong personality; the other, Anne, was quieter and enjoyed being the foil to Kate's humour. One day when they were 'up the Retro' – that means when they were cleaning the Retro-Choir, the wonderful 13th-century chapel behind the High Altar, a veritable forest of pillars – they were summoned to the main door in the nave. Assistance was needed as a 'flasher' had arrived and was showing his considerable *attributi* to the passing public. Kate took one look at him and shouted, 'You be off with you, we're not interested in what you've got!' She had five sons and a husband, so she added, 'I've got six of those at home.' At which the man, shaken by this harangue from an unexpected quarter, fled full tilt!

Life at Southwark was never dull, and my experience widened considerably. At Worcester, even in 1976, there were few people of colour, but at Southwark it was very different. I admitted many talented Afro-Caribbean boys into the choir. And many of the parish churches in inner-city areas would have been hard-pressed without all the people of colour who often formed a major part of the congregation.

The rural counties of the West Midlands were solid Conservative, though our MP for Worcester, Peter Walker, was very much a Tory 'wet'. In Southwark I came to see politics very differently. There was still considerable poverty and deprivation, with many of my choristers coming from homes which were far from affluent. I therefore ceased to vote Tory; in fact the last time I did so was in 1974, when Edward Heath was replaced by Harold Wilson with a slim Labour majority. For the next 20 years I voted Liberal Democrat. Simon Hughes was famously elected at a bye-election (for Bermondsey/Old Southwark) in 1983 when the Labour vote was split between Peter Tatchell, the official constituency candidate, and an independent Labour candidate put up by the outgoing Labour MP, Bob Mellish, who was appalled by the choice of Tatchell, a gay hard-left activist. In the event Hughes became popular, and over the years greatly increased his majority. I was glad to support him in my Southwark days. Alas he lost his seat in the General Election of 2015 and did not regain it in 2017.

Looking back, my 12 years in Southwark completely changed my attitudes. They also enabled me to develop as a musician and as a person. I was swept into a much more varied society from right across the social spectrum, and became equally at home when dealing with the dustman father of a chorister or the Archbishop of Canterbury or a Cabinet minister.

CHAPTER SIX

The Royal School of Church Music

THE CHALLENGE

During my time at Southwark, I became increasingly aware of the need to move on at some stage. The work there required a great deal of youthful energy, particularly in the recruiting of boys for the choir, then motivating and training them. During my forties, I was short-listed for three major posts: at York Minster, Durham Cathedral and Westminster Abbey. But having failed to secure a significant new appointment by the age of 50, the need to move became more urgent as I was uncertain of my ability, as I grew older, to maintain the momentum at Southwark for a further 15 years.

Then in 1987, the post of Director of the Royal School of Church Music (RSCM) was advertised – very early as Lionel Dakers did not intend to retire until February 1989 when he would be 65. I was most uncertain about whether this appointment would be right for me. I did not really want to lose my choir and organ. I hesitated, but having been leaned on by Lionel Dakers, I eventually applied on the final day set for applications! In the event, I was appointed from a shortlist of four. I then had 15 months to prepare for the change, but decided for the sake of Southwark that it had to be business as usual in 1988. I tried in fact to forget the RSCM for most of the year before I took up the appointment.

But I could not entirely ignore the formidable challenges which lay ahead. One which stood out was the relationship between the RSCM and churches within the Evangelical Tradition – particularly in the Church of England. Lionel Dakers had been aware of the pressures building up but did nothing, saying this was a problem for his successor! One challenge I had not envisaged was the necessity of moving from the RSCM's headquarters at Addington Palace, Croydon before the lease ran out in 2003. This was never mentioned at my interview – quite unbelievably, as I learned later that the Director and Council had realized for some time that this problem would have to be tackled. There were many other issues: the place of girls and women in church music and finance were two which called for immediate attention.

The place of evangelical church music had been much mentioned at the interview. Sir John Margetson, the incoming Chairman, had recently retired as Ambassador to The Hague and felt strongly that the RSCM should widen its scope. Though I had a traditional cathedral background, my work in the Southwark Diocese had made me aware of how musical styles were changing in churches. I was convinced that church music should communicate in a variety of styles, and the RSCM had to encourage quality music across a broad spectrum of traditions. The 'low church' tradition of robed choirs and choral Matins was very much on the way out. This change happened at Holy Trinity, Brompton in my early years as Director. But changes had already taken place in many places, and especially at All Souls, Langham Place which acted as something of a role model. The whole question of styles of music in church was one which would occupy me throughout my term at the RSCM.

In order to set the scene for my arrival at Addington Palace in February 1989, it is important to look at the background – particularly the work and the problems faced by my predecessors. Lionel Dakers, my immediate predecessor, took over from Gerald Knight as Director at the beginning of 1974. He had been Organist of Exeter Cathedral for sixteen years, and before that Organist of Ripon Cathedral and Assistant Organist of St George's Chapel, Windsor. There was no doubt that he was the right man for the job in 1974. Though deeply conservative by temperament, he had a flair for administration and good entrepreneurial skills. He too took over at a challenging time when the College of St Nicolas was becoming difficult to sustain. It was Sir Sydney Nicholson's idea that the School of English Church Music, as it then was, should have at its core the College where students could study both the theoretical and practical aspects of church music. This worked well at Chislehurst – the first home of the school – where there was a good group of boys and sufficient adult volunteers to form an efficient choir, able to maintain a round of services and available for the students to discover and improve their skills as choir trainers. In fact, from the early days, students were attracted from all over the English-speaking world, especially from Australia and New Zealand. At the outbreak of war in 1939, the College of St Nicolas was mothballed, but was revived soon after the war at a new home, Roper House in Canterbury. There were many students in the College in the late 1940s who went on to become distinguished church musicians – Dr Arthur Wills and Michael Fleming to name but two. But eventually in the early 1950s, when the Dean and Chapter of Canterbury wished to take back the premises occupied by the RSCM, a new home had to be found.

By this time Sydney Nicholson had died in 1947. It fell to his eventual successor, Dr Gerald Knight (Organist of Canterbury until 1953 and a protégé of Nicholson), to oversee the transfer of the College of St Nicolas to Addington Palace, Croydon. This move had been assisted and encourage by Archbishop Fisher. A 50-year lease was negotiated where the RSCM paid the owners, Croydon Borough Council, £1,000 in rent and undertook to maintain the interior of the palace, whilst Croydon Council were responsible for the external fabric. This was an amazingly good deal. I suppose in those post-war years it was hard to find an obvious use for the palace.

But the move to Croydon did entail a good deal of hard work and considerable expense. The driving force behind all this was Leslie Green, appointed in 1928 by Nicholson as the first Secretary. He believed passionately in the rightness of the move to Addington and worked hard to make it succeed – something for which he was in the past given far too little credit. He was eventually asked to leave the RSCM in 1966 after 38 years' service. He had done a good stint; but it was no secret that he and Gerald Knight did not get on. This was an instance of a rather unacceptable tendency which has dogged the RSCM throughout its history – too much in the way of politics and knee-jerk reaction.

In the early years at Addington, the College of St Nicolas continued to flourish. A good choir of local boys was formed and students from around the world continued to come to study. Some students combined study at Addington with tuition at the London music colleges. It was an excellent set-up in that it gave students real hands-on experience as organists and choirmasters. They also had the benefit of tuition from resident and visiting staff. These included a number of highly distinguished musicians, including Professor Derek Holman, who later moved to Toronto; Dr Roy Massey, subsequently Organist of the cathedrals of Birmingham and Hereford; Canon Cyril Taylor, a musical priest who will always be remembered for his inspiring tune 'Abbots Leigh'; and Michael Fleming and Martin How, who worked for much of their working life at Addington, becoming well-known throughout Britain and beyond. These last two gave so much inspirational musical leadership to generations of students in the College.

MY PREDECESSOR

When Lionel Dakers took over as Director in January 1974, the College was in crisis. There was insufficient money, and by this time the flow of good students was drying up. New universities and music colleges were springing up and the better students tended to go to these new institutions.

It fell to Lionel Dakers, therefore, to close the College. For this he had to endure severe criticism, not least from his predecessor, Gerald Knight, who continued to live at Addington Palace, working from 1974 to 1979 as Overseas Commissioner with responsibility for looking after the membership abroad. Of course the College of St Nicolas was a very good idea, but it was ultimately unsustainable. Dakers must be given considerable credit for setting up a new type of venture in musical education. He realized the potential of the residential facilities at Addington and set about organizing day courses and short-term residential courses which proved immensely popular. The membership liked the idea of spending a few days in the gracious surroundings of the palace and having the opportunity for some structured training in choral techniques or organ playing, or exploring the resources and repertoire available to the church musician. There were many distinguished lecturers who took part in this new arrangement, including Sir David Willcocks who himself had been a student at the College of St Nicolas just before the war before going up to Cambridge.

Lionel had a gift for *bonhomie* and provided just the right welcoming atmosphere for visitors to the palace. They felt they were spending a few days in a country house – and Lionel certainly liked to be thought of as the squire! In all this, the contribution made by Dakers' wife, Elisabeth, was outstanding. She acted as housekeeper, working long hours to keep the show on the road. She could be quite brusque – certainly a force to be reckoned with – but she inspired great affection. And of course when Dakers went on his frequent long journeys, she had to hold the fort. The personal factor she brought to life at Addington cannot be overestimated.

But it was not only at Addington Palace that Lionel Dakers brought new life. He revolutionized the Publications Department, both in terms of expansion and usefulness. He was also good at attracting money. So he was able to increase the staff and increase the number of those working in the field. The three Commissioners who worked around the UK, operating closely with the area RSCM committees, were a crucial factor in the increasingly successful RSCM of Dakers' early years in office. He was conservative, and was as 'political' as anyone I have met. He liked wielding power and influence, and this was an aspect of his personality that annoyed many people – particularly the Australian branch. Breaking away to form an independent body was very much on the cards in the late 1980s.

Dakers was, in my view, the man of the hour when he took over at the RSCM. He achieved much in making the organization relevant to church musicians in 1974. But his less agreeable traits and views did make for considerable difficulties when I succeeded him as Director early in 1989.

ARRIVAL AT ADDINGTON

I moved into Addington Palace in February 1989 and started work officially on 1 March. The change for me was very considerable. Previously I had worked in communities surrounding schools and cathedrals, where my duties were well defined locally. Having to operate on an international stage was something quite new. At first I missed the choristers of Southwark Cathedral and the regular music-making with a group who related to me. But I was quite used to administration, and aided by an extremely able PA, Marian Hughes, I threw myself into the daily work of managing the many different aspects of the RSCM. Marian had been in post for several years and had acquired a great deal of useful information about people and the business. I was not responsible for the day-to-day running of the RSCM. This was supervised by the Secretary and chief administrative officer, Vincent Waterhouse, who worked with an accountant and bursar and a sizable office staff. He had to oversee the financial side – and for this he had considerable flair, though when I arrived there were warning signs that all was not well with the balance sheet.

Waterhouse, a fellow Yorkshireman, was my principal colleague. He had been Secretary since 1968 so had worked closely with Gerald

ARRIVAL AT ADDINGTON

Knight and more so with Lionel Dakers. When I arrived he was 62 and had become rather set in his ways. He could at times be difficult. There was no doubt in my mind that he did not entirely welcome my appointment. I sensed that he thought I would upset the apple cart as I moved the RSCM away from its comfort zone. He had worked at the palace for 21 years and liked things as they were. But I would not wish to give the impression our relationship was disastrous. This was not the case. He took a great deal of trouble to prepare for my arrival and made sure that Nicholson House, the Director's home, was redecorated and in good order. And of course we both came from Yorkshire! But I felt he tried to play down his Yorkshire roots, whereas I was completely at ease with mine. He had managed to remove all traces of a Yorkshire accent – except when he was sometimes talking with me. As it turned out, we only worked together for just over a year. In the summer of 1990, he took the opportunity of retiring at the age of 63 and moved for several years to be clerk and administrative officer of the Royal College of Organists. His first task on arrival was to move the College from its grand premises in Kensington Gore to smaller accommodation at St Andrew's, Holborn. As I was by this time Honorary Treasurer of the College, we found ourselves working together again in a new environment. Here our working relationship was entirely harmonious and I was glad of the opportunity to get to know him better in circumstances where I was not the radical interloper.

When I officially started work at the RSCM, it was marked by a service in the Chapel of St Nicolas at the Palace – a Eucharist celebrated by the Bishop of Southwark. The liturgical arrangements were organized by Peter Penwarden, Vice-Provost of Southwark Cathedral, and other clergy. They arrived with a great portmanteau of vestments, and as they unpacked items of the Cathedral's cloth of gold, I became somewhat alarmed. I remarked that I did not want too much fuss – to which Penwarden said, 'Don't worry, we're not doing it for you!' The service was attended by a great gathering of former friends and colleagues, including Christopher Robinson and

Bernard Rose. Afterwards there was a finger buffet in the Great Hall. It was a good launch for my time at Addington.

The RSCM Secretary, Vincent Waterhouse, was initially not supportive of the launch service and said 'Who is going to pay for it?' – to which I replied that if the RSCM could not afford it, I would pay for it myself. The morning after, he was gracious enough to say how he thought it was a great success – and that it did the RSCM nothing but good.

My arrival at Addington was made easy for me by my PA, Marian Hughes. We immediately hit it off and very soon became an efficient duo. I think she welcomed a more relaxed approach and a greater degree of realism. She had got on well with Lionel Dakers, but he was rather grand and had clear ideas of how things should be done. She was my first experience of a personal, confidential secretary. At Worcester and Southwark I was my own secretary and wrote hundreds of letters by hand. I had never mastered the typewriter and was computer-illiterate. It was my salvation that Marian was such a good shorthand secretary. Emails were still at some distance, though at the time of my arrival the financial departments were fully computerized. I never learned the mysteries of the computer, though by the time I left in 1998 it was becoming imperative that those in important executive roles should have mastered the new technology. I am glad I escaped all that. Now that people key in their own letters, much has been lost.

I used to enjoy the time I spent with my secretary at the beginning of each day doing the post – it arrived early in those days! Marian naturally made quite a contribution to writing the letters which I so valued. I always believed in the 'ministry' of the post. It was much appreciated by the membership and created immense goodwill. I usually added a personal, hand-written postscript to all typed letters; in some cases I wrote complete letters by hand. Giving care to such a task reaped very great rewards. I still meet people who thank me for a personal letter I sent over 20 years ago. The recipient might show it to their friends, hand it round in the pub after the weekly choir practice and perhaps post it on the noticeboard in the vestry. This combined with regular visiting of affiliated churches built up the sense of belonging to a cause. As I have often said, the RSCM is not merely an advice bureau; it is a movement in which people march in step for the promotion of good music in church. The willing cooperation of the members during the RSCM Appeal in 1994 was largely due to the fact that they felt they were appreciated and cared for. I fully understand how useful electronic communication is today, but without the personal factor and face-to-face contact it can be unsatisfactory, and sometimes downright harmful.

At my daily letter writing sessions, Marian would discuss tricky matters where her knowledge of those concerned was most helpful. She was also able to keep me in order and remind me of things, and hence avoid dropping clangers. In sending invitations to special events, it is so easy to get things wrong and cause great offence. Being too trusting of a list pulled off the computer can be unwise; it needs to be scrutinized by those who know the membership so that no significant person is omitted. Which can happen, as I know from personal experience. Attention to detail helps to avoid these unfortunate lapses.

In the summer of 1996, just before we moved from Addington to Cleveland Lodge, my seven years with Marian came to an end; she lived nearby and felt she could not commit to the daily commute to our new home near Dorking. I was fortunate to be able to appoint June Williams as her successor, in a seamless transition. June was an experienced secretary with musical ability, and for two years we worked very harmoniously at Cleveland Lodge.

It was a magnificent setting, with my office on the first floor commanding a fine view of Box Hill. We carried on as before, turning round the morning post as efficiently as before. But it was quite a difficult two years, as we were effectively camping out in a building which was in the process of refurbishment. This brought challenges; but with the support of June, we survived very well. The actual building work was only finished after I retired in August 1998.

THE RSCM STAFF

Up to the time when the RSCM left Addington Palace in 1996, the workforce in the offices was considerable, occupying the whole of the basement. In addition to the Secretary who had his own PA, there was a highly efficient Accountant, Michael Kerrigan, assisted by a Bursar. He had overseen the computerization of the whole of the financial side. A similar process for membership records was in the future. Course administration and many similar matters were still done manually. There had to be a person in charge of each section. Duplicating the course material was still done on the Gestetner. The need for mechanization of such mechanical tasks was urgent, although the personal factor was still essential when dealing with people's enquiries.

The administration also contained the Publications Department, well managed by John Sansome and later Peter Wright, ably assisted by Dorothy Nicholls. This involved the selection, production and printing of music, which was a considerable financial prop to the RSCM. There was also a busy RSCM shop, holding music from other publishers, which was dispatched by a small team of packers. It was usually possible to respond quickly to orders, and this was appreciated by the membership.

And not least there were those who kept the Palace functioning well. The Warden was in charge of residential and day courses at Addington. When I arrived, this was done very efficiently by Janette Cooper, who had been Director of Music at Roedean School, Brighton. She was followed by Llywela Harris, who came from the Woodard School for girls at Abbots Bromley. She too was a very good organizer with an amazing grasp of detail. On her retirement in 1993 she was succeeded by Geoff Weaver, who did much to develop the educational programmes of the RSCM. He had at one time been Organist of Bradford Cathedral and then was on the staff of the Church Missionary Society (CMS) Training College in Selly Oak, Birmingham. He was a first-rate musician, a fine keyboard player and conductor, and contributed much. He was particularly successful at the Bath residential courses for male and female students, to which he brought great flair and charisma. He was also employed to run the music at the Lambeth Conference in 1998, and managed brilliantly to knock the Anglican bishops from around the world into shape – no easy task. He was ideally suited to this task as he had worked abroad and had a wide knowledge of world music. He was imaginative in his choice of material and moved away from giving them a watered-down version of the Anglican choral tradition.

When we ceased to run residential courses at Addington in 1993, the domestic staff was scaled down. We still needed a Housekeeper in particular, and Daphne Boniface and her husband Colin, who was brilliant at maintenance, formed a very effective team to keep the buildings in order. The long-serving chef Michael Benson stayed to provide good food for the courses, which had been much appreciated over the years. He took over the management of the palace on the retirement of the Bonifaces, and in fact stayed on as manager after the RSCM left when the palace became a centre for conferences, social occasions and weddings.

THE RSCM COUNCIL

A Chairman and a large council oversaw the running of the RSCM. In the past, the Chairmen had been bishops who had very little time to devote to the work, but who were supportive and sometimes influential. It was a system started by the RSCM's founder, Sir Sydney Nicholson (1927–1947), who gathered his friends around him as a supporting cast. When things were going well, the Council did not have to be proactive. Certainly, Sir Sydney Nicholson was very much the driving voice; though not seriously rich, he was a man of means and never in fact took a salary. Quite often he was prepared to put his hand in his pocket to fund a variety of projects. When he died, the RSCM could not afford to appoint a salaried successor. Three Honorary Directors oversaw things. They were the Organists of St Paul's Cathedral, Westminster Abbey and Canterbury Cathedral. Gerald Knight, organist at the latter, a protégé of Sydney Nicholson, was actually appointed a full-time Director when the move to Addington Palace took place in 1953. But the driving force after the death of Nicholson was Leslie Green.

The Council was far too large. Many members had had a lifelong association with the RSCM and were committed to its success. This was fine when the going was easy – and this was the case through most of the time at Addington (1953–1996), which at least up to 1980 had been a great success story. The membership increased greatly; courses were invariably full. But things started to change. Finance became more of a problem, particularly when new members of staff were not prepared to work for low wages. Outside bookings for residential courses decreased as people were no longer prepared to accept the archaic washing and lavatory facilities. The Council now found itself in a position where hard decisions had to be made. And this was really when the management of the palace and the extensive worldwide activities began to be fraught with difficulties.

There had always been a small General Purposes Committee drawn from the Council which dealt with financial and planning matters. This now became very important as decisions regarding the financial viability of the organization and its future home were now central to its agenda. All this called for a strong chairman with time to give to steer the ship through rougher waters.

THREE CHAIRMEN

Sir John Margetson
Sir John took over in 1988, the year he retired as British Ambassador to The Hague. He had taken part in the selection process for the new Director at the end of 1987, at which I was surprised to find myself the successful candidate out of a shortlist of four. At my

interview he quizzed me about my approach to 'renewal' music – and whether I would sanction support for all kinds of church music at a time when, particularly in evangelical churches, a broadening of the repertoire to include more popular styles of music was becoming increasingly prevalent. Sometimes known as 'happy-clappy' music, I felt this description unfair. Sometimes the introduction of folk and instrumental material was done very well, for example at pioneering churches like All Souls, Langham Place, London. And in fact there was nothing new about this: the high churchmen of the late 19th century used popular material at mission services, as exemplified by the *Mirfield Mission Hymnbook*, which forages far and wide for catchy material, often from the American revivalist tradition. Even the original *English Hymnal* of 1906, edited by Vaughan Williams, had a Mission section headed by the comment 'Not for ordinary use' and an Appendix of popular tunes headed by the comment 'additional tunes which do not enter into the general scheme of the book'. Obviously this material was added on sufferance.

When I started work at the RSCM, I immediately found Sir John a very great support. We became good friends and continued so till his death two years ago. After he retired, we met occasionally for lunch in London at either Brookes or the Athenaeum. I also visited him and his wife Miranda on many occasions at their home in Suffolk – most recently to attend a concert at the Snape Maltings, my first time there.

Sir John was very much a proactive Chairman. This was particularly so in the run-up to the Appeal, launched in 1994. There was a great dinner at the Guildhall, attended by the Duchess of Kent, and preceded by a concert by the choir of St Paul's Cathedral which I had been able to arrange with the support of my friend John Scott. This was a remarkable gesture of support from the Cathedral, which cost the RSCM nothing. The venture was organized by a small committee chaired by Sir John, which included the Lady Mayoress, whose husband was a member of the RSCM Council, and a variety of other distinguished people Sir John had cajoled into service. It was a great success and was one of many instances where he was prepared to work hard in support of the RSCM. It was a great sadness to me that shortly before the great Appeal Service in 1994, he was taken ill and was forced to retire as Chairman.

As a person he was cultured, well-read and deeply musical. He had been a choral scholar at St John's College, Cambridge. He was always the very best of companions. As a former diplomat, he had an inner core of steel which was usually invisible beneath his kindly and generous nature. But he was well equipped to deal when necessary with the sometimes unruly and opinionated members who were to be found on the Council. He could, when occasion demanded it, be very firm. Sir John was the first of the new type of Chairmen. He was not a clergyman, coming from a distinguished career in the world of diplomatic affairs. Though his tenure of six years was regrettably short, his appointment set a precedent: his successors were distinguished individuals from the world of music, education, the law and business. Sir John made a considerable contribution, for which I shall always be thankful.

Roger Butler (Acting Chairman 1994–1996)
Roger was thrown into the leadership role unexpectedly on the retirement of Sir John. He had for some years been Chairman of the General Purposes Committee, and was totally committed to the RSCM. He was a senior manager at the Bank of England and very musical too; as a boy he had been a chorister at New College, Oxford under my old tutor, Dr H. K. Andrews. It was vital to have an Acting Chairman whilst we went through the process of appointing a new Chairman. Originally, Sir Angus Stirling agreed to take on the role if we were prepared to wait a year until he retired as Director of the National Trust. He had also been Chairman of the Covent Garden Opera House. Shortly before he was to take over, he decided that he would have to withdraw for personal reasons; probably as it was a critical time of decision-making at the RSCM while we organized the Appeal and prepared for the move, he felt the job was becoming more taxing than he had originally envisaged. We were all disappointed – and

it did mean that Roger Butler had to serve for two years as Acting Chairman until we were able to fill the position of Chairman.

This interregnum was a difficult period. Roger was a committed Acting Chairman, but he was not always firm enough in his leadership. Admirably, he tried to achieve management by consensus, but very often this proved impossible. The large Council, and particularly the members of the General Purposes Committee, were understandably worried by their responsibility for managing the move to Cleveland Lodge, particularly with regard to finance and the possibility of the liability of the Council if things went badly wrong and the RSCM found itself in deep waters. This was the time for strong and even ruthless leadership, something which Roger's nature was not able to offer. Inevitably factions developed and there was fractious disagreement among the members of Council.

Michael Hockney, a businessman, had been the originator of the plan to move to Dorking. He had got to know the distinguished musician Susi Jeans, widow of the eminent scientist Sir James Jeans. Her home, Cleveland Lodge, boasted three organs and a pedal harpsichord, amongst the many musical instruments found there. Lady Jeans was a native of Vienna and a pupil of Franz Schmidt; she had come over to England before the war and was quite a sensation as a recitalist. I remember Francis Jackson telling me that when she played at York Minster she was 'the talk of the town'. She had been introduced to Sir James Jeans by Sir George Thalben Ball; he had shown her the Albert Hall organ and then took her to dinner with his friend, Sir James, at Cleveland Lodge. This led to a whirlwind romance and a happy marriage which produced three children – but as her husband was much older, it was relatively short-lived. She stayed on at Cleveland Lodge and developed it as a centre of music. I remember listening as a boy on the radio to organ recitals from Cleveland Lodge. I was quite mystified as to why a recital was coming from a private house.

This digression is important as it sets the background to the eventual move from Addington Palace and the negotiations with Susi Jeans and her family after her death about how to activate her generous offer to give Cleveland Lodge to the RSCM so that it could continue to be a place of music-making and educational work. This was made much more difficult by the fact she had not bequeathed Cleveland Lodge to the RSCM in her Will.

The period without a Chairman was very difficult for me personally. There were too many people volunteering their opinions and a very real degree of tension.

Sir David Harrison (1996–2005)

Our head-hunting for a new Chairman led us to Selwyn College, Cambridge. Roger Butler and I went there in the early summer of 1996 to see the Master, Sir David Harrison, with the intention of asking him whether he would consider becoming the new head of the Council. We arrived at the Master's Lodgings in a torrential downpour, which added considerably to the atmosphere of the ivy-covered Victorian gothic house. Inside we were given a friendly welcome. In fact we were delighted when after only a brief discussion Sir David agreed to take on the role of Chair. This turned out to be a very fortunate decision for the RSCM.

We had travelled to Cambridge in Roger's venerable Bentley. On the return journey, we took a delightful route through northern Essex, stopping at the Swan Hotel in Thaxted for a very agreeable, old-fashioned dinner. Even as late as the 1990s, comfortable hotels like this were to be found in county towns. In my day, Oxford had two – the Golden Cross in Cornmarket and the Mitre in the High Street. Both have since gone through interesting transformations: the former to a Pizza Express that boasts original 15th-century wall paintings; the latter to an up-market Italian restaurant.

Sir David's experience at Selwyn, but particularly his time as Vice-Chancellor of Exeter University, fitted him ideally to take over at a turbulent time. Though not a musician, he was deeply interested in church music – his father had been a church organist. He was genial and well-disposed in manner, but had the necessary determination to take tough decisions and bring some necessary order to the RSCM Council. Before I retired, he asked me for my views on the structure and size of the Council. Like him, I thought it was too big; I also thought, like him, that appointing Council members who in fact had a freehold was disastrous for the health of the institution. I suggested the Council should be no more than 12 in number, and that there should be a mandatory system of retirement after a designated period of four years with an option to remain for a further four. This system is something like that which was inaugurated after I retired. A slimmer Council has proved to be more manageable and more efficient.

I came to know Sir David well over the two years I worked with him. He supported RSCM events such as the Celebration Days and took a lively interest in the musical activities around the country and abroad. He was particularly kind and sensitive towards me in the way my retirement was handled. My farewell dinner given by the RSCM Council in August 1998 at the Salters' Company was a very pleasant gathering – as was the public retirement party at the Westminster Cathedral Hall for the membership when I was given many wonderful gifts, including a sheepskin rug by the Auckland RSCM Branch in New Zealand!

I cannot go into every detail of Sir David's tenure as Chairman, but in my view he was just the right kind of person for the time. He believed in the RSCM and was keen to bring stability at a time of great change and financial difficulties. He steadied the ship, and for that I and many others were grateful.

He was followed as Chairman by Mark Williams (2005–2010). He was a former chorister at St Chad's Cathedral, Birmingham under John Harper (Director 1998–2007), then worked in London as an investment manager before joining the Council in 2002.

It is now 21 years (2019) since I retired from the RSCM, but it has been a pleasure to get to know successive Chairs and Directors. I was on friendly terms with those who followed John Harper as Director – Lyndsay Gray and Andrew Reid. I have recently visited the present Director, Hugh Morris, in Sarum College, Salisbury. I met Lord Brian Gill (Chairman 2011–2019) on many occasions, and I am pleased to know that a friend of mine, Dr John Hall, soon to retire as Dean of Westminster, is to be the new Chairman. As Dean of Westminster and a parish priest in three parishes in South London, as well as serving for a time as Canon Residentiary at Blackburn Cathedral which he combined with Diocesan Director of Education, it was a logical move for him to become Director of Education for the Church of England at Church House, Westminster. Regrettably, ill health has more recently forced him to retire.

WORK IN THE UNITED KINGDOM

I always regarded the work at home of supreme importance. The largest concentration of our membership by far was in the UK, where there was much to be done. Like my predecessors I travelled frequently. I conducted a great variety of events, gave talks and attended social gatherings. This enabled me to make music and to get to know and to engage with the membership. Being a musician and a 'people person' was what I liked best.

Before I was Director, there had been occasional meetings for the Chairmen and Secretaries of the local areas held in London. I attended several myself as Chairman of the Southwark RSCM Committee. These were useful, but they were really occasions when Lionel Dakers and Vincent Waterhouse gave us our instructions. There was very little discussion – I felt that was something not to be risked.

When I took over, I decided to have meetings once a year and to have a varied agenda which encouraged a frank exchange of ideas. I established an annual pattern of a meeting for the North at York, a great railway centre; for the Midlands and the West of England at Gloucester; and for the South at Addington. There was a short act of worship with a hymn to open the proceedings. At York and Gloucester, the Deans and Chapters gave us permission to use their glorious Lady Chapels for ten minutes. To start the meeting before the vast East

Window at York or under the Lierne vaulting at Gloucester was indeed a privilege. It set the tone. I always got a Chairman who was a priest to take the short service. At Addington we were self-contained with our own chapel; at York we walked to St William's College for the meeting; and at Gloucester we used the historic Parliament Room. A light lunch was provided. These regular meetings did much to foster relationships and keep the membership walking in step. Over the ten years of my Directorship, these plus my visits around the country enabled me to get to know many people well. They felt regularly in touch, which increased morale. This was particularly important when we had to engage with the local committees about the Appeal for funds, starting in 1994. As I often said, the RSCM is not an advice bureau – it is a movement. Everything else follows from that.

Much of my involvement took place on Saturdays: usually a large Area Choral Festival. These were in those days very well attended. The Quire was filled with 500 singers at Canterbury Cathedral; there was a similar number at St George's Chapel, Windsor and King's College, Cambridge. The naves of Durham and Exeter were completely full from back to front. Often numbers had to be restricted. I loved these occasions, but they were very hard work. I remember at Durham I stood on a rostrum at the Crossing; I could hardly see the tenors and basses at the back under the West Window. Keeping them singing in time together was a nightmare. I recall Sir Sydney Nicholson's famous quip that it was rather like taking a jellyfish for a walk on a rubber band!

There were very few of the great churches I did not visit over my ten-year term. And it was always good to see my friends, the cathedral organists. I knew them well, in part because I was Secretary of the Cathedral Organists' Association, a job which had always fallen to the Director of the RSCM. This contact was extremely beneficial. Sadly this relationship has been discontinued – a truly great loss.

My regional work took many forms. Sometimes I visited a local committee, which might be followed by a visit to the local pub or curry house. There were many events for children. I remember two memorable occasions in Yorkshire: a singing day for boys and girls at Bridlington Priory, and a similar day further north at Grosmont, notable for its steam trains which accompanied us from time to time as they passed through the village. Sometimes courses for children were over two or three days, like the one I conducted in 1998 at Lincoln Minster.

Then there were musical events of a more general nature. The Lancashire area organized a large Christmas Carol Service in Blackpool's Tower Ballroom, accompanied by Neil Shepherd on the mighty Wurlitzer in aid of the RSCM Appeal. In fact they did it two years running. I was fascinated by the names of 19th-century composers which adorned the walls. All the great names were there, but quite a few had faded from the pages of history. On another occasion I went to Howells School, Denbigh, for the launch of their new school hymn book. I particularly enjoyed a visit to Sleaford in Lincolnshire, where Eric Sibley, organist of the parish church had been a long-time supporter. He remembered visits to the pub after choir practice with Nicholson in the 1930s. His wife Winifred had a reputation for providing superb buffet suppers. She did not let us down on this occasion. As I think back, the number and variety of these events was amazing.

Then remembering all these people, so many became friends. They were the lifeblood of the RSCM; they got things done. I was much helped in my regional work by the three Commissioners, later known as the Regional Directors. Their role was to look after their areas, which involved much travel by car, but this paid off. When it came to organizing the cathedral singers or recruiting boys and girls for residential courses, they were extremely useful. Up to the mid 1990s, there were 100 boys at the annual residential course at Rossall School, Fleetwood; and Martin How still attracted 150 at Haileybury. At Kingswood School in Bath there were also successful courses for boys and for girls. Two of my choirmen at All Saints, Margaret Street had been to the Bath course as young singers and spoke very appreciatively of Geoff Weaver, its Director. There are now fewer residential courses for boys and girls and numbers are down; this is an inevitable consequence of the fall in numbers in parish church choirs. But it is not quite the whole story. With the discontinuation of the role of Regional Directors after my time, the point of contact was lost.

All the Regional Directors used to be great visitors. I sometimes went with them, which would now be seen as uneconomical. I remember a very happy visit to the Isle of Man with John Cooke, Northern Regional Director. Apart from the work we did there, it enabled us to spend quality time together, enabling us to get to know one another better – essential for good working relationships between colleagues. As in any business, when RSCM members met at area events or at the annual Celebration Days, they got to know one another, swapped ideas and by so doing improved productivity.

I aimed to show my face as much as possible around the UK. This was good for the *esprit de corps* of the RSCM, but also I much enjoyed the opportunity to see the country, usually by train – a form of travel I have always loved. I remember once taking a night train after a festival at Carlisle Cathedral so I could be in Margaret Street for choir practice the next morning; or arriving at Durham station, with its impressive sightline of the Cathedral from the railway viaduct.

Working for the RSCM around the UK was demanding, and those who worked for it gave generously of their time. In my case the rewards of the work and the incidental pleasures of travel made it all worthwhile.

THE RSCM WORLDWIDE

Australia and New Zealand

The RSCM moved into the Southern Hemisphere very soon after Sir Sydney Nicholson founded it in 1927. In fact he undertook an extensive tour to both Australia and New Zealand in 1934. When I made the same journey in 1994 to celebrate his visit 60 years previously, I found much evidence of Nicholson's success. At Bendigo

Cathedral, the affiliation certificate signed by him is still on the wall in the choir vestry. In fact, he set up a great many outposts in both countries, which led to considerable development. He also attracted young people to come to the College of St Nicolas at Chislehurst to study. Some of them were still around in 1994. I particularly remember meeting Lin Saunders, a musician and writer of reviews for the Auckland press. He was a lively character and entertained us with stories of his time at Chislehurst. I gathered he found Nicholson not entirely to his taste!

The pre-war activity engendered by Nicholson continued to grow after the war. Both countries were organized into branches – though in Australia where the branches were established in each state, the vast distances involved precluded much inter-state activity except for occasional summer schools. Students from both countries still came to study at Canterbury and then at Addington. Gerald Knight was very proactive in recruiting students when on tour.

In New Zealand, the RSCM in my time still continued much as before, helped by a very good-natured coordinator, Nigel Werry, who lived in Wellington and who organized all my visits. He worked me very hard. I remember a frantic day in Christchurch when I visited four schools, at some of which I was expected to address the whole school – this in addition to performing an evening function. During a visit to the South Island in 1994, I was allowed a day off when I took the train from Christchurch over the Alps, descending to Greymouth, a town on the Tasman coast. But even here I found I was booked to take a singing evening at the local parish church.

In Australia on my first visit in 1990, I found a great deal of disgruntlement. The areas were beginning to ask why they should be run by an organization 11,000 miles away. There were also those who did not wish to be part of a body which called itself 'Royal'. Lionel Dakers, my predecessor, had considerably fanned the flames of disaffection. He treated them rather like colonials governed from the UK. Particularly irksome to them was his insistence on appointing the directors for the summer schools held after Christmas each year and organized in turn by the state committees. These events often included distinguished musicians who were well-known nationally, and they were perfectly able to choose their own directors. I told them this and immediately stopped the practice of imposing someone from the UK. This pleased them greatly. But basically they felt they were established enough to stand on their own feet. There was a real risk that the membership might vote to leave. As I gradually came to know the leading players, many of whom became great friends, the threat of leaving gradually diminished. I visited Australia in 1990, 1991, 1994, 1995, 1998 and 1999, and over this time, and after much discussion, I formed the view that the members would like to stay part of the RSCM but with very much greater autonomy and self-regulation. Thus RSCM Australia was born. New Zealand also decided eventually to go down this same path.

In Australia, we gradually worked towards a new constitution. The final steps to making this a reality were taken at a summit conference held in Sydney in February 1995, chaired very ably by the New South Wales Chairman, William Clark. Remarkably, we managed to gather the Secretaries and Chairmen from the seven Australian states – an indication of the importance given to this meeting. I was accompanied by Charles King, the Secretary at that time of the RSCM. It was resolved to create a new written constitution which defined the relationship with the UK and the autonomy which the Australian members sought. We were very much helped in the legal work by a member of the UK RSCM Council, the Hon. Mark Bridges, who put in a great deal of time to make the document a success. The consultation period took some time and it was not until 6 months after I retired that RSCM Australia was inaugurated at a great service in the Roman Catholic Cathedral in Melbourne in January 1999. I was touched that as the ex-Director I was invited to conduct the music at this, as well as to direct the summer school that year. The process which led to the establishment of RSCM Australia was crucial in safeguarding the continuing presence of the RSCM in Australia. I was proud to have had a part in this.

My seven visits to Australia and my three to New Zealand contained many highlights. They were hard work – but they were hugely enjoyable, leading to many good and lasting friendships. There were the usual round of talks, meetings and musical events, as well as social occasions when I could meet the membership. These I found exhausting. To meet many people, give them one's full attention and at the same time be interesting and amusing was quite an onerous assignment. I found it difficult to 'work' a room in a relaxed and easy-going manner, and I'm not sure that I was very good at instant *bonhomie* where nothing much below the surface was touched upon.

One of my most unusual exploits was to visit affiliated churches by air. The Queensland Chairman, Robert Boughen, Organist of Brisbane Cathedral, suggested that no visiting Director had visited the outlying membership in the bush. As he was a qualified pilot, he proposed he should fly us to meet the choirs in various churches. Never having been keen on aviation, I was considerably alarmed, especially as the flight was to be made in a twin-engined four-seater. Initially I declined, but he phoned again to say that if I would go, his son, a Quantas pilot, would fly the aircraft. At this I felt I had to agree. It turned out to be very agreeable, skirting over the top of the forests, avoiding great altitudes and the attendant unpleasant aural sensation associated with high-level flying.

Setting off from Brisbane, our first stop was a small rural town called Murgon where we were met at the airstrip by a choir member and taken to the church where I held a training session with the choir, followed by a good lunch. Eventually we returned to the aircraft and continued our trip westwards to Roma, about 150 miles from Brisbane. We then repeated the performance – a choir session followed by refreshments. Afterwards, we were taken home by a choir member to stay the night. She said her house was 'in the suburbs', which turned out to be 40 miles away. When we eventually arrived at her very modern farmhouse on a sheep station, we were made very welcome. It was a really remote location and to me quite exotic with large parrot-like birds making a lot of noise in the garden. On the way to the farm, we had been startled when three emus ran across the road in front of us! The next morning, after a very good breakfast of lamb chops, we returned to the aircraft and flew back to Brisbane.

There were many other highlights of these trips – like a visit to the 5-manual Hill organ in Sydney Town Hall. It just so happened that Simon Preston was practising for a recital. He very kindly let me run my fingers over the keys. Another great organ was the instrument by T. C. Lewis in St Paul's Cathedral, Melbourne, largely unaltered, and well restored by Harrison and Harrison in 1990. The organist June Nixon had visited me at Southwark to see the Lewis organ there when she was planning the restoration of her instrument. Then there were scenic delights – a visit to the Glass House Mountains near Brisbane with my friend Patricia Logan; a drive through the primeval forests of the Southern Highlands of the Blue Mountain range in the mist and rain, a truly Wagnerian experience; the delights of the Barossa Valley in Southern Australia; the Western Coast and the vineyards around Margaret River with my good friends Erik and Mary Leask of Perth, who I had got to know when they lived in Salisbury and who I always visited when travelling to and from Australia. A particularly good day out was the drive right across Tasmania from Launceston to Hobart with William Pierce in his splendid Bentley. There was so much of interest.

I was well looked after whenever I visited Australia. I stayed on most of my visits with Peter McMillan and his partner Alan Nipress. Peter co-owned with his brother the largest print works in Australia – McMillan Print. He was a fine amateur musician and a companion I prized highly. Alan had been a First Class Steward for Qantas but retired early to look after the sizable houses they inhabited. He too was a good musician and often delighted us with his playing of the piano and the Hammond organ. He had a gritty Australian sense of humour. He was also a brilliant host, looking after one's every need. Peter and Alan several times came to London, when I was taken to meals at the Dorchester and other quality hotels. Sadly both have now joined their ancestors. I still miss them very much.

I sometimes stayed with Geoffrey Cox in Melbourne when he was Australian President of the RSCM. He lived in a charming Victorian house with wrought-iron verandas. He was a university teacher of music and an organist who had come over to England to read Music at New College, Oxford. On my last visit in 2004, I travelled down from Sydney to Melbourne on the train and returned in the same way – an ideal way to see the country, particularly as the train travels at a leisurely pace with the added advantage of good buffet cars.

Another highlight was my visit to St James', King Street in Sydney to take a boys' practice – the first time I had ever met with an electric piano which was wheeled out into the middle of the chancel. The boys were excellent. I remember we rehearsed several movements of Byrd's *Five Part Mass*. The sadness was that the Director of Music, Walter Sutcliffe, was away playing the double bass with the Sydney Symphony Orchestra. Walter was an exact contemporary as an eight-year-old when we were both choristers in the choir of St Paul's, Shipley in the West Riding of Yorkshire. What a small world it can sometimes be. I did however meet his assistant, the young Peter Jewkes, who runs the largest organ building company in Australia. I met him on a number of occasions subsequently in his own country, but very frequently at All Saints, Margaret Street in London. He is a great fan of the organ and the music there.

Similar things could be said about my visits to New Zealand. I was warmly welcomed and always royally entertained. I stayed twice with Stanley Jackson and his wife Ruth in Auckland. He had emigrated from Lancashire and become Organist of Wellington Cathedral. In Christchurch, David Childs was Organist of the Cathedral, having read Modern Languages at The Queen's College, Oxford; he and his wife were wonderful hosts. And in Dunedin I met up with the Aitkin family, Bruce and Wendy; they loved a party and we had a great deal of fun.

The scenery in New Zealand was an endless source of delight – wonderful train journeys and visits to Hawkes Bay and the hot springs at Rotorua. One time I took the ferry from Wellington to the South

Island, and thence by bus through idyllic country to Nelson (where incidentally there is a Lewis organ!). These tours lasting four to six week were fascinating – but they were also exhausting. I was booked to do innumerable events most days, and then I had to be on my best form at the frequent social gatherings – something I found more tiring than the actual musical work. But it was all very worthwhile. I believe my visits forged a new relationship with the RSCM which was influential in keeping the RSCM members in Australia and New Zealand on board.

The United States
From the late 1950s, the RSCM had started to become involved in educational schemes in the US – the long-running Cedar Hills Course for Boys at Painesville in Ohio for example – and Gerald Knight (Director 1953–1974) built up contacts in California and along the eastern seaboard. However in 1980, under the Directorship of Lionel Dakers, it was decided to open an American Office in Lichfield, Connecticut run by Robert Kennedy. For some years this venture was a great success and the work very greatly expanded. Alas, it got into financial difficulties in 1985–1986; the precise reasons for this were not entirely clear, but a factor must have been an ambitious programme not sufficiently costed. The office had to be closed and the RSCM was left to pay off a debt of £120,000. From then on the American membership was administered from Addington Palace. This was the situation when I arrived in 1989.

Early in 1990 I made my first visit to America. I was accompanied by Vincent Waterhouse, the RSCM Secretary, with a view to reviewing the work in the US and possibly re-opening the American office. A meeting was held in the palatial study of the Rev'd John Andrew, RSCM American President, at St Thomas', Fifth Avenue, New York. At this it was resolved to re-establish an office, but this time with secure safeguards in place. Robert Quade, Director of Music at St Paul's Akron, Ohio, was appointed RSCM coordinator, and for the whole of my time ran an office at his church, staffed by a number of volunteers. This got things moving, and eventually other regions were identified and organizers appointed. This was a good start. But since I retired in 1998, the American Board of Directors have overseen a considerable expansion. Today (2017) there are 12 annual residential courses for male and female students, mainly in the north-east of the country. Before I became Director there were a number of courses up and running. I conducted the 1982 Ohio course for boys, and another course for boys at Winthrop College in North Carolina in 1988. The Americans particularly valued these courses as they made demands on the children in musical terms which were uncommon in the US. They were in fact treated as adults, like the boys in English cathedral choirs. The Americans saw the RSCM as the bastion of the great English church music tradition. The support came mainly from the Episcopal churches, but not entirely. Thirty years ago there were still a good number of what are called 'boy and men' choirs. Many survive. The best is at St Thomas', Fifth Avenue, which has the rare benefit of a choir school housed in a modern building in Manhattan, which has most of the features of a 5-star hotel.

I enjoyed my visits to America, particularly the making of new friends, distinguished musicians who did much to promote the RSCM. Foremost of these was Benjamin Hutto, then Director of Music at Christ Church, Charlotte in North Carolina. He became a great friend and after my retirement visited me in London during his annual expeditions to Europe. He was an enthusiast with a wonderful sense of humour, a good organizer and was good at personal relationships. My frequent visits to America quite often took in visits to his home in Charlotte, where I would do work for him at his church, but would also take the opportunity for rest and refreshment during a hectic US tour. He was very much a party animal so we had some wonderful occasions at his charming home, where I helped with the culinary preparations.

Another memorable visit was to Charleston, South Carolina, that fine 18th-century colonial town with its stately mansions and Wren-like churches. I was staying with Doug Ludlum, the organist of the

Lutheran church, in his charming Dutch-like wood house. Hardly had we arrived when we were bidden to a Martini party in the middle of the afternoon, when Doug, Ben and I were joined by Bill Gudger, organist of the cathedral in Charleston. I shall never forget Doug mixing (or as he would have said 'fixing') the martini. He had a large glass cylinder full of ice to which he added plenty of gin which he then stirred with a glass rod. Towards the end of this procedure he added very carefully drops of dry Martini from a pipette – making sure only to add a little. He then poured this lethal mixture into glasses. It was good, but it really did make your head steam! The only accompaniment was cloves of garlic roasted in the oven.

My knowledge of the mysteries of imbibing was definitely advanced in the US. One time I went to a bar with Jane Parker-Smith, the brilliant English organist who was a keynote player at the Centennial of the American Guild of Organists in New York in 1996. I ordered two martinis, and explained to the barman that I wanted it poured out of a cocktail shaker so that there was no ice in the glass. I also said I only wanted the rind of a lemon. He said 'Certainly, sir; you don't want it 'on the rocks', you want it 'straight up with a twist'!' This seemed to cause my companion some amusement. I found that Americans are either very abstemious or considerable 'arm lifters'.

In California I had three very interesting days rehearsing the boys of Grace Cathedral, San Francisco preparing for Evensong. This was in the time of John Fenstermaker, who looked after me very well. I did events in the Los Angeles area, though I never did succeed in finding the centre of that town. I was looked after by the Fosters, a husband and wife musical team at All Saints Beverley Hills, where I learned that David Hockney, who I had known a little at Bradford Grammar School, had been in the church the day before for a memorial service. His brother Paul Hockney, an accountant in Bradford, had once suggested to an old Bradford Grammar School friend of mine that he would give me David's phone number when I next visited Beverley Hills. I didn't take up the offer as I felt I didn't really know David well enough and did not want to push myself forward. I suppose I have a shy side to me and get nervous at the thought of such encounters.

Once when in California I was taken to dinner at a smart restaurant on St Valentine's Day. This turned out to be full of good-looking gay young men – 'ivy league' types, very well turned out – who sat looking at one another adoringly at tables for two over a bowl of red roses. On a number of occasions I had similar experiences. I remember going out to dinner in Charlotte at the invitation of a rich young man and his partner. There were two ladies present – very elegant, stylishly dressed with immaculately coiffed hair. I was very surprised to be told later that they were lesbians. I later learned the phrase to describe such couples as 'lipstick lesbians' from a knowing friend.

As well as the music, I took great pleasure in the topography and buildings of America. Georgia I found a highly attractive state with great trees and lush meadows. This was when I directed two Sunday morning services at the cathedral in Atlanta. Then there was an amazing journey by car on the Blue Mountain Parkway – a project initiated by President Roosevelt to ease unemployment during the Great Depression of the inter-war years. Travelling on the roads high up in the Appalachian Mountains with long vistas of trees stretching into the far distance was an unforgettable experience, ending up in Lexington, Virginia, a charming town with many red brick 18th-century buildings. One tends to forget how much Georgian architecture there is in the States, stretching up the eastern side of the country through Virginia, New England, and particularly Boston, right up to places like Portsmouth, New Hampshire. I found provincial America very attractive and loved the wholesome tasty food served in restaurants in such places. The metropolitan fad for *nouvelle cuisine* on both sides of the Atlantic was light years away, thankfully. I have always resented paying the bill at restaurants where the artistic design of the food on the plate seemed more important than its wholesomeness – the kind of places where one feels after dinner the need to order a plate of ham sandwiches!

On one of my visits to Newhaven, I spent a wonderful evening with the distinguished organist Thomas Murray at Yale. After exploring the delights of the large Aeolian-Skinner organ in the Wolesley Hall, we spent some time at his old house in Guildford, where I discovered for the first time a Chickering piano made by the reputed Boston firm. We then drove to the Connecticut coast to the village of Essex, where we had an excellent dinner at the Griswold Arms – a delightful inn set in a very well-manicured seaside village. I remember the smart old houses with white railings bordering the roads and gardens – always a sure sign of affluence.

I visited many churches, which I found by European standards very small and architecturally unimpressive. At such places the adjacent buildings – halls, classrooms, kitchens and even gymnasia – were usually four times the size of the church building and remarkably well equipped. To the English, American churches are vastly well attended with full congregations at several services on Sunday mornings. So spacious ancillary buildings are a necessity. Of course, some of the notable churches are large and superficially impressive. The National Cathedral in Washington is built in the grand manner. But I feel the design lacks depth in the detail both inside and outside – for example in the springing of the arches, the window tracery and the window design. Particularly the outside reminds me very much of a cardboard cut-out. I don't however feel this about the Cathedral of St John the Divine in New York. This cavernous building to me is very impressive – the vast nave leading to the byzantine east end, which was probably a cheaper option when funds were running low.

Many American churches have large organs which are often far too big for the confined space in which they are set. Hearing them made me think of the grandeur and brilliance of the Great organ of the Lewis organ at Southwark Cathedral, achieved from a mere thirteen stops. They can also be lethally loud. In New York, churches seem to have vied with one another as to who could have the largest reeds in the West End Bombarde division. I remember being virtually assassinated at a recital by the distinguished organist Frederick Swann at the Riverside Church, New York. Sitting near the back, I was totally unprepared for the eruption of noise when the heavy pressure reeds were drawn.

I could digress endlessly about my journeys – several by train across the plains of Michigan through beautiful pastoral scenery on my way to Chicago, where I performed for musical evenings at St Luke's, Evanston organized by Richard Webster, the Director of Music. The E. M. Skinner organ here is a wonderfully musical organ with fine voicing, particularly with regard to the subtleties of 'horizontal adding' of stops, which can lead to miraculous changes of tone quality. Sadly I didn't make it right into the middle of the country, where they are perhaps more interested in horses than music, but I did get to Evansville in Indiana, where I met the delightful organist Robert Nicholls, who continues as Director of Music at the First Presbyterian Church. I much enjoyed making music in his church.

One unexpected problem that arose was the American pronunciation of vowel sounds: how could I raise this with choirs without causing offence? I eventually found the answer. On one occasion I was rehearsing a setting of the Magnificat when the choir pronounced the opening words as 'My soul doth magnify the Lord and my spirit hath rejoiced in Gard my saviour'! I took my courage in both hands and dived straight in. I said I would like to discuss vowel sounds – and how Latin, Italian and English (as spoken in Yorkshire) have many open vowels which engender the right sound for the vowel. I then said that the English have great problems with vowels, especially when these are affected by regional pronunciation. I recalled boys from Worcester Voluntary Choir who sang 'for thoine is the kingdom'; a Cockney girl who pronounced 'apple' as 'ipple'; or a boy in Scotland who when asked by an examiner to play a scale of A major actually played E major. I finished with an experience I had when playing the piano for a rehearsal of *Belshazzar's Feast* by Walton at Worcester: seated behind me was a posh alto who sang something like 'Bai-eelsheeazzah'. This anecdote brought the house down. I was then able, without trepidation, to ask them to consider their own vowel sounds. My strategy worked and I used it time and again subsequently!

I might never have got as far as these experiences of America. When I started as Director in 1989, I noticed considerable dissatisfaction amongst some of the American membership. They resented the Royal connection and considered the US musicians were quite able to organize their own church music organization. But it gradually became clear that these dissenting voices were those of a minority. The link with the English choral tradition was appreciated. With the establishment of the new office and greater self-determination in RSCM America, the work has steadily expanded and talk of breaking away now seems a thing of the past.

South Africa

My first visit to South Africa was in fact before I became Director. Lionel Dakers asked me in January 1985 to run the summer school that year, in Grahamstown in the Eastern Cape. I was met at the airport in Port Elizabeth and driven through rolling countryside to Grahamstown. The base for the school was at a boarding school in the town, and all the events took place in the Cathedral, an impressive building by Sir George Gilbert Scott. It housed one of the few rings of bells in South Africa. I remember them pealing out on New Year's Eve, their sound mixed with the noise of shunting engines in the nearby marshalling yards – train travel was still in the age of steam. It was a picturesque place with white Georgian-style architecture.

For the first few nights I stayed with the Bishop, Kenneth Oram, and his wife in their Victorian villa on the outskirts of town. He was one of the last English bishops. But the slight air of Barchester which hung around him was deceptive: he was a radical campaigner against apartheid. I remember he preached a brave sermon at a broadcast service we did, in which he did not mince his words about the political situation. In 1985 racial segregation was still very much in force. Most of the black people lived outside the town in the townships, as they still do in many places. There was a great deal of discrimination: for instance, separate doors for whites and blacks at the railway station. The church however found a way round this. The summer school I conducted was multiracial, so Black and White lived side by side in shared accommodation. Somehow these Christian occasions inhabited a territory that the state found it difficult to invade.

Like all summer schools it was hard work, not helped by the high summer temperatures, but I met so many interesting people. The organ was played by Errol Slatter, Organist of St Paul's, Durban, who I got to know well and met later in Durban. The course was well attended by young people, but the choir was mostly adult. Probably at least half of the 100 or so on the course were Black or of mixed racial backgrounds. I noticed immediately the good singers: two very good boys from St Mary's Port Elizabeth; a tenor, Samuel Adams, from Cape Town; a primary school headmaster who I have continued to meet over the years on his travels to Europe. It was very much a social mix. One lady had arrived from Johannesburg in her Mercedes; others were only there because their churches had raised money to pay for them. As far as I could see, this considerable mix was mostly harmonious, unified by a common love of church music. The repertoire was traditional and Anglican; the move to have greater inclusiveness of style had not yet surfaced. It is interesting that Gerald Knight, when he visited as Director in the 1960s and 70s, thought it odd that all the music sung in the churches had been imported by the missionaries. *Hymns Ancient and Modern* came to have an almost Biblical status and was widely used!

The week revolved round practices and services, but there was also good social time. On a day off I was taken to a lagoon on the east coast near to Kenton on Sea. On our way there, as we passed through Port Alfred, I was amazed to see whites playing bowls dressed in boaters and striped blazers. It could have been Henley on Thames. This juxtaposition of traditional English dress and customs could be found frequently in South Africa. I was once travelling by bus across the Transvaal from Johannesburg to Natal and arrived at a bustling market town where I was being met by 'Bunney' Ashley-Botha, who took me to the Drakensburg Choir School where he was Director, high in the mountains. The town was thronged with people. of colour – smartly and brightly dressed. I then caught sight of a group of White prep school boys dressed in striped blazers and caps standing on a street corner. No one batted an eyelid!

One memory of Grahamstown was a visit to the house of Jill Westcott, Organist at Grahamstown Cathedral. She made no bones about the fact she lived with a woman. That seemed unremarkable by comparison with the fact that the house was populated by literally 20 cats; they were everywhere. My hosts soon cottoned on to the fact that I hate cats and actually made my life a misery! Coping with dogs and cats is a considerable hazard of staying in private houses.

After the Grahamstown course I was shown round Cape Town and the Cape Peninsula by Owen Franklin, an Anglican priest who has come to be a fairly regular visitor to England. I was overwhelmed with the beauty of the region, by the drive down the peninsula to Simons Town, and the university town of Stellenbosch.

I was in fact the third generation of my family to visit South Africa. My great grandfather, John Wakefield (1858–1904), fought in the South African war, and like so many soldiers in that campaign died of infectious illness. He was only 46 when he died at Standerton in the Transvaal. When I went on my long bus journey to Natal, I passed through Standerton where we had a break for lunch. In 1985, I was unaware that my ancestor was buried there. Had I known, I would have tried to find the grave. I only found out later about this when I discovered a card in family papers announcing his death. My grandfather, Richard Louis Wakefield, who was in the navy for 15 years, spent time at the base at Simonstown. He used to say that he would have liked to visit his father's grave but always found himself too far away.

After this short break in Cape Town, I paid a short visit to Bloemfontein where my old Pembroke friend, Tom Stanage, was bishop. He lived with his parents in a pleasant house in the suburbs. I had not seen him since he was a curate at St Faith's, Great Crosby near Liverpool 25 years earlier. He had a very successful ministry in South Africa as a parish priest at Somerset West in the Cape, and remarkably so as Dean of the Cathedral at Kimberley, which used to have 900 communicants on Sundays. He was perhaps less successful as a bishop – first Suffragan in Johannesburg to Timothy Bavin, and then Diocesan Bishop in Bloemfontein. It was a difficult assignment as the Orange Free State is predominantly Boer. But Tom was very musical and we enjoyed playing piano duets.

On one occasion we attended a performance of Verdi's *Aida* at the splendid new opera house. This was remarkable for having a 100 Black people bussed in from the township to take the part of the Ethiopian slaves. Their singing was electrifying. The Director at the Opera House had arranged this, providing the necessary training. It was clearly planned as a gesture of inter-racial solidarity. I came across this kind of cooperation a good deal, instigated by enlightened whites. The performance was also remarkable for having on stage horses and camels. One amusing anecdote I noticed in the local paper was a report of a camel arrested by the police. It had stopped with its keeper at a set of traffic lights. Asked by the police officer what he was doing with the camel on a public highway, he simply replied that he was taking it to a rehearsal at the opera house!

I visited the country three times, twice as Director in 1992 and 1996. Running the RSCM there as part of an international organization was financially difficult as the Rand was so low against the pound. I remember being taken to an excellent five-course lunch at the Mount Nelson Hotel in Cape Town by Barry Smith, the cathedral organist. The meal cost, in English value, about £7 a head, which even in 1992 was remarkable. My successor as Director, John Harper, did a good deal to help manage these financial problems caused by the exchange rate. Happily the RSCM still flourishes as a result, though I have noticed the numbers attending courses has considerably reduced since my time; but that is true also in the UK.

On my second visit in 1992, I found the political situation changing fast. Apartheid was now virtually gone. I started again in

Cape Town, doing visits and meeting the committee. A particularly memorable occasion was my visit to the Church of the Resurrection in Bonteheuwel. This was a new town on the Cape with flats built to house all the coloured residents of a district in Cape Town, though it could be called ethnic cleansing on a massive scale. The designation 'coloured people' in South Africa meant of mixed race.

I was taken on the Sunday morning to Bonteheuwel by car. The Director of Music had arranged for three young men from the choir to collect me. They eventually arrived and I was driven to the church very cheerfully in the most ramshackle of old cars. As we entered the town, the streets were filled with people making their way to church, many carrying Bibles and prayer books. The large building was packed. I had the daunting task of having to give an address at the service. The Mass included every conceivable type of music and liturgical style. Like most Anglican churches in South Africa, it was 'high'. There were clouds of incense, yards of lace and a pleasant mixture of the formal and informal. The music included traditional hymns and those in a more folk-like style; the large surpliced choir sang the well-known anthem by S. S. Wesley, 'Blessed be the God and Father of our Lord Jesus Christ'. It was on this occasion that, arriving back in Cape Town, I was taken to the Mount Nelson Hotel for lunch. What a contrast! Indeed, South Africa was a country of great contrasts in so many ways.

Later, on this tour, I experienced another remarkable Sunday morning service in Soweto. I was taken to St Paul's Anglican church, where I was the only white in a large black congregation. Virtually no English was spoken. In fact the congregation spoke two languages – Xhosa and Hutu. The sermon had to be translated line by line from one language to the other. Here again the service was a mixture of musical styles, but was rather more charismatic than I had previously witnessed in other churches. They still used the old *Ancient and Modern* hymn book. I remember one elderly server in a lace cotta getting rather carried away and walking up and down banging his hymn book like a tambourine. As usual, I was warmly received.

After the service I met some of the musicians in the adjacent convent where the nuns served refreshments. The main topic of conversation was about sight-reading staff notation. How could I help them? Surprisingly the tonic-solfa method was still widely used – a system I have always felt much more confusing than just reading the notes. It was a topic I encountered frequently, most memorably on a visit to a Roman Catholic basilica at Galeshewe near Kimberley. This was a large neo-classical building with a lively acoustic. The sizable choir of young men and women asked me to take their rehearsal. They attended the church every day after work at about 4.30 p.m. to rehearse for an hour. Like the singing of the Ethiopian slaves in the opera house at Bloemfontein, their singing was immensely impressive – wonderful natural voices with a very good ear for pitch and tone. I conducted them in several choruses from Handel's *Messiah* which they knew well. The elaborate runs were immaculate; their whole performance was marked by life and enthusiasm. They too used the 'tonic solfa' method and found this very difficult. I suspect they eventually learned the notes by rote. They were at that time engaged in learning some choruses from Haydn's *Creation* and asked me to help them. I have to be honest, I found it very difficult to get to grips with the process of learning the notes by tonic sol-fa. Looking back, the memory of this visit remains vivid; it was a deeply moving and humbling occasion and wonderful music-making in an unexpected place.

On all my visits I did one-day schools, talks, organ recitals and visits to individual choirs. It was also important to get to know the committees where I met many hard-working officers. On my first visit to Johannesburg in 1992 I met the formidable secretary of the local committee, Ella Hunt. She was highly efficient and even today many years after her death is remembered as someone one did not trifle with. I was reminded of this a few weeks ago when I bumped into a member of this committee who was attending a talk I gave in London. The committee were mystified as to why Ella and I from the outset became great friends. By the time of my visit in 1996, Ella had moved to a retirement home in Pietermaritzburg in Natal, having been replaced by another excellent Johannesburg secretary, Daphne Allinson. For my visit to the cathedral at Pietermaritzburg, Ella had come out of retirement to organize a one-day school. She managed to produce a capacity attendance; she had obviously worked very hard to get people out.

During this 1996 visit I gave an organ recital at the Anglican church in East London. On arrival there by plane, I noticed Ian Smith, last Prime Minister of Rhodesia, was a fellow passenger. The organist at East London had arranged a surprise encounter. A woman I had known years before in Yorkshire, Kathleen Long, was living in South Africa and came to tea with me at my hotel next to the Indian Ocean. She and I had both been associated with a coronation pageant, put on at St Paul's, Shipley in the West Riding of Yorkshire in 1953, when her sister played the Queen and I took the part of the Dean of Westminster. I was 16 at the time; I imagine she was in her late teens.

Occasional chance meetings abroad never cease to amaze me. Fifteen years ago, I was sitting having a beer at a café outside the cathedral in Seville when I heard a voice say, 'It's Harry, isn't it?' The Precentor of Exeter Cathedral just happened to be passing that way! On another occasion, I had just arrived at the railway station in Florence when a breathless taxi driver ran up to me. He said 'English professor would speak with you.' This turned out to be an elderly retired Classics master from the King's School, Worcester!

So many things in South Africa were remarkable – the visit to the multi-racial choir school high up in the Drakensburg country in the middle of Zulu territory, with its small houses with domed roofs – a journey made by bus from East London to Durban. I was noticing groups of children walking to school for many miles on the roadside, when at length I noticed their destination: a large school where the playground was thronged with boys and girls. (There were no 'school runs' in rural South Africa. Pampered children conveyed the short distances by car in the UK should take note – or rather their parents should.) When I was four years old, there were few cars; those who owned them couldn't get petrol in wartime. So we walked – in my case four times a day a distance of one and a half miles – four times, because I went home for lunch. I remember my Great-uncle Joshua (born 1876) telling me that when he was an apprentice carpenter, he had to walk five miles to get to his place of work each day. The children walking on the road was a sign of the hardship black children experienced as they went to and fro from their homes in the townships.

As I noted earlier, the church music I experienced was an import from the UK. Many of the musicians were white – but the music was enjoyed by those of all racial groups. Extreme contrasts in living standards were startling. A visit to the Johannesburg Club in the middle of the city with its manicured lawns and flowerbeds could quite easily have been in Cheltenham. But there were contrasts within the black community. On my way to Soweto, some very smart housing at the top of a hill was pointed out. I was told this was where affluent native Africans lived. The area was known locally as Beverley Hills! At the time of my visits 20 and more years ago, private education was mostly for whites, though in this respect things were beginning to change. Hilton College in the Midlands of Natal which I visited was then a carbon copy of an English public school – but of the 1930s. I think that this unequal situation was for the time tolerated because very many of the more privileged whites and the churches worked hard for social justice – to achieve a fairer society.

Many distinguished and admired musicians of the calibre of Richard Cock in Johannesburg and Barry Smith and Garmon Ashby in Cape Town were part of this movement to make musical opportunities more widely available to all, irrespective of background. Both Richard and Barry were cathedral organists and involved in a wide range of music-making; Garmon at the time of my last visit was Director of Music at the Diocesan College (Bishops) and Chairman of the RSCM Cape Town committee.

On my last visit to South Africa in 1996, I saw considerable evidence of change in churches and schools. In Bloemfontein the boys' school

(St Martin's) was changing slowly, but at the girls' convent school, St Michael's, change was well advanced. There were many black girls and the music being sung was much more varied, with native African material interspersed with more traditional fare.

It was a great privilege to visit South Africa three times between 1985 and 1996. Everywhere I went, I was received with warmth and interest. They worked me very hard. It was not the musical work I found tiring; it was the numerous receptions and meals that I found exhausting – enjoyable, yes – but having rightly to try to take a genuine interest in all the new people I met was draining. One of the committees wrote a report of my visit in which they remarked that I seemed very tired. With a packed schedule and much travel, it was hardly surprising. But sharing in the RSCM work worldwide is immensely important. Music as a common language which knows no frontiers is the ideal medium for forging links to create international understanding. The way the work has spread through the English-speaking world is an amazing story – of growth germinated from those seeds sown originally by the founder, Sir Sydney Nicholson, over 90 years ago.

Canada
The first time the RSCM reached Canada and America was during Sydney Nicholson's world tour in 1934. Some seeds were sown, but it was not until the 1950s when Gerald Knight started to travel abroad that these germinated and started to grow. In the past 30 years there has been remarkable growth, but perhaps not to the same extent in Canada as elsewhere. The vast size of the country and the scattered nature of the population have been great obstacles to growth. I made some visits to places where there was enthusiasm, for instance in Ottawa, where I visited St Matthew's Church, which still in those days had a noted boys' choir.

On that visit I also met the distinguished woman organist of the cathedral, who Dame Gillian Weir reliably informed me was one of only three women in cathedral posts worldwide! At this time there were none in the UK. Things have improved somewhat 25 years later, but organ playing worldwide still would appear, with very notable exceptions, to be mostly a male pursuit. Increasing the number of female organists is very important. Progress has been made, but not quickly enough. There are some brilliant women at the console these days. I recently heard the Canadian player Isabelle Demers give a whole recital of Reger at the Royal Festival Hall from memory – an amazing feat. And when I was about fifteen I heard the French organist Jeanne Demessieux play at Leeds Parish Church. She too had an amazing talent which I remember to this day. I have recently become a Patron of the Society of Women Organists, founded in 2019 by Anne Marsden-Thomas, Catherine Ennis and Ghislaine Reece-Trapp, aimed at raising the profile of women organists in the UK and helping them gain more prestigious appointments in British cathedrals.

I made time to go to other centres of excellence. I went to see Derek Holman, one time Warden at Addington Palace, subsequently a well-known musician in Toronto both at the University and at Grace Church on the Hill, which had a fine treble choir of boys. It was good to visit flourishing choirs in individual churches. But there was only one area of Canada where the RSCM had really taken root. This was the Niagara and South West Ontario Branch – a corridor stretching from Niagara and St Catherine to Stratford, Burlington and London – sizable towns on the route of the railway track from Toronto to Port Huron, which continued across Michigan to Chicago. In this region the support was considerable. There was a good committee headed by Peter Shepherd, a very hard-working chairman, ably assisted by Violet Naylor as secretary. There were keen people in all these cities, including Thomas Shilcock and Geoffery Steele in Burlington. They really got things moving. I conducted many well-attended events in this part of Canada. Many of the organizers became good friends. I suppose all this was possible because the distances were manageable.

On several occasions I continued by rail from Port Huron into the US to fulfil engagements in the Chicago area. I have already mentioned

Richard Webster at St Luke's, Evanston; but mention should also be made of Barbara and Charles Dickerman, who organized events in the Chicago region. Some went well; but here again the vast distances were an obstacle. The Dickermans were great RSCM supporters and actually came to the farewell dinner at Addington Palace in 1996. They had a dog I remember called Thatcher. Charles was a distinguished nuclear physicist and indeed spent time in Russia working to make Chernobyl safe after the nuclear disaster. Never be surprised by the unexpected talents of RSCM members worldwide!

The opportunity to see new places on RSCM tours was a great privilege. For me, a day spent on the train (ten hours) going from Toronto to Chicago was recuperative and gave me time to think and prepare as the Amtrak train rolled at a very genteel speed across the plains of Michigan – unsensational scenery, but quietly beautiful with meadows, forests and lakes. I always enjoyed my visits to this part of the world and everywhere was welcomed with generous hospitality.

Northern Europe and the Channel Islands
For many years there has been an RSCM presence in Belgium, Holland and Luxembourg. Martin Van Bleek throughout my time organized musical festivals in these countries. I conducted events in Utrecht, Brussels (at the pro-cathedral) and Luxembourg. There were British citizens working in Europe taking part, but also Europeans who like many in the Low Countries spoke perfect English. The RSCM could never have become a national organization in European countries because of the language barrier and perhaps cultural barriers too, but it is good to note the successful events supported by those who love the English choral tradition. My friend John Crothers, a former chairman of the RSCM in Ireland who now lives in Paris, recently organized several very successful residential courses in Provence. But here again, these were one-offs for a niche market.

It is very different in the Channel Islands, which were part of the Diocese of Winchester. There were about 25 affiliated churches in both Guernsey and Jersey – many medieval – and one in both Sark and Alderney. I made several very enjoyable visits to all these islands, and events were well supported. I remember particularly a visit to St Peter's, Sark where there was a large choir with a conductor from the UK and a very capable young organist from Sark. Afterwards we hitched a lift on a passing horse and cart towards the ferry back to Guernsey!

The 25 churches affiliated to the RSCM definitely enjoyed occasional visits from RSCM staff. I eventually ran into considerable opposition from the Addington management for arranging tours, as I was told that these were not cost-effective; in other words, their affiliation fees were insufficient to cover the cost of my travel. This is the kind of argument I have always found difficult to stomach. It seemed right to me that the total amount of the UK affiliation fee should be available for a reasonable amount of work anywhere. The spending of money in this way could be seen as an investment. So often accountants hold too much power; even though their job is to balance the books, they could surely do it more imaginatively.

The way the RSCM has developed worldwide over the past 90 years is a remarkable story. Rightly individual countries now have greater autonomy and are not ruled as a far outpost of empire from the British headquarters. But the bonds between those who make music in church are still strong, as is the thirst for new ideas and the desire to learn from one another in an international context.

THE EVANGELICALS

Up to the 1980s, Anglican churches from 'high' to 'low' tended to have robed choirs. In the evangelical churches the prayer book services of Matins and Evensong were still widely used; the worship had considerable formality. But increasingly this was seen as an obstacle to outreach and evangelism. A much greater variety of musical styles was beginning to be used, often involving instrumental accompaniment. Folk and popular material were of course nothing new: the revivalist hymns of the late 19th century echoed the tunes and harmonies heard in the opera house, just as hymnody from Luther to Vaughan Williams had used secular folk material. But the arrival of contemporary idioms inspired by lighter music from musicals, jazz and pop was something new. This jarred with many in the pews, but to others it brought musical and spiritual liberation. This conflict of musical preference in worship caused an irate reaction from the traditionalists, and also disdain from the innovators for anything which seemed old hat. Many saw the RSCM as a body opposed to change; the more evangelical churches of all denominations thought there was nothing in it for them. I had the difficult task of trying to prove this was not the case and that the RSCM was prepared to help to improve standards across the board.

My predecessor Lionel Dakers found 'renewal' music a difficult area. He played for time and postponed making decisions, saying once again this was something for his successor! I immediately started to write about the need for change in *Church Music Quarterly*. In this I was supported by Richard Morrison, the Editor at the time, who wrote an editorial entitled 'Bringing in the folk'. When I began to study the matter, I discovered that the contentious music in question was highly conservative in melody and harmony. Good new hymns and songs were being written, many of which have stood the test of time. Indeed, they have found their way into 'respectable' hymn books, including *Ancient and Modern* and the *New English Hymnal*. What was alien in this music was the orchestration, which made use of electric guitars and percussion along with the more usual acoustic instruments. For many this seemed too much like a discotheque. I have to admit that I sometimes feel very uncomfortable if this sound is like a jazz or pop combo. But then of course my whole background has been in cathedral music. Yet I have come to appreciate that there are many first-rate players in these groups who make beautiful and accomplished sounds.

How did I begin this programme of musical reconciliation? Well, I got around and widened my experience. One of my first visits was to a charismatic rally in Brighton. At the very beginning, as the first chords sounded, the whole assembly leapt to their feet and started raising their hands. I was surprised they felt moved before the event had hardly begun – perhaps a gesture of expectation. But the eagerness for hand waving led one wag to remark that one only knew they were moved by the Spirit when they put their hands down! The memorable thing about this rally was the leader, Graham Kendrick. I was impressed by his quiet, serious manner. I soon became familiar with his tunes, many of which like 'The Servant King' are now mainstream. I discovered he lived near Addington Palace and he came to visit us there.

Another early visit was to All Souls, Langham Place. I already knew the Director of Music, Noël Tredinnick, a former Head Chorister of Southwark Cathedral and an outstanding musician. He had developed a musical programme at All Souls which embraced all styles. There was hearty traditional hymnody accompanied by the well-maintained organ, and more popular material accompanied by instruments. The church prided itself on not being a church with a fondness for charismatic rave-ups, but for being a teaching church. The musical menu was all-embracing. There was a good choir which might sing an anthem; and on the occasion I visited, the All Souls Orchestra formed of London professionals played a movement from a Mozart symphony. The unifying factor was quality. Whatever was played or sung had to be the best attainable. I noticed this when another church, St Mary's, Reigate, played at Southwark Cathedral for the retirement service of Archdeacon Peter Coombs. I particularly remember two outstanding trumpeters. But in both these churches, good music is played in a relaxed ambience – rather like the Proms. It reminds me of Stravinsky's dictum that music should be 'loved' not 'respected'.

Increasingly I came to rely on the support of Noël Tredinnick, as also of Robin Sheldon, at that time Director of the Music in Worship Foundation. Both of them had a balanced approach: they wanted good music to enhance worship. They were 'both/and' people. George

Carey, Archbishop of Canterbury, once remarked to me that like him I was a 'both/and' person, and I took this as a great accolade. My personal musical preference was somewhat different, but I felt in my position of leadership at the RSCM that I had to be even-handed and supportive of every type of church musician.

What did more than anything to affirm the RSCM's support for church music across the spectrum was the festival organized in 1991 at the Royal Albert Hall jointly by All Souls and the RSCM. It was modelled on 'Prom Praise', which was the brainchild of Noël – but in this instance it was called 'Psalm Praise' as the original suggestion for the event came from the publishers, Hodder and Stoughton, who wished to publicize the launch of their two new books published in association with Jubilate Hymns: *Songs from the Psalms* and *Psalms for Today*. I assembled a robed choir of 500 singers from around the country. One choir, St Mary's, West Derby, travelled from Liverpool. They and the congregation were accompanied by the All Souls Orchestra and Martin How on the organ. There were also items in a lighter style, organized by Christopher Norton, which involved a small band. The event was compèred by Bishop Michael Baughen of Chester, formerly Vicar of All Souls, Langham Place. He did this superbly. He even remembered when time was getting on and the choir from Liverpool might miss their last train. So he thanked them and sent them away a little early. The whole occasion was an enormous success. All the music was set to Psalm texts ranging from Plainsong to Parry's 'I was glad', metrical psalms sung by all and items from the new Hodder and Stoughton books, accompanied by instruments and sung by soloists or the whole RSCM Choir. The Albert Hall was full. People came from far and wide, including a coachload from St Mary's, Bury St Edmunds. It was very much a case of actions speaking louder than words. It did the RSCM a great deal of good, making us many new friends. Our sphere of activity certainly widened. I remember the Bishop of Dorking, Ian Brackley, telling me he had recently visited a very evangelical church in the 'Bible belt' of Woking. He was amazed when a forthcoming RSCM workshop at the church was announced.

He said he had no idea the RSCM had any connection with churches like that.

We backed up this work by publishing material aimed at helping to bridge the gap between musical styles. Most significantly we produced two books of worship songs which included input for chorus. These were *Sing with all my Soul* and *Worship in Song*. Both were best-sellers, particularly the first. Archdeacon Norman Warren, a member of the RSCM Council, had selected the items. The musical editorship was in the hands of my friend William Llewellyn. He did some arrangements himself and farmed out the rest, many to cathedral organists, a fact that did not go unnoticed with those with a penchant for eyebrow-raising. I knew we had succeeded when one day, when visiting Oxford, I happened to look in the attractive 'classical' Baptist church near Carfax. I was delighted to see they had invested in a complete set of *Sing with all my Soul* for the congregation. We had promoted the book well. I remember two very well-attended events in the north at Leeds Parish Church and at the Church of Our Lady and St Nicholas in Liverpool. It had caught on.

Another influential event was the publication in 1992 of *In tune with heaven*, the report of the Archbishops' Commission on Church Music. This was instigated by Lionel Dakers just before he retired, and funded by *Hymns Ancient and Modern*. I was a member of this Commission, which met 14 times between July 1988 and October 1991. It included wide representation from the Anglican, Roman Catholic and Free Churches and embraced all traditions within those denominations. The Chairman was Rt Rev'd Timothy Bavin, Bishop of Portsmouth, who expended a great deal of time and energy on the project. It contained a wide range of background material, including the theological basis of music in church and a comprehensive survey of the practice of worship through the ages. There were many written submissions and presentations by individuals. I remember with amusement a talk on liturgical dance and the embarrassment of some of the more dignified members of the Commission when we were instructed in dance steps in the Great Hall at Addington. The report reads well and I think unlike many reports it did make an impact. What it stated clearly was that whilst safeguarding the great musical traditions of the church, the church music of the future would be more diverse and comprehensive. This tuned in exactly with what I was trying to achieve at the RSCM.

The popular RSCM liturgical planner, *Sunday by Sunday*, is an example of how far we have travelled. In addition to recommending organ music and choir anthems, it provides lists of hymnody, worship songs, psalm material and music suitable for children for each Sunday of the liturgical year. All traditions and all denominations will find there the information they need. Though this project started only just before I retired, its success gives me great pleasure as I had a strong wish to start a project to give the membership the help they needed in choosing music. During the RSCM Appeal, I was wondering where I might look for some financial assistance for a liturgy planner. It occurred to me that monks spend a great deal of their time in church and might like to help us plan services. So I wrote to the Abbot of Nashdom to ask whether the Trust he administered might give us a grant. I was astonished when by return of post I received a cheque for £5,000. This gave the idea a great boost. We had had some behind the scenes assistance I believe from a friend of mine, Very Rev'd Peter Moore, formerly Dean of St Albans, who was Chairman of the Pershore Nashdom and Elmore Trust.

At my interview for the job I was asked if I was willing to try to build bridges between classical music and lighter forms of church music. I am grateful that with the help of friends and a bit of luck I went some way to achieving this. I was of course criticized by the die-hards. But in fact though church music is now much more diverse, cathedral music has never flourished more, with congregations increasing rapidly. On a normal Sunday morning there are four times the number of people in Southwark Cathedral than when I was Organist there.

But there is no denying that choral music has greatly declined in parish churches. There are far fewer choirs. The reason for this is not to do with a takeover by the light music interest; it is to do with the sharp decline in church attendance over the past 30 years. There are fewer children in choirs because there are fewer families, but also because social and educational pressures are much greater these days. Children and their parents are less willing to commit to a weekly programme of rehearsals and services. They want to do other things on Sundays. But despite all this, church music is still very much around – and quite often the standards are higher than they used to be. And more children and adults contribute now as instrumentalists.

BRINGING IN THE GIRLS

Up to my arrival at the RSCM in 1989, very little had been done to even up the opportunities for boys and girls in church choirs. They were still dominated by boys and men. In the early days under Nicholson, the top line in Anglican choirs in the UK was usually sung by boys. This was a reflection of the cathedral tradition adopted for use in parish churches. When I sang in my local church choir at St Paul's, Shipley (1945–1952), we had a large number of boys. In all the surrounding Anglican churches in this part of Yorkshire, large and small, the treble line was sung by boys. This was the situation countrywide, which Nicholson took for granted when he initiated the work of the School of English Church Music from 1927 onwards. He went further – he vehemently supported this tradition. The note at the beginning of his Lenten Cantata, 'The Cross of Christ', states that the solo passages should be sung by a boy, and that if a sufficiently confident boy was not available, the solo passages should be sung by two or three boys together. He then added that on no account should these solos be sung by women! Of course you could never say such an outrageous thing these days.

Even when I began work at the RSCM in 1989, the cathedral choirs and the RSCM cathedral singers were boys only, a position that was rapidly becoming untenable. By now many girls were singing in parish choirs and three cathedrals had introduced girls to sing alongside the boys: St Mary's Cathedral, Edinburgh; St David's; and Bury St Edmunds. My predecessor, Lionel Dakers, deeply conservative in these matters despite having four daughters himself, did realize that change was inevitable but said it was something his successor would have to deal with. This was one of several hot potatoes I had to pick up in the early days.

My first step was to add a girls' section to the three cathedral singers' groups in the north, the south and the Midlands and west of England. Thus when Dr Richard Seal, Organist at Salisbury Cathedral, decided to found a girls' choir to sing independently of the boys who had been singing since the opening of the new Cathedral in 1358, I gave him my full support. I wrote an article in *Church Music Quarterly* in 1990 entitled 'Male and Female created He them'. For this I was widely criticized; there was much talk of the 'thin end of the wedge' by those who thought this would undermine the unique medieval tradition which had survived the Reformation in the 16th century and the Civil War in the 17th. Britain is the only European country in which these traditions of music in the greater churches are still intact. However, the Salisbury initiative has now been taken up by the majority of cathedrals. And far from undermining it, the tradition of cathedral singing has been reinforced; that roughly double the number of children are nowadays choristers must surely be a good thing.

I was always keen to emphasize the importance of the role of boys. Much of the choral repertoire up to the end of the 18th century and beyond was written for boys whose voices contribute very specially to the sound of this music. Listening to the choir of the Thomaskirche in Leipzig, the music of Bach sounds as he intended it; or the recent fine recordings of the complex liturgical music from the late 15th century from the *Eton Choirbook* sung by the boys of Christ Church Cathedral, Oxford capture perfectly the glorious and luminous sound world of the late medieval church.

Now 23 years after the setting up of a musical foundation for girls at Salisbury, this new tradition has definitely taken root. There will always be special circumstances in some colleges and cathedrals where the only choir will be male. Some cathedrals cannot afford the endowment necessary for a girls' choir, and wish to concentrate on maintaining the excellence they have inherited. In the great chapels of Oxford and Cambridge, a good case can be made for maintaining the choral foundations as intended by the founders: for example, Henry VI at King's College, Cambridge and William of Wykeham at New College, Oxford. But in such colleges there are also now opportunities for women undergraduates to sing in chapel on a regular basis.

Encouraging girl singers is already having important consequences, in that many are now developing into first-rate organists, choral directors and singers. Surprisingly, cathedral music is still male-dominated by men in positions of leadership. But things are changing with an increasing number of women being appointed. I believe that the situation will continue to change in favour of women, in the same way that female orchestral conductors are coming very much to the fore. The path to musical leadership must be open to all, irrespective of gender.

THE APPEAL

It became clear once a decision had been made to plan for the move to Cleveland Lodge, Dorking that the RSCM would have to raise an appeal for funds. From the outset, it was made clear that this would not only be for bricks and mortar. The Appeal Brochure, 'Sing with the Spirit', clearly stated that a proportion of the money raised would be given to the expansion of the educational programme. A committee was convened under the chairmanship of Humphrey Norrington which included those with a financial background who had an interest in music. The committee was responsible for overall planning and for trying to locate potential sources of funding in the business world. The day-to-day work was organized under two headings: an approach to the membership and an approach to trusts and charities. We were fortunate to secure the services of Jo Churchill to work with the area committees in the UK. I knew her from my days at Southwark Cathedral where she was Secretary of the Friends. Very soon she established a rapport with the membership and worked with the area representatives to arrange a great many fundraising events. We also appointed Tim McDonald, introduced to me by my good friend Nicholas Frayling; Tim had been very involved with raising money for Great Ormond Street Hospital for Children. He was with us for a year, during which time I worked closely with him as we approached trusts and charities. From 1994 onwards we worked hard on both these fronts, receiving a particularly positive response from the RSCM membership.

I thought we should inaugurate the Appeal at a great public occasion. This was the service in Westminster Abbey on Friday 3 June 1994, which turned out to be a great show of strength. The Queen (Patron of the RSCM) was represented by the Duchess of Gloucester; the address was given by the Bishop of Portsmouth, Rt Rev'd Timothy Bavin; and the Archbishop of Canterbury, Dr George Carey, President, pronounced the Blessing. The Dean and Chapter were fully supportive of this venture. One of their members, the Very Rev'd Colin Semper, was particularly helpful on an ongoing basis and formed a very good relationship with Tim McDonald.

The Abbey Choir directed by Dr Martin Neary sang at the service. The music was celebratory, including Walton's Coronation 'Te Deum', and an anthem which John Rutter wrote specially – a setting of the RSCM motto, 'I will sing with the spirit and with the understanding also'. This was made available to RSCM choirs by the Oxford University Press at a reduced price. It formed a kind of signature tune for the Appeal.

What made the occasion particularly memorable was the response of the membership. I had been nervous that we would not achieve a decent size of congregation; but as Roger Butler (Acting Chairman) and I stood for half an hour by the west door greeting people, I could hardly believe how many turned up, and from a distance, like Professor Ivor Keys from Birmingham. By the start of the service, the whole of the choir and transepts were full. It was I believe the last great RSCM gathering, and indicated the kind of support we would get. I was relieved and happy with the success of the occasion, which set the tone for the next few years when so many worked hard to raise money. In fact by 1996 around £560,000 had been raised to fund the move to Cleveland Lodge and to provide extra services and resources to benefit the membership.

The local committees had very good ideas. Jo Churchill wrote a regular column in *Church Music Quarterly* offering various suggestions for fundraising. There were the usual coffee mornings and sponsored sings, augmented by the sale of Addington Bears (wearing chorister robes and ruff) and even RSCM luxury chocolate bars bearing the Appeal logo. In the December 1994 edition of *CMQ*, it was noted that the membership had raised £200,000 with 648 members having donated and 304 having pledged to raise money. There were also some regional singing days. One took place in the fine medieval churches in Ipswich, many now redundant, which had been opened specially. I had previously not realized the extent of these buildings which testified to the prosperity of the port in the Middle Ages. A similar event was held in the churches of Brighton. But the biggest was in the City of London, where many groups made music in the Wren churches. The musical pilgrims were provided with an itinerary. The day ended in splendid fashion at Holy Sepulchre, Holborn Viaduct with a performance of Tallis's 40-part motet 'Spem in alium nunquam habui', ably conducted by Jonathan Rennert on minimal rehearsal. But the vast musical edifice did in the event hang together very well.

Perhaps the most memorable event was the Royal Reception in May 1996 hosted by the Queen at St James's Palace. I had wondered how I might secure the attendance of our Royal Patron. The only person I could think of who knew the Queen well was the Archbishop of Canterbury, Dr George Carey. When I asked him to write to Buckingham Palace, he agreed readily. The reply said that we could use St James's Palace, but it might not be possible for the Queen to be there. So I asked him to write again saying that she had supported us in the past at Addington Palace and the Royal Albert Hall, and we needed her support now more than ever. This worked and made the event a great success, raising £15,000 for the Appeal.

I met the Queen at the back door of St James's Palace and then introduced her to 20 RSCM members carefully selected from around the country. She was taken from room to room and in each one was introduced to the musicians who gave a short performance. There was a wind ensemble from Dulwich College, the choir of St Alphege's Church, Greenwich conducted by my old pupil Stephen Dagg in a performance of Byrd's 'Sing Joyfully', and a group of musicians from All Souls, Langham Place directed by Noël Tredinnick. At the end of the evening I escorted the Queen down a staircase to her car. At the halfway point on the stairs, we had arranged for the girls' choir of Croydon Parish Church to be singing as she walked past, conducted by Christine Phyllis. We were not intended to stop. But Her Majesty decided to do so. She then talked with Christine and the Vicar of Croydon, Canon Colin Boswell. The evening had in fact over-run by 40 minutes. I got the impression the Queen enjoyed the occasion. In fact, she seemed reluctant to leave. When we arrived at the door, she continued to talk with me for quite some time. I was impressed by her knowledge of those involved. I found her very easy, totally without 'side' and extremely friendly and relaxed in manner. It was a truly great occasion in the annals of the RSCM.

Then in 1997, Martin Neary directed a 'come and sing' performance of Fauré's *Requiem* in Westminster Abbey. The 1,000 singers' tickets rapidly sold out, giving a welcome boost to the Appeal. The great service at the Abbey and the singing events were free of charge to the RSCM. At all points we met with goodwill and generosity. We felt we could not possibly fail with support like this. When the Appeal closed in June 1997, £620,000 had been raised.

The other prong of the Appeal, the approach to charities, bore fruit but perhaps not quite so richly as we had hoped. It was difficult to convince trusts and charities to give to a 'network' rather than to a clearly defined project. At a time when so many charities were pursuing the same limited amounts of money, it was never going to be easy. But we did have our successes. A generous donation from the George Livanos Trust enabled us to restore and in one case move two organs.

It was essential that we took a limited number of instruments from Addington to Cleveland Lodge. In the case of a couple of grand pianos and a chamber organ, the expense was not great. Moving the Harrison organ from the Chapel at Addington to Dorking was a more costly matter. This instrument given to Sir Sydney Nicholson for the Chapel at St Nicolas College, Chislehurst was a fine and resourceful instrument very much *multum in parvo*, inspired by the ideas of Colonel George Dixon. It had followed us around. During the war it was set up in the crypt of Canterbury, where it sounded very fine. Then it travelled with us to Addington where it fitted perfectly into the chapel, the former conservatory of the palace. I felt strongly that it now should go to Cleveland Lodge. It was part of our history, and it fitted comfortably in the large music room there. A grant from the Livanos Trust of £25,000 made this possible. A further grant of £25,000 from the same source enabled us to restore Susi Jeans' organ at Cleveland Lodge, made in 1936 by Eule the East German organ builders. It had a gentle sound and was probably the first neo-classical instrument in the UK. This was the instrument I had heard as a schoolboy when Susi Jeans gave broadcast recitals. I felt it was right that we should bear the responsibility of putting this significant organ into good working order.

In addition to the money raised by the 'Sing with Spirit Appeal', in October 1996 it was announced that the RSCM had been successful in securing a Lottery award of £1,153,000. The first phase of the building work at Cleveland Lodge was entirely funded by the RSCM's own resources, principally from Appeal funds supplemented by legacies. One stipulation of the Lottery award was that funds could only be used for capital work – not for running the RSCM programme.

THE APPEAL

As with all charities in modern times, fundraising is always on the agenda. Though the main thrust of the Appeal was roughly over a two-year period, the need to raise money continued. In my last year as Director (1997–1998), when the administration of the RSCM was undertaken by Roger Butler, Vice-Chairman, and Ian Fraser, a member of the council who lived nearby, I arranged a series of 'Come and Sing' events in great churches. There were nine events in many notable buildings, including St Paul's Cathedral and King's College, Cambridge. In some places the piece sung was 'The Crucifixion' by John Stainer, in others Fauré's *Requiem*. The response to this initiative was amazing; all the concerts were a sell-out.

The Stainer at St Paul's involved a huge body of singers, filling the dome, and joined by the Cathedral choristers and two of the Vicars Choral as soloists. The event conducted by John Scott was truly memorable, as was that at King's College, Cambridge conducted by Stephen Cleobury when the assembled choir filled the ante-chapel. Numbers had to be limited. I conducted the Fauré at Christ Church, Oxford where David Goode, the Assistant Organist, managed miraculously to make their Austrian Rieger sound like Harrison and Harrison. I also conducted the Fauré at Dorking Parish Church, again with a capacity attendance of singers, many of whom lived in the vicinity of Cleveland Lodge. I asked Lionel Dakers to return to his old cathedral at Exeter to conduct the Stainer; James Lancelot conducted it at Durham and Ian Tracey at Liverpool. At the other venues, at Lichfield and Guildford, the event was similarly directed by the Cathedral organists Andrew Lumsden and Andrew Millington

Remarkably these occasions, again administered by Jo Churchill, cost the RSCM nothing, with the result that there was a clear profit of £27,000. There were no facility fees and all the performers gave their services; any necessary expenses were covered by the Deans and Chapters. Being a strong believer in eyeball to eyeball conduct, I got on the train and visited all these places to make the necessary arrangements. The business was always conducted speedily. At Liverpool Ian Tracey readily agreed to give his services; he then telephoned the Dean, who said he would be pleased to make the Cathedral available and to pay the cost of the soloists.

Again, all this was a remarkable gesture of support for the RSCM. The money raised gave a boost to the cashflow in that financial year. In fact 1998 was the only year in the last 40 years that the RSCM broke even. Unfortunately this was achieved by making cuts to areas like the publishing of music. This was unfortunate, but the need to get on top of the annual finances was a serious matter. The success of the money-raising efforts during 1994–1998 was heart-warming, and at the time it seemed to augur well for the RSCM's future stability. That this was sadly not the case is a matter which must be taken up elsewhere when the subsequent record of the RSCM's affairs comes to be written.

THE MAGAZINE

Church Music Quarterly has been a significant factor in the workings of the RSCM, particularly during the past 25 years. The technological advances in printing and the now universal access to colour reproduction have greatly facilitated the production of the magazine and enhanced its attractiveness. The dissemination of news and the writing of instructive articles has made the publication indispensable in binding together and informing the membership worldwide.

Richard Morrison was briefly Editor before he moved to important work as music critic of *The Times*. I enjoyed working with him. His successor, Trevor Ford, with whom I worked for almost all of my time, turned out to be a great asset and a good friend. He was supportive of what I was trying to do, deeply interested in the RSCM and full of good ideas. From the outset, I used the magazine to set my agenda. So instead of random jottings from the Director, I determined to write a serious article each quarter. This could be of a theological or philosophical nature outlining the basis of what we were trying to achieve. But generally the subject was topical or practical – or even contentious. The use of popular music in worship and the introduction of bands were both matters which raised the blood pressure. I dived in head first to tackle them head on. For some of the more traditional members, I was insufficiently hard line. I was often accused of selling the RSCM down the river. This I thought unfair, as I made it clear from the outset that I was committed to the organ and the choral tradition of the church. Sometimes my articles reflected these differences, like the article I wrote in support of girls' choirs in cathedrals. And sometimes I examined a matter in depth, like the disagreements between the protagonists of the electronic organ and the supporters of the pipe organ. I spent a good deal of time writing these articles; they were important to me. So I thought it worthwhile reprinting four of these in an Appendix.

But as well as being a vital forum for ideas, I very much valued the 'parish magazine' aspect of the publication. This humanized it and was to be the source of many good ideas used elsewhere. It also emphasized the worldwide dimension and gave a sense of belonging to a great movement. It is a great pleasure to me to see how, since my retirement, the magazine has continued to develop and expand. It is an indication of health and wellbeing. The latest *Church Music Quarterly* to arrive through my letterbox leaves me in no doubt that the RSCM is in good shape – brimming over with life and new initiatives.

THE MOVE TO CLEVELAND LODGE

The move to Cleveland Lodge actually took place in July 1996. This was ably masterminded by Charles King, Secretary at the time. To get ourselves to a point where we were in a position to move was a colossal exercise. Coping with the size of Addington Palace with its large public rooms, 40 bedrooms and innumerable cubbyholes – wine cellars, butlers' pantries, gunrooms etc. – was no mean feat. Over the 43 years the RSCM had occupied the palace, a great deal of clutter had been accumulated. I set about trying to investigate this material, in which I was ably assisted by Jean Castledine, Secretary of the Southwark RSCM committee. We had to look at everything. In so doing, we amassed a very considerable archive, most of which moved with us. There was a huge photographic record going back to 1927. There were also things like Sydney Nicholson's Doctor of Music robes, found in a drawer in an attic. I gave this clearing out as much of my attention as possible, as I felt strongly that knowledge of the past is essential for charting a suitable route into the future.

In addition to truckloads of archives, there was the whole library that had to be transported, undertaken with great care by the long-serving librarian Dr John Henderson. He arrived somewhat out of the blue towards the end of my time at Addington and continues to care for all this remarkable material, now at Salisbury. The preservation of the valuable archive has been very much down to him. He has organized and written with the help of Trevor Jarvis, assistant librarian, three very interesting historical books: *They fly forgotten, as a dream*, on 46 church musicians born between 1840 and 1870; *The Chislehurst Years* (1928–1939) on Sir Sydney Nicholson, based on his unfinished autobiography *Musings of a Musician*; and most recently *The Addington Years* (1954–1996).

The task of reallocating many of the organs and pianos at the palace fell to me. I managed to place three of the organs: the largest by Harrison found a home at Stoke Gabriel in Devon; the original Chislehurst organ went to a church at Cheshunt in Hertfordshire; and pipes from the organ in the basement (known as the Dungeon) were used in the restoration of an instrument in Cape Town. I took the two best grand pianos to Dorking; the 18 uprights eventually found good homes.

The palace also contained some fine furniture which had belonged to Sir Sydney Nicholson, I believe originally from his family home at Totteridge, High Barnet. I chose the best of this to go to Cleveland Lodge; regrettably some of it had to be sold. But I thought it important to safeguard our heritage and the link with the founder. All this sorting and relocating added greatly to my workload. But I felt that unless I did it assiduously, many of the archives, instruments and furniture would have been lost – even abandoned to a skip.

The arrival at Cleveland Lodge was somewhat chaotic. For the next two years we were living in a building where reconstruction work dominated our space. Much planning had been done leading up to this by Michael Hockney, a member of the Council, who was determined to achieve the best possible transformation. At the time I had my doubts about this, and now, with the benefit of hindsight, I feel we should have employed a local builder to do the essentials on the building: making it rainproof, doing essential plumbing work and repainting the whole structure inside and out. We could then at least have moved in and seen how we felt about it. Leaving the building more or less in the shape we found it would also have enabled us to renegotiate with the Jeans family, had we decided that it would be in our best interests to find another option.

This is all past history – and hindsight is a blessed thing. Its location next to Boxhill railway station and close to the M25 meant that Cleveland Lodge was easily accessible and could in the long term have become a good administrative and musical centre. But this is not how it turned out, much to my regret. Ultimately the RSCM decided to leave Cleveland Lodge and move to Sarum College, Salisbury in the first week of June 2006, not long before John Harper himself retired as Director in 2007.

So many things could be said on this subject, but it is better they should remain unsaid and the eye should now be firmly on the future. Ultimately the RSCM is built of people, not bricks and mortar. And no retired person, if wise, should pass judgement on decisions made by successors.

AN RSCM POSTSCRIPT

The years I spent as Director from 1989 to 1998 were the busiest period of my life. Much of the work I enjoyed – that which involved music and people. We managed to change the image of the RSCM and prevented the overseas branches from leaving. We also raised a great deal of money.

But I was from the beginning a reluctant Director. My trade is that of an organist and choirmaster and importantly a teacher. I hesitated about applying for the job and only did so under persuasion on the final day for the receipt of applications. I was surprised when I was appointed from a strong shortlist of four candidates. The Chairman of the selectors, Montague Durston, tried to phone me the night before with the news, but I was not home till late after attending the opera at Covent Garden. I was actually handed the letter offering me the job next morning by the Bishop of Wakefield, a member of the panel, at the consecration of George Carey as Bishop of Bath and Wells which took place at Southwark Cathedral, where of course I was directing the music. Once the news had sunk in, I felt honoured and determined to give of my best. If I were asked whether I enjoyed my time at the RSCM, the answer would be an emphatic 'yes'. The personal and musical factors were something I relished.

But I have never held a job where such a vast range of skills was required. I had to be helpful when required to act as 'agony aunt'. On quite a number of occasions I was consulted by distinguished church musicians who had run into difficulties of one sort or another. I was not sure how helpful my responses were, but at least I was able to lend a listening ear. I once remarked to a cathedral organist that I was never sure what advice to give; his response was that if I was prepared to meet and listen, this was the main thing, which was reassuring. The cases where parish organists came to complain about their vicars I handled more cautiously. The early 1990s were years when the choral and organ tradition of the Church of England was being questioned in some parishes by priests in favour of a more varied musical menu. I could sympathize with the organists who felt threatened, and with the clergy who had to live with inflexible attitudes and poor musical standards. I discussed the issues, but I refused to write letters in support of complaining organists. I knew from experience that there are always several sides to every argument.

When I retired from the RSCM I was given a good send-off and farewell party at Westminster Cathedral Hall, at which I was given several very generous gifts. I also attended many regional farewells and presentations. The Devon area committee arranged a trip by steam train down the line from Buckfastleigh to Totnes, at the end of which they presented me with a coffee machine which I still use every day. The Auckland committee in New Zealand sent a sheepskin rug. And in the final days just before I retired at the end of August 1989, the Chairman and Council gave a dinner at the Salters' Company Hall in the City. There was so much kindness from many areas, too numerous to mention individually. But I was immensely grateful for it. The details of my retirement plans were sensitively handled by the Chairman and Council. I felt they marked the close of a major period of my life in fitting style. For this I shall always be grateful. The varied experiences and enjoyment I received from the work remain firmly in my memory. I have no doubt in my mind that, though a decent organizer and administrator, I was not born to be a managing director. I was first and foremost a musician, and thank goodness there were plentiful opportunities to use this gift. At the end of the day, the making of music is what the RSCM is all about.

CHAPTER SEVEN

All Saints, Margaret Street

A LONG-TERM CONNECTION

David Hutt, the Vicar of All Saints, I knew well as he was on the staff of Southwark when I arrived in May 1976. We were working colleagues for my first year and a half in the job. I had had a long-term connection with All Saints, first visiting it in 1960 when the choir school was still functioning. From my arrival in London, I became closely associated with the church. Dr Eric Arnold, the Director of Music, was a great admirer of Christopher Robinson's work with the choir at Worcester and had in fact as Assistant Clerk arranged for the Musicians' Company to sponsor a concert by the Worcester choir at St Johns, Smith Square. The moment I arrived at Southwark, he got in touch with me and invited me to play. We soon became good friends. I played the organ for a Christmas concert at All Saints in 1976, and then at a special Evensong when the restored chancel roof was rededicated in 1978 at which I had to play Elgar's 'Te Deum', which I knew well from our 1969 Worcester recording. The choir made an LP in 1980 on which I played some of the accompaniments, particularly of Mozart's *Missa Brevis in D*. Margaret Street became an important port of call throughout my Southwark years.

Dr Arnold, the Organist and Director of Music, was actually a chemist by profession. But he was also an able musician with high professional standards. His role was pivotal in reforming the choir after the closure of the choir school at Easter 1968. Until that time, the music had been under the direction of Michael Fleming, who had done an excellent job. The singing of the boys was much admired. It therefore came as a mighty bombshell when he heard during Lent from the Vicar, Fr Kenneth Ross, that the following day the parents would receive a letter announcing the closure of the choir school at Easter. There was no discussion. The Vicar thought it inevitable that it must close; he wanted to avoid endless discussion of the matter. Naturally Michael was upset and left when the school closed, but not before he had secured places for all the younger boys in cathedral choirs. The congregation was outraged and there was much ill feeling.

But Kenneth was right. The facilities in the school were prehistoric and liable to be condemned; the cost of maintaining it was not sustainable. There had also been difficulties getting suitable staff. It was all held together by the much-loved matron, Mary Baddeley, who did much to keep the show on the road. Discipline was draconian. The good boys put up with this, but it was difficult for those less musical. If boys looked at the congregation they were punished – also when they turned the page at the wrong point. The copies were marked with a sign to indicate when the page should be turned – the 16 boys were expected to do so at precisely the same moment!

It was at this point that Eric Arnold, Michael Fleming's assistant, came to the rescue. Though he deplored the disappearance of the boys, he undertook to rebuild the choir, with four sopranos taking the place of the boys. He did this with considerable success – but without losing the very special style of singing and the characteristic musical repertoire which had evolved over the years from the time of Walter Vale, William Lloyd Webber and John Birch. Much of that which made the choir special was salvaged, and although girls now sang the top line, it still sounded like the choir of All Saints, Margaret Street. Eric continued in post for 20 years until his death in 1988.

To many he appeared formidable and gruff; but it was a classic case of his bark being worse than his bite. He was a traditionalist and didn't care for change. He was sometimes heard to remark that 'this is how it is done at Margaret Street'. But when one got to know him, he was much less formidable. The choir, at least the inner cabinet, was very sociable in those days, with long lunches on Sundays at a restaurant in Soho. One wonders how they found the strength for a 5 o'clock practice followed by Evensong and Benediction. Margaret Street, like many Anglo-Catholic churches in those days, had a coterie of hard-drinking, hard-smoking inmates. When I sometimes went to lunch with the churchwarden, Denzil Freeth, and other members of the congregation, there was a smoking break between each course! How times have moved on. Towards the end of my time, the choir was very moderate in its drinking habits and quite a few members were teetotal.

I was glad to be able to write an obituary of Eric Arnold in the *Church Times* when I stressed the important work he had done to maintain the musical tradition. I also mentioned some of his eccentricities, particularly that he kept a pet owl in an aviary in his garden at home! He was an interesting man, an important link in the musical chain which stretched back to the first organist, Richard Redhead, in 1859. Without him, the tradition could well have been lost.

But there were other factors which linked me to All Saints. About the same time as I moved to Southwark Cathedral in May 1976, my old Oxford friend David Sparrow was instituted as Vicar of All Saints, Margaret Street. He was a contemporary at Pembroke College where he read History and then Theology, arriving there after military service in 1956. He hailed from Finchley, where his parents ran two grocers' shops. He was very much a London boy, boasting a grammar school education, as did so many at Oxford in those days. He had developed a vocation for the priesthood, so naturally became part of the college chapel congregation at a time when services were well attended by the undergraduates. In fact there were a good number of ordinands at Pembroke in those days, when many students of real ability were deciding to serve the church. It is not so today; but still a small number of able students find their vocation while at university. I regularly meet some of them in the Diocese of Southwark, which still has a magnetism for younger clergy, both men and women.

David sang tenor in the chapel choir as an enthusiastic but not (he would have agreed) the most accomplished of choristers. He was quite a character: sociable and noted for dispensing drinks or afternoon tea at his lodgings in Pembroke Street. The keen chapel types were usually known as the 'God squad'. Those who attended services poured out of the chapel after said Evensong on weekdays before massing for dinner; and similarly a group of perhaps 40 who had attended the Holy Communion service at 8.30 a.m. on Sundays had their own corporate breakfast in one of the fellows' dining rooms attached to the hall. In retrospect, I am not sure this was a good idea; it was a rather flagrant display of their supposed piety.

On graduation, David went to Lincoln Theological College before being ordained to a curacy at St Stephen's, Rochester Row in Westminster where the able Tony Tremlett was Vicar and later became Bishop of Dover. It was Tony I believe who influenced David's promotion to second chaplain to Archbishop Michael Ramsey at Lambeth Palace. Here he worked as Secretary of the Doctrine Commission, at which he was punctilious; but the day-to-day administrative chores were not much to his liking. Michael Ramsey had a rather low opinion of his abilities in this area. However he did not stay long. He was soon off to be Chaplain of St Catherine's College, Cambridge. I believe Tony Tremlett had a hand in this too. Here, David was very happy. He was remarkably successful in this work – perhaps one of the last of the great 'Oxbridge' chaplains. He went down well in the Combination Room and was additionally elected to a fellowship of the college. I still meet people all these years later who benefited from his remarkable ministry there. I occasionally visited him, staying in a college guest room. I practised on what was their fine Harrison organ and enjoyed occasional meals on High Table. On one of these occasions I was sitting next to an English don, Tom Henn, who was very gracious and tried to put me at my ease. Knowing I was a musician, he came out with the wonderful remark – 'I had a cousin once who was rather musical; his name was Stanford!'

After nine years in Cambridge, David was offered the prestigious living of All Saints, Margaret Street at the age of 40. As I was now Organist at Southwark, we started to meet a little more often. His time there was from the outset marked by tragedy and difficulties. He had hardly been there five minutes when it was realized that the stone vaulting of the chancel was becoming unsafe. He had to initiate an urgent appeal for funds for its repair. But more tragic personally was when, at the age of 42, he was diagnosed with cancer. From then on he had to cope with terminal illness. But he put on a brave front and remained until his death in office three years later. He showed amazing stoicism. Months before his death, he had to preach from a cushioned chair at the chancel gate, so frail had he become. This upset many in the congregation with weaker sympathies; but the stronger members admired his courage and fortitude, and still speak with great affection of him. Perhaps he should have retired sooner; but he didn't because he never gave up hope.

There were those who argued David was not the right person for Margaret Street. He had received his formation in the Church of England in a 'middle-of-the-road' parish at St Luke's, Finchley. His perception of the church changed at Oxford, and he became very much a Catholic in his thinking. He became doctrinally 'high church', but although he didn't object to the ceremonial practices in Anglo-Catholic parishes, I felt the trappings were not a natural part of his interests and habits. Nevertheless, I believe his time at Margaret Street was good for the parish. His frank intellectual vigour and his pastoral gifts brought much-needed humanity and reality – even if the reality was sadly blended with mortality. After his funeral and memorial service in 1981, I went less to Margaret Street, though I did keep in touch from time to time.

I would subsequently discover another link with Margaret Street when I became Director of the Royal School of Church Music. Sir Sydney Nicholson, founder of the RSCM, was actually related to

Dr Walter Vale, the legendary organist of All Saints (1907–1939), who had married his niece, daughter of his elder brother, Sir Charles Nicholson, the well-known architect. Sir Charles was married to the sister of the actor Sir Laurence Olivier. That explains why Laurence as a child became a chorister at Margaret Street and starred in the choristers' theatrical productions, produced by their ambitious Vicar, Father McKay. Sydney Nicholson visited the church from time to time and wrote a certain amount of music for the choir. Two small pieces, an 'O Salutaris' and a 'Tantum ergo', are still sung regularly. So in becoming Nicholson's successor but two at the RSCM, I found I eventually followed him to Margaret Street when I was appointed Organist in 1989. My move there for all the reasons outlined seemed pre-ordained!

HOW I CAME TO ARRIVE AT MARGARET STREET

Within days of leaving Southwark at the end of January 1989, I received a surprise visit from David Hutt, Vicar of All Saints. I had seen him six months previously when he invited me to join John Birch (a former Organist and subsequently Organist of Chichester Cathedral) to help him and the churchwardens appoint a successor to Eric Arnold. As usual the congregation had views, and the process was politically not entirely straightforward. However, it was decided unanimously to appoint a strong candidate, Murray Stewart. He took over in September 1988, but by Christmas he had decided the post was not the right place for him. He had underestimated the time commitment: he had many irons in other fires and had to be away quite often. I think also the musical and liturgical tradition of the church was unfamiliar to him. He decided to leave and handed in his notice at Christmas, giving three months' notice that he intended to finish on Easter Sunday.

It was this that occasioned the Vicar's unexpected arrival on my doorstep. He spoke for around half an hour of how difficult it had all become and how some in the congregation had told him he ought to have appointed another candidate. Eventually he came to the point and said, 'I suppose what I'm really trying to say is will you come yourself?' Recovering from the shock, I explained that I was just about to take over as Director of the Royal School of Church Music, an organization with worldwide connections. I did however say, knowing I had an interval before starting my new job, that I would be prepared to be Acting Organist to help them out for a while. But I made the proviso that they must create the post of Assistant Organist, as I knew I would have to be away a good deal. If they were prepared to accept these terms, I would do the job for a short period, then take stock of how things were going.

I had a good deal of assistance from the former Assistant Organist (Norman Caplin) and a former Organist (Michael Fleming) who was one of my colleagues at the RSCM. Importantly, on my suggestion, the church appointed my second assistant at Southwark (Nicholas Luff) to help me. We were vetted on Mothering Sunday 1989, and started work in earnest on Low Sunday, which was early that year on 2 April. Things went well and eventually I allowed the Parochial Church Council to confirm my appointment – unlike Widor who was technically Acting Organist at St Sulpice, Paris for 67 years as the authorities forgot to confirm his appointment!

It was hard work – and I did have absences, sometimes of up to a month. But it gave me a choir of my own. I had fretted greatly about losing my Southwark choir, but suddenly this other was placed in my hand. Continuing as a practising church musician preserved my sanity, and I think the benefits to the RSCM were considerable. Had I been married with a family it would have been impossible as sometimes it meant a seven-day week, though of course there were pleasant interludes and holidays. When I retired after ten years at the RSCM in 1998, I continued at Margaret Street for another five and a half years. In fact my 15-year tenure was the longest in the whole of my professional career.

TWO ASSISTANT ORGANISTS

Nicholas Luff

The appointment of Nick was an essential factor in making it possible for me to take on Margaret Street. It was good of him to respond to my request for help. We were close friends of 11 years' standing. He was ideal as it was essential to have someone I could trust. The need for an assistant was never more obvious than on my first Sunday. As it was in the Easter holiday, Nick was away taking a necessary break as he was a full-time school teacher. That meant I had something of a baptism of fire, particularly as a soprano who was leaving that Sunday had chosen Gounod's *Messe Solennelle* for her final service. The choir were used to conducting themselves, but it did mean I had to learn the Mass – quite a handful, but I much enjoyed it. I certainly touched the ground running. Some musicians are snooty about Gounod's Mass, but I can't agree. It goes very well on the organ, especially the rather Handelian parts of the Gloria. It is full of memorable tunes and ingenious harmonic sequences. If one omits the Credo, it is of a very manageable length for the liturgy on a great occasion – for instance All Saints' Day.

I first met Nick in November 1978, when I had been at Southwark for two and a half years and was approaching my 42nd birthday. After the arrival of John Scott as Assistant Organist in September 1978, I increasingly felt the need for an extra pair of hands. There were times when John had to be away and occasionally I was involved in work elsewhere. My meeting with Nick happened by chance – and in the light of subsequent experience maybe it was providential. I walked into the Cathedral one day at the beginning of November and heard someone practising the Fauré *Requiem* in preparation for the annual Trinity College of Music performance under James Gaddarn at the lunchtime Eucharist on All Souls' Day – 2 November. I paused to listen and thought it rather good. So out of curiosity I went to the organ loft and found Nick, then in his final year at Trinity College of Music. We introduced ourselves. I found he had lodgings with the family of Godfrey Hurst, a primary school headmaster who was organist of a church in Mottingham. I knew him well as he was on the RSCM Diocesan Committee, of which I was Chairman. Eventually I asked Nick to play for a service, and as he continued to play for us we gave him the title of Deputy Organist. This was on the suggestion of John Scott, who thought the title appropriate as Nick deputized for him or me when one of us was not available. One such occasion was when the Southwark choir toured East Anglia in 1981 and sang Evensong in Ely Cathedral; meanwhile John was required to play for the wedding at St Paul's of Prince Charles to Lady Diana Spencer!

Nick soon became a much-loved figure at Southwark. In fact wherever he worked he was much loved. He was very much a 'people person', quiet and caring in manner with considerable awareness – also with a delightful down to earth sense of humour. But above all, he was highly professional in his music-making. He was a good sight-reader, a fluent improviser and an extremely sensitive accompanist. Later on, when he played every Sunday at Margaret Street, Rex Stephens, a repetiteur and voice coach at the Royal Academy of Music who attended the High Mass fairly regularly, commented to me that Nick was the best choral accompanist he had ever heard. He said 'he listened to the choir carefully, watched the beat and was completely at one with the singers'. At Southwark, there were many occasions when we witnessed this expertise. In 1985 John Scott went on a short sabbatical and it fell to Nick to play the organ for a broadcast of Choral Evensong, which he did superbly.

As we worked together over 11 years, Nick and I became great friends. I was fortunate in that my assistant and deputy both thoroughly understood this eccentric Yorkshireman they found to be their boss. Later on at Margaret Street, the churchwarden Denzil Freeth remarked on Nick's loyalty. He made the telling comment that during my long absences away on RSCM business, the choir would find it impossible to drive a wedge between the Organist and the Assistant Organist. In fact we gave Nick a special title – that of Associate Director of Music. This seemed right in that he had to take full responsibility when I was away for a significant period – on one occasion for six weeks in Australia and New Zealand. Actually I must confess that I pinched the title 'Associate Director' from All Souls, Langham Place round the corner. My friend Noël Tredinnick invented it for his assistant, who he regarded as an equal part of the team.

Nick was very practical. He was able to do repairs on his car, for instance, or help put up pictures in my flat when the walls needed to be plugged and drilled. As another of his friends, Nicholas Frayling, said in his address at Nick's funeral: 'He was as good under a bonnet as at a console.' Well endowed with common sense, he was a very good judge of character. To discuss difficult personal matters with him, when perhaps a singer had been troublesome, was always helpful and reassuring. Throughout my time at Southwark and during the decade or so we worked together at Margaret Street, he was a wonderful sounding board and a great support. And he was much appreciated by the congregations in both places.

Sadly his stay at Margaret Street came to an end at the beginning of 2000 – in fact the last Sunday before Lent. It was no secret that he had developed a drink problem. However much his friends tried to help, it was of no avail. His retirement was sparked off by an almost unheard of altercation I had with him about a broadcast of Choral Evensong. He felt things were becoming too much for him. But I did persuade him to stay for three months so we could thank him properly. He went out in a blaze of glory with the thanks of all of both choir and congregation.

In the following 14 years he and his long-term partner Christopher Caine kept in close contact with me. I used to visit them every three or four weeks at their home in Forest Hill. We would then go out for a meal, usually at our favourite curry house, Gurkha's in Sydenham Road. But before that, in 2001, he became seriously ill. He had to retire from his school post at St Bartholomew's Church of England Primary School, Sydenham and later in the year underwent a liver transplant at King's College Hospital, which successfully restored his health. I visited him on several occasions in the intensive care unit at Kings, after which his partner Chris and I would go out for a meal, usually at the Greek restaurant at the bottom of Camberwell Grove. It was occasions like this which deepened my friendship with Chris.

But there were also many happy occasions, such as my visits to see them in Normandy with Nick Frayling, at their cottage in Neuville-sur-Tonques, 30 km south of Lisieux. When they decided to sign a Civil Partnership in 2009, they asked Nick Frayling and me to be witnesses. We were deeply moved that they should want us to do this. We all went off to the Registry Office in Lewisham, just the four of us, to sign the legal documents. They did not want a fuss – not even the optional 'versicles and responses' articulating their decision. But it was one of the most solemn occasions I have witnessed. We all put on our best suits. We were greeted by the Registrar, a friendly and helpful young woman who led us through the formalities. It was an austere business; but we then celebrated the importance of what they had done. We went round the corner and caught the train from Ladywell station to Charing Cross. I was then able to provide a bottle of champagne at the Athenaeum before we went off to the Dorchester for a long lunch!

The years that followed were times of increasing illness and frequent stays in hospital. However, Nick kept his organ playing going as Organist of the South London Crematorium, morning organist at St Clement's, Dulwich and evenings at St Giles' church, Farnborough. He was still much in demand for special occasions, at some of which I deputized when he was unable to cope, such as the Red Cross Christmas concert at Westminster Central Hall and the annual carol service of the Prince's Trust at Holy Trinity, Sloane Street. In my mid-1970s I was able to cope with all the stairs and the impressive organ at the Central Hall – but nowadays my nerves would probably not be adequate for such high-powered exposure. Nick in his good days took it all in his stride. He was much in demand.

Life all became very difficult. Chris had to hold down his senior post at Trinity Laban School of Music. He was however helped by

Brenda Renshaw, Nick's deputy head in Sydenham; and I made sure I was on hand when needed, as did Nicholas Frayling. In the end Nick died on 1 January 2014, his 57th birthday. Though we expected this, that did not soften the shock or the sadness. His subsequent funeral at All Saints, Margaret Street in January was impressive beyond belief. The church was completely full; people had come from far and wide, including two young men from Gambia who had been supported financially in their education by Nick and Chris. I helped Chris to choose the music for the High Mass of Requiem, during which at Chris's request I conducted Edgar Bainton's anthem 'And I saw a new heaven'. The Mass was celebrated by the Vicar, Alan Moses, and a memorable address was given by Nicholas Frayling, marked by its understanding and humour while not shirking the difficult issues. The two incumbents with whom Nick had worked in South London also took part – Maria Coulter of St Clement's, Dulwich and Matthew Hughes of St Giles, Farnborough. In addition to Nicholas Frayling, Dean of Chichester, two other Deans, of Southwark and Westminster, were present. I mention this because it underlines the breadth of the congregation when friends from far and wide meet to honour a special person. The following day at the committal at the South London Crematorium, the whole of the office staff came. And within a week, a memorial plaque marking Nick's time as organist had been placed on the wall behind the organ in the chapel. Nick would hardly have believed the affection with which he was surrounded in his death. Would that things might have been different. But I count it a rare privilege to have known Nick and to have worked with him for 22 years.

Andrew Arthur
Having advertised for a new Assistant Organist, we interviewed four strong candidates. They had to play the organ, rehearse the choir and most importantly accompany the choir in the Gloria of Mozart's *Coronation Mass* which I conducted. To these musical tests was added an interview with the Vicar.

Since the beginning of the 20th century there has been a strong tradition at All Saints for the performance of Mozart, Haydn and Schubert. It was important that the candidates should feel comfortable in this repertoire. We also asked them to accompany a hymn, again very necessary as the art of congregational accompaniment has gone into considerable decline in recent years. Hymn singing has always been important at the church. Even in the 19th century, the quality of the congregational singing was remarked upon. A friend of mine visiting from the US said he was totally unprepared for the explosion of sound all around him – like the Southern Baptists, he said.

In the case of Andrew Arthur, the decision to appoint was unanimous. The choir were asked for feedback on the basis that there would be no discussion of their views. In all the recent music appointments made at the church, the views of the choir have been in tune with those of the appointing committee. This is not always the case. I once was adviser at a cathedral where the selectors were of one mind about who they wanted, but the men in the choir indicated that on no account should this candidate be appointed. I think they feared that their comfort zone might be disturbed. However, it was decided to disregard their views. The following Sunday when the Dean announced the appointment to the choir, the boys cheered. And that was that! 'Out of the mouths of babes and sucklings hast thou ordained strength'!

Andrew Arthur soon became a good team player. He had been Organ Scholar of Gonville and Caius College, Cambridge and also a keen Head Chorister of Chelmsford Cathedral. He kept up his singing skills and deputized as a counter-tenor at St John's College, Cambridge for Christopher Robinson. After graduating, he stayed in Cambridge for a while to teach Music undergraduates Techniques of Composition, Fugue etc. He continued this work when he was with us.

On arrival at All Saints, he found his boss to be about 40 years older than himself; naturally he took some time to adjust to my old-fashioned ways. Like most just out of university, he was full of new ideas. I would not say he knew it all. I think my Romantic approach to music and repertoire came as something of a shock. But he soon got used to playing the anthems of Bairstow and Stanford and was exceptional in his accompaniment of the Viennese Masses. We soon shook down and I came to rely on his professionalism. He was always well prepared, and particularly so for the annual BBC broadcast of Evensong.

Andrew had developed a passion for the music of J. S. Bach making a speciality of the organ works. He occasionally travelled to Holland for lessons from Jacques van Oortmerssen, and every year he took part in the Carmel Festival in California which featured the music of Bach. But he did play a wide repertoire; I remember with pleasure his commanding performance of Messiaen's 'Dieu parmi nous' at Christmas.

When the time came for me to retire, he wrote me a wonderful letter in which he said that he had come to appreciate my Edwardian Romanticism, which I considered to be a very great compliment. Knowing of my admiration for Sir John Barbirolli as an Elgar conductor, he bought me a boxed set of CDs of Sir John conducting Elgar. As a sixth-former I had regularly heard his performances at St Georges' Hall, Bradford. When I moved to Worcester, it was frequently said that Sir Adrian Boult was the quintessential Elgar conductor. When he performed at the Three Choirs Festival, his well-tailored suits and Edwardian manner made for comparisons with the outward appearance of Elgar. But my friend Edgar Day, who knew Elgar well and often heard him conduct, was adamant that Boult was nothing like Elgar. There was none of the fire and passion which were the hallmark of Elgar's own performances.

I have been fortunate to work with good assistants, especially at Southwark. I was glad that Andrew, as successor to Nicholas Luff at All Saints, more than maintained the high standards to which I had been accustomed. A few years after my retirement, he moved back to Cambridge as Director of Music at Trinity Hall, to which shortly afterwards was added a fellowship of the college.

FIVE ORGAN SCHOLARS – A SOUND INVESTMENT

After the new Vicar, Alan Moses, had been with us two years, he suggested we institute an organ scholarship for young musicians. He rightly said we had to hand our expertise on to future generations. I had known this all along, but being rushed off my feet at the RSCM I had hesitated to take on a new project. So in 1997 our first scholar arrived, Mark Laflin, who I had previously met on courses for young organists at the RSCM. He was on the Royal Academy gap year course, during which he was awarded the Organ Scholarship at Keble College, Oxford.

I met him once there when I was doing research into organ pipe decoration. The original organ at All Saints had painted front pipes, which during the 1910 restoration were removed to the inside of the organ. The question was whether the architect, William Butterfield, made his designs follow the contours of the pipework, or did he maintain a horizontal scheme though the pipes increased in length? We needed to find out as we were planning to paint the exterior pipes at the suggestion of Mark Venning of Harrison and Harrison. The Butterfield pipes at Keble gave the answer – the horizontal option.

After Oxford Mark became a successful schoolteacher at Godolphin and Latymer School for Girls in Hammersmith, and later at Kingston Grammar School. Happily he still plays the organ, until recently at St John the Divine, Richmond where he encountered the interesting organ of 1896 by William Thynne, a brilliant voicer originally trained by T. C. Lewis.

Mark was followed in 1998 by Justin Luke, who came to us after an organ scholarship at Rochester Cathedral. He had a real feel for the sound of the organ and was a good accompanist and improviser. At this stage the assistant organist was often unwell, so Justin assumed a pivotal role: playing very well for a live broadcast of Evensong in 1999. He was a friendly and constructive person and we became good friends. Since he left in 1991 we have met only infrequently. He has been Assistant Organist of the Savoy Chapel for many years, whilst holding a day job as a schoolteacher.

His successor David Pipe was about to leave school at just 18. He came from a family who were members of the United Reformed Church; both his parents were hospital consultants. He was not particularly advanced when I interviewed him, but I could see that he had what it takes. He did a year with us, during which he made great progress. He went to Downing College, Cambridge as Organ Scholar, eventually ending up as Assistant Organist at York Minster. In May 2016 he moved to a new job at Leeds Roman Catholic Cathedral, where he runs a very successful diocesan training scheme for organists, which he inaugurated. He has kept in touch with me from time to time.

In early spring 2016 David drove me to Acklam, 17 miles from York, to visit Francis Jackson, then in his 99th year. Francis was waiting for us at the gate, took my hand and led me down the garden to his cottage where he lived alone – but looked after by his children and the farmer's wife next door. It meant a great deal to me to make this visit. I had known Francis for 65 years since his early days as Organist at York. I remember meeting him for the first time when he was practising for a recital at Leeds Parish Church. My teacher, Dr Melville Cook, Organist at Leeds, at the end of my weekly lesson asked me to take a programme to the organ loft. I knocked and went in to deliver it. But instead of just thanking me, Francis held a little conversation with me, asking where I came from etc. It was a little thing, but I was greatly impressed. In my later teens, I was a frequent visitor to the organ loft at York. I learned so much watching him play for Evensong. One day he asked me to play a voluntary. I was so thrilled that my feet hardly touched the ground from York to Bradford! From these early experiences, Francis and I and his wife Priscilla became lifelong friends.

Our next organ scholar was David Humphreys, who arrived in 2002 after a year as Organ Scholar at St Albans, where he had been a chorister. He went on to be Organ Scholar at Jesus College, Cambridge.

At first I found him slightly abrupt in manner and thought he was bored with the liturgical goings on at Margaret Street. But he had real ability and gradually we began to get on. He has subsequently done well and is currently Assistant Organist of Peterborough Cathedral.

Our last appointment, in 2003 five months before I retired, was Peter Dutton. He had done things rather differently. He had gone up to Trinity College, Oxford to read Theology and whilst there had become Organ Scholar. We got on well. He did a great deal to bring himself up to speed during his year with us. He eventually did well in school teaching and is currently organist of Christ's Hospital, Horsham.

I have gone into some detail to show just how right the Vicar was. The young scholars who came to us have all done well and would acknowledge that the church gave them opportunities to further their musical education. It was a sound investment and one which continues to bear fruit, with many of them distinguishing themselves as organists and several of them achieving distinguished academic posts in universities. It was all very worthwhile. It made extra work for the Director of Music, but after I retired from full-time work at the RSCM in 1998 I had the time to give. I always saw the scholars on Sunday afternoon and quite often in the week as well to see how they were getting on. It was work I enjoyed and in which I had plenty of experience, especially from my Worcester days.

TWO VICARS

Canon David Hutt

Since we met in 1976 at Southwark, David Hutt had kept in touch. I visited him when he was Chaplain of King's College, Taunton and later when he was Vicar of St Albans, Bordesley in Birmingham. In fact I played a small part in his move there. We had gone for a short holiday at Lake Vyrnwy in mid-Wales when he told me he had just received a letter from Keble College, Oxford who were the patron of the parish, asking him whether he might be interested a post there. His immediate reaction was that he didn't want to go to Birmingham. I asked him whether he knew the church, one of Pearson's very best buildings. He didn't, so I said he ought to look into it. He eventually took the living and I think did some of his finest work there. He built a new parish centre and brought the parish into the realms of sanity. He also planted a thousand daffodil bulbs in the vicarage garden. He was always an expensive vicar!

Eventually the move to Margaret Street came in 1986. It was not a straightforward task. The church was in the grip of several powerful figures whose motto was 'this is how it is done at All Saints, Margaret Street'. He made few changes, but he did improve the look of Butterfield's fine church which had got rather dowdy and very unkempt. The Organist, Eric Arnold, did not like interference; the Master of Ceremonies, Derek Bevan, thought his reign in the sanctuary was beyond question; and the senior churchwarden, Denzil Freeth, was a strong character who could express himself very forcibly. I saw this at first hand when I became Organist three years later. The Vicar had little room for manoeuvre without a row of epic proportions. I think David opted for the quiet life. But he ran the church well – he had after all been a professional soldier – and it was not unusual to see him around with a clipboard in his hand. The church was still very well attended and things ticked over comfortably.

But things changed. Several of the grandees joined their ancestors and then in 1992 the vote in the General Synod in favour of the ordination of women caused unsettling tremors. It was no secret that the Vicar favoured the priesthood of women, though he did not express his opinions often in public. But it was inevitable that things were never going to be quite the same.

David was a great supporter of the music and really just let me get on with it. But by creating the Choir and Music Trust Fund in 1992, he did much to safeguard the fine musical tradition – and he certainly avoided having to discontinue sung Evensong on Sundays. The trust fund was very successful. It had the support of most of the congregation, for whatever their differences, they were united in their love of the music. Several members of the congregation died around this time – very conveniently, as the money they left amounted to around £350,000, enough to get things off to a good start. Since then there have been many benefactors, enabling the fund to rise to a market value of 1.6 million pounds, producing in the region of £60,000 per annum interest to help pay the musical expenses of the choir and organists. This was all down to the imaginative initiative of David Hutt. It will always stand as a testimony to his nine years as vicar.

David was a great character with a quirky sense of humour. There were many enjoyable moments. He didn't like trouble, so tended to avoid it; but he was capable of taking a stand when it was really necessary. His transfer to Westminster Abbey to a residentiary canonry where he ultimately became Sub Dean was a surprise move. I think the Dean wanted an Anglo-Catholic representative on the Chapter. David enjoyed Westminster, as he liked the grandeur and the great occasions. But he did make sure he retired just before the Dean, Dr Wesley Carr, as he had no wish to hold the reins as Sub Dean during an interregnum.

At Margaret Street, the church benefited from David's ability to think big. It also benefited from the fact that he was his own man and could be relied on not simply to maintain an unthinking Anglo-Catholic orthodoxy. He had vision and knew things must ultimately change.

Prebendary Alan Moses

The arrival of Alan Moses in July 1995 was very much the beginning of a new era. He was the first married Vicar since the end of the 19th century. His wife Theresa and two children were a welcome addition to the parish community. Both Alan and his wife came from County Durham. He had studied Theology at the University of Hull, trained for the priesthood in Edinburgh Theological College, after which he was appointed curate and later vicar of Old St Paul's in

Edinburgh in the heart of the city just off the Royal Mile. His Vicar was the redoubtable Richard Holloway, later Bishop of Edinburgh – a distinguished thinker and author. Alan eventually moved to Dundee to be a parish priest before arriving in Margaret Street.

His whole experience had been in the Scottish Episcopal Church. In church terms he was liberal and inclusive and a supporter of women's ordination, which didn't go down well with the many conservatives in the congregation at Margaret Street. But despite this agenda he was himself very wedded to the catholic tradition of the Church of England, particularly in the daily recitation of Matins and Evensong and the celebration of the Mass. In his day the clergy had a punishing schedule: starting at 7 a.m. with meditation, followed by Matins, leading up to the morning Mass at 8 a.m.; at lunchtime a priest was available to hear confessions before the Midday Mass; in the evening Evensong (preceded by another opportunity for confession) leads into the evening Mass at 6.30 p.m. The Masses are celebrated by one of the clergy or another priest from outside the parish, but the in-house clergy attend the daily offices. The surprising thing is that people still come to these services, but not in such numbers as 20 or 30 years ago. It is a remarkable fact that the Mass has been celebrated every day since the church opened in 1859. Many clergy would have thinned out the daily schedule, but it is a sign of Alan's commitment to the Anglo-Catholic spiritual tradition that this has not happened. But in the sung services, changes have been made to make them more user-friendly, without in any way devaluing the musical and liturgical tradition for which the church is famous worldwide.

As was to be expected, changes have ruffled feathers – for many the comfort zone is all important. But he decided early on that if changes were not made in his first year, they would never happen. The greatest furore was over the service in Commemoration of the Faithful Departed on All Souls' Day. This was a macabre affair at which there was a fake funeral. A catafalque and coffin covered by a beautifully embroidered pall was set up, intended as a potent reminder of mortality. When I first experienced this custom, I did not like it.

It seemed to stretch symbolism beyond the credible. Several vicars would have liked to get rid of the catafalque, but their courage failed them. Alan grasped the nettle and completely reformed the service to give more hope to it. There was of course an outcry, but Alan stood firm. He was adamant that things should change. He once said to me that the service was rather like a necrophiliac's night out!

In all the changes that took place in the sung services, he involved me fully. We formed a very good relationship over the eight and a half years that we worked together. He was an interesting person with a lively academic mind. He read widely and was very well informed. I often formed the impression that he would have liked to have been an academic. I also thought the church could have served him better by eventually facilitating a move to a post which suited his talents. The Church of England lacks perception over career paths, and what is worse they often end up making disastrous appointments to important jobs. Some might have considered Alan too difficult and perhaps a touch stubborn. He was also very much a Northerner, which the more lah-di-dah might have found off-putting. But there was no doubt in my mind that he was a very considerable person and ought to have had significant preferment.

Perhaps his greatest strength was the way in which he cared for those who were ill, the elderly and the dying. For them he would drop everything. I have never personally experienced another priest who showed such steadfastness and compassion at the difficult moments in life. The addresses he gave at funerals were agreed by all to be outstanding. He had the gift to get things just right from his personal understanding of the person. He gave much interesting information and when appropriate a touch of humour. I heard many of these words of appreciation at funerals and memorial services. Often they were for well-loved members of the parish community; sometimes they were for well-known public figures. But whatever the occasion, they were perfectly crafted, well delivered and always deeply moving.

Alan was a good preacher at Sunday services too. He could always rise to the occasion. Sometimes he was on the long side, and occasionally he got into theological lecture mode which showed erudition but for some was on the heavy side. On quite a number of occasions he tackled the book of Ecclesiastes – and each time he quoted a comment I heard in a lecture at Oxford from Cuthbert Simpson, that characterful Dean of Christ Church, when he summed up the book by saying that its theme is 'life is just one damned thing after another'! Sitting at Alan's feet I have learned a good deal over the years.

During the 25 years that Alan has been in post, the complexion of the congregation has changed markedly. It has attracted a wider range of people, many of whom are not card-carrying Anglo-Catholics of the old school, but who are attracted by the place and the high standard of the services in which good music has always played a key role. I think it is a great tribute to Alan's ministry that he has appealed to a wider clientele, who like what they find but are also inclusive in their thinking and prepared to admit they are still seeking. Not everyone would agree, and it would be odd in a church like All Saints if there were not people of firm opinions and conservative by nature who look back to the glory days of Anglo-Catholicism. Despite differences of opinion, there has been mutual respect and a desire to make things work for the good.

I would be wrong to conclude an account like this without mentioning Alan's whole-hearted commitment to the restoration of Butterfield's great building – a programme which has continued for 20 years, including the re-roofing in Welsh slate, the restoration of the organ and the complete renovation of the interior, including the stained glass, the uncovering of the stencilled patterns in the walls and the return to the original colour scheme in the decoration of the nave roof to the architect's revised scheme of 1895. Some may think that Alan will be remembered for his restoration work. He will be, but also as a bold and compassionate priest who did not shirk the difficult decisions but transformed the thinking of many in the congregation. I had a good relationship with him, eased along by occasional give and take.

I have been fortunate in the clergy I have worked with, in seven places of worship, and organist over a period of 65 years, starting from the time when I was a very green 17-year-old at All Saints, Bingley where the Vicar Canon William Gunter first set the tone with his gentle encouragement.

THE CHOIR

The professional choir of 12 men and women at All Saints could not be described as 'rent-a-choir'. There has always been a high level of commitment to the music, but also to many other things which make the choir special. In my time the musical sound was recognizable as that of All Saints. It had deep roots in the past, both in repertoire and in the manner of performance; there was a devotional feel to singing which had been handed down. There was also a high degree of discipline in the deportment and behaviour, unlike anything I had previously experienced. There was silence in the sacristy whilst we waited for the service to begin. This set the whole tone – the careful way of walking in, the way the hands were held in front of the chest when not singing and the complete absence of talking in the choir stalls, let alone the reading of books and newspapers during the service. Occasionally one had to work at maintaining the standard. If someone had been behaving inappropriately, it was easy to check it. I merely suggested that the choir was front of stage, clearly visible and that they had to remember that there were sometimes in the congregation those who had come there for solace from grief or great trouble, perhaps recently bereaved or getting to the end of their tether trying to deal with an autistic child. There were sometimes people who had walked from the Middlesex Hospital round the corner, having been given bad news about the progress of their cancer. To an approach like this the response from singers was immediate.

When someone came for audition for a place in the choir, I gave them an indication of what was required. I said that even if they could not affirm many points of doctrine, they had to take the worship seriously. Like the members of an opera chorus, matters of deportment and direction were not optional; they were necessary, including the requirement to genuflect.

When I started in 1989 there were some very good singers, some of whom went on to sing in opera or on the concert platform. But there was also a tradition of 'staying'. Those who had active freelance work, as with the BBC Singers or The Sixteen, mostly managed to keep up their commitment to All Saints. This meant a degree of flexibility in granting leave of absence. One girl, a brilliant jazz pianist, occasionally went on a tour of *Evita* and other musicals. But if she was within striking distance, she would drive long distances after the show on a Saturday night to be in her place in the choir stalls on Sunday morning. There were also good singers who earned their living outside music – for instance former Oxbridge choral scholars who worked in the City but wanted to keep up their music. Throughout my 15 years as choirmaster, we were greatly blessed by good singers who were interesting as people and often considerable characters. I got great pleasure from working with them week in, week out.

Recruitment was never a great problem, but one had to keep on the lookout for talent. When I first started, we had no basses and a vacancy for a soprano. In time, good people were found. In fact one person I appointed in 1990, Ian Lyon, is still there 35 years later! As with most choirs, the members created a good social life. Many of the singers regarded the visit to the pub after services as obligatory. In my early days I suppose we drank far too much, but in recent years, as with many young people today, the choir has become much more abstemious. When I left, a number of the choir were teetotal. But it was natural that musicians should want to get to know one another; as Sir Adrian Boult once remarked, 'music making is 70% personal relationships' – though I imagine his preferred beverage would have been Horlicks. I never thought singers were at the top of the drinking league. Rugby players, bellringers and brass players always seemed to be way ahead. The *esprit de corps* generated by after-work fraternizing had a good effect on the music-making; but it showed in other ways too. Under my successor, Paul Brough, the whole choir often put on a cabaret evening in the large basement of the Phoenix pub in Margaret Street in aid of the church restoration fund. This was a highly professional affair which raised a lot of money from capacity audiences. The choir worked for weeks perfecting their act. When professional musicians give freely of their time to this kind of venture, it is clear that attitudes and commitment must be of a high order.

The choir was very much an integral part of the worship at the church. The renowned organist Jane Parker-Smith, who often worshipped at the church, was clear in pointing out that she did not come solely for the music – she came for the whole package: music, liturgy, the building and the preaching, all of which blended seamlessly into a satisfying whole.

THE CONGREGATION

When I arrived in Margaret Street, there were some in the congregation who had been there for around 50 years. Some of these were remarkably advanced in their thinking: then in their mid-60s, they were passionate advocates of women's ordination. The leaders of this faction were former Assistant Organist Norman Caplin and his wife Lily, and Patrick Spencer, a long-term server, and his wife Margaret. They loved All Saints and did not wish to upset the apple cart, but they longed for change. Equally stalwart were two women, Helen Clayton and Frances O'Neil, churchwardens in the 1990s, who were both keen advocates of women's ordination and for women an enhanced role in the life of the church. This indicates that All Saints has never been set in concrete. The Vicar from 1952 to 1969, Fr Kenneth Ross, was also a keen reformer and Chair of the Church of England Liturgical Committee. All Saints has always prided itself on its Anglican roots, but over the past 25 years the congregation has gradually become more diverse.

There have been so many notable characters in the congregation – some very colourful – I must describe some of these. I will start with the churchwardens. Denzil Freeth had been in post for many years when I arrived. He had been a junior minister in Harold Macmillan's government, but had retired from politics at the 1974 election. Thereafter he worked as a stockbroker. He was a generous donor to the church anonymously. But everyone knew who had provided money for the current project – usually to do with the restoration of the church. He was for quite a number of years a churchwarden with Christopher Rawll, whose day job was medical officer at Heathrow airport.

He was followed by Helen Clayton, a lecturer at Roehampton College in the Theology department. She was charming and intelligent – and there was no doubt of her support for the women's ministry. But she is too rarely known for proposing Resolution A and B (no woman vicar and no woman administering the sacraments), because she felt the most important thing was to make slow and steady progress. This worked well. At that time, All Saints was not ready for women clergy. She played a leading role in the appointment of the new vicar – a fact not without significance. This was done in company with Denzil Freeth – they were chalk and cheese, but both saw the need to pacify the congregation. But on the retirement of Denzil, the parish selected Frances O'Neil, making two women in post, a striking fact already noticed. It was not long before Helen retired – she was in declining health.

At that point, John Forde, a younger traditional member of the congregation, was elected as churchwarden. Eventually Frances felt the need to retire. At this, the Vicar Alan Moses caused an immense stir when he arrived at the election of the churchwardens to say that he was going to exercise his right and appoint to the vacancy himself. He realized there was a push to get another traditionalist elected, and he thought this was not right for the parish. Amidst considerable uproar, he appointed Christopher Self, who it should be noted was re-elected by the parish the following year! Eventually John Forde and he certainly settled into a good relationship. They didn't agree, but John felt that Christopher was very reasonable in the way he reached out to those who wished to make difficulties. This partnership lasted many years and has provided the basis for reconciliation, taking into account the views of all members of the congregation.

Now for a quick snapshot of the many characters I have enjoyed knowing. Jean Harmsworth immediately comes to mind. She had been a teacher in a prison; she also had an extremely loud singing voice. Some winced when she got going. But I felt she gave a good lead. This led her to give herself the title of 'the organist's favourite congregational singer'! There were so many who gave their services. Kate Burling came every day after work to keep the washing and ironing of the sacristy in order. Christine Ellis cleaned the church every Monday, into her 80s single-handed. The servers were a loyal band who were organized by Cedric Stephens, a former floor manager at John Lewis. He was of a generous nature, and was with his partner Alan very much respected in the parish. There were a number of doctors – one a Welshman, Michael Duggan, who used to read a lesson each year on St David's Day wearing a leek in his button hole! Another, Stephen Miller, with a great interest in music was there as a young man when I arrived. There was the usual coterie of precious young men who might wear a boater and carry a silver-headed cane. But they fitted in, kept in order by Cedric who was not pleased by frivolity. There were Rod and Beatrice whose wedding I played for, and surprised me by choosing Palestrina's 'Missa Iste Confessor'. They became regular members of the congregation, bringing up a charming daughter, and to this day they all cycle to the church from their home in South London. There were also many single men. And single women, many of whom were Oxbridge graduates, and some I had known a long time, like Jean Castledine who I had invited to be Secretary of the Southwark Diocesan RSCM Committee. When she moved to live at Morden College, she changed church from All Saints, Dulwich where she had been a member for many years. There were of course traditionalists, many of whom were good friends. Kate

Hodgetts ran the bar. She made her views well known; they were not mine, but I always had time for her as she represented an aspect of the parish which had to be respected. There were times of course when the bar became a conspiratorial chamber. But we lived with that!

A married couple, Martin and Jasmine Cullingford, leads me on to the subject of church plants. Nowadays, church planting (that is, a certain number from an existing successful church moving on to revive or create a new congregation) is seen as an Evangelical pastime. But originally church plants were almost always in Anglo-Catholic parishes. Richard Redhead, first organist of Margaret Street, moved after only a year in the new church to the recently built St Mary Magdalene, Paddington where he established the tradition of the church which included a choir school. In recent years, All Saints has become linked with both the Annunciation and St Cyprian's, Clarence Gate. All are outstanding buildings (Butterfield, Walter Tapper and Ninian Comper). Originally the Vicar of All Saints was asked to take over as Priest-in-charge of the Annunciation, as the Vicar with a freehold was no longer able to perform his duties. This meant some attendance. But most of the work was done in conjunction with an assistant. Then Fr Gerald Beauchamp arrived to be Assistant Priest at Margaret Street. He had been a distinguished Vicar of St Mary-le-Bolton, Kensington before going to the Cowley Fathers in Boston Massachusetts to test his vocation to the religious life. In the event, he returned to the UK and found his way back into the Church of England via Margaret Street as assistant priest. Eventually he took over as priest-in-charge at the Annunciation with a growing congregation, and later was put in charge also at St Cyprian's. Thus, almost by accident, three famous churches have joined together in a church plant operation which is bringing much new life to these parishes. There are occasional shared services. The whole venture was creative and successful.

Before leaving this rapid sketch of the kind of people who can be found at All Saints, I recall with pleasure the old friendships I sustain. Elaine Caplin is now on the PCC; she is married to Philip

Norman, who frequently appears. Then Colin Symes, a friend with Caplin connections, now on the PCC. They are part of the progressive vanguard of the church, which leads us to the subsequent development. In 2016 the Church of England required parishes to scrap Resolutions A and B and just pass a resolution to apply for alternative episcopal oversight, which meant a whole package of no women celebrants at Mass, no visiting women clergy, and oversight by an alternative bishop with unsullied Catholic credentials. At this stage, there was a very large majority of traditionalists on the PCC. When the more progressive and inclusive element of the congregation realized what was going on, they awoke from their slumbers; the result was that at the PCC elections in 2016 and 2017, this majority was almost wiped out. This has led to much greater dialogue and to a realization that around 70% of the congregation, to various degrees, belonged to a modern church seeking for a solution to modern theological thinking and modern life. It has been a remarkable episode. But it all goes to show that nothing can be taken for granted when contemplating the All Saints congregation.

Any piece about the congregation at Margaret Street must give prime place to Pat Thompson. I first met Pat in 1984 when she organized Eric Arnold's 70th birthday party in the downstairs bar. I was struck by her vivacity; but I did not get to know her until I was Director of Music at All Saints in April 1989. We had two things in common – a love of music and Worcester. She had grown up there. Her music mistress at school, Marjorie Potts, sang in the Worcester Festival Choral Society, and so did Pat until she moved to London in 1967. She lived in a flat at Margaret Street and soon became useful in the parish office. In fact she was asked by the Vicar, Fr Kenneth Ross, to type the letter to the choirboys' parents announcing the closing of the choir school on Easter Sunday 1968.

The probability of closure had rumbled on for years. At Father Ross's induction by Bishop Wand of London in 1952, in the sermon the Bishop had said 'of course we all know the choir school will have to close'. It was kept going for a further 16 years. But Father Ross knew that closure was inevitable. When the news was out, there was a furore. But it was too late. Shortly afterward, Kenneth moved to a residentiary canonry at Wells Cathedral; alas, he didn't live more than a year. Many thought the strain had been too much for him. And by the way, Fr Ross was an old boy of the King's School Worcester. He came to speak at the memorial service in 1968 for a classics master who had taught him. That was the only time I met him. I only remember one thing he said of the deceased master. 'One sometimes says a person was dead from the neck upwards. In his case, he was dead from the neck downward!'

Pat was wonderful company and a wonderful hostess. Her lunches were highly liquid in content. For a while after the General Synod of the Church of England decided to ordain women, I took the conservative view – i.e. against. But once I played regularly in South London as an itinerant organist, I saw the value of women's ministry. Pat was tolerant of my changed views. This had to be the case in her family too. Her middle sister, Linda, was married to Richard Clarke, Bishop of Meath and Kildare, later Archbishop of Armagh. He and Linda were very pro women, as were their two children. But they always respected Pat's point of view.

Pat remained a colourful personality. In appearance, she was uncannily like the Spanish singer Montserrat Caballé. You could not miss her in a crowd. She likes to meet for a good lunch. She is one of the traditionalists who have been at Margaret Street for many years. I hope the greater tolerance of inclusiveness of the parish today will still be home to those of conservative views – still a significant minority.

THE RESTORATION OF THE HARRISON ORGAN OF 1910

When I took over in 1989, it was clear that not all was well with the organ. Three of the keyboards had been converted to direct electric action – cutting out the pneumatic stage. This caused many problems, with many notes ceasing to work. The dedication of Harrison's tuner, David Chapman, meant that by 2002 when the organ was taken down for restoration, the actions had become very much more efficient – constant cleaning of the magnets – and in one case more extreme methods. We were about to do our annual BBC broadcast of Choral Evensong. The quietest pedal stop, the Subbass, had suffered water damage, and when the felt of the pallets dried out it became hard, causing a very audible clunk when the pallet fell as the note was discontinued. Unbelievably David took all 30 pallets home and steamed them, hoping to make their vertical fall quieter. How many organ tuners would go to such lengths!

When the major restoration of 1957 was undertaken, most of the pipework remained as it had been voiced by Arthur Harrison in 1910. Ten stops were altered. This was significant as they all contributed to the sound of 'full' organ, the backbone of the instrument. The loudest of these was the Large Open Diapason. Many of the pipes are on display in the front case. Their appearance will be familiar to anyone who has looked round churches. The sound of this stop (a rank of 61 pipes) had become 'hooty' because the 61 pipes had been moved up one note, making the pipe longer and the note therefore louder. Reversing this change slightly softened the sound. By careful attention to the mouths of the pipes, it was possible to improve the brightness and life of the sound by changing the way the pipe begins to come onto speech. If one wanted to be scientific, this could be illustrated by a graph which would show how the pipe gradually settles down to a constant note.

The higher register of the 'flue' stops (those which make the sound as on a recorder or flute) benefited greatly from this treatment. The most daring thing I did was to reinstate the 'Harmonics' which combine in the four pipes sounding a unison note, a third (Tierce), a fifth, and a twelfth (Nazard) with the note flattened by half a tone. Playing C on this four-rank Mixture (that is what a stop with more than one note is called) the other notes above would be E, G and B flat. When chords are played, the result should be utterly cacophonous. But this is not so if the stop is well composed with organized downward breaks when the pipes become too small. If the more discordant notes (e.g. the third and the flattened seventh) are quieter, a remarkable effect can be achieved where resultant sounds are produced when a note an octave lower is heard to sound. It is difficult to explain precisely such a technical matter. But when well done, the chorus of the organ is knit together in a remarkable way. I asked for this 'Harmonics' stop to be modelled on that at the Caird Hall, Dundee which has a remarkably successful example of this stop; it impressed me greatly when I heard it about 25 years ago, and the replica at Margaret Street has been much admired. There is also a simpler 'Mixture' on the Great manual (the second from the bottom) composed only of fifths and unisons. This is brilliant and melodious in sound.

The reed stops (those which sound like the clarinet, which only has a single reed) had also been tampered with in an attempt to make them more brilliant. There is a letter in the Harrison archive from Dr John Birch, a former organist (1953–1958), who said that he wanted the 'Harmonic Trumpet' to be 'flashed up'. The result was nondescript. By increasing the loading of the weight attached to each individual reed, the tone was much improved in warmth without losing all the fire.

I very much enjoyed working with Mark Venning (Managing Director), Peter Hopps (Head Voicer) and Andrew Scott (then the London Tuner, now Head Voicer). What was done brought the whole thing together and improved the tonal quality and excitement in the sound. We had a clear idea what we wanted to do. How on earth could we raise the £380,000 necessary? In fact I was amazed we managed to achieve this in just over a year. I was visited by eight organists who individually came to ask me how we managed it. My simple answer was that the project had to be 'owned' by the whole parish. People realized that All Saints without the organ would be unthinkable. It all stemmed from that.

A very good example of parish involvement was when the proprietor of the local Kerala Restaurant decided to have a fundraising event at his restaurant. He was a Syrian Orthodox Christian from Kerala, south-west India, and used to visit the church to say his prayers every morning. One Sunday evening he closed his restaurant to the public and charged £20 to church members – all of which was profit. It was a sell-out. In addition he gave all the profits on the wines, so that £2,500 was raised to support the organ restoration. The success of this event made the owner (David Tharakin) decide to do it again, and £2,500 was the result again. An amazing story, and heart-warming to think such a community spirit can still exist in central London, far removed in spirit from the crowds who flock to Oxford Street to engage in retail therapy. Many of the congregation took out monthly standing orders. The Vicar and I approached trusts and charities with a degree of success. The choir of St Thomas, Fifth Avenue in New York City were giving a concert at St John's Smith Square which we went to. We were both well-known to the clergy and musicians of St Thomas'. This resulted in a generous gift of £15,000 which they wished to give in honour of Dr Gerre Hancock, the notable organist who was about to retire after many years of distinguished service at Fifth Avenue.

The inauguration of the organ was on Saturday 29 March 2003. This was given by Dame Gillian Weir and Jane Parker-Smith, both of whom had been married in the church. John Scott, then Organist at St Paul's, was the third player. John opened the afternoon with a great performance of the Overture to *St Paul* by Mendelssohn arranged by W. T. Best. He then played Bach and finished his allotted 25 minutes with part of the 'Whitlock Sonata'. In fact, being a composite recital, I had to help with the programme. I actually chose Gillian Weir's two pieces, the Mozart Fantasia in F minor (K 608) and the Reubke Sonata. The recital sold out: all 300 seats went like hot cakes. There followed an excellent recital by Thomas Trotter, in which he played the Bairstow Sonata. The opening series concluded with a concert for choir and organ with solos by Andrew Arthur. Looking back, I feel we did justice to the restoration of the organ as we launched it into its second century.

THE WILLIAM BYRD 450TH ANNIVERSARY (1992)

To celebrate the occasion of William Byrd's 450th anniversary, the Church Music Society published an edition of the four propers for the Feast of All Saints – usually sung to plainsong but here set polyphonically. We were asked to sing a High Mass including these pieces during the context of Byrd's Five Part Mass, which we sang in its entirety. This caused Professor Henry Chadwick to remark that it was a veritable 'Byrd bath'.

The service attracted a very large congregation, amongst them Sir David Willcocks. He spoke warmly to me of the singing of the choir. I said I had wondered whether I could continue at All Saints in conjunction with the Directorship of the RSCM. On most Saturdays I was conducting a large choir festival in a cathedral, after which I had to get back to Margaret Street for the 10 a.m. rehearsal on Sunday morning. I was also heavily involved in plans for the RSCM Appeal. Hearing me speak in this way, Willcocks rounded on me and said it would be a mistake to give up at Margaret Street. He said that having conducted a vast amateur choir from the parishes on Saturdays, I needed to get back to All Saints to make music of a higher professional standard on Sunday mornings. Having agonized about whether to carry on, when I heard what Sir David said, I immediately put all thought of moving out of my mind. It turned out to be a happy decision, for in retirement from the RSCM I was able to achieve so much at Margaret Street, not least the restoration of the organ.

There were of course many important events at the church; but the Byrd anniversary was special in that it clarified my own thinking. And of course it was very important for my future and for the future of All Saints.

FINAL YEARS AT MARGARET STREET

I retired from All Saints on 25 January 2004. Much of my activities in the final years has already been chronicled in these pages. In January 2003 I decided to give notice that I would retire at the end of January the following year. This gave the church time to look for my successor; it also gave me time to acclimatize. My actual day of retirement was well planned. In the morning the High Mass included the whole of Byrd's Five Part Mass. It also included some excerpts from Mendelssohn's oratorio *St Paul* suitable for the Feast of the Conversion of St Paul. The highlight for me was the address by my old Pembroke chaplain, Professor Colin Morris, later Professor of Medieval History at Southampton University. He, his wife Brenda and their middle child Gillian, my goddaughter, have been regularly in touch over the years. Colin took as his theme Christian friendship. He started by saying that David Sparrow and I, both of Margaret Street, were former pupils but also his friends.

He explained that in the Middle Ages one could propose friendship in the same way as people propose marriage. It was a fascinating survey laced with a good deal of humour.

Evensong was sung by the choir of All Saints plus 24 former members who had come back for it. Described by the Vicar as a 'wall of sound', they did ample justice to the Evening Canticles by Hugh Blair and William Harris' 'Faire is the heaven'. The Caplin Benediction music went well with large forces. I was glad to do it as a tribute to Norman Caplin, who was there. The service was very well attended. Afterwards, a good many walked round the corner to the University of Westminster building in New Cavendish Street for an excellent hot buffet. The evening was rounded off by the choir, organized by James Sherwood, giving an amusing take of me which featured a good deal of my music which they had cleverly worked into the script. It was a fitting close to my 15 years as Director of Music.

When I stood down, I said I would not go into the church for a choral service for a year. I went occasionally to the Temple Church and found myself enjoying Prayer Book Matins. One Sunday when Stephen Layton was away I actually played for the service. By this time I was getting requests to deputize on Sunday mornings in South London. This continued until I ceased to live at Margaret Street in July 2007. But at the request of the churchwardens, I did return to choral services before the end of the year. They said I had been out long enough.

The final period was marked by my good relationship with the new Director of Music, Paul Brough. He asked me to write music for the choir. I was quite taken aback when he requested an anthem ('This is the day the Lord hath made') for the 150th anniversary of the church in 2009. I owe much to him for igniting my interest in composition. This led to the launch of a CD of my music in 2011 (*The Church Music of Dr Harry Bramma*, Priory Records PRCD1060). Here again there was a very good attendance. Christopher Robinson sat next to me. After a particularly fast and slick performance of Byrd's 'Laudibus in Sanctis', he turned to me and whispered, 'They do things rather faster these days!' Paul and I had a good relationship; he welcomed my presence and I didn't feel threatened by him. After this, I moved to South London and went to All Saints less. But I am grateful for what Paul did to make my final years at Margaret Street such happy ones.

CHAPTER EIGHT

Retirement from full-time work

LONDON LIFE

The Athenaeum

I have been a member of the Athenaeum since 1989. When I was about to become Director of the RSCM, Lionel Dakers, my predecessor, suggested that it would be a good idea if he were to propose me for membership. He and the first two Directors, Sydney Nicholson and Gerald Knight, had been members. It was kind of traditional, and also useful for entertainment purposes, especially for branch officers from overseas who appreciated a visit to Pall Mall. I found it pleasant to give dinner to friends also, or to use the clubhouse for rest during busy days in London. Since I retired from full-time work in 1998, I have found it a useful resource, particularly as a place to think and write in comfort.

Sitting at the club table with very good meals at reasonable prices, one meets and gets to know over time many distinguished and interesting people. Many have a deep knowledge and love of music. David Trimble, when away from Northern Ireland, talks always of music, particularly his interest in English opera. He went to see Vaughan Williams' *Pilgrim's Progress* twice when it was on some years ago. I also met a businessman who is an amateur organist with a passionate interest in Wagner; as a Friend of Bayreuth he managed to get tickets after a long wait for *Parsifal* and *Meistersinger*. Another former Oxford college head was extolling the virtues of the Wexford Festival. I often meet a violinist from the London Philharmonic Orchestra, and sometimes his wife who is a musical journalist. There are also clergy, judges and many others with whom one can usually find some link. It is a place where one gets to know things and keeps up to date.

There are a good many church and cathedral organists and several very accomplished amateur musicians. One such, Brian Henry, a friend of mine, conducted a fine performance of *Tosca* last year in the Drawing Room and in the spring of next year is planning to do Mozart's *Cosi fan tutte*. I now go to the club about once a week. It is a wonderful central location for work, reading and conviviality – in magnificent restored surroundings. The membership now hovers under the imposed ceiling of 2,000 men and women. Since the admission of women as members 25 years ago, many men who would not be part of a single-sex organization have now joined. The majority of those (a significant minority) who originally opposed women have changed their minds once they have encountered these impressive professional women. They have much enhanced the life of the club and have stood for office on various management committees. There will always be those who say the concept of any club is elitist. In my view it would be a poor kind of society which wanted a dull uniformity in all departments of life. And alongside their professional credentials, many members engage in voluntary work, which benefits people from all walks of life and all age groups. Overall I choose to see clubs as an invigorating force in society.

Becoming a composer
Since I started to learn the piano at the age of eight, I have had a feeling for harmony. Many people who play by ear have this. If it prevents them bothering to learn how to read musical notation, it is a pity. When natural harmonic instinct is wedded to fluent sight-reading,

the art of composition may emerge. There are some universities where technical matters such as doing composition exercises, or playing an instrument and reading notation at sight, are not required. In taking this view, they are flying right against the traditional view of how the talented composer is formed. Studying the works of composers and imitating their style has been common practice for as long as music has existed. This method of study has usually been in the context of teacher and pupil: Bach taught his sons; Beethoven begged Haydn to take him on as a pupil; César Franck was a pupil of Lemmens in Belgium; Marcel Dupré had almost daily lessons with Alexandre Guilmant. Nearer home, Vaughan Williams and Holst almost taught one another on their field days, whilst Britten was much inspired by Frank Bridge. But the received wisdom has been that originality of style emerges as a pupil absorbs a range of influences from the works of other composers. Elgar was largely self-taught; he just had what it takes, but he was constantly acquainting himself with the work of many composers. He, like many English musicians, was influenced by German music. But he was unusual in his attention to the works of Wagner, whereas others almost exclusively idolized Brahms. Elgar cast his net wide. He knew Verdi and Rossini well, but he also had a penchant for lighter music such as that of Delibes. I mention all this as I feel it makes those academics in universities who shun these methods seem rather misguided.

I had always dabbled with putting notes on paper. I had a wonderful tutor in Bernard Rose, with whom I studied for three years when I read Music at Oxford. When I became a cathedral organist and schoolteacher, I wrote music when it was required; as when the Vice Provost of Southwark Cathedral asked me to write an anthem to cover the lighting of the candles at Candlemas on 2 February 1982, as I have described earlier.

Sporadic anthems and arrangements followed from time to time. But in the early years of the 21st century I received more invitations to write. I composed two anthems for the choir of Dorking parish church at the request of the Director of Music, Martin Ellis. He produced two fine texts: 'Late have I loved thee' and 'I will go unto the altar of God'. Both of these have been published. The first has been sung several times at King's College, Cambridge, most recently at the beginning of a broadcast of Choral Evensong. Two of my most extensive pieces were written at the request of Paul Brough for the choir of All Saints, Margaret Street. The first, 'This is the day the Lord has made', was written for the 150th anniversary of the church in 2009. It has been sung elsewhere, notably in a magnificent performance at Trinity College, Cambridge, directed by Stephen Layton. The other large-scale piece was a setting of the Benedicite which was written specially for a record of my music made by All Saints choir. Subsequently it was sung at Matins in Christ Church Cathedral, Oxford under the direction of Stephen Darlington.

It is always good to hear one's music performed. But getting a large number of performances in my case seems difficult. This is because most of the music was written for All Saints choir, who were technically up to singing difficult music. The compositions are written in an approachable style, but I have never bothered much about making the music easy enough for amateurs. My music demands a large range in all the voices and it requires people with good voices. Gradually the pieces are getting an airing. But I don't want to adopt a commercial attitude, worrying whether the music will sell.

It was not until I was approaching 70 that I really got going as a composer, and hearing my music sung now gives me a considerable thrill. I shall continue to write the occasional pieces to meet the requirements of a particular circumstance. I am grateful to those who have asked me for music: especially Paul Brough, one of my greatest encouragers. To him I remain deeply grateful.

The Musicians' Company

I joined this livery company in 1985 at the suggestion of Dr Eric Arnold, Director of Music at All Saints, Margaret Street. He was Deputy Clerk of the company and had recently asked me to be an adjudicator for the W. T. Best Organ Scholarship, which carried a very good annual stipend of £3,000. Strangely, the company had very few organists in those days and it was necessary to bring in an outsider like me to fill the gap. I have enjoyed attending the dinners and seeing the company grow in size and usefulness over the past 30 years.

It now gives financial assistance to a great many students and has recently initiated a scheme to take classical music into schools by funding professional musicians to play and demonstrate their instruments. There have been visits to 40 maintained schools on a regular basis, making overall 120 school visits involving almost 7,000 children. The musicians have been very well received by the schools and the children, including a Special Educational Needs and Disability (SEND) school in Camden. This work with disabled people is increasing. Recently there was a special performance at the Royal Hospital for Neuro-disability patients and their carers which led to an interactive music session on the wards. I support this charitable work financially – but I wish I had been able to play a more active part in the affairs of the company.

When I was around 55, the Master enquired of me informally whether I would welcome being proposed for membership of the Court. This might, if they had liked me, led to office and ultimately the position of master. However, at that stage I was so involved with the affairs of the RSCM, which included the major appeal, that I felt it would have been virtually impossible to attend meetings of the Court during the day. Sadly there have been other professional musicians who have felt the same. But more recently more musicians have come forward and high office in the company has been held by professional musicians – or amateur players of professional standard.

The livery companies of the City of London are a remarkable survival of the medieval guild system. Some of the very wealthy companies – the big 12, such as the Mercers and Skinners – are able to do amazing charitable work, including the running of major schools. They are also a colourful survival, with the Livery Halls and customs passed down over the centuries. Behind the pomp and ceremony, much is done to promote education and the trades they represent. I suppose some feel there is a certain cachet to being a liveryman. But this is as nothing when one considers the work that company members do to promote the crafts their companies represent.

The Omphiangelum Society
The idea for this curiously named club grew out of meetings which took place during the restoration of the Harrison organ at All Saints, Margaret Street between 2001 and 2002, when the organ dating from 1910 underwent a major tonal and mechanical refurbishment. Ian Bell, engaged to act as consultant, frequently came to meet me in the church when the instrument was returning from Harrison's works in Durham in the autumn of 2002. We were often joined by Andrew Scott (Harrison's London tuner), Mark Venning (managing director), Peter Hopps (head voicer) and a good friend William McVicker (curator of the Royal Festival Hall organ). When our meetings ended, as is the custom with organists, we adjourned to the Cock Tavern in Margaret Street where Yorkshire bitter was available – Sam Smith's of Tadcaster – at prices way below those normally found in London pubs. As the opening of the organ drew near, we were sorry that our meetings would come to an end.

At this point Ian Bell suggested we ought to start a small club at which we could continue our very enjoyable gatherings. Ian also suggested it should be called the Omphiangelum Society. Why such a strange name? Obviously Greek in origin, it is taken from the name of a stop on the Harrison organ built in 1870 for the new Bodley church of St Martin, Scarborough. It is not known whether it was a reed or flue stop and whether loud or soft! Mark Venning who read classical Mods and Greats at Oxford came to the conclusion that *omphiangelum* means something like 'glory to God in the highest'. Whether it was given to undulating Célestes or to a lively reed, we shall probably never know. But it is a splendid name for a society of organists. The first meeting was on Wednesday 10 December 2003, when we visited first to collect a splendid leather-bound volume from a craftsman in Gipsy Hill which was presented by William McVicker. We then repaired to The Railway Bell where I was elected President, William McVicker Chairman and Ian Bell Secretary. We had one guest, Geoffrey Mitchell, the distinguished singer and teacher. The managing director of Harrisons became an *ex officio* member. The three officers always attended meetings. So the pattern evolved.

On 27 June 2017 we celebrated our 60th meeting, followed by the 61st meeting on Wednesday 27 September at The Colonies, Wilfred Street, London SW1. On this latter occasion our guests were Geoffrey Mitchell, Nicholas Thistlethwaite, the distinguished organ historian, and Maurice Merrell, the octogenarian head of Bishop & Son, the longest running British organ building firm. We have visited many London pubs of character serving good beer and food. We have also visited unusual locations – a box at the Royal Albert Hall for the re-opening of the Harrison/Willis organ, and the stage of the Royal Festival Hall just before the acoustic retuning of the building and the re-configuring of the shape of the auditorium, both of which have brought tremendous improvement to the sound of the instrument.

It has become the custom at our meetings to write a summary of our conversations, a job which usually falls to me. After 18 years, these make interesting reading. They are frank and sometimes libellous – a fine historical record. But were any publication of our deliberations to be considered, a considerable amount of time would have to elapse, or else the text would have to be severely edited. It is far too rich in content – particularly about what is said of well-known individuals – to be sanitized!

Having considered elsewhere here the merits and demerits of democratizing clubs and societies, I feel almost guilty speaking of the exclusivity of the Omphiangelum Society. It is very much a Dickensian organization with non-elected officers and occasionally distinguished women guests. But as a private coterie, it seems unnecessary to get worked up about political correctness. It is just a group of three friends forming the core membership who can invite whoever they like to meetings that are a mixture of seriousness, fun and gossip – nothing more than that!

The Madrigal Society

There are so many clubs and organizations which have flourished over the centuries in London. The Madrigal Society was founded in 1741 by a group of people who enjoyed choral singing – particularly of English music dating back to the Elizabethan period, the golden age of the madrigal. I am not a member, but from time to time I get invited by a friend, Hubert Chesshyre, who was a Herald at the College of Arms – his grand title was Clarenceux King of Arms. He sang as an amateur in the choir of Southwark Cathedral, where I first met him. I rather dreaded the arrival of these invitations! The evening started with sherry, followed by a three-course dinner in the Hall of the Apothecaries Company, at which white and red wine were served. The tables were cleared before the singing began. For refreshment, decanters of port were left on the table. The society had an extensive library of bound volumes from which the selected items from the evening's programme were taken.

I found having to sing difficult tenor parts after a substantial dinner almost more than flesh and blood could stand. The madrigal repertoire is so difficult. It does not easily trip off the tongue. The master gave the order to start and controlled the proceedings by banging a gavel on the table, which he used to stop the singing when the performance broke down – or when he thought we ought to do something again. Musically the singing was often of a low standard. But I imagine the exercise was considered a good thing because it gave the members hands-on experience of a wonderful choral repertoire. The evening's singing usually lasted about two hours.

There was another reason for finding things difficult. In the past choirboys had been borrowed from church choirs, particularly St Paul's Cathedral, to sing the soprano parts when these occasions were exclusively male. In more recent times, this practice became untenable and women were recruited to sing soprano and alto. But they were not invited to the dinner – just given sandwiches and coffee in an adjoining room. In my view this was preposterous. I am told they are now invited to the dinner, but such are the heavy traditions of the society that I am told that some of the women actually preferred having their own gathering.

Of course such societies are wonderful survivals. They are also proof of the vibrancy of the tradition of singing in London, going back to the time of Purcell and Blow, and beyond to the golden age of the madrigal in the Elizabethan and Jacobean periods.

SALISBURY

After I had worked for three years at the RSCM, I decided I ought to get my foot on the property ladder. A colleague at Southwark, Canon Peter Penwarden, had recently retired to a flat in the Close at Salisbury. It was during a visit to him and his sister Margaret in 1993 that I happened to say that I was thinking of buying a second home. I lived in tied accommodation at the RSCM, and had done so at both Southwark and Worcester Cathedrals. Peter replied that Mrs Piggott across the courtyard was thinking of selling. Hearing this, I went to see her and there and then arranged to buy her ground-floor flat – number 177. I had had a low salary at Southwark: £1,500 per annum in 1976. In fairness I had the house with all expenses paid. At Worcester I had been much better off. However, now at the RSCM, I was on a realistic salary which enabled me to take out a ten-year mortgage on the property. I had savings enough to put down almost half the purchase price of £158,000. My solicitor thought I ought to have attempted to get the price down, but I didn't want to get into this kind of negotiation. In fact my decision turned out to be a remarkably good investment, just before the dramatic rise in property prices towards the end of the 20th century.

The flat was not very large, but it had been converted to a high standard from the former teachers' training college of Sarum St

Michael. From the front were wonderful views of the Cathedral. Sitting at my kitchen table I could see the whole western aspect of the building, from the west front up to the top of the spire. I loved my occasional visits to Salisbury, though they were restricted as during the lifetime of my mother I had to make regular visits to Yorkshire, which I was often able to combine with RSCM visits in the north of England. I was able to furnish Salisbury by thinning out the contents of my large house in the grounds of Addington Palace.

I already knew quite a number of people in Salisbury. Lionel Dakers, my predecessor, and his wife Elizabeth had a house on the way to the station. The Organist of the Cathedral, Richard Seal, was an old friend, as was the Precentor, Jeremy Davies. And of course I quickly got to know many others who lived around and people connected with the Cathedral.

When my mother died on 8 December 1998, I decided to sell our home in Guiseley near Leeds. Some of the proceeds from this enabled me to pay off my mortgage. I kept Salisbury for another nine years. I had retired from the RSCM before my mother died, and I had intended in semi-retirement to spend more time in Salisbury. I did to some extent, though I had frequently to travel to London as I was Organist of All Saints, Margaret Street from which I retired on 31 January 2004. For a period from April 1998, when my mother went into a nursing home, until I sold the Yorkshire house in August 1999, I had three homes, two of which I owned. The London flat I rented. I soon discovered the difficulty of one person trying to live in three homes. My visits to Salisbury became less frequent as I had to keep my eye on the Yorkshire house. Sometimes on Sunday evenings I played for Evensong at All Saints. I switched off the blowers which provide the wind for the organ at about 7.20 p.m. and got the Tube to King's Cross where I easily caught the 8.10 p.m., non-stop to Wakefield then on to Leeds, which meant I managed the whole journey in two hours. I then changed to the local train to Guiseley, which went at 10.10 p.m. On one occasion the London train was early and the Guiseley train was late, so I managed to open the kitchen door at our house in Tranmere Park at 10.35 p.m., having walked the half mile from the station.

The next-door neighbours were very good at keeping an eye on things. Our cleaner, Sheila Brooksbank, stayed on and went in twice a week to keep the house tidy and clean. Eventually in August 1999 I sold the Yorkshire house in two parts: the major part of the sizable garden, where a new house was built; and the actual house and part of the garden to a Leeds solicitor and his family. Life then became simpler and I did go to Salisbury more. In fact I kept my flat there for three years after I retired as Director of Music at All Saints, where I still rented a flat at the church.

Eventually at the beginning April 2007, I decided to find a buyer for my Salisbury flat. In fact it all happened very quickly. Some friends of my neighbours upstairs bought it, with the result that I had to get out rather quickly. I put furniture in store in Croydon whilst I looked for a new flat in South London.

It was clear that my life now centred on London. My close friends were there. Eventually I found a suitable ground-floor flat in Beckenham, which was actually the first I looked at. I went with my friends Nicholas Luff and Brenda Renshaw, and Nick said my furniture would look wonderful in it. It was spacious with three bedrooms, two reception rooms and a large hall and kitchen. Having made an offer that was accepted, I had to wait four months as there was a queue. This turned out to my advantage, as I was able to invest the proceeds of Salisbury when good rates were still available. Eventually I moved the furniture from store in Croydon, and a few days later from Margaret Street. I had already taken the best things from my mother's house to Salisbury.

Had I had more considerable means, it might have been wise to keep the Salisbury flat. But my finances would not stretch to it. On reflection this was a good thing, for as a bachelor with no close relations, I would eventually have become weighed down by too many possessions!

TEACHING AT KING'S COLLEGE, CAMBRIDGE AND CHRIST CHURCH, OXFORD

The moment I retired from the RSCM at the end of August 1998, I was asked by my old pupil Stephen Cleobury at King's in Cambridge to help teach the undergraduates reading Music. He felt that since I had taught composition exercises (harmony, counterpart and fugue) to sixth-formers, himself included, I might have the experience to help those arriving at the university with little facility in these areas. I enjoyed my Friday afternoon visits to Cambridge and found the work congenial. Some undergraduates had been at schools where they had done musical exercises; to others this was a foreign area, but most of these caught up very quickly. An added pleasure of my visits was my weekly lunch in the Combination Room with Dr John Butt. In addition to hugely enjoying his company, I found I learned a lot too. Sometimes I went to the chapel for Evensong.

In the summer of 2000, they no longer needed me at King's. Immediately I was asked to go to Christ Church, Oxford by Stephen Darlington to do similar work. I continued this for five years until I was nearly 70. I thought I had better resign rather than have them say 'I do wish he'd go'! I was fortunate to be given university teaching in my 60s. I very much enjoyed getting to know the undergraduates and being in touch on a weekly basis with Oxford – a place which has played a big part in my life.

THE DIOCESAN ADVISORY COMMITTEE

When I arrived at Southwark Cathedral in May 1976, I was asked to join the Diocesan Advisory Committee (DAC) as Diocesan Organ Adviser. I had little idea what this involved. But I always had an interest in organs, which went well with my love of church architecture. The idea appealed to me, so I took the job on. I soon realized that I had walked into something very demanding.

The Provost of the Cathedral, Harold Frankham, was Chairman. He had been Vicar of Luton, where he presided over the neo-classicalization of the venerable Norman and Beard organ. He thought he knew a thing or two. He had a very good ear and knew for instance when the Choir 2-foot stop needed tuning. But he had little time for the historical approach to organ restoration. We usually got on very well, but at times he could be extraordinarily imperious. There was an occasion at Evensong when John Scott played the hymn 'Jesus Christ is risen today' to the fine German tune 'Wurtemburg'. At this Harold shouted out 'wrong tune'. We took no notice and carried on. After the service I told him that shouting things out in the service was unacceptable. I also told him that we had sung this tune on a broadcast of choral Evensong some weeks earlier. This led to a heated exchange in the north choir aisle. He didn't like being contradicted. He had wanted the fine medieval tune 'Orientis partibus'. I went home feeling very upset and wrote a letter of apology. He did the same. Next morning I discovered we had both put letters through our front doors – we lived next door!

My debut on the DAC was made difficult by the fact that meetings always took place on the second Tuesday of the month at 2 p.m. I had to leave at 4 p.m. and hurry though the back streets of Southwark to be in time for the rehearsal of the boy choristers at 4.30 p.m. before Evensong.

There were wonderful characters on the DAC in those days, and a very good Secretary in Hilary Aggett. Philip Whitbourne, an architect, had a wonderful turn of phrase. The windows he always referred to as 'fenestration' and the churchyard boundary as the 'curtilage'. Attending the monthly meetings was a mere fraction of what was required. There were frequent site visits. My first, to St Mary's, Balham, was extremely problematic. The church had gone ahead with major and controversial work without a faculty. This led to a consistory court. The fall-out from this is still being felt 42 years later: the result of bad decisions which left the church without a pipe organ – something today they would very much like.

Eventually as Director of the RSCM I had to resign from the DAC. Dr William McVicker took over from me in 1993. Eventually, retired from full-time work, I went back to help William in 1999. I finally retired in 2016 at the age of 80. I was touched by the award of the Lancelot Andrewes Medal by the Bishop of Southwark – in fact I was the first recipient of this award which honours service to the Diocese: 40 years in my case. It put a dignified full stop to what I had done and gave me much happiness.

A PERIPATETIC ORGANIST

I retired as Organist and Director of Music at All Saints, Margaret Street on 31 January 2004. It took only a few days for churches to realize I was now free on Sunday mornings and available to deputize. I once played the organ at the Temple Church when Stephen Layton was away and the Assistant Organist, James Vivian, needed someone to accompany the choir whilst he conducted. Sometimes I helped out at St Giles, Cripplegate when Anne Marsden Thomas was away. But most of the requests came from South London, where I was remembered as Diocesan Organ Adviser. My first call came from St Dunstan's, Bellingham. I then settled down to a regular pattern in a number of churches, mostly within striking distance of my home in Beckenham. But sometimes I ventured further afield – to All Saints, Tooting with its fine Harrison organ of 1906; and even to St John the Divine, Richmond. Travel by minicab is not expensive on Sunday mornings. I continue to welcome these opportunities to keep my organ playing alive and feel part of a number of church communities where I play regularly. Where I live now in Chislehurst I am well connected by bus and train and enjoy getting to know new routes.

Organists tend to be resilient, though few will echo Francis Jackson's achievement of giving his final recital at the age of 95 – and indeed of continuing to play the harmonium in his village church at East Acklam at the age of 101! I have been retired from full-time work for nearly 25 years and am grateful I can still play and advise parishes on making appointments. All this is good for my social life, keeping me in touch with good friends and with what is going on. And for that I am thankful.

CHAPTER NINE

A spiritual pilgrimage

FAITH AND DOUBT 70 YEARS AGO; IS THERE A PLACE FOR GOD IN THIS?

Those of us who grew up in the 1940s and 50s have experienced an amazing transformation of the church in many matters. The culture after the war was still one of acceptance – but now many battled with the Theology of Creation, with ideas about sex and other ethical matters, all of which were becoming untenable on a 'handed-down' basis. Challenging concepts of God, the book *Honest to God* published by Bishop John Robinson in 1960 articulated doubts which were increasingly experienced by serious thinking people in the 1950s. It caused an outcry; it moved people suddenly away from their comfort zones. Many were relieved that a bishop of rigorous intellect could seriously challenge long-held beliefs, but assure people it was still possible to remain within the church. It was a serious shock from which the faith of many never really recovered. Suddenly nothing was sacrosanct, especially doctrines of a supernatural nature, like the Virgin Birth. Or indeed was the Son of God just a great teacher who taught love as the key to all? His was a humanitarian gospel, as outlined in the Sermon on the Mount.

The remarkable discoveries made by scientists about the workings of the universe might eventually provide answers to what has evolved over 20 million years. More discoveries will be made – about the birth of stars or the chemical substances found on the planets. We already have moondust! But whether the meaning of existence or the complexity of human nature will become clearer is not a question for scientists. They cannot prove if there is such a state as life after death. Those who witness the birth of new human lives perhaps experience the greatest sense of wonder and closeness with the cosmos.

In his book *Leaving Alexandria*, Bishop Richard Holloway of Edinburgh described watching his three children walking up the hills behind their home, which evoked the thought for him, 'This is what I'm for!' Maybe 'everlasting life' can be explained by saying that our lives are continued in the lives of our children. It is possible to grasp this; but it is something which gives eternal life not an existence in its own right but a concept which can relate to the here and now.

For each of us, these ideas can become clearer as we age and develop a sense of wonder at the glories of creation. Those who have musical gifts will appreciate beauty in sound, or the logical subtleties of harmony. Some musicians have a highly developed experience of sound and tone colour as well as a developed harmonic sense. These skills may be genetically based. They give pleasure and form the basis of musical performance and composition. For this we should be grateful; they lead to new ways of life and enjoyment – and indeed the very basis of the musical profession. But remarkable as these facts are, they may not lead to understanding. That is a different channel of thought, open to everyone who gives time to deeper thinking.

MEMORIES OF SOCIAL UNEASE

I remember that attitudes could be hard at Oxford for talented pupils who came from homes that felt less privileged than their confident peers'. Young people could find the sophistication of more well-to-do undergraduates gave them feelings of inferiority, which sometimes prompted competitive social climbing. It was not only the attitudes that felt alien; it was also the more conspicuous trappings of possessions and clothes sported by wealthier undergraduates.

I remember being told off by my father for wanting to buy a linen suit I had seen in a shop window in the High Street which cost £13. We did not have that sort of money for such extravagances, he said. My father had a decent income as a lecturer in the Textile Department of Bradford Technical College. As a state scholar which followed from my open scholarship, I did not have to pay tuition fees. But I did have to pay for my board and lodging in term-time. My father worked out that I would have enough for this from my grant, which I seem to remember was £69 a term. He then said he would keep me in the holidays – board and lodging and buying new clothes. Here we come back to the £13 linen suit. My father had strong ideas about what I required, but we did not always see eye to eye. However, I always had a decent tweed jacket and flannel trousers for working days. He bought me several new suits, in which I had some say, and these were tailor-made. I realize now that I should have been grateful for being so well clothed, and I eventually found money to vary my dress. Lack of a linen suit did not mean I went around feeling sorry for myself, but I am saying that I found it difficult being catapulted into upper-middle-class society.

I had a wonderful tutor for three years in Dr Bernard Rose. Though he was always smart and rather upmarket in his manner, I always felt he was interested in what I could do rather than what I looked like. My years at Oxford certainly broadened me as a person and helped me to feel at ease with whoever came my way.

An interesting coda to this section should be a brief account of experience working in the mill during vacations. My father thought I ought to do this, and as my grandfather was Weaving Manager at Salt's Mill in Saltaire, this was easily arranged. I was given a job working in the Pattern Room where we made swatches of cloth samples for the salesmen to take out. I had to learn how to do it, but soon got the idea. In my first summer I worked for eight weeks, 8.30 a.m. to 5.30 p.m. with an hour off for lunch. An eight-hour day was something

I had never experienced before. There were four others in the room: Walter Bell the manager, a delightful older man and two young men of about 20, one of whom I was distantly related to. They were great characters. Occasionally my grandfather would visit us, and it was then I learned that he had a reputation for being an old-fashioned manager who was rather feared in the mill.

The following year (1956) I went back for four weeks. My parents were disappointed I did not go back in 1957 in the long vacation before my third year at university. They were right to be disappointed: I ought to have gone for a third time. But my parents thought that life in the mill cut me down to size, and they were right!

THE IMPORTANCE OF SPECIAL FRIENDSHIPS

In what I have written about Nick Luff (in Chapter 7) I have spoken of my close friendship with him and with Chris Caine. Nick died on 1 January 2014. In the five years since then I have been much sustained by close friendships dating from around this time. Those of us with no close family members living near need the support and happiness which derives from deep mutual friendships. I want to write something about these.

Christopher Caine – Chris was Head of Undergraduate Studies in the music department at Trinity-Laban College in Greenwich until 2019. Increasingly, he has become a very good friend on a day-to-day basis. We enjoy one another's company and find each other good sounding boards when we need to talk about personal matters or share information. We often have meals together, either at home or at restaurants, and we speak frequently on the telephone.

There have been particular moments when I could not have done without Chris. When I went into London Bridge Hospital just after my 81st birthday, it was the first time I had been in hospital. I had to arrive by 7 a.m. So Chris came to stay with me the night before and went with me in the cab. He also accompanied me to two early morning appointments at the Princess Royal University Hospital, calling for me in his car at 8 a.m. This was when I had to see a doctor to discuss plans for treatment for CLL – described by one haematologist as 'friendly leukaemia'! I have now (November 2018) completed a very successful six-month cycle of chemotherapy. It would have been terrible to have to go to appointments alone.

Nicholas Frayling – I first met Nick when I moved to Southwark in 1976. He was Vicar of the fine grade 1 listed church, All Saints, Tooting and a member of the RSCM Diocesan Committee. We soon became good friends. In fact we have gone on holiday together for over 40 years, latterly mainly to his cottage in Normandy. He has given me wise advice when I encountered problems, and I believe I have done the same for him. We meet quite often and speak frequently on the phone. He knew my mother well and was well aware of my family background. He retired as Dean of Chichester in 2014. He too is a close friend of Chris Caine, who was for a time choirmaster at All Saints, Tooting. He knew Nick Luff well – see his address at his funeral in Chapter 7. He has been a very good companion for many years, but particularly so in the past five years, and especially in 2017–18 when I had to cope with major knee surgery, my move to a new flat and my treatment for leukaemia. He is a person on whom I need to lean from time to time – a very great support.

Brenda Renshaw – Brenda is the third person in the trio of friends who were closely connected with Nick Luff, along with myself and Chris. At the end of Nick's teaching career in 2001, she was Deputy Headteacher of St Bartholomew's C of E Primary School in Sydenham. This was when Nick was struggling with his drink problem and becoming very ill. She maintained a caring watch over him until he retired, and was very much around when Nick had his initially successful liver transplant at King's College Hospital, Camberwell. I mention all this because my friendship with these three people was long-term, and towards the end of Nick's life fashioned in the 'furnace of adversity'. We have continued to be close. Brenda has helped me greatly, particularly with the massive downsize from

Raleigh Court, Beckenham when I moved to a brand new flat with fewer rooms in Chislehurst. Brenda is a Methodist whose attitude to the faith is inclusive and liberal but very serious. It is similar to my way of thinking. As a widow she has a son and daughter and several grandchildren; but like many married people she has time for a larger family. Chris and I are fortunate to count on her support and enjoy her friendship.

Lionel and Jill Bourne – I got to know Lionel in 2007 when I started to deputize for him at the church of St John the Divine, Kennington where he had recently been appointed Organist and Director of Music. A good friendship quickly developed and later with his wife Jill. They were a great support in 2018 when I was recovering from major and successful knee surgery. In fact Lionel accompanied me on two occasions when I had follow-up appointments with the knee surgeon at London Bridge Hospital. He was willing to drive me around, especially when I went weekly to see Frank Hall, a remarkable leg nurse at Beckenham Hospital. And on the day I moved to Chislehurst, he came to help put books on shelves etc. Both he and his wife have always been ready to give me meals. There are so many ways in which I am grateful to Lionel and Jill.

Val Neale – Val is the fifth person I must mention. After discharge from London Bridge Hospital, I went to the nursing home wing at Morden College, Blackheath. My friend David Hutt, who lives in the Wren Quadrangle there, arranged this. I could not have gone home to an empty house. When I was fit enough to leave, Val made this possible. She lived in a flat opposite mine in Raleigh Court, Beckenham. She had recently retired as a district nurse. At her own suggestion, she came in every day at 9 a.m. and 6 p.m. to see if I was all right. She soon had no need to come in the evenings, and it was not long before she only needed to come about once a week in the mornings to help to put on my support stockings. This was a generous act of kindness which had a pleasant spin-off. Though I had known Val for ten years as a neighbour, she now became a much valued friend.

Peter Barker – Peter comes again into this narrative because of our continuing lifelong friendship. He was musical but not marked out for a professional career in music. We shared interests, particularly music. Whilst still at school he was in fact seriously considering becoming a Methodist minister. His father was a 'big' Methodist, as they say in Yorkshire, and wanted him to take this career path. He did eventually go to Hartley-Victoria College in Manchester, a 'low church' Methodist theological college. Subsequently this turned out to be a mistake. He would have been more suited to a 'middle-of-the-road' college. He was ordained and served in six churches in Lancashire and Yorkshire, retiring in 2009, since when he has lived in Kendal after the break-up of his marriage of 35 years to Rosemary. Over the years he has kept in touch by visiting me at my homes in the West Midlands and the south. And I saw him at his various churches from time to time. As is true in many long-term friendships, over the years we have become very different people as a result of our contacts, work and way of life. And though the expression 'old friends are best' is very questionable, length of friendship does in most cases add a special dimension to a relationship. Peter is now really an Anglican manqué.

CHAPTER TEN

Envoi

UPWARDS AND ONWARDS

Trying to span a long life of over 80 years is a formidable task. Reliving past events in these pages has been mostly enjoyable, but sometimes painful. With the benefit of hindsight I feel I could on occasions have made better decisions. I have always been fortunate in my powers of recall – words remembered, faces seen in a variety of expressions. The sentiment Cardinal Newman recalled in the last verse of his hymn 'Lead kindly light': 'And with the morn those angel faces smile, Which I have loved long since, and lost awhile'.

My memory of musical sounds is good, particularly those of an organ heard before the original voicer's work had been changed out of all recognition. Over the past 30 years I have often been consulted about quality of tone – particularly plans for the revival of something like the original sound of the organ at York Minster, before considerable alterations were made in 1960. Of course the pipework can provide clues, but it is useful to consult those who remember the organ well before the changes. Ian Bell who grew up in York (and is consultant for the project) and I who played the organ in the 1950s can offer a valuable insight to help guide the instrument back to the spirit of the original.

My aural memory can also be used to describe orchestral sound. I often heard Sir John Barbirolli conducting the Hallé Orchestra in St

George's Hall, Bradford when I was 17 and 18 years old. The speeds, nuances and style as well as the characteristic sounds of the orchestra remain clear in my memory. Of course gramophone records can provide accurate evidence – but this is more useful if supplemented by personal recall. The Hallé sound was golden, very expressive and luminous, altogether different from other British orchestras of the time. These memoirs have I hope a value as a historical record, which will enable future generations to recall the sound world of the mid 20th century.

A much often heard witticism in my youth, often from the lips of waggish Anglo-Catholic clergy, was that with advancing years one believes more and more about less and less. In my case it is the opposite. I believe less and less about more and more! We may have a sense of wonder as we contemplate the vastness of the universe, more limitless as it now is known to be than we thought even recently. Human existence and life in myriad forms are facts we are able to comprehend. We can also see that the workings of the cosmos are fearsome, in that earthquakes, volcanoes, floods and other disasters are part of the natural process. The traditional theological concepts where original sin and the disobedience of man could be blamed for what has gone wrong no longer seem plausible. Even the later medieval doctrine of 'original righteousness', where the essential divine goodness in man has escaped complete obliteration by sin, is also difficult. It is perhaps comforting, but ultimately no more helpful to our understanding of our place in the cosmos. The 4th-century Father of the Church Athanasius in his treatise 'De Incarnatione' ('about the incarnation') has a moving passage where he imagines the human condition to be like a painted image on a panel which has faded. It is revealed again in its original colour and beauty by the saving work of Christ. But though we may find joy in our relationships with those we love, and though we may find a sense of purpose and satisfaction through the exercise of our talents as musicians, craftsmen, thinkers, cooks, painters and cricketers and so on ad infinitum, the questions as to why and how it all began are always at the back of our minds.

The glib fundamentalism and indeed the bigotry of Christians and followers of all other faiths in the end provide no answer.

As someone who has attended Christian worship all my life, how do I account for my continued attendance at Church on Sundays and other Holy Days despite this capacity for rational thought? I continue to attend against a background of doubt because I feel it helps me to put a value on my own life and on those of the many close friends who are important to me. I have also found it helpful as a teacher. It has always been my strong belief that there is no person or pupil, whether brilliant or less gifted, who does not have something which is innately worth developing. I have thought of this as discovering the 'divine' in every child or person. This has been brought home to me constantly.

I remember a severely handicapped married couple who attended Southwark Cathedral every Sunday in wheelchairs. They could hardly sit still and found great difficulty in speaking. Then one day the wife wrote me a letter which she had typed. The wonderful intelligent person within was suddenly revealed. Then I was recently on a crowded train from Leeds to Blackburn over the top of the Pennines. I was surrounded by many teenagers from families who had probably arrived in Yorkshire from Pakistan several generations ago. They were making a lot of noise in their seats and I was trying hard to fight off irritation or even a touch of racism. At that point I dropped my walking stick in the aisle. The young man sitting opposite immediately picked it up and handed it back, looking me straight in the eyes and giving me a charming, considerate and very genuine smile.

Such experiences have made me realize that Christian worship and scripture still have a value for me. And particularly the practice of prayer at bedtime I find gives comfort in the familiar words of hymns and scripture. I am led to think of those who are ill or in various ways need help. I recall some words of Archbishop Michael Ramsey at a mission to the University of Oxford in 1957, held in the Sheldonian Theatre which he packed four nights running. He was explaining that prayer was not only 'vertical' but travelled 'horizontally' helping one to reach out to those in need. It occurred to me then that prayer is not really like dialling a celestial telephone exchange, but conditioning the mind to do what is right to those in need, or even to give thanks. That is why I still pray. Others might for the same reasons take up yoga. I am reminded of my place in relationship to my very existence and to those I am privileged to know.

As I come to the end of this memoir, I am reminded of my good fortune: of where I have been, those I have known and what I have been able to achieve musically. But I have also been reminded of a wide variety of experiences in many areas. If these reminiscences are not self-indulgent but objective and informative, I feel I will have succeeded in what I set out to achieve. I also hope that the mixture of perception and individuality will add enjoyment to the historical record.

Appendix

[These articles I wrote for the RSCM Magazine are reprinted here with the permission of the Director of the RCSM]

'MALE AND FEMALE CREATED HE THEM' – IN SUPPORT OF DR RICHARD SEAL AND THE GIRLS' CHOIR AT SALISBURY CATHEDRAL

I am writing this in the shadow of Salisbury Cathedral during a break from duties at the RSCM Summer Course here. It seems inevitable, then, that this quarter I should try to assemble some thoughts on the subject of girls in the choirs of cathedrals and greater churches, and on the implications for the musical life of all churches. A good deal of what I have to say about boys and girls is relevant to the local churches, and particularly to those which have magnificently maintained the great tradition of boys singing in church. I would like my views to be seen as an affirmation and support for this tradition, which brought me and many others to musical birth. But I would also like at the same time to sound a clear note of support for the development of girls' voices alongside. Peaceable coexistence should be the aim in all cases.

As is widely known, Salisbury Cathedral hopes, funds permitting, to establish a choir of girls to work alongside the famous boys' choir which has been in existence since the Cathedral was built in the 13th century. As was only to be expected, this bold move has sparked off a considerable amount of discussion in the newspapers and on the air. It has also released a good deal of prejudice, as was also to be expected. My reaction, when telephoned by innumerable newspapers seeking my views, was to say that I wholeheartedly backed Richard Seal and the Chapter of Salisbury – so long as the decision led to a doubling of the numbers of children singing in the choirs of great churches. To reduce the number of boys at present singing in our cathedrals and greater churches would be nothing short of iniquitous, as I will attempt to explain. It would, however, in my view, be equally wicked to continue to exclude young girls from the type of musical education their brothers have received for centuries. In contemporary society it has come to be accepted as inevitable and right that equal opportunities must be available in education for boys and girls. To continue to exclude girls from choir schools will become increasingly hard to justify in all countries. I would point out that I am not only speaking of the United Kingdom and Ireland. Major churches, with and without choir schools, in the United States, Canada, Australia, New Zealand and South Africa, still continue the boy chorister tradition, and the problems facing the church authorities in these countries are the same as those facing us in Europe.

The importance of the all-male tradition
At an early stage in this discussion, I wish to emphasize that I am passionately concerned that the noble tradition of boys singing in church must continue in all the churches where it is maintained. Girls must be added to bring new opportunities and richness. They must not cause boys to be subtracted.

I believe that the first reason for wishing to keep the male tradition alive is entirely musical. The sound of a choir of boy trebles is special, and whatever some may say to the contrary, the *timbre* is very different from that of young girls. It would be ironic, in these days of authenticity in musical performance, if boys' choirs were to disappear. To get the right sound in Byrd, Palestrina and Lassus, and even in Bach, Mozart and Haydn, boys' voices are preferable. Having worked with both boys' and women's choirs, I have no doubt in my mind that polyphony especially has a haunting and luminous quality when sung by the male voices for which it was written, and that a comparable effect is much harder to achieve with the average mixed choir, unless one goes in for selecting girls with 'boy-like' voices, something which has always seemed to me to be a considerable insult to women. Let us get our thinking straight: our musical resources would be immensely impoverished without the all-male choirs, and the proper performance of much music would be impossible.

My second reason for my commitment to the boys' choir tradition is to do with the musical and artistic nurturing and training of young men. Very few intelligent people would doubt the wisdom of encouraging boys in artistic pursuits. But many perceptive and articulate leaders in churches and education have not sufficiently grasped the fact that the boy chorister is an 'endangered species'. Very often a boy will be discouraged from his love of singing because he is ridiculed by his peers. It is sad that in society, particularly in English-speaking countries, music is seen as an occupation for women and something to be spurned by the manly – an attitude found in the philistinism of the pre-war English public school, mercifully in most cases now almost a thing of the past. But still the myth persists in many areas. A few years ago, when I was an examiner for the Associated Board, I was appalled when visiting co-educational state schools to find the names of only two or three boys on a list of around 70 candidates. Enquiry always provoked the same reaction – that it was very difficult for boys to be musical in a mixed-school environment. I have never been able to decide whether this reflects inbred tribal tendencies which have been with us from the dawn of civilization, or whether it is more to do with the deification of sport and the ingrained philistinism and blinkered conservatism of the majority of male teachers. I suspect the latter.

Against this true and devastating scenario, it will be obvious to all that a reduction in the number of places where boys are encouraged to sing would be terrible indeed. It would also lead to a serious diminution of tenors and basses available in the future. I believe that up to the age of 13 or 14, boys are best taught to sing in male groups. To a boy in an all-male choir or a single-sex school, singing is a perfectly normal pursuit. The introduction of girls at this stage can spark off a 'gender crisis' leading to a reluctance to continue to sing with an unbroken voice. Boys and girls at this age are very different and need, at any rate in subjects like music, to be treated differently. The marked difference between young boys and girls was brought home to me at the BET/RSCM Chorister of the Year Award Finals in London last year. Twenty 12- to 14-year-old children were assembled on the platform. Half were girls, half boys. The girls looked like young adults – very sophisticated – and made a beautiful, quite mature sound, rich in fundamental tone. The boys on the other hand looked like a collection of children, and made a sound that was much more child-like – bright and rich in overtones.

I believe we must continue to train young male and female singers separately, just as in many other activities it is accepted that single-sex participation is desirable. But, unlike in sporting activities, it is possible for young male and female voices to be combined for special occasions. The resulting blend of sound is different, but interesting. I very much hope the boys and girls of Salisbury Cathedral, though forming their own distinct and special identities, will occasionally combine to sing the *Nelson Mass* on a great Festival of the Church!

Girls and women should be given equal opportunities
Having, I hope, made out a strong case for the *retention* of the all-male choir in our churches, I will now try to demonstrate why I believe an equally strong case can be made out for the introduction of choirs of girls. I am fully aware of the brilliant work Dr Dennis Townhill has done in recent years at St Mary's Cathedral, Edinburgh, training a choir in which girls sing alongside the boys. I don't, however, believe this should become normal practice – particularly as I suspect success in this area is only achieved by a very remarkable choir trainer, and, as in the case of St Mary's Cathedral, by keeping the proportion of girls

to less than one fifth of the total number of choristers. I am strongly of the opinion that all cathedrals should now try to provide resources, both financial and in staffing, to cope with the introduction of a choir of girls, who would sing with the lay clerks at certain services during the week, whilst the boys sang at the rest. When ultimately established, they should not be seen as the second team. And with tourists in ever-increasing numbers visiting our cathedrals, it would be excellent if the second daily choral service, which disappeared in the years following the war, could be revived – not I hope as an early Matins, but as a Sung Eucharist at noon. Yes, the introduction of an expert additional choir of children could open exciting and challenging musical and liturgical prospects for our great churches.

In the case of girls, my first reason for wishing to introduce them would be to do with fairness and equality of the sexes. It is well known that education in a good choir has given boys in the past wonderful opportunities, enabling them to scale great heights in the musical and other professions. In an era when co-education is becoming normal – even many choir schools take girls – it seems inevitable that girls should be given equal opportunities. This might encourage more parents to allow their boys to join the choirs, if they felt their daughters could be included. And it would certainly get rid of the heartache and, in some cases, severe depression which has resulted from the boy-only policy. I can think of several families where the sons were cathedral choristers and where their sisters, equally musical, suffered mental and emotional damage because they were kept out of something they desperately wanted to do. In an age when boys and girls expect to be educated side by side in school and university, it would seem to make sense that, in the sphere of church music, it should be made possible for girls to be alongside.

The second reason for bringing the girls in would certainly be musical. Though we are still in under-developed territory, my guess is that, given equal training, girls aged 8 to 14 would cultivate a beautiful sound, different but equal to the boys. There has been a good deal of mythology in this area, perhaps encouraged by male chauvinists not wishing to be taken over! But having listened to young girls singing on courses at Addington recently, I shall be very surprised if the development of girls' choirs, based on daily training and the highest professional standards, does not lead to exciting new discoveries in the world of musical sound.

Churches should have the courage to innovate

I realize that I have taken a moderate view throughout this article. The traditionalist would wish to keep only the male tradition of the great churches. The radical progressive would doubtless pour scorn on the idea of wishing to continue segregated singing. The sensible innovator, listening to the spirit of the age, yet having deep consciousness of European Christian tradition, would wish to make bold experiments to bring women fully into the musical life of the churches, whilst realizing the importance of maintaining the all-male choral tradition. When contemplating a great church like Salisbury, which was at the centre of musical and liturgical experiment in the Middle Ages, it is entirely right to be traditional, to wish to maintain the sound of the cathedral which has been its soul over the centuries. The sound of a boys' choir in this building is as much part of the medieval legacy as the stone carving, the spire, the glass and the Sarum service books and, like them, must be maintained. But just as it was recently possible to enrich the architectural splendours of the building by introducing the magnificent new east windows by the distinguished French stained-glass artist, Gabriel Loire, so must it be possible to add to the musical richness and life of this noble place by augmenting the number of young singers in the choir. I believe Salisbury Cathedral, in planning a girls' choir, will set a trend which might well become universal. I hope the vision of those concerned will be crowned with success.

Harry Bramma
August 1990, Salisbury

APPENDIX

'LET OUR MERRY ORGAN BLOW' – A DETAILED EXAMINATION OF THE MERITS OF PIPE AND ELECTRONIC ORGANS

And now for something completely different. I would like to make a contribution to the lively debate which is currently taking place in the correspondence columns of this magazine and national newspapers relating to the relative merits of pipe and electronic organs. Sadly, there is so much ignorance and prejudice on both sides. Only the other day, when I was in Yorkshire, I saw a letter in a local paper from two churchwardens complaining bitterly that the diocese was making it difficult for them to remove their pipe organ, the work of a first-rate 19th-centry builder. They saw this objection as a move against progress, and made it quite clear that, in their view, any sensible person would consider an electronic instrument to be the organ of the future.

In his letter in the last issue of *CMQ* my friend Norman Warren, Archdeacon of Rochester and member of the RSCM Council, made many valid points which I readily accept both on pastoral and musical grounds. But as he knows, I cannot travel all the way with him! I intend to respond to his challenge that the RSCM 'will face these issues with realism and give guidance in a fair, unbiased way'. I shall do my best to be both fair and unbiased.

There is no doubt that in a large building, the organ remains the only satisfactory instrument which can be played by one person to accompany massed singing. And for most people, the organ retains its popularity as a liturgical instrument. At no time have so many known so much about the glorious history of the European organ. The splendours of Cavaillé-Coll, Silbermann or Father Willis are now readily available on compact disc, and the 'King of Instruments' still evokes great interest amongst the general public as the hugely successful TV series of recitals by Gillian Weir on historic instruments recently testified. Yet, whilst the pipe organ and its repertoire are appreciated as never before, there are many in positions of authority in the Church who do not acknowledge the importance of this tradition.

I would therefore like to try to analyse the main issues of the debate in the hope that such a discussion will help those who find themselves having to install, repair, or replace an organ.

Quality of tone

Let us start with quality of tone; and here I will make my views quite clear. If the great literature of the organ is to be played – or church music in the classical tradition is to be accompanied – *in ideal circumstances* there is no substitute for the sounds of the pipe organ. If, on the other hand, light music or modern hymns in the folk tradition are what is most often played, the electronic organ may be more suitable. For here there is no question of comparison, as the pipe organ is not normally used for jazz and light music. It was, of course, so used in the heyday of the theatre organ – but no one could confuse a large organ by Wurlitzer for one of similar size by Father Willis! I find electronic sounds extremely suitable for light music. Listen to some of the excellent playing of this type on the enterprising radio programme 'The Organist Entertains'.

At this moment, I can hear some saying that this is arrant nonsense. Many believe the electronic organ is now so good that it is virtually impossible to distinguish its sound from that of the best pipe instruments. And have not several major cathedrals installed electronic instruments in their naves? Yes they have, and, let it be said with great sincerity, the technology which goes into the making of electronic instruments is one of the great scientific achievements of modern times, and the musicality and quality of these instruments has improved very greatly, even in the past few years.

However, I personally cannot agree that the two kinds of instrument are now virtually indistinguishable. I will try to explain why. On the best electronic organs, individual stops can be very impressive. I have heard Open Diapasons and Gedackts which come extremely close to pipe organ sound. This has been achieved by studying the way a pipe blown by wind starts to speak. It does not immediately produce a note where the sound waves are regular. Indeed, they are very erratic as the pipe comes on to speech. This way in which a note *begins* in the pipe is very important, as it gives clarity to the speech, particularly when playing music with a complex texture like a fugue.

Very ingeniously, the makers of some electronic instruments have now simulated this special way a pipe speaks, and that is why their results are often much more convincing. What cannot be achieved, however, is the subtle change in tone quality from note to note often found in a rank of pipes. In a pipe organ, every note has its own pipe which is carefully made and voiced, and frequently the harmonic composition of the pipes is subtly altered as one ascends the scale, producing an effect of increasing brilliance or the reverse as one moves up the compass. The Father Willis Tuba from the old Gloucester organ, now at All Saints, Margaret Street, takes off in a quite remarkable way from Middle C upwards. Many other instances could be cited of both flue and reed stops where the same is true. Yet on an electronic instrument, since even on the best examples the harmonic composition of the stop is only changed once an octave, this kind of effect is not possible – and it does show. On inferior electronic instruments, moreover, the same harmonic composition is maintained throughout the compass.

But the main drawback in the electronic instrument is found in a different, though related, area. I have often been impressed by individual stops on good instruments but have wondered why there was something unsatisfactory, for instance, about Full Great. This can be explained quite simply. On a pipe organ, a six-part chord played with 15 ranks of pipes sounding will cause 90 pipes to speak in a variety of positions on the soundboard. The sound waves from these pipes interact and build up a great pyramid of sound, at the same time throwing down resultant tones an octave lower, thus binding the chorus together whilst amplifying the sound. A simple experiment on a well-voiced organ will prove my point. Draw all the strops of the Diapason chorus on the Great from 4-foot up to Mixtures. Then play some chords. Immediately it will be noticed that a considerable amount of 8-foot tone is present. To achieve this essential effect requires wind and sound waves emanating from many different sources.

The kind of phenomenon I am trying to explain can also be experienced on the acoustic piano. Open the lid of the instrument, depress the sustaining pedal to lift the dampers off the strings, then sing a note into the piano. Immediately, many strings will vibrate in sympathy with the sound waves of your voice! The same thing occurs when a piano is played. Many more strings are sounding than those actually hit by the hammers. This gives greater richness and brilliance, and is an important factor in true piano tone.

I hope I have been able to show that the musical superiority of pipe organ sound is based on scientific fact – not the taste or prejudices of the listener. If music in the classical tradition is to be played in church, a *good* pipe organ is the correct instrument to choose if at all possible. A friend of mine, Peter Comerford, who has been one of the most important minds behind the recent astonishing advances in electronic sound, was a few years ago called in to give an opinion about the restoration or replacement of an organ. Some PCC members secretly hoped that he would advise in favour of an electronic replacement, and were astonished to hear him say that there was no way he could reproduce the sounds of their 1880 Hill!

Instances where it is right to install an electronic organ

Lest those who have read so far think I have been expressing opinions biased in favour of the pipe organ, let me say with great emphasis that I rejoice that there are so many good electronic organs now on the market; there is no doubt they are the right answer in many cases. Let me give you some instances.

I will start with a recent case which I encountered in a church in South London, which highlights most of the problem. The church building was of moderate size, built about 30 years ago. In one corner there was a small, two-manual pipe organ by a minor 19th-century builder, which had been transferred from another building. Though it made quite pleasant sounds, it certainly was in no way distinguished. It had, however, considerable drawbacks. It was very sharp in pitch which made it impossible for instruments to be played with it; it made an inadequate sound to accompany the large congregation; and it took up a good deal of space needed to seat extra people. In dealing with the parish's application to install an electronic instrument, I could have said that the pipe organ must stay – or I could have decided that pastoral, musical and architectural considerations tipped the balance in favour of an electronic instrument. In the end I felt the latter view was the only sensible course of action.

Or take another instance. The very large Edwardian organ, by a minor builder, in a huge Victorian church, was coming to the end of its working life. The tubular pneumatic action was worn out. To restore it to full working order would have required at least £100,000. The organ was capable of pleasing effects but, overall, it was an undistinguished piece of work. To spend a vast sum of money on such an instrument would, in my view, have been a criminal waste of resources. The best solution might well have been to build a smaller pipe organ with mechanical action. Musically and economically this would have been a good solution, as the church would have had an organ with a potential life of several centuries. (This is a proven fact, as many organs built between 1764 and 1883 in the diocese of Southwark bear witness.) But the £75,000 required for a new pipe organ simply was not available. So in this case, a good electronic organ was quite emphatically deemed to be the right answer.

Similarly in a new church where funds are limited, it may well be best to install a good-quality electronic instrument. This would certainly be preferable to an inferior pipe organ and, in my view, generally better than a small one-manual pipe organ of 3 or 4 stops. Such organs, of course, can be very effective. But, in a church where a variety of styles of music is used, and where a choir needs to be accompanied, the greater flexibility and tonal variety of the electronic instrument would be preferable. This is a fact not always recognized by organ advisers, some of whom seem to think that the staple musical diet of all churches consists of straightforward hymn tunes and the organ works of Froberger!

The organ, as the most expensive internal fitting of the church, often poses great problems for those responsible for these buildings. Many churches possess magnificent instruments, dating very often from the late 19th century. These organs are of the highest quality and are part of our national heritage. It would be unthinkable to break up a fine organ by T. C. Lewis, J. W. Walker, or any of the other good Victorian builders. When funds are not available, it is best to leave the instrument to await restoration at a future date. And here a good electronic organ must be the best short-term solution. There are many fine organs which await their resurrection. For instance, the historic organs of Christ Church, Spitalfields and St Anne's, Limehouse cry out for attention. It is nothing short of scandalous that these instruments are silent. In France or Germany they would have been restored long ago, with assistance provided by national or local government funds.

Occasionally, it might be better to try to find a fine organ a new home where it will be appreciated, though of course it is always risky transferring an instrument voiced for one building into another. Some years ago, a small church in London was faced with the problem of what to do with its huge four-manual organ, installed in 1930 by a first-rank builder and paid for by the extremely wealthy organist of the church. There was no possibility of enormous sums being raised for its restoration. And, had money been available, would it have been right to restore an instrument far bigger than necessary, and only required for one hour per week? Mercifully, a buyer was found and the organ is being given new life in a more appropriate home.

Complicated decisions need to be made
I could go on! The problems facing churches over the restoration and provision of organs are complicated – and virtually no two cases are similar. *It is therefore impossible to generalize*; every church must seek

the right solution for their particular circumstances, remembering that quality is never cheap.

Above all we must work for toleration and peaceful coexistence. The achievements of modern technology must be recognized. But let no one be in any doubt about the skills, both manual and musical, which go into the making of the pipe organ. The highest levels of craftsmanship, patience, time and musical imagination are needed to achieve success. I have no fears that the success of the electronic organ will mark the demise of the pipe organ. All over the world pipe organ building flourishes and there has almost everywhere been a welcome increase in the number of really good small builders. The electronic organ, however, now plays a different and complementary role. This must be recognized.

Just a few words of theological postscript. There is a tendency these days for the Church to think as the world thinks. Is it cost-effective, is it practical, does it make sense? Might I suggest that if our medieval ancestors had thought thus, none of their great cathedrals would have been built. There is a sense in which only the best is good enough for God.

I will end with a personal anecdote. On the evening of my first day as Director of the RSCM, many of my friends came to a Eucharist in the Chapel at Addington, celebrated by the Bishop of Southwark. The arrangements were masterminded by my friends from Southwark Cathedral. Before the service I became a little alarmed as a second portmanteau of gold vestments was unpacked. I protested that I did not want too much fuss. 'Don't worry', one replied, 'we're not doing it for you!'

Harry Bramma
1990, Addington

Footnote: Since writing, the instruments at Christ Church, Spitalfields and St Anne's, Limehouse have both been restored.

'THE LABOURER IS WORTHY OF HIS HIRE' – WHY CHURCH MUSICIANS SHOULD RECEIVE PROPER FINANCIAL REMUNERATION

Amateur and professional – these words defined

In this article I intend to come down to earth with a bump! I shall attempt a discussion of the vexed question of the financial payment given to organists, choir leaders and musical directors. It has often been observed that when money is the matter under discussion, even nice people turn nasty! And the remuneration of church musicians is no exception to this fact of life. Or if people do not turn exactly nasty, they become illogical and confused in their thinking. Both amateur and professional musicians are very much at the mercy of clergy, church councils or cathedral chapters, and though there are many these days in such bodies whose views are enlightened and progressive, it is still possible to find attitudes which are either ill thought out or quite simply archaic.

In any discussion of this nature it is essential to define the status of the musician concerned. The terms *amateur* and *professional* have to do with *how* a person's living is earned – not in this case with musical standards. There are, of course, many amateur musicians who maintain the highest musical standards, and sadly some professionals whose quality of work is not what it should be. But the amateur musician may have a highly paid job as an accountant, stockbroker or whatever; the professional actually depends on what is earned as a musician to provide all the essentials of life – food, housing, clothing, holidays, pensions, etc., etc. This distinction between those who depend on their musical earnings and those who do not must always be kept right at the front of one's thinking. Our discussion must therefore fall into two parts – the treatment of the professional musician and the attitude churches should take to amateur musicians who have a considerable weekly commitment.

Financial support for music in larger churches

Larger churches and cathedrals still have no difficulty in recruiting professional musicians, though it is sometimes difficult to find people of the right musical calibre. But there are still many organists and musical directors who have a real vocation to a type of work they love, and this fact has in the past (and even today in some instances) been used as an excuse for paying inadequate or even shameful salaries. Church authorities have often salved their consciences by saying that, for example, a cathedral organist might earn extra fees by teaching, playing and conducting. This may be true, but very often it has led to neglect of the musician's principal duties at the cathedral – or in the case of the dedicated, to insufferably long working hours, often away from home, leading to stressful family situations and even marriage breakdowns. Happily things are improving in the larger churches as the authorities come to realize the value of the ministry of music. In most cathedrals these days (but not all, I fear), it is accepted that, if an organist is prepared to devote a great deal of time to daily duties, the remuneration should be comparable to that of the clergy. But outside cathedrals in the greater churches of all Christian traditions where music plays an important part, there is still a long way to go. If high musical standards are expected from a voluntary musical set-up, a professional musician will find that recruiting and training a choir of children and adults is a highly time-consuming business, especially when one considers all the hidden tasks. A director of music often has to act as public relations officer, transport manager, matron, wardrobe mistress, headmaster and pastor! I know this from personal experience as organist of Southwark Cathedral.

A friend of mine who used to run a fine choir in a large church reckoned that he had to spend 20 hours a week on the work. If to the choral and organ work other duties are added – for instance the organization of orchestral players and the arrangement of instrumental parts for music groups, the work really ceases to be part-time. Many of our churches in the evangelical tradition are beginning to realize the need for expert leadership for music in larger churches, and how time-consuming this is, and are in fact beginning to offer financial remuneration which is much more realistic.

A clerical friend of mine once remarked that a good choir director was worth two curates – a considerable exaggeration of course! But, what he meant was that a person who leads the music in church has a unique opportunity to make contact with people of all ages – particularly with the young. Thankfully there are still many pied-pipers around who attract hundreds of children into our churches, giving them musical training and enjoyment certainly, but also a wider vision and the beginnings of real understanding of the faith. It is no accident that many Christian leaders, both lay and ordained, made their first step on the Christian pilgrimage as a result of being attracted to make music in church. Enlightened, spiritually-aware musical leadership in church is immensely important. I very much hope that in all the larger churches, congregations will make every effort to make it possible for professional musicians to devote enough time each week to this vitally important area of work.

Finding the money in smaller churches

In the smaller local churches of all denominations, there has been a tragic decline over the past 40 years in the number of professional musicians holding regular appointments. The reasons for this are complicated. There *are* more opportunities for professional musicians in the educational field, and many have opted for regular employment instead of the old-fashioned way of making a living as church organist and private music teacher. But an important factor in the decline is financial. When I was organist and choirmaster of a parish church in Yorkshire during my final year at school, my annual stipend was £100. That was in 1954. I was astonished to discover last year, when speaking with the present organist of the church, a highly-respected, long-standing professional musician, that the salary has only increased to £500 – 35 years after I had been receiving £100! Had the remuneration kept up with inflation, the 1989 figure should have been £1,150 approximately. This instance is typical of what has happened in hundreds of churches. It is not surprising therefore that professional musicians are unable to afford to take this kind of appointment.

Recently, I was invited to help with the appointment of an organist in a prosperous suburban parish with a fine organ and a large congregation. The salary being offered was £1,000 per annum. Though several highly qualified professional musicians were on the shortlist, none of them felt able to accept the appointment – not because their attitude was mercenary but because they could not afford to take it.

A minimum of two Sunday services and two weekday practices would involve a musician in at least seven hours' work. This represents one fifth of the salary of, for instance, a school teacher. If this were fixed on the low side at £10,000 per annum, the organist's fee in the suburban parish I have cited should have been in the region of £2,000 per annum. For a person living some distance from the church, travel expenses alone might well eat up most of £1,000 during the course of a year. It is not surprising therefore that for a person making a living from music, a remuneration of £1,000 per annum is totally unrealistic – especially when one considers that the cost of living has risen way beyond inflation in some areas, notably housing. My parents were able in 1936 to buy a substantial semi-detached house for £500 on an income of £175 per annum. If inflation alone were to be considered, the house today would cost around £14,700 and my father's salary would be approx. £5,145. In fact our old house was recently sold for £60,000 – I need say no more. Even if the salaries paid to professional musicians in local churches *had* kept up with inflation, they would still be inadequate for today's living costs. I very much hope thriving local churches will try to do more to make it possible for professional musicians to give their time to provide creative musical leadership at the local level. The worship of our churches is often greatly impoverished simply because the necessary skilful leadership is not available.

The proper treatment of amateurs

So far I have been speaking of professional musicians. I would now like to consider the position of the amateur. And here we immediately come up against much prejudice, often thinly disguised by a veneer of piety. In recent years, church newspapers and musical periodicals have often printed letters from irate church members asking why the organist should be paid when the treasurer of the church council or the churchwarden are quite prepared to give their services. It is often suggested that it is unchristian that pay should even be considered. Quite often, those who make such statements speak from positions of considerable financial stability and can afford to pontificate. The local organist may not be so well-placed, and may in fact face considerable expense in making three or four journeys to the church each week. But the question is really a matter of the commitment involved. The church musician has to be present week by week, year in, year out, and if he or she wishes to be absent has to find and pay a deputy. It is a very demanding assignment, and even considered at the level of civility and courtesy, it is entirely right that the church should recognize the extent of this commitment by saying an annual financial thank you. In many instances this will hardly cover the expenses incurred, but most musicians are glad to make a contribution as part of their Christian stewardship. But let us be quite frank when dealing with those in churches who think it wrong to pay the organist. The musician's time commitment is formidable and quite different from that of the churchwarden, who will expect to be away from time to time to attend a dinner party or to catch up with the gardening during a period of fine weather.

It may of course be that the devoted organist of the local church is well off and does not need remuneration. In such instances, the person concerned will very often, in my experience, pay back the money by increasing a covenant, or by paying for new music. But what such a person must not do is to decline to take the remuneration. The next organist may not be in a position to be so generous, and it would be unfair to the church if suddenly the annual budget had to be increased to cope with the organist's honorarium. In the same way, it is quite wrong for clergy with private means to refuse expenses. I have known several churches where there have been severe financial problems after the departure of a wealthy incumbent.

Fair pay for musicians is a moral issue
I hope I have given sufficient reasons to allay the fears of those who have qualms about the morality of paying musicians to work in church. I am well aware that these qualms stem from a fear of employing musicians who only do the work for the money. Such people do exist and they are a menace. But in my experience, the payment of professional singers and musicians in our churches has been entirely compatible with a truly spiritual and devotional attitude to worship. Indeed it is quite remarkable that hundreds of lay clerks in cathedral choirs throughout the country are prepared to turn up five or six days a week for an honorarium in the region of £1,600 per annum. Those who lead the worship in churches have a responsibility to make sure attitudes are right. When employing musicians for work in church, one must make sure that the thinking and commitment are spiritually based. This can be done without turning an interview into a kind of spiritual inquisition which infringes on matters that quite rightly are of a highly personal nature.

It is good that in some areas things seem to be improving, because the church has had a terrible record on the question of the fair treatment of musicians. Bach complained about his finances, Mozart quarrelled with the Archbishop of Salzburg and, nearer home, S. S. Wesley did not mince his words on such matters. Until recently, the idea did linger on that musicians were members of the servant class and should be treated like gardeners, coachmen or parlour maids. Musicians have now left social serfdom behind – though vestigial traces survive here and there. But much progress still remains to be made in the area of fair and adequate financial remuneration.

It is not always easy for churches to raise extra money, burdened as they are with the maintenance of large and often historic buildings, and with all the other calls on the budget. Earlier this afternoon when I was looking round the church of St Sulpice in Paris, I saw a notice announcing the restoration of the 1862 Cavaillé-coll organ at a cost of £220,000. The notice went on to say that half of this would be given by the Département and half by the city of Paris! It may be that all historic churches in many different countries, and particularly in Great Britain, should be maintained by the government. I realize there are strong arguments for and against this. Yet were such support to become universal, I doubt whether more money would automatically be channelled into the salaries of church musicians, for we are talking about changing attitudes, not necessarily the provision of more cash. Of course, in some churches, there is real financial hardship. There is no doubting this. But all the churches wherever one goes have more than their fair share of those most lamentable of creatures who say 'It can't be done!' Where there's a will there's a way, and more often than not, things can be done. Churches which are alive and growing very rarely let financial matters worry them over much. At one suburban Anglican church near where I live in South London, during the past year the congregation has doubled and the annual income has increased from £40,000 to £80,000!

Most church musicians do the work because they love the church they serve. They are not in general a grasping or greedy lot. But I believe the time has come when the churches need to reassess this whole question of just financial rewards for musicians. And this reassessment should include provision of funds for training musicians, especially young people with limited resources. If the church is to attract the musical leadership it needs, to enable well-qualified men and women to devote time to improving the musical quality of worship and to teaching the young, more money will have to be found. Adequate reward for those who serve the church as musicians is a moral matter. I hope the churches of all traditions will increasingly address themselves to the issues involved in this important area.

APPENDIX   345

Harry Bramma
May 1990, Amiens

Footnote: I realize that some of the situations described in this article are particularly relevant to the conditions found in Great Britain and Ireland. But I believe that conditions in other countries are often similar and I hope members will find what I have said helpful. This article was written in 1990. The figures of course need to be upgraded.

'BE STILL AND KNOW THAT I AM GOD' – THE IMPORTANCE OF SILENCE IN WORSHIP

It is estimated that several million people in the British Isles regularly go fishing. Most of them would be ready enough to speak enthusiastically about the sport – the choice of tackle, the best stretches of water or the legendary catches! The majority, I suspect, would be embarrassed to explain why they really enjoy their pastime. The truth however is that, in many cases, the fishing is incidental – what they really enjoy is the solitude and the silence of the river, lake or canal. Whether it be the steelworkers of Sheffield making their weekly pilgrimage to the banks of the Trent, a small boy playing by the mill dam, or expert anglers wading in remote mountain streams – all are seeking what many people inwardly yearn for: the peace and tranquillity which grows out of silence, especially the particular kind of silence found near running water. I believe it was Jung who said that humans would be much happier if they could all live near to the sound of running water. (It is true, one occasionally sees anglers plugged in to headsets – in these cases they must rate solitude more highly than silence!)

All through history human beings have yearned for silence. The Bible is full of instances where people have gone off to seek solitude, and in the monastic tradition of many of the world's great religions, silence has been an important ingredient in the daily round of work and prayer. It is, however, the one ingredient which is normally absent from most Christian worship today. I believe it is essential we do something about this as soon as possible. I will try to explain why.

Silence can be felt

Firstly, I would stress that silence can be a powerful element in preparation for worship – either spoken word or music. In some churches, the choir observes silence for several minutes in the vestry before the service; in others, at a given signal, perhaps the ringing of a bell, the congregation falls to silence. In such a way, thoughts are collected, and the mind prepared. I have noticed in some churches, particularly in the evangelical tradition, the words 'Let us pray' are the signal for the members of the congregation to compose themselves very consciously in collective recollection. Music or words which grow out of silence have magical quality, immediately lifting the worship to a higher plane. But we can all think of instances where a service never gets off the ground, where there is no effective preparation for worship, and where constant clatter and chatter make it difficult to come into the presence of God. It is undesirable and certainly unrealistic to expect worshippers to greet one another in stony silence when they enter the church building. There needs to be a clear understanding however about the value of silence at the beginning of worship, and clear instruction in this matter from those responsible for leading worship.

It is important to remember that silence in church is a *corporate* activity – just as much as singing or speaking together. This is particularly so when silence follows words or music. Those who have attended a performance of Britten's *War Requiem* will know what I mean. At the end of the work, after over an hour of corporate listening, the choir brings the piece to an end with a most moving few bars of hushed unaccompanied writing. The effect of the final cadence, moving from F sharp major to F major is electrifying and never, in my experience, fails to reduce the listeners to the kind of silence which can be felt. Only after some seconds do people feel able to applaud. Another similar instance, recounted by a friend, concerned a performance of Donizetti's opera *Mary Stuart*. After an aria sung with great emotion by Dame Janet Baker, some insensitive fan shouted 'bravo'. The frost which descended on the auditorium immediately indicated the audience's intense disapproval of one who was out of step with the communal feeling. Such a chilling response was expressed through silence. No words were necessary, not even for the insensitive creature who dared to break the spell!

Experiences such as these when translated to the corporate worship of the Church become vital ingredients in Christian devotion. Many churches now have a short silence after the reading of the Word – or after the sermon. And it is increasingly common to have a substantial silence after all have received Holy Communion at the Eucharist. Many find this helpful and very moving, coming as it does at the climax of the service.

Increasingly the use of silence is seen as an important element in developing spirituality within the framework of public worship. Some of the most profound (and, dare I say, enjoyable) silences I have experienced have been in the great Benedictine monasteries of northern France, particularly at Solesmes and Bec. There is something about these churches which is peculiarly conducive to silence and tranquillity. Significantly both are set in areas of outstanding natural beauty – and both stand beside a river. The beautiful interiors of these churches and the sound of plainsong all combine to make the places where deep silence is naturally felt. But in the end, one has to admit it is impossible to analyse precisely why certain places have such a powerful impact on the soul. I believe, in common with Christians down the ages, that there *is* such a thing as a holy place. Indeed, this idea is best expressed in the book of Genesis in the account of Jacob's dream. 'When Jacob awoke from his sleep, he thought, "Surely the Lord is in this place and I was not aware of it." He was afraid and said "How awesome is this place! This is none other than the House of God; this is the gate of heaven"' (Genesis 2: 16 and 17).

The importance of place

Though I am aware there has always been a tradition in Christianity which has distrusted the externals of worship – and rightly so when they become an end in themselves – it is clear that what is *seen* is an important factor in creating the right atmosphere for contemplative silence. Beautiful surroundings, though not essential, are a great help to many people in bringing them to the silence which leads them closer to God. The Victorian architect, J. L. Pearson, said that his aim in designing a church was to bring people to their knees. Many church buildings have precisely this effect. That is why we must look after them, keeping them clean and tidy. One doesn't often find beer bottles under the verger's seat these days, though a 19th-century visitor to Christ Church Cathedral, Oxford complained of this! But, one does see much untidiness – piles of hymn books and hassocks left anywhere, and lots of dust. A casual approach to the interior of a church is indefensible and does nothing to enhance the presentation of worship. A clean, neat building can do much to heighten the spiritual quality of a service by providing the right setting for music, speaking and silence.

So far I have spoken of the immense spiritual value of silence in the context of worship. I would now like to consider why silence is important for the proper performance of much music – though not all, as you will see.

Sound out of silence

I readily admit that there is such a thing as background music – in a restaurant, at a dance, or as a congregation leaves the church during a final organ voluntary. But for the most effective performance of much music, silence is essential. A composer creates sounds in the silence in the same way that a painter creates a picture on a blank piece of paper. I believe that in a church service, there is room for both background and foreground music. Too stuffy an attitude puts many people off. I think it was Stravinsky who said music should be loved, not respected. It is quite unrealistic for a congregation after the Sunday service to sit in solemn silence during the final voluntary. Music at this point must be a joyous accompaniment as the people of God leave the church. I remember once hearing a recording of a mighty congregation happily leaving the Cathedral at Strasbourg – the organ pealed out a glorious toccata, the bells rang out, combining with the voices of the people to produce an atmosphere of great excitement. Or what about the use of organ music as a background to the spoken voice? I have sometimes heard the Eucharistic Prayer spoken to the accompaniment of quiet sounds on the organ – very beautiful and deeply moving. Yes, it is possible to be creative about combinations of music and other sounds.

The importance of foreground music
At the present time, however, congregations need most of all to learn the value of foreground music in church, where all listen with rapt attention. They also need to recover a sense of the numinous. So much worship these days is noisy and earthbound. Of course there must be warmth and informality – the giving of the Peace is, for example, one of the oldest features of the Eucharist – but there must also be elements of quiet and repose. So often the effect of fine music is impaired by talking or off-stage voices. This very often happens during the prelude before the service, whether played by organ or a combination of instruments. At this point congregations should be encouraged to recollect themselves as they prepare for worship. The musicians should also be encouraged not to play for too long, otherwise it will be unrealistic for the congregation to be silent. (It is of course possible to prepare for worship by singing together. This is common in some churches. In my view both private and corporate preparation are equally valid means of heightening awareness of the presence of God at the beginning of the Liturgy.)

It is obvious that the most effective musical performances grow out of silence. How does one reconcile this undoubted fact with the presence of children in church, who naturally tend to be somewhat noisy? I personally don't believe a few isolated whimpers from a baby are sufficient to destroy a motet by Byrd. Sustained cacophony from a number of children however makes such a performance impossible. What is the answer? It is important that children come to church from an early age so that they naturally grow up to feel part of the family of God. But I have been to services where children have got out of hand, and where attention to the spoken word and private and corporate prayer proved very difficult. At my request Canon Peter Price of Southwark Cathedral has written a short article exploring how children are best integrated into Sunday worship, drawing on his experience as a parish priest (see *Church Music Quarterly*, April 1990, p.18).

I hope I have said enough to explain why I consider creative silence in worship important, both for its own sake and as the context in which music is sung. Of course the cultivation of silence poses great practical problems for those who organize worship. The place of children is an important issue which is not always sufficiently addressed. But alas the children are not the only source of inappropriate noise in our churches! Much needs to be done to educate people of all ages into a more spiritual approach to corporate worship.

Silence is golden
Silence *is* golden, not only because of the relief it brings from constant noise but also because it can be the means by which people enlarge their vision, looking beyond themselves to the greater context in which they live. Sir Walter Scott expressed something of this when he said, 'Silence is deep as eternity; speech is shallow as time.' There are welcome signs that Christians are beginning to appreciate silence and contemplation much more. The amazing growth of interest in Taizé music is an indication of this. Let us hope the trend continues. Thirty years ago, much public worship was over-formal and arid. The pendulum inevitably (and rightly in my opinion) has swung to the opposite view, where warmth and informality are all-important. The time has now come to restore a balance and to explore areas of

human personality and Christian devotion which have been unjustly neglected.

Harry Bramma
February 1990

Index

Addington Palace 123, 159, 182, 186, 188, 198–208, 211, 214–15, 218, 223, 238–40, 242, 244, 251–2, 255–6, 306, 330
Adlington, David 146
All Saints, Margaret Street 2, 41, 181, 222, 261–96, 300, 302, 306, 310, 333
All Saints, Tooting 310, 317
All Souls, Langham Place 198, 209, 242–3, 251, 270
Andrews, Dr H. K. 38, 52–4, 56, 210
Andrews, Robert 32, 36
Annett, David 71, 106
Archbishops of Canterbury 143, 150, 162, 181–2, 186, 196, 243, 249–50
ARCO diploma 45, 49, 188–9
Armstrong, Very Rev. Christopher 89
Armstrong, Claude 76, 78
Armstrong, Sir Thomas 44, 48, 98
Arnold, Dr Eric 261–3, 266, 278, 289, 300
Arthur, Andrew 272–3, 293
Associated Board exams 56, 186, 190, 327
Athenaeum 124, 209, 271, 297–8
Australia 4, 199, 202, 217–23, 270, 326

Bach, Johann Sebastian 6, 31, 34–5, 38, 44, 60, 101, 115, 121–2, 148, 168, 247, 274, 293, 299, 326, 343
Baildon Green 17, 28
Bain, Roly 145–6
Baker, Thomas 83, 85, 92–4
Barbirolli, Sir John 35, 274, 321
Bardsley, Cuthbert 148–9
Barker, Peter 20, 319

BBC 78, 110–11, 143, 155, 274, 284, 291
Beckenham 2, 62, 307, 310, 318
Beeching, Dr 22, 26, 60–1, 116
Bell, Ian 302–3, 321
Bell, Robert 20
Beverley 24
Bingley 11, 13, 32, 36, 283
Birch, Dr John 262, 266, 292
Blackpool 2, 7, 29, 191, 216
Boult, Sir Adrian 35, 39, 120, 274, 284
Bourne, Lionel and Jill 318
Bowen, Colonel Bill 91
Bowlby, Ronald 180–2
Bradford 11, 13, 18, 22, 34–7, 74, 163, 274
Bradford Cathedral 10, 143, 206
Bradford Grammar School 2, 5, 16–18, 20, 26, 32, 43, 45, 73, 225
Bradford Technical College 5, 14–15, 315
Braley, Dr Evelyn, 76
Braley, Isabel 74, 120
Bramma ancestors 3–16
Bredon Hill 116, 134
Britten, Benjamin 39–41, 85, 96, 107–8, 113, 121, 165, 299, 346
Brough, Paul 42, 285, 296, 300
Burnham, David 69
Butler, Roger 210–12, 249, 253
Byrd, William 38, 53–4, 67, 75, 144, 222, 251, 295–6, 326, 350
Byrd Anniversary 294

Caine, Chris 270, 316–17
Campbell, Dr Sydney 137
Canada 165, 237–9, 326

353

Canterbury Cathedral 199, 208, 215, 218, 252
Caplin, Elaine 288–9
Caplin, Norman 267, 285, 295
Carey, Archbishop George 242–3, 249–50, 258
Chancellor, Philip 192
Channel Islands 239–40
Chapman, David 291
Charles-Edwards, Mervyn 75, 77, 90
Cheltenham 22, 236
Chislehurst 2, 199, 218, 252, 256, 310, 318
Christ Church, Oxford 42, 44, 48–9, 53, 55–6, 62, 110, 125, 247, 253, 282, 300, 308, 348
Christ Church, Spitalfields 336–7
Church Music Quarterly 241, 247, 250, 254–5, 350
Churchill, Jo 249–50, 253
Clark, Kathleen 13
Clark, William 219
Clarke, Richard 290
Clarkson, W. E. 33
Clayton, Helen 285–6
Cleobury, Nicholas 82, 105, 107, 110
Cleobury, Stephen 82, 103, 107, 113–14, 253, 308
Cleveland Lodge 205, 211–12, 248, 250, 252–3, 255–7
Cocker, Norman 37–8
Coggan, Archbishop Donald 150
Cole, Dr William 186
Cook, Dr E. T. 137–8, 169, 194
Cook, Dr Melville 36, 96, 129–30, 276
Coombs, Peter 177, 242
Croft, Fredrill 9
Croydon 148, 162, 181–2, 186, 199, 251, 307

Dakers, Lionel 190, 197–8, 200–4, 214, 218, 223, 229, 241, 244, 247, 253, 297, 306
Darlington, Jonathan 82, 110
Darlington, Stephen 42, 110, 127, 300, 308
Davies, Coliss 76–7
Davies, Jeremy 306

Davies, John 82, 126
Day, Edgar 71, 84, 99, 102, 125, 131–2, 274
Dexter, Harold 137–8
Dickens, Charles 11, 152, 177, 186, 192, 303
Diocesan Advisory Committee 183–5, 308–9
Durham 14, 17–18, 57, 68, 76, 107, 110, 190, 197, 215, 217, 253, 279, 302
Dutton, Peter 277

Edwards, Adrian 128
Edwards, David 152–5
Edwards, Frank 121
Elgar, Edward 35, 39, 41, 55, 77, 81, 85, 96, 98–101, 103, 111, 117, 119, 131–2, 178, 261, 274, 299
Eliot, Lady Alethea 75, 77, 89
Eliot, Peter 77
Eton 52, 55–6, 112, 166, 180, 247
Evesham 77, 112, 116–17, 134

Fauré, Gabriel 39, 67, 251, 253, 268
First World War 11–13, 19, 75, 100, 131
Fleming, Michael 199–200, 262, 267
Ford, Trevor 254
Forde, John 286–7
Frankham, Harold 136, 138, 146, 148–52, 309
Fraser, Ian 253
Frayling, Nicholas 123, 249, 270–2, 317
Freeth, Denzil 263, 269, 278, 286

Gilbert and Sullivan 40, 107, 155, 183
Girls' Choir, Salisbury 247–8, 255, 325–6, 328–30
Gloucester Cathedral 22, 37, 71, 81, 95–8, 100, 110–12, 130, 145, 214–15, 333
Goode, David 253
Gover, John 66
Green, Leslie 199, 208
Greenwood, Frank 23–4, 37
Guest, Douglas 71, 76, 80, 125, 132
Guest, George 113, 185

Hallé Orchestra 35, 321–2

INDEX

Hammerstein, Dorothy 162
Handel, Georg Frideric 33–4, 40, 50, 234, 268
Harper, John 213, 232, 257
Harrison, Arthur 102–3, 291
Harrison, Dr Frank 51–3
Harrison, Sir David 212–13
Harrison and Harrison 47, 101–3, 136, 169–70, 172, 184, 221, 253, 275, 292, 302–3
Harrison organs 38–9, 96, 102–4, 190, 252, 256, 264, 290–4, 302–3, 310
Hartley, Walter 24
Haydn, Joseph 35, 50, 115, 140–1, 234, 273, 299, 326
Heath, Edward 109, 196
Henderson, Dr John 256
Hereford Cathedral 22, 26–7, 71, 87, 95–8, 100, 104, 112, 116, 129, 135, 144, 160, 200
Hill, David 160
Hill, William 24, 34, 99–104, 121, 183–4, 221, 334
Hockney, David 19, 225
Hockney, Michael 211, 257
Hope-Jones, Robert 101–3
Hopps, Peter 170
Hughes, Marian 202, 204
Humphreys, David 276–7
Hunt, Dr Donald 81–2, 93, 95, 129–31
Hutt, David 119, 139, 145, 261, 266, 277–9, 318

Jackman, Eric 31
Jackson, Dr Francis 23, 114, 211, 276, 310
Jeans, Susi 211, 252, 257
Jeffery, Robert 94
Jenkins, David 57–8
Jenkins, John 26, 60–1
Jennings, Annie 10, 33–4

Kemp, Eric 83, 85, 89–94, 129, 135
Kerrigan, Michael 206
King, Charles 219, 255
King Edward VI Grammar School, Retford 2, 38–9, 65, 70–2
King's College, Cambridge 19, 44, 49, 53, 62, 70, 93, 112, 114, 152, 166, 215, 248, 253, 300, 308
King's School, Worcester 2, 15, 19, 40, 71, 74, 77, 81, 84, 96, 103–11, 113–16, 121, 124, 134, 137, 142, 166, 235, 290
Knight, Dr Gerald 198–203, 208, 218, 223, 230, 237, 297

Laflin, Mark 275
Layton, Stephen 166–7, 296, 300, 310
Leeds 1, 4, 13, 24, 30, 35–6, 93, 129–30, 149, 238, 244, 276, 306–7, 323
Leigh-Spencer, Harriet 142
Lewis, T. C. 24, 136, 167–73, 184–5, 221, 223, 227, 275, 336
Lichfield 165, 253
Lincoln 54, 92–3, 216, 264
Luff, Nicholas 162, 267–72, 274, 307, 316–17
Luke, Justin 275
Lumsden, Andrew 164–5, 253
Lyndon, Barry 187–8

Macmillan, Harold 173, 286
Madrigal Society 304–5
Malvern 22, 78, 100, 105, 112, 116–18, 122, 134, 166, 183
Manchester 31–2, 35–7, 319
Margetson, Sir John 198, 208–10
McDonald, Tim 249
McVicker, Dr William 184, 302–3, 310
Mendelssohn, Felix 11, 35, 37, 82, 99, 126, 130, 293, 295
Milburn, Dean Robert 71–2, 83, 85–92
Millington, Andrew 110, 127, 253
Morris, Colin 44, 62, 295
Morrison, Richard 241, 254
Moses, Alan 272, 275, 279–82, 286
Mozart, Wolfgang Amadeus 34–5, 40, 52, 70, 107, 130, 141, 178, 242, 261, 272–3, 293, 298, 326, 343
Muenthe, Guy 136
Musicians' Company 261, 300–2

Neale, Val 318
Neary, Dr Martin 249, 251

New College, Oxford 38, 53, 55, 70, 107, 110, 164, 210, 222, 248
New York 161–2, 223, 225, 227–8, 293
New Zealand 199, 213, 217–20, 222–3, 259, 270, 326
Nicholson, Sir Sydney 30, 108, 125, 199, 207–8, 215–18, 237, 246, 252, 256, 265–6, 297
Nicholson organs 78, 103, 108, 134, 183
Norman, Herbert 183
Norman and Beard 103, 184, 309
Nottinghamshire 2, 38, 65–72

O'Brien, Garrett 139, 158–9
O'Neil, Frances 285–6
Ogden, Jim 17, 28
Omphiangelum Society 302–3

Palestrina, Giovanni 38, 53, 75, 287, 326
Parker, Revd T. M. 58–9
Parker-Smith, Jane 225, 285, 293
Parrott, Gerald 144, 150, 155–6
Pembroke College, Oxford 2, 15, 38, 43–8, 55–6, 58, 90, 110, 120, 155, 231, 263, 295
Penwarden, Peter 136, 150, 152, 154–5, 203, 305
Petty, Reginald 43
Pipe, David 276
Porter, Roy 58
Preston, Simon 70, 98, 221
Purcell, Henry 53, 305
Purcell, William 77–8

Queen Elizabeth II 166, 235, 249–51
Queen's College, Oxford 48–9, 57, 222

Ramsey, Archbishop Michael 135, 264, 323
Renshaw, Brenda 272, 307, 317–18
Retford 2, 39, 65–73
Richardson, Frank 137
Robinson, Christopher 70–1, 80–2, 84, 88, 95–7, 103, 106–7, 125–9, 131, 169, 203, 261, 273,296
Robinson, Bishop John 43, 128, 176, 313
Rose, Barry 143, 160, 164

Rose, Dr Bernard 38, 48–51, 54, 70–1, 204, 299, 315
Ross, Fr Kenneth 262, 285, 289
Royal Albert Hall 148, 243, 251, 303
Royal College of Music 45, 110–11, 142
Royal College of Organists 61, 106, 109, 171, 185–9, 203
Royal Festival Hall 143, 147, 169, 238, 302–3
Royal School of Church Music 2, 30, 62, 125, 142, 159, 161–2, 166, 181–2, 186–90, 197–259, 265–7, 269, 275, 277, 287, 294, 297, 301, 305–6, 308, 310, 317, 325, 328, 331, 337
Royal Schools of Music 56, 190
Runcie, Archbishop Robert 162, 181

Salisbury 50, 61, 76, 81, 87, 93, 109, 149–50, 158, 213, 221, 247–8, 256–7, 305–7, 325, 328, 330
Saltaire 5–6, 12, 14, 17, 133, 315
Sanders, John 98, 130
Sanderson, Michael 89
Sandon, Henry 80
Schulze, Edmund 168, 170
Scott, Andrew 172, 292, 302
Scott, Sir George Gilbert 75, 87, 92, 104, 168, 184, 229
Scott, John 114, 119, 143–4, 148, 160–4, 178, 209, 253, 268–9, 293, 309
Seal, Dr Richard 247, 306, 325–6
Self, Christopher 286
Severn Valley 78, 82, 89, 111–12, 116, 120, 126
Shepherd, Dr Arthur 76
Shepherd, Neil 216
Shepherd, Peter 238
Shipley ix, 7–8, 11–13, 16, 23, 29–30, 36, 114, 163, 222, 235, 246
Smith-Cameron, Ivor 157, 160
South Africa 6, 153, 162, 182, 229–37, 326
Southcott, Ernest 137, 149
Southwark ix, 2, 5, 15, 41, 51, 79, 110, 114, 119, 123, 125, 129, 135–98, 202–4, 214, 221, 227, 242, 245,

INDEX

249, 256, 258, 261, 263–70, 272, 274, 277, 287, 299, 304–5, 308–10, 317, 323, 335, 337, 339, 350
Sparrow, David 263, 295
St Anne's, Limehouse 336
St George's Chapel and Hall, Windsor 129, 169, 198, 215
St John's College, Cambridge 107, 110, 113, 160, 164, 190, 210, 273
St John's College, Oxford 58
St John's Smith Square 261, 293
St Paul's Cathedral 26, 58, 68, 119, 143–4, 160, 164–5, 167, 171, 208–9, 221, 253, 269, 293, 304
St Paul's, Shipley 7, 13, 29, 31, 114, 163, 222, 235, 246
St Saviour's, Retford 68–9
Stamford 25
Stanage, Tom 231–2
Stanford, Charles Villiers 30, 37, 50, 75, 82, 103, 127, 265, 274
Stockwood, Mervyn ix, 79, 137–8, 143–4, 149, 158, 173–82
Stuart, Bishop C. E. 76
Sumsion, Herbert 71, 81, 97–9, 130

Tasker, Derek 157–8
Tewkesbury 26, 112, 116, 166
Thompson, Pat 289
Three Choirs Festival 39–40, 77, 95–101, 109, 112, 129–32, 160, 274
Tolley, Christopher 107, 110, 164
Townhill, Dr Dennis 328
Tredinnick, Noël 242, 251, 270
Tremlett, Tony 264
Trollope, Anthony 24, 74, 86–7
Turnbull, Eric 78–9

United States of America 101, 161, 165, 181, 209, 223–9, 237

Vaughan Williams, Ralph 35, 39–40, 67, 96, 99, 111, 121, 148, 178, 209, 241, 297, 299
Venning, Mark 170, 275, 292, 302
Verdi, Giuseppe 40, 98, 107–8, 121, 127, 232, 299

Voluntary Choir, Worcester 72, 75, 78, 83–5, 90, 95–6, 130, 132–3, 166, 228

Wagner, Richard 41–2, 115, 221, 298–9
Wakefield 160, 258, 306
Wakefield family 6–7, 12, 231
Walker organs 113, 120–1, 184, 336
Walker, Peter 109, 196
Wall, Fonce 12–13
Wall, Jim 13, 163
Warren, Norman 244, 331
Waterhouse, Vincent 188, 202, 204, 214, 223
Watson, Derek 158
Watson, Dr Sydney 48, 55
Weir, Dame Gillian 191, 237, 293, 331
Wesley, S. S. 29–30, 80, 100, 125, 130, 162, 181, 233, 343
West Riding 1, 18, 24, 28, 46, 143, 160, 222, 235
Westminster Abbey 26, 70–1, 80, 93, 108, 113, 119, 125, 144–5, 152, 165, 197, 208, 214, 235, 249, 251, 272, 279
Westminster Cathedral 113–14, 213, 259
Westminster School 141
Westrup, Sir Jack 54–5
Williams, June 205
Willcocks, Sir David 76, 80, 132–3, 181, 201, 294
Willis organs 23, 69, 96, 100, 103, 125, 136, 150, 167, 169–71, 184–5, 303, 331–3
Winchester Cathedral 165–6, 239
Winchester College 55, 107, 110, 164
Worcester ix, 2–3, 15, 19, 22, 26, 39–41, 62, 71–137, 142, 166, 177, 190–1, 195–6, 204, 228, 261, 274, 289, 305
Worksop 65, 67, 69
Worn, Nigel 146
Wurlitzer organs 101, 191, 216, 332

York Minster 23, 35, 108, 114, 130, 143–4, 190, 197, 211, 214–15, 276, 321